SKYE
SCRAMBLES

*Scrambles, Easy Climbs and Walks
on the Isle of Skye*

including
The Cuillin, The Red Hills,
Strathaird, Minginish, Duirinish
and Trotternish

Noel Williams

SCOTTISH MOUNTAINEERING CLUB
SCRAMBLERS' GUIDE

Published in Great Britain by The Scottish Mountaineering Trust, 2011
Reprinted with corrections 2017, 2020 & 2022

ISBN 978-0-907521-99-0
A catalogue record for this book is available from the British Library

Route descriptions of scrambles and climbs in this guide, together
with their grades and any references to in situ or natural protection, are
made in good faith, checked and substantiated where possible
by the author. However, routes lose holds and are altered by rockfall,
rock becomes dirty and loose and in situ protection deteriorates.
Even minor alterations can have a dramatic effect on a route's grade
or seriousness. Therefore, it is essential that scramblers and climbers
judge the condition of any route for themselves, before they start.
The authors, editors, friends and assistants involved in the publication of
this guide, the Scottish Mountaineering Club, the Scottish Mountaineering
Trust and Scottish Mountaineering Trust (Publications) Ltd, can therefore
accept no liability whatever for damage to property, nor for personal injury
or death, arising directly or indirectly from the use of this publication.

This guidebook is compiled from the most recent information and
experience provided by the author, members of the Scottish
Mountaineering Club and other contributors. The book is published
by the Scottish Mountaineering Trust, which is a charitable trust.
Revenue from the sale of books published by the Trust is used for
the continuation of its publishing programme and for charitable
purposes associated with Scottish mountains and mountaineering.

Production: Scottish Mountaineering Trust (Publications) Ltd
Diagrams: Mark Hudson, Jean Thomas, Colin Ballantyne and Doug Benn
The Maps are derived from Ordnance Survey OpenData™
© Crown copyright and database right 2010
Photographs unless otherwise indicated: Noel Willams
Typesetting, diagram & map graphics: Noel Williams
Printed & bound by Latitude Press Ltd.
Distributed by Cordee Ltd.

Front Cover: The third pinnacle on Pinnacle Ridge, Sgùrr nan Gillean (Difficult).

CONTENTS

List of Maps & Diagrams 11

Introduction 15

Acknowledgements 16

Geology 17

Human History 29

Wildlife *by Gordon Rothero* 35

Weather 47

Mountaineering History 50

Environment, Safety & Technical Notes 61

Amenities 68

Strath Suardal and Strathaird 71
  Strath Suardal 72
    Suisnish and Boreraig 72
  Strathaird 76
    Kilmarie to Camasunary 76
    Elgol to Camasunary 77
    Suidhe Biorach 77
    Spar Cave 78

THE RED HILLS 81
  Eastern Red Hills 82
    Beinn na Caillich 82
      The Round of Coire Reidh .82
  Western Red Hills 83
    Meall a' Mhaoil 83
      Allt Darach Gorge 83
    Glàmaig 85
      South-East Rib 85
    Beinn Dearg Mhòr 86
      North-East Ridge 86
      The Beinn Deargs via Druim na Ruage 87

Marsco 88
   Fiaclan Dearg, North-West Shoulder 88
   Fiaclan Dearg, Odell's Route 91
   South-East Ridge 91
Druim Eadar Dà Choire 93
   Coire na Seilg Slabs 93
Ruadh Stac 94
   South Face 94
Meall Dearg 95
   North Buttress 95

Cuillin Outliers 96

Belig 97
   South-East Ridge 97
   North Ridge 97
   South-West Ridge 99
Garbh-bheinn 99
   North Ridge 99
   North-East Ridge 101
   South-East Ridge 101
Sgùrr nan Each 101
   North Buttress 103
   East–West Traverse 103
Clach Glas 104
   North Ridge 104
   South Ridge 106
   Sid's Rake 109
   Ramp Route 112
   Athain Slab Route 116
   Pilkington's Route 116
Blàbheinn 117
   Forked Pinnacle Ridge 117
   North Face 120
   Dog-Leg Gully 122
   North-East Face 124
     a) 18m Chimney 124
     b) Gap by the Half-Crown Pinnacle 125
     c) Left-hand Variation 125
   Scupper Gully 125
   East Ridge 125
   East Flank 127
   Dyke Route 129
   Great Gully Slabs 129
   South-East Flank 131

Southern Buttresses: D Buttress 131
C Buttress 133
B Buttress 133
B- Buttress 133
A Buttress 133
South Ridge 133
South-West Buttress 135
Traverse of the Cuillin Outliers 137

THE CUILLIN 140
Sligachan to Camasunary 141
Sligachan to Coruisk via Druim Hain 142
Camasunary to Coruisk via the Bad Step 143
Glen Brittle to Coruisk via the coast 144
Sligachan to Glen Brittle via Bealach a' Mhaim 145

Northern Cuillin 146
Sgùrr na h-Uamha 147
South Ridge 147
North-East Face 149
North Ridge 151
Sgùrr Beag 151
North–South Traverse .151.
South-East Flank 152
Sgùrr nan Gillean 152
South-East Ridge 152
Eastern Spur 154
Nead na h-Iolaire 156
Riabhach Rib 156
Basteir Gorge, Cooper's Gully 156
Pinnacle Ridge 158
Knight's Peak via 4/5 Gully 162
West Ridge 164
a) Nicolson's Chimney 164
b) Tooth Chimney 164
c) Tooth Groove & Arête 165
d) Lota Ledge & Chimney 165
West Ridge Continuation 165
South Face 166
Sgùrr Coire an Lobhta 167
Am Basteir 167
East Ridge 167
Lota Corrie Route 169
Naismith's Route, Basteir Tooth 171

Basteir Nick to Am Basteir 171
King's Cave Chimney 175
Base of the North Wall 175
Sgùrr a' Bhasteir 176
Traverse by the North-East Ridge 176
North Face 176
Sgùrr an Fhionn Choire 178
Traverse via the West Ridge and North Face 178
Bruach na Frìthe 178
East Ridge via Fionn Choire 180
North-West Ridge 180
South Ridge via Sgùrr na Bàirnich 182
An Caisteal 184
North Ridge 184
South Ridge 184
West Buttress 186
East Face, Central-South Buttress 189
East Face, North Butress 190

Central Cuillin 191
Bidein Druim nan Ràmh 192
North Peak 192
Central Peak 195
West Peak 195
Northern Flank 198
Sgùrr an Fheadain 198
The Spur 198
Edgeway 200
Waterpipe Slabs 202
Pipeline 202
Bealach na Glaic Moire Slabs 203
North Buttress 203
Tuppenny Buttress 205
South Buttress 205
Sgùrr a' Mhadaidh 206
North-West Buttress & the Upper Rakes 206
Foxes' Rake 208
Traverse of the Four Tops 209
Sgùrr Thuilm 212
Traverse via Black Slab 212
Sgùrr a' Mhadaidh 215
North-West (Thuilm) Ridge 215
West Face 215
South-West Ridge via An Doras 217

Sgùrr a' Ghreadaidh 217
  North-North-East Ridge 217
  West Flank via Sgùrr Eadar da Choire 219
  South Ridge via Sgùrr Thormaid 223
  Diagonal Buttress 223
  Coire a' Ghreadaidh Headwall 225
  Bealach Thormaid via Coire a' Ghreadaidh 226
  An Diallaid, North Rib 226
Sgùrr na Banachdaich 228
  North Ridge 228
  Western Shoulder via Coire an Eich 230
  Sgùrr nan Gobhar Ridge 230
  South-West Flank 232
  South Ridge, the Three Tops 235

Southern Cuillin 236

Sgùrr Dearg 237
  Banachdaich Slab 237
  North-West Flank 238
  Window Buttress 238
  South-West Ridge via Sgùrr Dearg Beag 241
  South Flank, Central Buttress 241
  South-East Flank 243
The Inaccessible Pinnacle 244
  East Ridge 244
  West Ridge 244
An Stac 245
  East Buttress 245
  An Stac Chimney 247
Sgùrr MhicCoinnich 247
  North Ridge 247
  West Buttress 249
  Hart's Ledge 250
  King's Chimney 250
Sgùrr Theàrlaich 253
  North Ridge 253
    a) Eastern Traverse 253
    b) East Wall & Slab 256
    c) Western Route 256
  South Ridge 256
Sgùrr Alasdair 258
  South-East Ridge 258
  South-West Ridge 261
Sgùrr Sgumain 261

North-East Ridge 262
North Ridge 262
North-West Ramp 264
Lochan Traverse 264
West Buttress 266
South Ridge 268
Sròn na Cìche 268
Collie's Route, The Cioch 269
Arrow Route 271
Cioch Slab Corner 271
South-West Face, The Cioch 272
Cioch Gully & South-West Chimney 273
Amphitheatre Arête 273
Western Gully 275
Traverse by the South-West Flank 276
Stony Rake 277
Central Buttress 278
Pinnacle Rake 281
Stack Buttress Direct 281
Slab Buttress 282
Sgùrr Theàrlaich 285
Traverse below the South-West Face 286
South-East Ridge via the Theàrlaich–Dubh Gap 286
Sgùrr Dubh na Dà Bheinn 289
North-West Ridge 289
East Ridge to Sgùrr Dubh Mòr 289
South Ridge 289
Caisteal a' Gharbh-choire 291
North-East Ridge 291
South Ridge & West Face 291
Sgùrr nan Eag 292
North Ridge 292
Western Buttress 294
West-South-West Flank 296
East Ridge 299
Coire nan Laogh 299
Western Slabs 300
Eastern Route 302
Sgùrr a' Choire Bhig 302
North-West Ridge 302
South Ridge 305
Gars-bheinn 305
North-West Ridge 305
Rubh' an Dunain 306

Coruisk 308
  Sgùrr Hain 310
    South-East Ridge 310
    South-East Slabs 313
  Sgùrr na Strì 313
    North Ridge 314
    South-South-East Buttress 316
  An Garbh-choire 317
  Gars-bheinn 317
    North-East Ridge 317
  Sgùrr a' Choire Bhig 319
    North-East Ridge 319
  Sgùrr Dubh Beag 320
    The Dubh Slabs 320
  Sgùrr Dubh Mòr 327
    East Ridge 327
    North-North-East Flank .327
  Sgùrr Theàrlaich 328
    East Face 328
    North-East Rib 330
  Sgùrr Coire an Lochain 330
    South Ridge 333
  Sgùrr MhicCoinnich 333
    East Face Rake 333
  Sròn Bhuidhe 335
    Peridotite Buttress 335
  Sgùrr na Banachdaich 335
    Midget Ridge 336
  Sgùrr a' Ghreadaidh 336
    Terrace Buttress West 336
    South Face 339
    South-East Ridge 339
  Coire an Uaigneis 342
  Bidein Druim nan Ràmh 342
    Druim nan Ràmh 342

Cuillin Main Ridge Traverse 346

Greater Traverse 370

Cuillin Round 370

North-West Minginish 371
  Preshal Mòr 372
    Boswell's Buttress 372
    Summit Buttress 375
    Finger Wagging Buttress 375
  Preshal Beag 375
    Southern Flank 375

Duirinish 376
    Duirinish Coast Walk – Orbost to Ramasaig 377
    MacLeod's Tables – The Round of Glen Osdale 379
    Waterstein Head 381
    Neist Point & Oisgill Bay 381

Trotternish 385
  Ben Tianavaig 386
    South Ridge 386
  The Storr 388
    The Old Man of Storr 388
    Northern Flank 388
  Meall na Suireamach 389
    The Quiraing – The Needle & The Table 389
    North–South Traverse 390
  Sròn Vourlinn 391
    Leac nan Fionn and Sròn Vourlinn 391
  Meall Tuath 392
    Rubha Hunish 392
  Beinn Edra 394
    The Round of Corrie Amadal 394
  The Trotternish Ridge 396

Index 397

List of SMC Publications 400

MAPS & DIAGRAMS

The orientation of the Cuillin cone-sheets 21
The Cuillin Icefield 12,000 years ago – Doug Benn 25
The Trotternish Landslips – Colin Ballantyne 28
Skye Population 34
Skye Wildlife – Jean Thomas 36, 41,42 & 45
All crag diagrams as listed below – Mark Hudson

Strath Suardal & Strathaird
Strath Suardal – Map 71
Strathaird – Map 75

The Red Hills
Eastern Red Hills – Map 81
Western Red Hills – Map 84
Marsco
   West Face, Fiaclan Dearg 89

Cuillin Outliers – Map 96
Ruadh Stac & the Cuillin Outliers 100
Sgùrr nan Each
   North Buttress 102
Clach Glas
   North Ridge 105
   South Ridge 107
   East Face 110
   West Face 115
Blàbheinn
   North Face 118
   North-East Face 123
   East Ridge, North Face 126
   East Face 128
   Eastern Slabs 130
   Southern Buttresses 132
   South-West Flank 136

THE CUILLIN – Map 140

Northern Cuillin – Map 146

An Garbh-choire   318
Sgùrr Dubh Beag
   The Dubh Slabs   322

Coruisk North – Map   325
  Sgùrr Dubh Mòr   326
  Sgùrr Theàrlaich
     East Face   329
  Sgùrr Coire an Lochain
     East Face   331
     South Ridge   332
  Sgùrr a' Ghreadaidh
     South-East Ridge   337
     Coir'-uisg   340
  Bidein Druim nan Ràmh
     Druim nan Ràmh   343
     South-West Flank   344

Main Ridge Traverse
  Southern Cuillin – Profile   347
  Theàrlaich to MhicCoinnich – Sketch map   351
  Central Cuillin – Profile   354
  Tops of Mhadaidh – Sketch Map   358
  Bidein Druim nan Ràmh – Sketch Map   362
  Northern Cuillin – Profile   364
  Am Basteir & Basteir Tooth – Sketch Map   366

Minginish – Map   371
  Preshal Mòr
     North-West Flank   373

Duirinish – Map   376

Trotternish – Map   385

MAPS & DIAGRAMS

The orientation of the Cuillin cone-sheets   21
The Cuillin Icefield 12,000 years ago – Doug Benn   25
The Trotternish Landslips – Colin Ballantyne   28
Skye Population   34
Skye Wildlife – Jean Thomas   36, 41, 42 & 45
All crag diagrams as listed below – Mark Hudson

Strath Suardal & Strathaird
    Strath Suardal – Map   71
    Strathaird – Map   75

The Red Hills
    Eastern Red Hills – Map   81
    Western Red Hills – Map   84
    Marsco
        West Face, Fiaclan Dearg   89

Cuillin Outliers – Map   96
    Ruadh Stac & the Cuillin Outliers   100
    Sgùrr nan Each
        North Buttress   102
    Clach Glas
        North Ridge   105
        South Ridge   107
        East Face   110
        West Face   115
    Blàbheinn
        North Face   118
        North-East Face   123
        East Ridge, North Face   126
        East Face   128
        Eastern Slabs   130
        Southern Buttresses   132
        South-West Flank   136

THE CUILLIN – Map   140

Northern Cuillin – Map   146

Sgùrr na h-Uamha,
   South-East Face   148
   North-East Face   150
Sgùrr nan Gillean
   Eastern Spur   155
   North Face of the First Pinnacle   157
   Pinnacle Ridge   159
   West Ridge   163
Am Basteir
   South Face   168
   West Ridge & Basteir Tooth   172
   North Face   174
Sgùrr a' Bhasteir
   North Face   177
Bruach na Frìthe   181
An Caisteal
   West Buttress   185
   East Face   188

Central Cuillin – Map   191
Bidein Druim nan Ràmh
   North Flank   193
   North-West Face   194
Sgùrr an Fheadain
   North-West Flank   199
Coire a' Mhadaidh
   Bealach na Glaic Moire Slabs   204
Sgùrr a' Mhadaidh
   North Face   207
   South-West Face   210
Sgùrr Thuilm
   South-West Buttress   213
Sgùrr a' Mhadaidh
   North-West (Thuilm) Ridge   216
Coire an Dorais   218
Sgùrr a' Ghreadaidh
   North-West Flank   220
Coire a' Ghreadaidh   224
An Diallaid
   North Rib   227
Sgùrr na Banachdaich
   Coir' an Eich   229
   South Ridge   234

Southern Cuillin – Map   236

Coire na Banachdaich   239
Sgùrr Dearg
North-West Flank   240
Sgùrr Dearg
South Face   242
An Stac
South-East Face   246
Sgùrr MhicCoinnich
West Face   248
North Ridge   252
Upper Coire a' Ghrunnda
North Side   259
Sgùrr Sgumain
North-West Face   263
Lower Coire Lagan   265
Sgùrr Sgumain
West Buttress   267
Sròn na Cìche
The Cioch & Cioch Slab   270
Coire Lagan Face   274
South Crag, Coire a' Ghrunnda   279
North Crag, Coire a' Ghrunnda   283
Sgùrr Alasdair
Coire a' Ghrunnda Face   288
Sgùrr Theàrlaich
South-East Flank   290
Upper Coire a' Ghrunnda
South-East Side   293
Sgùrr nan Eag
Coire a' Ghrunnda Face   295
West-South-West Flank   297
Coire nan Laogh   301
Sgùrr a' Choire Bhig
South-East Face   303
Gars-bheinn
North-West Face   304

Coruisk South – Map   308

The Cuillin from Elgol   311
Sgùrr Hain
East Face   312
Sgùrr na Strì
South-South-East Buttress   315

An Garbh-choire 318
Sgùrr Dubh Beag
The Dubh Slabs 322

Coruisk North – Map 325

Sgùrr Dubh Mòr 326
Sgùrr Theàrlaich
East Face 329
Sgùrr Coire an Lochain
East Face 331
South Ridge 332
Sgùrr a' Ghreadaidh
South-East Ridge 337
Coir'-uisg 340
Bidein Druim nan Ràmh
Druim nan Ràmh 343
South-West Flank 344

Main Ridge Traverse

Southern Cuillin – Profile 347
Theàrlaich to MhicCoinnich – Sketch map 351
Central Cuillin – Profile 354
Tops of Mhadaidh – Sketch Map 358
Bidein Druim nan Ràmh – Sketch Map 362
Northern Cuillin – Profile 364
Am Basteir & Basteir Tooth – Sketch Map 366

Minginish – Map 371

Preshal Mòr
North-West Flank 373

Duirinish – Map 376

Trotternish – Map 385

INTRODUCTION

The Isle of Skye is arguably the finest of the many and varied islands lying off the western seaboard of Scotland. Second only to Lewis in size, Skye boasts the most rugged group of mountains in all the British Isles – the Cuillin. This compact massif has attracted the attention of mountaineers for well over a century. Its sharp peaks, narrow ridges and ice-scoured corries are fashioned out of rough, bare gabbro – one of the finest of all rocks for scrambling and climbing on.

Two other spectacular but contrasting kinds of scenery are displayed by the granite intrusions of the Red Hills and the basalt lavas of Duirinish and Trotternish. The coastline of Skye is scarcely less impressive. Its remarkably convoluted outline is many hundreds of kilometres long. The Gaelic name for the island, An t-Eilean Sgitheanach, means 'The Winged Isle', which refers to the shape of its major promontories. The coast is peppered with countless caves, arches, geos and stacks. There are long stretches of vertical cliffs, which in places reach several hundred metres in height.

The seaward vistas are especially varied too. Numerous smaller islands, such as Raasay, Scalpay, Soay and Wiay, lie close in to Skye whilst, among the more distant ones, Rum, Eigg and the Outer Hebrides are conspicuous. The mountains of Wester Ross and Lochaber form a prominent backdrop on the mainland.

The landscape found in the southern part of the island, although geologically more complex, is perhaps less dramatic. However, an interesting type of landform occurs in Strath, where exposures of limestone are riddled with small caves.

This guide is concerned mainly with scrambling routes in the Cuillin. Only a selection of walks and lower grade climbs is included. The Cuillin main ridge offers the longest, and most continuously absorbing, scramble in the country, and this is fully described. However, there are all sorts of interesting outings in the flanking corries and on adjoining ridges. Indeed, the Cuillin can be regarded as a scramblers' paradise. The walks described from elsewhere on the island have been chosen to give a taste of the many delights to be found there. To explore all the corners of the island properly would take a lifetime.

Noel Williams
March 2011

ACKNOWLEDGEMENTS

This new edition has allowed a number of route descriptions to be updated and some additional outings to be included. The description of the main ridge traverse has also been expanded and new diagrams added.

Grading scrambles is fraught with difficulties because the lines of some routes may be varied. Sections that seem straightforward on a warm summer's day can be completely different propositions in wind and rain. Damp basalt can test the best of mountaineers. Having said all this there were some rogue grades in the previous edition and thanks to comments made by users some of the worst offenders have been corrected. Most notably the North-East Ridge of Sgùrr a' Choire Bhig was poorly described and woefully undergraded in the previous edition.

I thank the following for feedback and helpful suggestions: Rab Anderson, Robin Campbell, Mike Dixon, Jim Duffy, Simon Fraser, Martin Hampar, Willie Jeffrey, Al Matthewson, Scott Muir, Tom Prentice, Mark Shaw and Iain Thow.

I am also very grateful to a number of people for company on numerous outings – both repetitions and new discoveries – in particular Dick Allen, George Archibald, Robin Campbell, Peter Duggan, Simon Fraser, Willie Jeffrey, Peter Macdonald, Archie Marshall, Pete McLeod, Richard Merryfield, Oliver Overstall, Tom Prentice, Rob Richardson, John Temple, Iain Thow, Les Watt, Andrew Wielochowski, Fay Wielochowska and Lucy Williams.

The use of full colour has made it possible for the original artwork to be improved. I am extremely grateful to Mark Hudson and Jean Thomas for creating coloured versions of their delightful crag and wildlife diagrams respectively. Their sketches remain an important feature of the guide.

I thank Gordon Rothero for kindly updating the wildlife section. I also thank Colin Ballantyne and Doug Benn for allowing me to use their geological diagrams, and Neil Clark and the Hunterian Museum and Art Gallery for permission to use his photograph of dinosaur footprints.

I thank Martin Moran for allowing me to adapt his sketch maps showing the key sections of the Cuillin main ridge.

The location maps were created using Ordnance Survey OpenData. Although this data is now freely available for use without charge, it remains Crown copyright. Many thanks to Matt Munro for much help with technical aspects relating to the use of this data.

I am extremely grateful to Stuart Pedlar for so generously sharing the results of his meticulous research on the history of exploration in the Cuillin.

Many thanks also to Tom Prentice for processing all the photographs used in the guide, and for his help in trying to ensure that the Gaelic names are correct. We thank Peadar Morgan, Peter Drummond and Alasdair Grant for their words of advice on Gaelic spelling and the use of accents.

Last but not least, thanks to Peter Duggan, Stuart Pedlar and Tom Prentice for scrutinising the manuscript and making many helpful comments.

GEOLOGY

The landforms of Skye are strongly influenced by geology. The jagged Cuillin peaks, the rounded Red Hills and the layered plateau lavas in the north all owe their dramatic and distinctive forms to the different rocks from which they are built. Not surprisingly the island attracted geologists and scientists from early in the nineteenth century. MacCulloch, Forbes, Geikie and Harker are some of the famous names associated with the first phase of discovery. Subsequent researchers have continued to unravel the fascinating story behind the island's matchless scenery.

The rocks of Skye fall into three broad age categories; i) the oldest and most complex group is more than 400 million years old, ii) the middle group consists mainly of sedimentary rocks laid down when dinosaurs roamed the Earth, and iii) the youngest group is made up of igneous rocks associated with an outburst of volcanic activity which took place some 60 million years ago just prior to the opening of the North Atlantic.

Mountain Building

The oldest rocks on Skye are of Precambrian and Cambrian–Ordovician age. They are confined mainly to Sleat and the south-eastern part of the island. They have an extremely complex structure because they were involved in the Caledonian Mountain building events some 450 million years ago. Moine metamorphic rocks were thrust in a north-westerly direction on top of rocks belonging to a more stable foreland region comprised of very ancient Lewisian gneisses, Torridonian sandstones and shales, as well as Cambrian-Ordovician quartzites and limestones. All these rocks were caught up in a zone of thrusting and faulting known as the Moine Thrust. This major thrust feature was first mapped in detail more than a century ago in the Assynt area of Sutherland. It extends all the way from Tongue on the north coast of the mainland down through the North-West Highlands and across onto the Sleat peninsula of Skye.

The only significant hills belonging to this group are formed from Torridonian rocks, and they occur at the eastern corner of the island overlooking Kylerhea. Younger Cambrian quartzites form a minor ridge of hills to the east of Ord. One distinctive type of quartzite, known as 'Pipe Rock', is characterised by long tube-like structures believed to be fossil worm burrows. Numerous small caves have developed in the overlying limestones and dolostones of Strath and Ord. These better-drained rocks tend to produce grassy rather than heathery terrain. In the neighbourhood of later granite intrusions the limestones were changed by the heat from the large bodies of magma (i.e. thermally metamorphosed) to create a distinctive rock with yellow and green markings known as 'Skye Marble'. Various quarries have been worked in the Strath district over the last two centuries to exploit this rock as a decorative stone and for agricultural purposes.

Two sets of dinosaur footprints in rippled Jurassic rocks on the coast near Staffin
© Hunterian Museum & Art Gallery, University of Glasgow

Time of the Dinosaurs

There is a 200-million-year gap in the geological record of Skye until rocks belonging to the Mesozoic Era are found. Only minor exposures of Triassic age occur, but the succeeding Jurassic sandstones, limestones and shales are more widespread. They outcrop in an arcuate strip south and west of Broadford as well as on the Strathaird peninsula, and again beneath the lavas in the northern part of the island. They can be seen easily at Elgol, for example, where limy sandstones have weathered to produce an unusual honeycombed surface. The limestones and shales are especially rich in marine fossils, such as bivalves, brachiopods, ammonites and belemnites. Other remains found include marine reptiles (ichthyosaurs, plesiosaurs and a turtle). Of particular interest are the various dinosaur remains which have been found in Trotternish. These include a vertebra and various leg bones as well as sets of dinosaur footprints. These fossils show more similarities with dinosaurs found in North America than with those found in other parts of Britain. There is a small museum at Ellishadder, near Kilt Rock, where many local artefacts and superb fossil specimens are exhibited. It is well worth a visit.

Any deposits laid down in Cretaceous times were largely removed by the period of uplift and erosion which took place at the close of the Mesozoic Era. This set the stage for the third and most spectacular episode in the geological history of Skye.

Palaeogene Igneous Rocks

Some 60 million years ago forces deep inside the Earth were starting to break Greenland apart from north-western Europe. This process began with great outpourings of **basalt lava** throughout the Inner Hebrides, as well as in Northern Ireland, Greenland, and the Faroes. This would eventually lead to a great tectonic plate (Laurasia) rifting apart and creating the North-East Atlantic Ocean.

The lavas of Skye and Raasay today outcrop over more than $1,000 \text{ km}^2$, but geophysical surveys show that the same group of flows extends for a further 700 km^2 on the sea floor beyond Canna. Before they were worn down by erosion, the lavas on Skye probably exceeded 1,200m in thickness. It has been suggested that this spectacular burst of volcanic activity was caused by a large plume of molten material which developed within the Earth's mantle. This same feature may be located under the volcanic island of Iceland at the present day.

After an initial explosive phase, which produced deposits of volcanic ash, the basalt lavas probably erupted relatively quietly from long, deep fissures. Individual flows seen today are around 10–15m thick, although some can be more than double that. Bubbles of gas were frequently trapped in the upper section of a lava flow as it cooled. In many cases the resultant holes or **vesicles** in the basalt were filled at a later date by various minerals (such as zeolites, calcite and quartz) to create conspicuous white **amygdales**. Some of the zeolite amygdales consist of very delicate and attractive needle-shaped crystals.

The uppermost section of a lava flow is slaggy, and more easily eroded. Sometimes the intervals between flows were long enough for their upper surface to break down into red soil (laterite), and also for plants to grow. In some cases the remains of plant material were thick enough to eventually form thin beds of primitive coal called **lignite**. Plateau lavas now dominate the northern and western parts of Skye. They form distinctive flat-topped hills with stepped sides – excellent examples being MacLeod's Tables in Duirinish.

The magma not only erupted at the surface, but at a later stage also forced its way sideways, between the layers of Jurassic sediments underlying the lavas, to form thick **sills** of **dolerite**. Some of these sills developed strong **columnar jointing** when they cooled. This feature is seen clearly at Kilt Rock near Staffin. Indeed, the name Staffin means 'place of the upright pillars'.

A major **magma chamber**, some 12km across, developed within the base of the lava pile in the Cuillin area. Most of this magma had a similar composition to the basalt lavas but, because it cooled much more slowly, it crystallised into a much coarser-grained rock known as **gabbro**. It was intruded in a series of stages as funnel-shaped masses. Also included within the gabbro is a wide band of **peridotite**. The magma which produced this rock is thought to have originated from the Earth's mantle. Geologists describe it as having an ultrabasic rather than a basic composition, which means it contains more olivine and less silica than gabbro. It may have been the first pulse of magma to crystallise. It weathers to produce a very rough, pitted surface with a most distinctive brown-orange colour. It outcrops from An Garbh-choire (*rough corrie*) to Coireachan Ruadha (*brown/red corries*) – both these localities getting their names from the characteristics of this rock.

Numerous minor intrusions were subsequently injected into the Cuillin pluton after it had crystallised. These cooled more quickly than the gabbro and so formed either very fine-grained basalt or slightly coarser dolerite. One kind of intrusion produced large horizontal and inclined **sheets of tholeiite** (a variety of basalt poor in sodium). These sheets occur notably on the western side of the Cuillin, and also along long sections of the main ridge crest from Sgùrr Sgumain to Sgùrr na Banachdaich. In places the sheets have numerous **amygdales**. The surrounding gabbro, into which the sheets were injected, was also broken up in places to form volcanic breccia.

The whole gabbro mass was also permeated by funnel-shaped intrusions of basalt/dolerite known as **cone-sheets**. These are generally less than one metre thick, and run parallel to the layering in the gabbro. They are rather more common in the north-western and south-eastern sectors of the Cuillin pluton. The cone-sheets all dip towards a common focal point below Meall Dearg. Those near the centre of the complex dip more steeply (65°) than those near the outer margins which dip at only 10°. In the east on Clach Glas a cone-sheet forms the steep step at the start of The Impostor, and also extends as a broad slab dipping down the western flank of the mountain. On

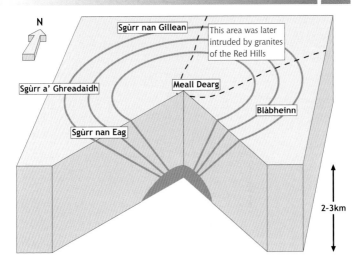

The orientation of the Cuillin cone-sheets

the southern Cuillin peak of Sgùrr na Stri the cone sheets dip to the north, so they form inward-dipping bands on the southern flank of this peak. On the western peaks such as Sgùrr a' Ghreadaidh they dip to the east and on the northern Cuillin peaks they dip to the south.

Magma was also injected into countless narrow, parallel-sided, vertical fissures, and cooled to produce basalt and dolerite **dykes**. The trend of the main Skye dyke swarm is in a north-west to south-east direction. It extends beyond Skye to the Outer Hebrides in one direction, and to the Great Glen in the other. A smaller subswarm with a south-west to north-east trend has been identified in Glen Brittle. Dykes are usually softer than the gabbro, and tend to weather out into chimneys and gullies. Some dykes, however, seem to be more resistant to erosion and do not form gullies. Generally, only the later dykes, which cut the cone-sheets, give rise to conspicuous gullies. Good examples include Willink's Gully on Blàbheinn, Waterpipe Gully on Sgùrr an Fheadain, Eag Dubh on Sgùrr a' Ghreadadh and Shadbolt's Chimney on the Basteir Tooth.

Both dykes and sheets, because they are fine-grained and usually well-jointed, tend to be rather brittle. They are also notoriously slippery when wet, so they generally have to be treated with much more care than the rougher and sounder gabbro.

The orientation of dykes and cone-sheets has an important influence on how easy it is to traverse along a section of ridge in the Cuillin. Where cone-

A dyke and cone-sheet intersect on the south ridge of Sgùrr na Banachdaich

sheets dip in towards the ridge crest they weather to form convenient ledges (Hart's Ledge on the west flank of Sgùrr MhicCoinnich for example), but where they dip away from the crest they form exposed slabs. Where dykes cut across a ridge they tend to form deep gaps, such as on the Pinnacle Ridge of Sgùrr nan Gillean. Where dykes run parallel to the ridge they may erode to leave steep faces such as on the two sides of the Inaccessible Pinnacle.

The Cuillin complex is also penetrated by a large number of pipe-like structures filled with a jumble of rock fragments of various types, ranging in size from fine dust particles to huge blocks. These structures are thought to represent **volcanic vents** from which a froth of lava and broken rocks was erupted. A good example of one of these pipes is exposed high up on the west ridge of Sgùrr nan Gillean.

A dyke in the floor of Coire a' Ghrunnda

Granite Intrusions

A change in composition from basic to acidic magma signalled the next episode of igneous activity. It led to the formation of rocks loosely termed 'granites'. The first pulse of this acid magma partly invaded the Cuillin complex and crystallised to form rocks now seen forming the peaks of Meall Dearg and Ruadh Stac, which overlook Glen Sligachan, as well as the lower slopes of Blàbheinn. The second group of intrusions formed the granites of the Western Red Hills, which lie between Glen Sligachan and Loch Ainort. The third and final group of intrusions led to the formation of the granites of the Eastern Red Hills, which are centred around Beinn na Caillich, west of Broadford.

These granite intrusions took place after the main phase of dyke injection had passed, and so dykes are much less common in the Red Hills. Where dykes do occur they tend to project slightly from the surface. Ring-dykes, composite sills and pyroclastic deposits complicate matters in some localities, but not sufficiently to influence the final rounded outlines of the Red Hills.

No further igneous activity took place in the subsequent 50 million years up to the present day. Instead, uplift, faulting and prolonged erosion deeply dissected the lavas. The granites were laid bare, though the summits of Glàmaig and Beinn na Crò still retain caps of basalt. The root of the Cuillin complex was also exposed. One more dramatic episode was still to provide the finishing touches to the scenery.

Glaciation

The Earth has been completely free of ice for much of its history, but at widely spaced intervals it has experienced ice ages. The Earth's climate began to cool significantly around 50 million years ago, shortly after the igneous activity along the west coast of Scotland had ceased. By some 34 million years ago an ice sheet had begun to form on Antarctica. Further cooling led to the growth of the Greenland ice sheet some 3 million years ago. North America and northern Europe have experienced an oscillating pattern of glacial periods and rather shorter temperate interglacial periods for at least the last 0.75 million years. Water locked up in the ice during glacial periods caused sea levels to fall worldwide by up to 150m.

When glaciers were most extensive, Skye was probably overwhelmed by ice over 1600m thick. During the last glacial maximum, some 18,000 years ago, an ice dome centred on the Cuillin and Blàbheinn deflected mainland ice to the north and south. Many peaks stood out as **nunataks** above the ice, including most of the crest of the Cuillin main ridge, Blàbheinn, Glàmaig, the Trotternish summits and Healabhal Bheag.

By 14,000 years ago glaciers had largely melted away throughout Scotland. Then a minor glacial episode (the 'Loch Lomond Stadial'), that lasted from 12,900 to 11,500 years ago, caused the regrowth of a large icefield over the centre of Skye, and the development of a dozen other ice masses on the island. All the western Cuillin corries, from Coire na Creiche to Coire nan Laogh, cultivated their own glaciers.

A very obvious terminal moraine dating from this time can be seen on the moor below Coire a' Ghrunnda. This feature was first identified by the pioneering Scottish glaciologist Professor Forbes in 1845. (Forbes had made the first recorded ascent of Sgùrr nan Gillean in 1836.) At that time, the idea that Britain had suffered glaciation was very contentious. Archibald Geikie described Forbes's observations in the Cuillin as *'the most detailed and satisfactory account which has yet been given of the proofs that the highlands of Britain once nourished groups of glaciers.'*

Corries, arêtes and U-shaped glens are now readily recognised as being of glacial origin, as are extensive deposits of moraine. The floor of Loch Coruisk has been excavated to a depth of some 30m below present sea-level by the passage of ice. Where rocks have been scoured by ice they are generally smooth and sound. However, the peaks which remained above the ice were subjected to freeze-thaw action, and hence are more broken. The upper limits

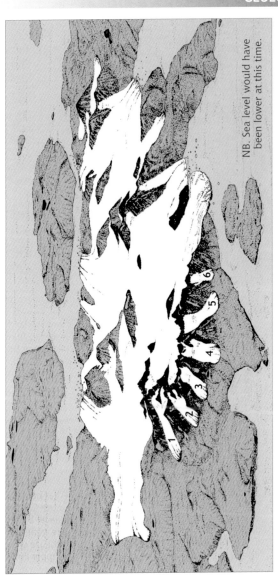

The Cuillin Icefield & neighbouring corrie glaciers around 12,000 years ago

NB. Sea level would have been lower at this time.

1. Coire na Creiche
2. Coire a 'Ghreadaidh

3. Coire na Banachdaich
4. Coire Lagan

5. Coire a' Ghrunnda
6. Coire nan Laogh

Ice-smoothed gabbro in the floor of Coire a' Ghrunnda

of ice are marked by what are called **periglacial trimlines**. A superb example descends southwards from about 400m to about 250m on the west flank of Blàbheinn.

Raised Beaches

A number of former shorelines – up to 30m above present sea level – can be identified around the coast of Skye. Dating these features with any precision is difficult because there were huge fluctuations in sea level during the multiple episodes of ice build-up and decay. The land surface was depressed by the weight of ice added to it during glaciations. Where the ice was thickest the land surface was depressed the most.

When the ice melted the land began to bounce back up to its former level. At the end of the last glacial episode sea level rose rapidly until some 6,000 years ago. This rise was countered by slow uplift of the land as it re-adjusted to the weight of ice being removed. Postglacial raised beaches on Skye tilt gently towards the north-west falling from 10m OD at Kyleakin in the south-east to about 6m OD on the Duirinish peninsula in the north-west.

The terminal moraine below Coire a' Ghrunnda

Landslides

The most spectacular landslides in Britain are to be found in the northern part of Skye. All along the east side and also parts of the north end of the Trotternish escarpment, there are major slipped rock masses. The two most famous areas are below The Storr and Quiraing. A subsidiary area of landslides on the south side of Glen Uig is known as the Fairy Glen.

The Trotternish escarpment is built of a thick sequence of westward-dipping basalt lavas resting on relatively weak Jurassic sediments. The slides took place along curved surfaces, and as many as five successive major blocks have been identified below the Quiraing between the present day escarpment edge and the sea. In many cases the bases of the slides correspond with the presence of dolerite sill – a tougher rock – within the weak Jurassic strata. The landslides were probably initiated in preglacial times, and the outer ones have certainly been modified by the passage of the last ice sheet over the area. The most recent ones, closest to the escarpment edge, are thought to have finished moving soon after deglaciation last took place. The land around Flodigarry, however, still appears to be unstable and this causes ongoing engineering problems with the main road in that area.

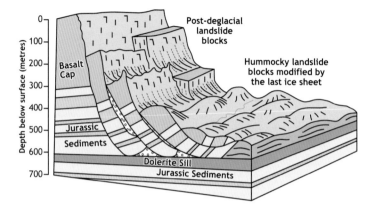

The multiple landslips on the east flank of the Trotternish Ridge

Diatomite

In early postglacial times the remains of microscopic unicellular algae called diatoms began to accumulate in several freshwater lochs in parts of Trotternish. The siliceous remains of these algae eventually collected in sufficient quantities to form deposits of a white, porous and inert material called diatomite. When the climate became cooler and wetter around 5,000 years ago conditions were less favourable for diatoms and peat began to accumulate instead.

The thickest deposits of diatomite were laid down in Loch Cuithir below Sgùrr a' Mhadaidh Ruaidh, near Leallt. The extraction of diatomite began there in the late nineteenth century and a railway line was used to bring the material to drying facilities near the shore at Inver Tote. Production finally ceased in 1960. Diatomite has many uses including filtration, as an abrasive, and in the manufacture of dynamite.

Maps & Guides

Various geological maps are available for Skye. See the website of the British Geological Survey <http://shop.bgs.ac.uk/Bookshop/>.
The Skye Central Complex 1:25,000 map (2005) is strongly recommended.

Several geological guides to the island are also available:
An Excursion Guide to the Geology of Skye (Bell & Harris) 1986.
The Quaternary of the Isle of Skye (Ballantyne, Benn, Lowe & Walker) 1991.
Skye: A Landscape Fashioned by Geology (Merritt & Stephenson) 1993.

HUMAN HISTORY

Prehistory

Stone Age people started to move into northern latitudes soon after the last ice age ended some 10,000 years ago. The island of Skye has a wealth of archaeological remains, but they are poorly preserved compared with more famous examples found in Lewis, Orkney and Shetland. A Mesolithic (Middle Stone Age) shell midden recently discovered at An Corran near Staffin, and dated as 8,500 years old, is the earliest evidence of human presence in the Hebrides. These first visitors were hunter-gatherers, and they used simple implements made from antlers and stone, including pitchstone from Arran and the bloodstone of Rum. They used rudimentary boats such as dug-out canoes for some of their travels, which must have been exciting given west coast currents.

Some 6,000 years ago, Neolithic (New Stone Age) farming settlers started to travel north and introduce new skills. They sought out fertile islands, and settled in Islay, the Uists and most notably in Orkney. They reared cattle, sheep and goats, and also grew grain. No evidence of their dwellings has been found on Skye, but several stone tombs known as chambered cairns have been discovered. There is a good example of a chambered cairn at Rubha an Dùnain, only a few kilometres from the camp site in Glen Brittle.

Only very poorly preserved standing stones and stone circles are found on Skye. Examples of these structures include a stone circle near Kilmarie, Strathaird, and standing stones at Borve, near Portree.

The remains of ornate pottery and stone coffins (cists), which are found in some of the chambered cairns, are assumed to have been inserted at a later date. They indicate that 'Beaker People', originally from the Rhine valley, had arrived on Skye about 2000BC. They had knowledge of metal working, and could smelt copper and tin to make bronze. The climate began to deteriorate from 1500BC onwards, and the colder and wetter conditions made arable farming less productive and caused peat to accumulate. The growth of peat may well have covered traces of earlier human settlements.

During the last thousand years BC, communities began building stone fortifications to protect themselves and their livestock. This need may have arisen due to pressure from neighbours competing for land and resources, or more probably because of seaborne attacks from outsiders. A variety of structures were built, including hill forts, duns and brochs.

More than twenty Iron Age brochs have been identified on Skye. Most of them are badly ruined, but it is clear that at one time they must have been fairly substantial circular towers, shaped like the cooling towers in a modern power station. They had an internal diameter of some 10m, and walls about 4m thick with an internal staircase and gallery. The best example on the island, Dun Beag, is only a few minutes from the roadside near Struan, and is well worth a visit. Those travelling to Skye via the Kylerhea ferry need only make a short detour from Glenelg to examine two spectacular brochs on the mainland in Gleann Beag. The larger of the two is over 10m high.

The term dun is used to describe a great variety of other structures. (Dun is the Gaelic word for 'broch', which is rather confusing.) Many of the duns were built on promontories overlooking the sea, such as at Rubha an Dùnain. Interestingly, the brochs are found mainly in the north and west of Skye, whilst the promontory duns are found mainly in the south. The age of these structures is uncertain, though most of the Skye brochs are believed to date from 100BC to 100AD.

The Roman presence further south around 100AD may have reduced forays to the north, and a more peaceful period seems to have ensued. The brochs were abandoned and some of their stones re-used. Hut circles, which took the place of brochs, were mainly wooden structures built on a circular stone base. The souterrains associated with them are long, narrow stone-lined passages of uncertain purpose. They may have been used as underground shelters, or as communal food stores. The best preserved example on Skye is above the Allt na Cille about one kilometre north of Glasnakille, in Strathaird. *In Search of Prehistoric Skye*, by Ian Donaldson-Blyth, gives details of how to find this souterrain and over forty other prehistoric sites on the island.

History

In the late third century AD, Roman writers referred to the people living north of Antonine's wall as the Pictae (painted people). Clach Ard, a stone slab with carved symbols, found at Tote, near Skeabost Bridge, is evidence of their presence on Skye. A finer example of a symbol stone occurs on nearby Raasay.

The Scots spread up the west coast of Scotland from Ireland around 500AD. They brought with them their Gaelic language, and the art of writing. Christianity spread to Skye a short time later. St Columba visited in 585AD, and other saints soon after. An early monastic site has been identified at Loch Chaluim Chille (now drained), near Kilmuir, in the north of Trotternish.

The relative peace of the next few centuries was shattered by the start of the Viking raids from Scandinavia. Although the Norse occupied Skye for more than four centuries, there is remarkably little tangible evidence remaining of their presence. The main signs of Norse influence that survive are the large number of Norse place names found on the island. The names of the major regions of the island – Minginish, Bracadale, Duirinish, Waternish, Trotternish, Sleat and Strath (or Strathordil) – are all of Norse origin, as are some 60% of the village or township names. The main hills were also named by the Norse. Healabhal and Storr, for example, are obviously of Norse origin, but Cuillin too is probably a derivation of the Norse word *kiolen* meaning high rocks.

Norse rule came to an end with the defeat of King Håkon of Norway in 1263 at the battle of Largs. The Sudreys (i.e. the Hebrides and the Isle of

Man) were ceded to Scotland by the treaty of Perth three years later. The clan system had evolved by the time Skye fell under the dominion of the Lord of the Isles. The inhabitants of Skye continued to regard themselves as separate from Scotland. Resistance to mainland rule continued through the fourteenth and fifteenth centuries, but feuding between clans also caused much strife. At the battle of Sligachan in 1395 a large invasion party trying to usurp the ruling MacLeods were cut to pieces. The spoils were divided at Creag an Fheannaidh (rock of the flaying), which some have identified as The Bloody Stone in Harta Corrie.

James IV, who came to the throne in 1488, was the last Scots king to speak Gaelic. He had some success in subduing the island chiefs, and in 1493 the Lordship of the Isles was finally forfeited to the Crown. However, clan warfare continued on Skye for another century, until a final battle in 1601. A party of MacDonalds, after raiding MacLeod properties in Bracadale and Minginish, had arranged to meet up with their spoil in Coire na Creiche (corrie of plunder) below the Cuillin. In the late afternoon they were set upon by a party of MacLeods, and the battle continued into the night. The MacDonalds eventually came out on top and captured the MacLeod leader and thirty of his followers. James VI, alarmed by their constant feuding, commanded the two clan chiefs to surrender themselves. They were made to settle their quarrels, by arbitration through the intermediary of other island chiefs, and the prisoners of the battle were released.

With the death of Elizabeth I in 1603, James VI of Scots also became James I of England. He then made further efforts to tame the Western Isles. In 1609 the Hebridean Chiefs were summoned to Iona, and signed up to the Bond and Statutes of Icolmkill. The direct intention of these measures was to eradicate the Gaelic culture, and make the islanders conform more with the Lowland life-style. The importation of *aqua vitae* (whisky) was banned, eldest sons had to be sent to the Lowlands to learn English, and obedience to the reformed kirk was demanded.

Attempts to restore the Stuarts to the throne in the eighteenth century were to pose a further threat to the Gaelic way of life. Charles Edward Stuart (Bonnie Prince Charlie) landed on the Scottish mainland from France in 1745, and gained the support of sufficient Highland chiefs to launch a rebellion. His eventual defeat at Culloden the following year had great repercussions throughout the Highlands. Skye did not experience the harsh reprisals suffered elsewhere, because the MacLeods and MacDonalds of Skye had not supported the Jacobite cause. Raasay, however, was completely devastated by government forces. All property there was razed to the ground, and the livestock destroyed.

The Prince only escaped to France with his life after an extraordinary journey through Lochaber to the Outer Isles, and back again via Skye and Raasay. A young woman from South Uist, Flora MacDonald, was instrumental in the Prince's escape from the Outer Isles to Skye. Although she was captured soon after, and taken to London, she was released unharmed after a year's detention. By then she was something of a national celebrity.

As a consequence of the rebellion, Jacobite estates were forfeited, and the government banned the wearing of Highland garb and the carrying of arms. The clan chiefs had their powers removed, and they became mere landlords. The Highlands and Islands, however, were an important source of manpower for the British army so, when the Seven Years War broke out in 1757, numerous Highland regiments were raised. By the end of the war the restrictions on dress were being relaxed, although it was a further two decades before they were repealed.

Highlanders had been emigrating to the Cape Fear district of North Carolina in small numbers since the 1730s. Some of the soldiers who fought in North America against the French now settled there too. Word spread back to Skye and, after a particularly harsh winter in 1771, hundreds of islanders tried to improve their lot by sailing off to the new world.

Flora MacDonald and her husband Allan, a local tacksman, were among those who followed in 1774, '...as we cannot promise ourselves but poverty and oppression.' These early emigrants had the resources to pay their own way and left voluntarily. Many of them became embroiled in the American War of Independence. Allan MacDonald and his sons fought as loyalists, and were captured and held prisoners by the colonists.

The population of Skye doubled in size between 1755 and 1831. This is remarkable considering the numbers that emigrated during that time, and also the repeated draining of men to the army. An important factor in this population explosion was the introduction of inoculation against smallpox, which was practised on Skye by the early 1760s. The preservation of life was further improved with the introduction of vaccination, which began on the island in 1800. The potato had been introduced shortly after 1750, and by 1770 it had become the staple diet of the people. The runrig system of allocating land to a different tenant every few years still prevailed. The trade in black cattle was lucrative throughout the second half of the eighteenth century, and some 4000 head a year followed the droving route from Skye to the southern markets.

During the Napoleonic wars there was a period of relative prosperity. Men found employment in soldiering, and, due to the disruption of imports, the kelp industry and cattle rearing thrived. Herring shoals were frequent visitors to the sea-lochs and fishing was successful. Land was divided into crofts, and the tenants could sub-divide their holdings among their relatives. Cottars held no land or grazing rights, but could live in cheap rented property.

After the peace of 1815 these various livelihoods went into sharp decline and great hardship ensued. The potato crop was ruined by blight in 1835. By 1837 half the people of Skye were destitute. In 1845 and during the three succeeding summers the blight returned and distress became even more acute. Landlords found their incomes falling, and sheep farms became an attractive alternative. It was found that the Cheviot breed of sheep could withstand the rigours of a Highland winter. The more fertile land was in great demand for sheep grazing, and people were moved onto the poorer ground.

Several wealthy farmers from the mainland took possession of tacks on Skye. So began the clearances. Crofters were evicted from Duirinish, Trotternish, Bracadale, Minginish and Strath. In 1852 two whole communities were forcibly cleared from Boreraig and Suisnish, and their dwellings razed to the ground. This kind of brutality was perhaps exceptional, but it is estimated that 3500 were dispossessed of land and home on the whole island. The evicted were in some cases pushed onto poorer quality crofting areas near the shore, and great overcrowding took place. Multitudes had little alternative but to emigrate. Some idea of the heartbreak they suffered can be imagined from this contemporary account of a scene on board a ship as it sailed south with emigrants bound for Adelaide, Australia:

> 'The Collen [Cuillin] mountains were in sight for several hours of our passage; but when we rounded Ardnamurchan Point, the emigrants saw the sun for the last time glitter upon their splintered peaks, and one prolonged and dismal wail rose from all parts of the vessel; the fathers and mothers held up their infant children to take a last view of the mountains of their Fatherland which in a few minutes faded from their view forever.'

On the mainland genuine concern was shown for the starving and dispossessed people of the island. Schemes were devised to give employment in building roads, constructing piers and draining land. Much money was raised to assist emigration, and the bulk of the emigrants had their fares paid by the state, or by their landlords. Norman, Chief of MacLeod, was a notable philanthropist who, it is said, spent about £200 a week to alleviate the suffering. When he was warned of impending financial disaster, he said 'ruin must be faced rather than let the people die'.

Great hardship was suffered on the voyages to North America and Australia. Many died through sickness either at sea or during the early months after arrival at their destinations. Many vessels were shipwrecked with hundreds of lives lost.

The main wave of clearances had finished on Skye by the late 1870s but, when the economics of sheep farming deteriorated, landlords were squeezed to survive. Crofters then began to resist the poor treatment they received. Skyemen became leading agitators for reform in the 1880s. There were major disputes over grazing land, notably at Braes and Glendale, to which police, marines and gunboats from the mainland were called in. All this unrest resulted in the Napier Commission being set up to investigate the crofters' grievances. One of the commissioners was Alexander Nicolson, the early Cuillin explorer. The resulting Crofters Act, which was passed in 1886, gave important rights to crofters: security of tenure, the right to pass on land to descendants, the right to compensation for improvements should land be sold, and a new body, the Crofters' Commission, able to fix fair rents. Despite this landmark victory, there were still grievances, and land raids took place as late as 1920.

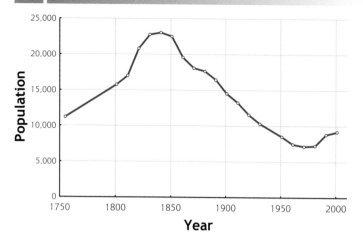

How the population of Skye has changed over the last 250 years

As recently as 1924 there was widespread distress in Skye and the Western Isles and many were on the verge of starvation. A relief fund was set up and appeals for help reached right round the world. This information appeared in a letter published in an Australian newspaper – the *Argus*:

In the Isle of Lewis alone fully 20,000 people are threatened with starvation. In the Isle of Skye probably 10,000 are in a similar plight. There is distress in a similar degree throughout remaining islands of the west....No man living ever saw such hardships in the Western Isles as are to be seen in many parts of them today.

The population of Skye continued to fall for most of the twentieth century. Two world wars took their toll, as the war memorials on the island starkly testify. The decline appears to have halted, however, and resident numbers may soon return to the level of 250 years ago. Land ownership is still a contentious issue, although crofters have been entitled to purchase their land since 1976, and a new and influential Scottish Crofters Union was formed in 1985. An interesting development took place in 1997 when Orbost farm estate was bought with public funds. There were lengthy teething problems agreeing the best way forward and some have questioned the long term viability of the estate, but the hope is that resettlement will be encouraged.

Tourism continues to play a big part in Skye's economy. The dramatic scenery and the superb opportunities for all aspects of mountaineering on the island are certain to remain big attractions for visitors.

Tufted hair-grass on the summit of Sgùrr a' Ghreadaidh   Photo: Peter Duggan

WILDLIFE

Plants

This short account has been written with scramblers in mind and consequently it emphasises those plants which grow in the more rocky hills. However, on Skye, as throughout north-west Scotland, many plants that are normally associated with a mountain habitat are found right down to sea level. Indeed, the plants that you can expect to see when walking and scrambling on Skye, particularly the more interesting ones, are often determined more by the geology than the altitude. The marked differences between the plant communities on the major hill groups are due largely to the varied nature of the underlying rocks, such as Torridonian sandstone above Kyleakin, gabbro in the Cuillin, or basalt in Trotternish. However, there are also some plants that are common over much of the island and these warrant a brief mention first.

It will probably not have escaped your notice that it rains a lot on Skye, and this excess of precipitation over thousands of years has led to the formation of extensive areas of peat, particularly on lower and flatter ground.

A   Devilsbit Scabious
B   Northern Rockcress
C   Mountain Avens

The dominant plants growing on the peat may vary but the commonest species tend to be ubiquitous and will be familiar to most hill-goers. **Heather** (Calluna vulgaris), **deer-grass** (Trichophorum cespitosum), **cotton grasses** (Eriophorum species), **cross-leaved heath** (Erica tetralix), **bell heather** (Erica cinerea), **purple moor grass** (Molinia caerulea), **bog myrtle** (Myrica gale) and **bog-mosses** (Sphagnum) are more or less abundant everywhere on the peat. In the wettest areas the bog-mosses form large lawns and hummocks of green, ochre and red. Skye can even boast its own eponymous bog-moss in Sphagnum skyense, first found in Strath Suardal and only known from a few sites in the west of Britain and Ireland. A closer look at the bogs will reveal other plants of interest. These include all three British species of the insectiverous **sundew** family (Drosera species), the starry yellow flowers of **bog asphodel** (Narthecium ossifragum) and, in bog-pools, the three-lobed leaves and the pink flowerheads of the **bogbean** (Menyanthes trifoliata).

In the bogs and also in most areas of hill grassland the small, yellow four-petalled flower of the **tormentil** (Potentilla erecta) is common and enlivens the scene from early summer to late in the autumn. Another common plant on boggy ground, which can also be abundant in a number of other habitats, is **devilsbit scabious** (Succisa pratensis), a tall plant with dark green lanceolate leaves and a rounded head of small, blue-purple flowers. The **heath spotted orchid** (Dactylorhiza maculata) is also very common, adding a splash of colour on the peatlands and damp grassland, its spikes of flowers varying in hue from white through pink to pale purple.

In drier grassland, **thyme** (Thymus polytrichus) is often so abundant that the distinctive aroma of its leaves accompanies each footstep. On better-drained ground there are areas of heather moorland usually with abundant bell heather, but much of this has been converted over the years by burning and grazing into grassland with the common grasses being **fescues** (Festuca species) and **bents** (Agrostis species).

The richest woodland on Skye is on the Sleat peninsula. Over the poorest soils the dominant trees tend to be **birch** (Betula pubescens), **oak** (Quercus petraea) and **rowan** (Sorbus aucuparia) with scattered **hollies** (Ilex aquifolium). **Alder** (Alnus glutinosus) is generally common on the wetter soils. Over the richer soils, and particularly over the limestone at Ord and Tokavaig, **hazel** (Corylus avellana) can be abundant – often with **ash** trees (Fraxinus excelsior) and, more rarely, **gean** (Prunus padus).

The more interesting flowers occur on the limestone where spring produces an abundance of **primroses** (Primula vulgaris), **wood anemone** (Anemone nemorosa) and **bluebells** (Hyacythoides non-scripta) and, more locally, **ramsons** or **wild garlic** (Allium ursinum). Later in the season, flowers of **meadow-sweet** (Filipendula ulmaria), **marsh hawksbeard** (Crepis paludosa) and, on ledges, **globeflower** (Trollius europaeus) appear. Rarities here include **herb paris** (Paris quadrifolia) and **long-leaved helleborine** (Cephalanthera longifolia), a large, beautiful, white orchid.

The rocky nature of the woodland, in conjunction with the oceanic climate (wet cool winters and wet cool summers!) and freedom from pollution, has led to the development of beautiful carpets of **mosses**, **lichens** and **liverworts** on both rocks and trees. Not only are these plant communities very attractive to look at, but they are also extremely rare in global terms and some species are close to their northern-most limits in the world on Skye. More easily identifiable as separate plants are the flat fronds of the **Tunbridge filmy-fern** (*Hymenophyllum tunbrigense*) growing amongst the mosses, the most northerly colonies of this plant in Britain.

There are also large areas of limestone through Strath Suardal and down to Loch Slapin at Torrin. These are pleasant to wander over and have much botanical interest. **Mountain avens** (*Dryas octopetala*) is locally abundant, growing right down to sea level at Camas Malag, the large white flowers and neat, dark green leaves providing a wonderful display in early summer.

The grassland over the limestone is fertile and has an abundance of common flowers like **thyme**, **fairy flax** (*Linum catharticum*), **bird's-foot trefoil** (*Lotus corniculatus*), **selfheal** (*Prunella vulgaris*) and **devilsbit scabious** and some less common plants like **northern bedstraw** (*Galium boreale*), **grass of Parnassus** (*Parnassia palustris*), **alpine bistort**

Early Purple Orchid

(*Persicaria vivipara*), **field gentian** (*Gentianella campestris*), **early purple orchid** (*Orchis mascula*) and **twayblade** (*Listera ovata*).

In the crevices of the limestone, protected from grazing, there are many ferns and flowers like primrose, **sanicle** (*Sanicula europaea*), **wild angelica** (*Angelica sylvestris*), **enchanter's nightshade** (*Circaea* species) and rarer plants like herb paris and the beautiful **dark red helleborine** (*Epipactis atrorubens*).

The Red Hills are built of granite and have rounded, exposed ridges but

Top: Sphagnum skyense   Left: Roseroot   Right: Grass of Parnassus

also crags and areas of block scree. These hills are not botanically rich but they do support a few of the more common montane species. In rocky places the dominant plant is often the conspicuous **woolly hair-moss** (*Racomitrium lanuginosum*), growing with **stiff sedge** (*Carex bigelowii*), **blaeberry** (*Vaccinium myrtillus*), **least willow** (*Salix herbacea*) and **mountain everlasting** (*Antennaria dioica*). Other frequent species include **heath bedstraw** (*Galium saxatile*), common in all hill grassland, **alpine lady's mantle** (*Alchemilla* *alpina*), **crowberry** (*Empetrum* species) and, more rarely, **alpine cudweed** (*Gnaphalium supinum*). On the wind-blasted ridges and bealachs there are prostrate plants of **juniper** (*Juniperus communis alpina*) growing with other low shrubs in an attractive, open vegetation. The faces of the larger boulders in the screes are a good place to look for **Wilson's filmy-fern** (*Hymenophyllum wilsonii*) and, where mounds of bog-moss occur under the heather, the **lesser twayblade** (*Listera cordata*), a tiny orchid, can be abundant.

Scrambles in the Cuillin form a major part of this guide but climbing and plants often do not mix, and the vast expanses of bare rock which are such a feature of the Cuillin bear witness to this. The gabbro which delights climbers is a very solid rock; it is slow to weather and produce the soil that plants need; it is also a basic rock and the minerals that it does release into the soil are not to the liking of all plants. One plant that thrives in these conditions is the **northern rockcress** (*Arabis petraea*), an uncommon arctic-alpine plant that is more abundant in the Cuillin than anywhere else in Britain. Its purple-tinged white flowers and its wild habitat more than make up for its rather close resemblance to certain garden weeds. A close relative, and even more rare, is the **alpine rockcress** (*Arabis alpina*), common in the Alps but having its only British site in the recesses of the Cuillin corries where it was first found by H.C. Hart, the Irish mountaineer and botanist, in 1887.

The ledges on crags in corries are more productive than exposed ridges and slabs but even relatively sheltered ledges may have little more than woolly hair-moss, crowberry, alpine lady's mantle and **goldenrod** (*Solidago virgaurea*). Alpine lady's mantle can be abundant – its deeply divided leaves with their silvery lower surface being unmistakable. The spikes of yellow flowers of goldenrod here seem larger and more attractive than the lowland plant.

Broken crags with damp ledges, and the wet areas at the base of larger crags are more interesting; here you can find plants like **starry saxifrage** (*Saxifraga stellaris*), **roseroot** (*Sedum rosea*), **stone bramble** (*Rubus saxatilis*), **mountain sorrel** (*Oxyria digyna*), **moss campion** (*Silene acaulis*) and, more rarely, **alpine sawwort** (*Saussurea alpina*), **arctic mouse-ear** (*Cerastium arcticum*) and **purple saxifrage** (*Saxifraga oppositifolia*). More sheltered sites can also harbour a few small trees, usually rowans, sometimes growing at an altitude of over 600m.

Glen Sligachan has numerous dubh-lochans and mire areas where the pale-green, spiky rosettes of the **pipewort** (*Eriocaulon aquaticum*) form large mats on the bottom of the pools. Some of these rosettes produce very long flower-stems with a head of small blue flowers. The pipewort is an American plant with its only European sites in Skye, Ardnamurchan, Coll and similar oceanic areas of western Ireland. Bogbean often grows with the pipewort while lochs with a stony floor usually have the slender flower-stems and pale blue flower of the **water lobelia** (*Lobelia dortmanna*).

Wet, stony areas with **black bog rush** (*Schoenus nigricans*) often contain

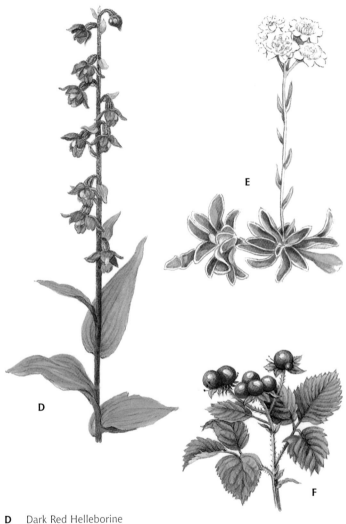

D Dark Red Helleborine
E Mountain Everlasting
F Stone Bramble

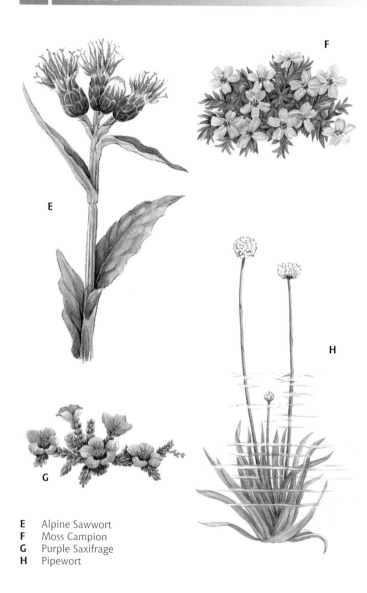

E Alpine Sawwort
F Moss Campion
G Purple Saxifrage
H Pipewort

both the **common butterwort** (Pinguicula vulgaris), with its star-shaped rosette of yellow-green leaves and violet flowers, and the smaller, **pale butterwort** (Pinguicula lusitanica) which has lilac flowers. Both species supplement their nutrient uptake by trapping insects in the sticky mucous that covers their leaves.

The richest sites on Skye for mountain plants are the basalt crags and corries of the Trotternish ridge from The Storr in the south to Quiraing in the north. Almost all of the plants of the Cuillin occur here, and usually in greater abundance. The Storr is perhaps the best known site, but Quiraing and the area above Loch Cuithir are also very rich. The lush vegetation on the ledges is richer than that in the Cuillin, and in the grassland there are cushions of moss campion, covered in pink flowers in early summer and, in a few places, creeping stems of **sibbaldia** (Sibbaldia procumbens). **Mossy cyphel** (Minuartia sedoides) resembles moss campion but the cyphel produces rather dull, greenish flowers that are easily overlooked. Where there is less competition from larger plants, mountain sorrel, purple and **mossy saxifrages** (Saxifraga hypnoides), northern rockcress, **hoary whitlow-grass** (Draba incana) and **moonwort** (Botrychium lunaria) can all be locally abundant. In a few places there are scattered plants of **alpine saxifrage** (Saxifraga nivalis) with its tight cluster of dull white flowers, and also tiny mats of **alpine pearlwort** (Sagina saginoides). The plateau area of the Trotternish ridge and its associated stony springs has a special plant in the **Iceland purslane** (Koenigia islandica), the only other British site for this arctic species being in similar terrain on the island of Mull.

A number of plants find the habitat they need both on the mountains and on the coast. Common seashore plants that also occur in the hills are **scurvy grass** (Cochlearia species), **kidney vetch** (Anthyllis vulneraria), **sea plantain** (Plantago maritima), **sea campion** (Silene unicolor) and **thrift** (Armeria maritima). The latter forms carpets of pink on rocky shores and coastal grassland in early summer but looks equally at home growing in mats of woolly hair-moss on a windswept summit at 900m. Similarly, mountain plants like roseroot, purple saxifrage and moss campion also occur on ledges of the less exposed sea cliffs.

Lower down, where the influence of salt spray is greater, the common plants are thrift, sea plantain, **English stonecrop** (Sedum anglicum) and more occasionally sea campion. Where sea-birds nest and there is an accumulation of 'organic material' there can be large stands of **red campion** (Silene dioica) and **stinging nettle** (Urtica dioica). One northern plant that is common on some rocky coasts is **Scottish lovage** (Ligusticum scoticum), a large 'umbellifer' with an attractive shiny foliage. At the heads of some of the sea-lochs there are areas of salt-marsh with **sea aster** (Aster tripolium) and frequent large stands of **yellow iris** (Iris pseudacorus).

Animals

In the nature of things, climbers, scramblers and, to a lesser extent, hill-walkers tend to visit those exposed and least productive areas that most animals tend to avoid. In the mountains on Skye, once embarked upon a walk or climb, most of the larger wildlife seen is likely to be airborne unless one is lucky (and quiet) enough to stumble across a **fox**. One animal is an unfortunate exception to this rule. Most visitors to Skye in the summer months are aware of the misery the teeming **midge** can cause in damp, still weather (and in many other sorts of weather too), but otherwise perfect days can also be marred by biting **clegs**, particularly on the lower ground.

In common with most islands, Skye is poorer in most mammals than the adjacent mainland. Though there have been records in the past, relatively common animals on the mainland like badger and rare ones like the wildcat are not now thought to occur on Skye and there are no historic records of red squirrel. Other species have been introduced, largely during the 19th century, with mixed results. **Rabbits** have spread throughout the island wherever suitable habitat occurs, and the **hedgehog** is now sparsely spread over the island. The **mole** has spread only 15km since being introduced at Lyndale House in 1903. Other insectivores – the **common**, **pygmy** and **water shrew** – are found across the island. The **mountain hare** is another introduction that apparently did well at first but now seems to be restricted to Raasay, Trotternish and the Cuillin.

The lowland **brown hare** is also an introduced species to Skye but it has a very patchy distribution which is probably linked to the pattern of cultivation, now more common in the north of the island with the Sleat population in the south probably extinct. Of the smaller mammals, the most frequently seen by the hillwalker is the **short-tailed vole**, which is found everywhere except on some of the islands and can be particularly abundant in new forestry plantations. The **field mouse** is limited to the richer, wooded areas and to the better crofting land, and is a frequent visitor to houses in the winter months. The **bank vole** is limited to the islands of Raasay and Scalpay where it has been isolated long enough to have evolved as a distinct race, being slightly larger and darker than those on the mainland.

Our two native species of deer occur on the island but again populations are much smaller than on the mainland. The **roe deer** is a shy and quiet animal of woodland and is thus difficult to see but it is present in much of Sleat, in Glen Varragill between Sligachan and Portree, and is reported from Raasay. Much of the **red deer** population is again in Sleat, close to the mainland, but smaller herds occur further north and numbers are apparently increasing. Some can even be seen in the quieter Cuillin corries such as Coire nan Laogh and Harta Corrie.

Of the predatory mammals on Skye, the **stoat** and **weasel** are present in small numbers with perhaps the stoat, larger and with a black tip to the tail, being the more numerous of the two. The **pine marten** arrived on Skye as

Otter

the bridge neared completion in 1995 and has subsequently spread in to Sleat and is now heading northwards. **American mink** have reached Skye and, having successfully colonised the island, they are moving north on the mainland. The most successful predator without doubt is the **fox**, which is present in greater or lesser numbers all over Skye but is apparently absent from Raasay. The efforts of crofters and keepers to control the numbers of foxes have been thwarted, probably by the abundance of both carrion for food and of rough and rocky terrain for cover.

One mammal with a Skye population density probably exceeding that of the adjacent mainland is the **otter**. Otters, or otter signs such as spraints, have been seen over the whole of the island but virtually all sightings are coastal and apparently numbers tend to be greater where the underlying rock is Torridonian. Recent surveys suggest that the first glimpse a climber is likely to have of an otter is as a casualty on the faster stretches of road between Kyleakin and Luib where currently eight a year are found dead. This rate of mortality, albeit regrettable, presumably reflects a very healthy total population, probably over 250 on Skye and Raasay. Forest Enterprise run a popular otter-viewing hide near Kylerhea.

The coastal waters around Skye offer the possibility of seeing a number of other mammals. Seals are the most conspicuous, both swimming and in haul-out colonies. They can be seen round most of the Skye coast with the **common seal** being much more numerous than the **Atlantic grey seal**. **Harbour porpoise** are fairly common around the coast, and other species which can be seen include **white-beaked** and **Risso's dolphins**, **minke whales** and the **basking shark**, the latter particularly off the Elgol coast. A pair of **northern bottlenosed whales** aroused great interest when they spent several weeks in Broadford Bay in the summer of 1998. You are much more likely to see all these species, and possibly **killer whales** too, from a boat when sailing around the island.

The birds with which climbers become most involved tend to be those that are interested in the remains of your lunch. It is remarkable how quickly a **herring gull** appears once the sandwiches are in evidence, but other birds like **hooded crows** and even the magnificent **raven** are all attracted to favourite lunch spots. **Golden eagles** are more stand-offish but Skye does have a good population and, though they may be difficult to see in the more popular mountain areas, visits to the less frequented parts of the hills and coast can often result in a sighting. The re-introduction of the **sea-eagle** on Rum has meant that sightings on Skye are now quite frequent and they have nested here since 1987, indeed, in 2006 the 200th Scottish sea-eagle chick fledged on Skye. **Buzzards** – the tourists' eagle – are much more common, and there will be few days when these adaptable birds are not seen or heard, particularly on lower ground. The **peregrine** has undergone a steady recovery in Scotland in recent years and, though still rare on Skye, its noisy alarm call may accompany a walk past a big crag or coastal cliff.

The **meadow pipit** is ubiquitous in grassland on the hills and its descending trill and 'parachuting' flight are redolent of fine days in the early summer. The **wheatear** is also common on open stony ground, the white flash of its rump and the distinctive call, like stones being knocked together, attracting attention. Other less common birds include the **ptarmigan** and **ring ouzel**, the former preferring open ridges and boulder fields, and the latter bouldery and craggy ground in the more sheltered corries. The wild call and 'head down' flight advertises the presence of nesting pairs of **red-throated divers** on a number of the more remote dubh lochans.

The remarkable seabird colonies of the islands out in the Minch are largely absent from Skye. However, out to sea from the larger headlands, rafts of **guillemots**, **razorbills**, **puffins** and **shearwaters** can sometimes be seen, going to and from the huge colonies on the Shiants and other islands. **Black guillemots** nest all around the coast, particularly the more remote north and west, but nesting guillemots and razorbills are limited to a few sites in the north, often accompanied by **fulmars** and **kittiwakes**. Herring gulls are common round most of the coast and **common gulls**, **great** and **lesser black-backed gulls** also have scattered breeding colonies. Flotillas of **eider duck** are a common sight off most of the coasts and noisy **oystercatchers** attract attention on the flatter coasts and offshore skerries, but the large flocks of wading birds, characteristic of the Scottish east coast, are absent from Skye.

The River Sligachan – April 2008

WEATHER

My personal experience of Skye weather is that it is the driest place in the British Isles, for I have been there three times, spending at least ten days on each occasion, and have only had four hours' rain in the three visits.[1]

The name 'Skye' is thought to be derived from the Norse word ski meaning 'cloud' and ey meaning 'island'. The island is also known as Eilean a' Cheo (Isle of Mist). These associations with cloudiness are probably related to the tendency for the high ground of the Cuillin to attract a capping of cloud, rather than implying that the island generally has a misty character. Indeed, the island has a better sunshine record than the neighbouring mainland.

[1] Charles Pilkington, one of the early Cuillin pioneers, describing his experience of Skye weather in *The Black Coolins*, AJ (1888), Vol XIII, No. 99, pp. 433–46.

*A lightning strike high up on the north-east
ridge of Garbh-bheinn, June 2005*

Skye has a typical maritime climate, which means that its weather is greatly influenced by the sea. It has relatively mild, wet winters, whereas maximum temperatures in summer tend to be tempered by cool sea-breezes. Otherwise, Skye's weather is difficult to make simple rules about. It can vary dramatically from one end of the island to another. Even opposite ends of the Cuillin can experience very different conditions. When the wind is from the south-west the southern Cuillin can be enveloped by cloud while the northern peaks bask in sunshine. Just the opposite can be the case when the wind is from the north. It often pays to have flexible plans. Pouring rain in the Cuillin can contrast with bright sunshine at Neist. It can be hailing in Portree when there are clear skies over Quiraing. A dreich morning can be followed by a brilliant afternoon. When only the highest peaks protrude above the clouds, a dull ascent can be rewarded with the sight of spectacular Brocken spectres. On the other hand, the whole island can be blasted by wind and rain, or, conversely, bathed in sunshine, for weeks on end.

The north has a general tendency to be drier than the south. Broadford, in the lee of the big hills, has about twice as much rainfall as Staffin in the north. In the summer, the eastern side of the island tends to be slightly warmer than the west coast.

When a long term view is taken, May seems to be the driest and sunniest month, with April and June not far behind. The main summer months of July and August are warmer, but wetter. This may not be true in any one year, and variations from the average are considerable. Sconser, which lies north-east of the Cuillin, had only 32mm of rain in December 1995, but it recorded 240mm of rain in May 1996. Only 93mm fell there in the following August, but a phenomenal 970mm of rain fell in February 1997, with a further 98mm falling in 24 hours on 1 March 1997. (Data collected at Sconser by Dr Hartley.)

Snow rarely lies long at sea level, but in some years significant quantities can build up in the Cuillin corries and persist until late spring. Remnant snow patches can sometimes be a welcome source of moisture on a traverse of the main ridge in June. Cold spells of a week or more are unknown after March.

The direction of the airstream over the island may help in anticipating the weather. This is what William Inglis Clark discovered on an early visit.

The weather continuing inclement, we next day moved on to Sligachan, and planned an immediate attack on the ridges. But, alas, for man's proposals, the morning broke wild and stormy, and so continued till we left ten days later. A stone-breaker by the road was consulted as to the prospects.

"Ah weel, ye see, it's a nor'-west win' the day, and that's a baad win' for Skye. It's aye wet and stormy."

"But," said I, "I thought the south-west wind was the wet wind here."

"Ou aye, the soo'-west win' is an awfu' wet win' here."

"I suppose the east wind is the best wind."

"Na, na, the nor'-east win' is aye rainy, and the south-east win' poors for days at a time."

"But the east wind must surely be good."

"Aweel, aweel, I hev' seen it fine wi' the east win', but no aften."

To prove this statement we tested the wind in every direction, and found hail, rain, and storm continuously, with the exception of one fine day when the wind was due east.

Stormy June Days in Skye and on Ben Nevis, W. Inglis Clark, SMCJ (1901), Vol VI, No 36, p218–30.

MOUNTAINEERING HISTORY

Legend has it that the remains of a Norse princess are buried beneath the massive cairn on the summit of Beinn na Caillich above Broadford. If true this must be one of the most impressive early mountaineering feats on the island.

Some of the clan battles are reputed to have been fought at the base of the Cuillin, the last one being in Coire na Creiche in 1601. It is probable that clansmen or shepherds visited many of the Cuillin corries, but it is unlikely that they ventured onto any of the major summits of such a barren range.

The Romantics & the Surveyors

1746 Bonnie Prince Charlie and his escort, Captain Malcolm, walked at night from Portree to Elgol. They skirted to the west of Sligachan to avoid government troops, and probably passed through the hills to the east of Marsco, down to Loch Ainort and along Srath Mòr. This was a distance of well over 40km, and they both fell into deep bogs on the way. The Prince then took a boat back to the mainland, and from there later sailed for France.

1772 Thomas Pennant ascended Beinn na Caillich above Broadford, and described the prospect to the west as 'that of desolation itself; a savage series of rude mountains, discoloured, black and red, as if by the rage of fire'.

1773 Samuel Johnson and James Boswell visited Skye on their tour of the Hebrides. Boswell described the Cuillin as 'a prodigious range of mountains, capped with rocky pinnacles in a strange variety of shapes'. Boswell ascended Preshal Mòr above Talisker with Donald Maclean, the young Laird of Coll.

1814 Sir Walter Scott visited Loch Coruisk (after the geologist MacCulloch had described it to him in awesome terms). The following year he published *The Lord of the Isles*.

1816 After several years work, Dr John MacCulloch produced the first geological map of Skye. He did so without managing to reach any Cuillin summits, although he walked round Loch Coruisk and climbed part way up Sgùrr na Stri.

1819 Thomas Colby led a party of men from the Ordnance Survey on an epic 'station hunt' across the Highlands. They tried to climb Sgùrr nan Gillean, and reached Bealach a' Bhasteir, but could not get past the Gendarme (or Tooth) on the west ridge. The next day they ascended Glàmaig.

William Daniell published dramatic sketches of the Cuillin.

1831 Turner painted Loch Coruisk to illustrate Scott's poems. He nearly came to grief when he slipped trying to find a good location for his composition.

The Forester, the Scientist & his Barometer

1835 The Reverend Lesingham Smith and local forester Duncan MacIntyre visited Coruisk and returned to Sligachan by crossing the Druim nan Ràmh ridge into Harta Corrie. This is the first recorded scramble in the Cuillin.

1836 Duncan MacIntyre had tried repeatedly to ascend Sgùrr nan Gillean, but without success. He was then engaged by Professor James Forbes, and together they made the first ascent of the mountain by its south-east ridge. Forbes noted, 'the extreme roughness of the rocks rendering the ascent safe, where with any other formation, it might have been considerably perilous. Indeed, I have never seen a rock so adapted for clambering.'

1841 Lord Cockburn visited Coruisk. He learnt that a local fisherman had been washed away and drowned three days before, in trying to cross the Scavaig River when it was in flood.

1845 Forbes ascended Bruach na Frìthe along with MacIntyre and a barometer. Then they descended into Lota Corrie and climbed to the summit of Sgùrr nan Gillean by its west ridge, presumably gained from its southern flank. Forbes used his barometer to calculate the heights of the two peaks.

Forbes intersected the Cuillin in several directions. He also circumnavigated the range with Necker, a Swiss geologist, and found convincing evidence of glaciation.

1846 Forbes published his observations on glacial phenomena in the Cuillin, together with the first good sketch map of the range.

1857 Professor John Nicol and the poet Algernon Swinburne reported an ascent of Blàbheinn, though the peak is known to have been climbed by shepherds in the early 1830s as described in Black's guidebook of 1834.

1859 Captain Wood, a surveyor for the Admiralty, was working on a chart of the coastline of Skye using triangulation methods. He mapped the southern Cuillin peaks, and identified a 3212 feet high inaccessible peak. Charles Weld, an Alpine Club member, spoke with Wood, and also ascended Sgùrr na Strì. Weld later wrote a rapturous description of the Cuillin peaks which included a mention of the unclimbed Inaccessible Pinnacle. 'Surely some bold member of the club will scale this Skye peak ere long and tell us that it is but a stroll before breakfast.' He did not try it himself.

The Sheriff & his Plaid

1865 Alexander Nicolson started his exploratory campaign among the Cuillin at the age of 38. He was a Skyeman, born at Husabost, and later became sheriff-substitute of Kirkcudbright. With the gamekeeper at Sligachan, Duncan MacIntyre's son, he ascended Sgùrr nan Gillean, and then made the first descent of the west ridge by Nicolson's Chimney. They continued below Am Basteir and ascended Bruach na Frìthe.

1866 John Mackenzie began his long and distinguished Cuillin career by ascending Sgùrr nan Gillean at the age of 10. He went on to become a mountain guide, and spent more than 50 years climbing in the Cuillin, most notably with Norman Collie.

1870 Newton Tribe and John Mackenzie possibly made the first ascent of Sgùrr a' Ghreadaidh. It was ascended by Professor Heddle the following year.

In September a fatality took place on Sgùrr nan Gillean. A scrambler continued when his companion turned back. He left his name in a bottle at the summit, but slipped and died on the descent.

1871 Cundill and Hall made the first ascent of Sgùrr na h-Uamha.

1873 Professor Knight managed to bribe a local guide, Angus Macpherson, to descend from the summit of Sgùrr nan Gillean with him, and make the first ascent of Knight's Peak. (This was originally known as Needle Rock, but Nicolson also called it the *Little Horn*.) They returned the same way.

Nicolson and Angus Macrae, a local shepherd, ascended Sgùrr na Banachdaich and Sgùrr Dearg. They then skirted below the Inaccessible Pinnacle ('it might be possible with ropes and grappling irons to overcome it, but the achievement seems hardly worth the trouble'), before descending into Coire Lagan and making the first ascent of Skye's highest summit via the Great Stone Shoot. Nicolson suggested that the peak be called Scur-a-Laghain. It was later named Sgùrr Alasdair in his honour.

A few days later Nicolson made his most audacious ascent ('the hardest adventure I have had among these hills'). He walked with a geological friend from Sligachan to Coruisk, and at 4pm they set off up An Garbh-choire. After sheltering from a shower of rain, they reached the summit of Sgùrr Dubh Mòr at 7pm. They then descended to Coire an Lochain in the gathering gloom. From eight to half-past ten they descended in almost total darkness.

> About half-way down we came to a place where the invaluable plaid came into use. My companion, being the lighter man, stood above with his heels set in the rock, holding the plaid, by which I let myself down the chasm. Having got footing, I rested my back against the rock, down which my lighter friend let himself slide till he rested on my shoulders. This little piece of gymnastics we had to practise several times before we got to the bottom of the glen above Coruisk.

The floor of Coir'-uisg was bathed in moonlight. They then tried to find a way over Druim nan Ràmh, but had to retreat right back down to Loch Coruisk. They eventually escaped over Druim Hain and reached Sligachan at 3am.

The Willink brothers traversed Blàbheinn from east to west by its two very prominent gullies. They baulked at a drop part-way down the western gully, and had to reascend some distance. They then traversed out on the north side and descended a scree gully on the north-western end of the mountain.

1879 Nicolson made his final contribution (aged 52) – the first ascent of his own chimney on Sgùrr nan Gillean – along with the Reverend Black, David Hepburn, and Angus Macpherson as guide. Hepburn described their technique:

> We had with us a strong staff about six feet in length and a long highland plaid. The chimney when arrived at gave rise to a long consultation, but eventually we decided to attack it. By means of the crook the plaid was hitched over an overhanging point, and after considerable difficulty Angus Macpherson succeeded in drawing himself up, and reported that an advance was feasible. By means of the plaid, firmly gripped by Angus, we remaining three scaled the Chimney one by one and without much further trouble reached the summit.

Nicolson found 'the rockwork a good deal abraded and softened since 1865'.

The Pilkingtons, the Alpine Club & the Rope

1880 William Naismith paid his first visit to Skye. He made the first ascent of the north top of Bidein Druim nan Ràmh, although, because the map of the time was inaccurate, he thought he had ascended Sgùrr a' Mhadaidh.

Charles and Lawrence Pilkington, members of the famous Lancashire glass-making family, paid their epoch-making visit to Skye. They were among the foremost mountaineers of their day. The Pinnacle Ridge of Sgùrr nan Gillean repulsed them, but they reached the summit via the west ridge the next day. They then made the first ascent of the Inaccessible Pinnacle by its east ridge, having approached it from Sligachan via Coruisk and Bealach Coire na Banachdaich. They had to throw down a lot of loose rock as they climbed. 'The noise was appalling; the very rock of the pinnacle itself seemed to vibrate with indignation at our rude onslaught.'

The ascent was watched by John Mackenzie, who had guided the Pilkingtons to the foot of the climb.

1881 A local shepherd (almost certainly John Mackenzie) made the second ascent of the Inaccessible Pinnacle after taking off his boots.

1883 Lawrence Pilkington returned to Skye, and had rather poor weather, although he did manage to climb the central and highest peak of Bidein Druim nan Ràmh with Eustace Hulton and Horace Walker. He also re-climbed the east ridge of the Inaccessible Pinnacle in very different circumstances. 'Not a single loose rock on the ridge; ... The cloud stretched away and away all round us, a silver sea with the tops only of the highest peaks standing out like black, rocky islands. No sound!'

1885 The Ordnance Survey produced the first one-inch map to the Cuillin. However, the surveyors had not visited many summits, and it soon became apparent that the map had many shortcomings.

1886 W.P. Haskett Smith climbed up and down the Inaccessible Pinnacle by its east ridge in twelve minutes, which included a two minute rest on top. This was the same year that he made the first ascent of Napes Needle in the Lake District.

Stocker and Parker made the first ascent of the shorter, but steeper, western end of the Inaccessible Pinnacle. They then descended the east ridge to complete the first traverse of the peak.

Norman Collie visited Skye for the first time, and was inspired by watching Stocker and Parker make a first ascent on Knight's Peak from Coire a' Bhasteir. He telegraphed for a rope, and then made unsuccessful attempts to climb the west ridge and the Pinnacle Ridge of Sgùrr nan Gillean with his brother. After consulting John Mackenzie, he managed to follow the normal south-east ridge to the summit.

1887 Charles Pilkington returned to Skye with Horace Walker and James Heelis. They employed John Mackenzie and were blessed by excellent weather. Several first ascents were among their list of outings. Charles led the way up the north-east summit of Sgùrr Alasdair by a gully leading off from the Great Stone Shoot. This peak was later named Sgùrr Theàrlaich (Charles's Peak) in his honour. The party finished off by traversing Sgùrr Alasdair and Sgùrr Sgumain. The next day they became only the second party to traverse the Inaccessible Pinnacle. They then made the first ascent of a 'nameless peak' by its long north-west ridge. This peak was called Sgùrr MhicCoinnich (Mackenzie's Peak) after John Mackenzie.

Members of Pilkington's party were also the first to tread the summit of Clach Glas. They started their ascent by a gully on the west face. High up near the summit they discovered – to their surprise – that what appeared to be a knife edge of tremendous steepness was in fact the edge of a relatively straightforward slab. This feature has since become known as the Impostor.

To round off an impressive effort they made the first ascent of the north-east face of Sgùrr na h-Uamha – and the second ascent of the peak – by a slanting break in the rocks. The outing had been suggested to them by Alfred Williams, an artist who based himself at Coruisk in the summer months.

Later the same season John Mackenzie made some lengthy traverses with a very capable climber called Henry Chichester Hart from Dublin. At no time did they use a rope. One outing started up Sgùrr nan Gillean and continued by way of Am Basteir, Bruach na Frìthe, Bidein Druim nan Ràmh and Sgùrr a' Mhadaidh to Sgùrr a' Ghreadaidh.

Their finest effort took them from Sgùrr na Banachdaich, over the Inaccessible Pinnacle, Sgùrr MhicCoinnich, Sgùrr Theàrlaich and Sgùrr Alasdair. Mackenzie's boots were unsuitable for climbing and Hart had to give him a leg-up on the Inaccessible Pinnacle. They retraced their steps from the summit of Sgùrr MhicCoinnich and reached Bealach MhicCoinnich by traversing the western flank along a line which is commonly referred to as Collie's Ledge. It should more appropriately be called Hart's Ledge.

Collie, Mackenzie & the SMC

1888 Collie teamed up with Mackenzie, and so began an extraordinary partnership. They spent five hours one afternoon prospecting a route up the Basteir Tooth (the summit of which had only been reached for the first time from Am Basteir by Collie and King the previous year). They eventually succeeded by following a slanting weakness on the south face of Am Basteir.

Their final outing of the year together proved to be one of the hardest of Collie's mountaineering career. They started from Sligachan and reached Bealach na Glaic Moire from Coire na Creiche. They then followed the ridge all the way from Sgùrr a' Mhadaidh to the Inaccessible Pinnacle. A very strong wind made things difficult, but John took off his boots and led the steep western end. Collie admitted that he went up on the rope.

They continued to Sgùrr MhicCoinnich, and used Hart's route from the summit to reach Bealach MhicCoinnich. They crossed Sgùrr Theàrlaich, but had to retreat from the Theàrlaich–Dubh Gap. So to continue their traverse they descended the south-west ridge of Sgùrr Alasdair and contoured beneath the summit rocks to Bealach Coire an Lochain. From there they descended by Coire an Lochain to Coir'-uisg. They went up and over Druim nan Ràmh to Harta Corrie, and eventually reached the Sligachan Hotel at midnight.

1889 After Naismith published a letter in the Glasgow Herald at the beginning of the year, the Scottish Mountaineering Club was formally constituted on 11 March.

An important pioneer by the name of Wickham King teamed up with Collie, and between them they finally solved the problem of the T–D Gap by climbing up both sides.

1890 The Scottish Mountaineering Club Journal was published for the first time. The second one appeared in May and contained an article by Naismith entitled 'Three Days among the Cuchullins', the first of many relating to Skye.

Charles Pilkington organised a meet for an accomplished group of Alpine Club members. They had many fine days out, with Charles starting them off on the Pinnacle Ridge of Sgùrr nan Gillean. Charles's wife became the first woman to climb the Inaccessible Pinnacle, and a party of three had an unusual aquatic outing up the Basteir Gorge.

1891 Charles Pilkington published his 'Corrected Map of the Coolins'. '... it is probably the most correct map of these mountains obtainable.'

Collie, King and Mackenzie had a fright on an ascent of Clach Glas. King described the incident:

> On the slabs leading to Clach Glas we were not roped. J. Mackenzie was the last man. His unsuitable shepherd's boots caused him to slip, and then he slid with face to rock for some distance. He arrested his descent himself. He needed my aid to reach a safe resting place, for he was much shaken. ... Collie soon after gave him proper climbing boots.

The sixth SMCJ was published containing the first version of Munro's Tables.

1893 Collie wrote an article for the SMCJ 'On the Height of some of the Black Cuchullins in Skye', in which he explained how he made his measurements. He established that Sgùrr Alasdair is higher than the Inaccessible Pinnacle, and hence the highest Cuillin summit.

1895 Mrs Rose, guided by Mackenzie, became the first woman to negotiate the Gendarme on the west ridge of Sgùrr nan Gillean. Kelsall and Hallitt heralded the start of more difficult climbing in the Cuillin by their bold ascent of Waterpipe Gully on Sgùrr an Fheadain.

Sir Archibald Geikie suggested that Alfred Harker be appointed to the Geological Survey to map the Cuillin.

1896 This was a very productive season. Sidney Williams was camped with his artist father at Scavaig. He made numerous ascents, mainly in company with John Mackenzie. These included a traverse of Sgùrr Dubh Beag (avoiding the drop at its western end by a traverse on the southern side), and Sgùrr

Dubh Mòr. He also climbed the north-east ridges of Gars-bheinn, and Sgùrr a' Choire Bhig, which gave 'some excellent sport'. Lamond, Rennie and Douglas sailed a yacht into Loch Scavaig, and heard from Williams about his exploits. They then traversed Sgùrr Dubh Beag and Sgùrr Dubh Mòr from east to west, but they took the drop off the former directly. They concluded, 'It gives as interesting a scramble as any in the Coolins ...' On the same day Williams and Mackenzie crossed the TD Gap without much difficulty, and on hearing of the other party's success, they too made the direct descent off Sgùrr Dubh Beag the following day.

Collie and a friend, E.B. Howell, climbed one of the longest mount-aineering routes on the island when they ascended Sgùrr a' Ghreadaidh from the floor of Coir'-uisg. Then, along with Parker and Naismith, they climbed the north-west buttress of Sgùrr a' Mhadaidh. Parker and Naismith also found a new route on the west face of Clach Glas. They then visited the summits of four pinnacles on the north-east side of the peak.

A notable event took place on 12 September, when Collie, Howell, Naismith and Mackenzie scaled the north-east face of the north top of Sgùrr Coire an Lochain, and so conquered the last unclimbed mountain summit in Britain. They completed their day by traversing the Inaccessible Pinnacle, and following the ridge to Sgùrr a' Mhadaidh, before dropping down the Thuilm ridge to Glen Brittle.

1897 A detailed list of the Cuillin peaks was prepared by Douglas, and appeared as an appendix in the SMCJ. Many of the heights had been calculated from aneroid measurements taken by Collie.

The famous SMC yachting meet in April failed to set foot on Skye, because of bad weather. The summer meet fared little better. Portable huts were erected at the head of Loch Coruisk, but the weather was appalling during July and August. 'Rain! Rain! Rain! Real Skye rain and no mistake, and all the water-works of the Coolins were going at high pressure. It continued like this all day ... On our return to camp we found that the loch has raised its level by nearly three feet.' Amazingly, they did manage some climbing, including the first ascent of Brown's Climb on Sgùrr a' Mhadaidh. Harold Raeburn made his first appearance on Skye.

1898 The SMC reproduced the OS six-inch map of the Cuillin at a reduced scale, with additional information added by its members. The month of August was especially fruitful. Among the many new routes completed were two sensational climbs on the main ridge. King led Douglas and Naismith straight up to the summit of Sgùrr MhicCoinnich from Hart's Ledge to produce King's Chimney. After inspecting the upper part from above with a rope, Naismith climbed his intimidating route on the Basteir Tooth with A.M. Mackay. Naismith's Route gained a companion climb when King, Gibbs and Mackenzie completed their epic ascent of Basteir Nick Gully, now known as King's Cave Chimney.

Harold Raeburn set out from Sligachan and soloed the north ridge of Sgùrr nan Each, before traversing Clach Glas.

1899 On 10th September, a Gurka, called Havildar Harkabir Thapa, set an astonishing record by running up and down Glamaig from the Sligachan Hotel in 55 minutes in bare feet. His record stood for 90 years, although it has not yet been beaten by a barefooted runner! Collie ascended Sgùrr Alasdair with Harkabir Thapa and Major Bruce. Descending from the lochan in Coire Lagan late in the day, he noticed a strange shadow cast on the face of Sron na Ciche. It was a further seven years before Collie followed up his observation.

1900 Harker wrote some informative 'Notes, Geological and Topographical, on the Cuillin Hills, Skye' for the SMCJ. Sidney Williams carried out some important explorations on the east faces of Blàbheinn and Clach Glas.

1901 Dr and Mrs Inglis Clark had an exciting time on Clach Glas in June. They climbed a route just north of B Gully. Caught in a fierce storm at the summit, they were unable to descend either the south or north ridges of the mountain. 'Conversation was impossible, while the dash of hail and roaring of the wind tended to stupefy.' They eventually found a way down the east face, reaching its base by means of Sid's Rake.

1903 The OS published the third edition of their map of the Cuillin: '... this latest map represents a great advance upon its predecessors.'

1905 Harold Raeburn led a team up the central buttress of An Caisteal in April. He changed his footwear to climb the delicate lower slab.

> ...the leader removed his boots and put on Kletterschue. A traverse had soon to be made to the left, across and up some steeply inclined slabs. This, none of the party would have cared to attempt, and would have considered it unjustifiable to lead up in boots. With the cloth-solers, however, it was quite safe and went all right, and passing under the overhanging slabs, barring the direct route, the climbers found themselves above the great pitch in the gully on their left, which had stopped their first attack.

The party had to contend with snow and ice higher up. From the summit they made their way down to Lota Corrie and marched out to Camasunary.

The Keswick Brothers & their Camera

1906 The Keswick brothers, George and Ashley Abraham, had visited Skye a decade earlier. They took remarkable photographs of their climbs with a very cumbersome glass plate camera. Now they began to put up new climbs as well. One of their first was West Buttress, a long route on Sgùrr MhicCoinnich.

The most notable event this year, however was the first ascent of A' Chìoch. Collie had seen the shadow of this extraordinary rock feature some seven

The Cioch and its shadow

John Mackenzie, Mrs Urquhart, Archie Mackenzie and Hugh Munro descending Sgùrr nan Gillean via the Gendarme, 11 June 1906 Photo: SMC Image Archive

years previously. After an exploratory probe alone, Collie teamed up with Mackenzie to reach its summit. They followed a devious route up what must have felt a very intimidating face. Collie was so excited by his discovery that he led numerous other climbers to the summit over the following weeks.

1907 Collie continued where he had left off, and climbed Amphitheatre Arête up the main face of Sròn na Cìche. Harland, Bartrum, Binns and Ashley Abraham between them added several important new climbs including two Severes – Cioch Direct on Sròn na Cìche, and Slanting Gully on Sgùrr a' Mhadaidh. They also ascended Spur and Summit Gullies on Sgùrr an Fheadain.

Douglas published the first climbing guide to Skye as a special edition of the SMCJ. Most of the routes were at the northern end of the Cuillin, closest to Sligachan. The climbs were graded for difficulty using a simple (1–4) numerical system. Accompanying the guide was a reduced version of the OS six-inch map on which Harker, who was not a climber, had marked in red all the easy routes he used for getting about the Cuillin.

1908 Ashley Abraham published his inspirational book – *Rock-Climbing in Skye*. It contained many superb photographs, as well as a graded list of climbs. Naismith reviewed it for the SMCJ: 'Some of the descriptions of rock climbs – the Cioch direct ascent for example – are abundantly exciting, and will be apt to cause the reader to wedge himself across his arm-chair while he gropes about for a good hitch.'

Abraham's book was largely responsible for making Skye more widely popular with mountaineers. A burst of new route activity took place over the next few years, which was only halted by the First World War. However, Abraham's comments about traversing the main ridge in one outing were soon to sound dated.

> I must admit that it is doubtful whether the various qualifications necessary to success will ever be possessed by any one man.
>
> Amongst other things he would need to have exceptional physique and staying power; to be a quick, skilful, and neat rock-climber (particularly would he need to be neat, for otherwise his hands would be torn to pieces before he got half-way); to possess an intimate knowledge of the entire length of the ridge, and a familiarity with its various 'mauvais pas'. Perfect weather, a light rope to 'double' for descents, and a carefully arranged commissariat would be essential. Moreover, I think it would be advisable to start at the southern end of the ridge, because a fatigued man might find himself 'pounded' at the short side of the Tearlach–Dubh Gap.
>
> Whether the game would be worth the candle, for the attendant risks would be considerable, and whether it is desirable that the Coolin should be treated with such disrespect, are points which each must settle for himself; but personally I think that the expressive 'Dummheit' of the Swiss guides would justly describe such a performance!

1911 On 10th June Leslie Shadbolt and Alastair McLaren made the first continuous traverse of the main ridge. They started from Glen Brittle at 3.35am and reached Sligachan at 8.20pm, having taken 12hrs 18mins from Gars-bheinn to Sgùrr nan Gillean. They were Cuillin campaigners of old, having pioneered a new route on the Basteir Tooth in 1906.

Steeple, Barlow & the Guidebook

Two English climbers, E.W. Steeple and Guy Barlow, were very active on Skye around the time that Abraham's book was published. Sometimes in company with Bowron, Buckle and Doughty, they opened up whole new climbing areas. Their output of new climbs was so prolific that the SMC soon involved them in producing a new guidebook to the Cuillin. They camped in the high corries to carry out much of their work.

1923 The SMC published *The Island of Skye*, edited by Steeple, Barlow, and MacRobert. So thorough had Steeple and Barlow been in their explorations that only a trickle of new climbs were added in the following two decades.

The Finishing Touches

1939 Ian Charleson and Woodhurst Forde completed the first Greater

Traverse, which included Clach Glas and Blàbheinn. They took exactly 20 hours from Gars-bheinn to Blàbheinn.

1943 The Red Hills yielded their first climb when Noel Odell carried out a geological examination of Marsco. He found the rock to be surprisingly good.

1944 Menlove Edwards, though a troubled man, completed the Greater Traverse solo in under 13 hours. He returned to his starting point in Glen Brittle in 24 hours. Later, in squally weather, he spent 18 hours at sea crossing to Rum and Canna, and back again, in a hired rowing boat.

1949 W.A. Poucher produced a fine book of photographs called *The Magic of Skye*. (A new edition appeared in 1980.)

1952 Ben Humble produced a fascinating book, *The Cuillin of Skye*, describing the history of climbing in the Cuillin. (A facsimile edition appeared in 1986.)

1965 The first winter traverse of the Cuillin main ridge was completed in two days by Crabb, MacInnes, Patey and Robertson.

The Glen Brittle Memorial Hut was formally opened. It was built to commemorate climbers who had died in the war.

1975 The OS published *The Cuillin and Torridon Hills* in their Outdoor Leisure Maps series.

1987 The Gendarme fell off the west ridge of Sgùrr nan Gillean.

1988 The Glamaig Hill Race was inaugurated – inspired by Harkabir Thapa's phenomenal performance in 1899.

1991 Robin Campbell conquered the Cuillin's last unclimbed peaklet, and named it 'Sgùrr Coire an Lobhta'.

1994 Gordon Stainforth published a photographic study of the Cuillin. It included a useful description of the main ridge, which graded all the difficulties.

1995 Skye was finally linked to the mainland by a bridge.

1997 Harvey produced an excellent new-style map entitled *Skye : The Cuillin*.

1999 Rob Woodall completed The Cuillin Round (i.e. a circuit of the Red Hills overlooking Glen Sligachan, the Cuillin Outliers, and all the Cuillin main ridge) in 23hrs 28mins. He had a team of nine people to resupply him at various points.

His route included Glamaig, the Deargs, Marsco, Belig, Garbh Bheinn, Sgùrr nan Each, Clach Glas, Blàbheinn, Sgùrr Hain, Sgùrr na Strì, and all the Munros and Tops of the Cuillin main ridge, plus many others including Sgùrr Beag and Sgùrr na h-Uamha: 59 tops in all (53km/7060m of ascent).

2000 Yiannis Tridimas – one of Rob Woodall's supporters – started from Coruisk and extended The Cuillin Round to include Sgùrr a' Bhasteir, making a total of 60 summits in 21hrs 22mins (55km/7920m of ascent).

2007 A lightning strike hit the summit of the Inaccessible Pinnacle destroying some of the rock. The neighbouring 'Bolster Stone' has now become the highest point.

2013 In October, Finlay Wild set a phenomenal new record of just 2hrs 59mins for completing the Cuillin main ridge traverse.

ENVIRONMENT

Access

The Land Reform (Scotland) Act 2003 gives you the right to be on most land and inland water for recreation, education and for going from place to place, providing you act responsibly. This includes climbing, hillwalking, cycling and wild camping. Guidance on where access rights apply, and what being responsible entails, can be found in the Scottish Outdoor Access Code (SOAC). See

Stalking, Shooting & Lambing

The stag stalking season is from 1 July to 20 October, although few estates start at the beginning of the season. Hinds continue to be culled until 15 February. There is no stalking anywhere on Sundays. The National Trust for Scotland has no property on Skye, but hillwalkers are never requested to use alternative routes on its land elsewhere.

The grouse shooting season is from 12 August until 10 December, although the end of the season is less used.

It is also important to avoid disturbance to sheep, especially from dogs and particularly during the lambing season between March and May. Dogs should be kept under close control (i.e. a short lead) wherever they might encounter livestock.

Bird Life

When scrambling or climbing, don't cause direct disturbance to nesting birds, particularly the rarer species, which are often found on crags (e.g. Golden Eagle, White Tailed (Sea) Eagle, Peregrine Falcon, Razorbill, Guillemot, Puffin, Fulmar, Kittiwake, Cormorant, Shag, Buzzard, Kestrel, Raven). Often this is between 1 February and the end of July. Disturbance of nesting birds (intentional and possibly unintentional) is a criminal offence and, if convicted, you face a fine of up to £5,000 and confiscation of climbing equipment.

It is the individual's responsibility to find out about nesting birds on crags they may scramble or climb on. The MCofS provides advice on the law relating to birds, bird behaviour and what constitutes disturbance.

Vegetation

In Scottish law it is illegal to kill, remove or damage plants without the landowner's permission, even if they are not rare species. There are rare and 'specially protected' species on cliffs, and many crags are Sites of Special Scientific Interest (SSSI). However, you also have the right to climb, so it is important to do so responsibly, by minimising damage to vegetation. The MCofS gives advice in 'Minimal Impact Mountaineering Advice' (MIMA) – see below.

Footpath Erosion

Part of the revenue from the sale of this and other Scottish Mountaineering Club books is granted by the Scottish Mountaineering Trust as financial assistance towards the repair and maintenance of hill paths in Scotland. However, it is our responsibility to minimise our erosive effect, for the enjoyment of future climbers.

Camping, Litter & Pollution

Responsible wild camping is permitted under the new access legislation, although 'No Camping' signs can still be found in the hills. If camping, do not cause pollution, and bury human waste carefully out of sight and far away from any habitation or water supply. Avoid burying rubbish as this may also pollute the environment.

Cairns

The proliferation of navigation cairns detracts from the feeling of wildness, and may be confusing rather than helpful as regards route-finding. The indiscriminate building of cairns on the hills should be discouraged.

Car & Bicycle Use

Do not drive along private roads without permission and, when parking, avoid blocking access to private roads and land or causing any hazard to other road users. The use of bicycles is covered by the Land Reform (Scotland) Act 2003. Bicycles can cause severe erosion when used 'off road' on footpaths and open hillsides and are best used on vehicular or forest tracks.

General Privacy

Respect for personal privacy near people's homes is nothing less than good manners.

Bothies

The Mountain Bothies Association has about 100 buildings on various estates throughout Scotland which it maintains as bothies. The MBA does not own any of these buildings. They belong to estates which generously allow their use as open bothies. Bothies are there for use by small groups (less than six) for a few days. If you wish to stay longer permission should be sought from the owners. The increased number of hill users have put a greater strain on the bothies and their surrounding environment. It is therefore more important than ever that the simple voluntary bothy code be adhered to,

• If you carry it in, then carry it out and have respect for the bothy, its owners and its users;

- Leave the bothy clean and dry, guard against fire and don't cause vandalism or graffiti;
- Bury human waste carefully out of sight far away from the bothy and the water supply and avoid burying rubbish.

This and more information can be found on the MBA website:
<www.mountainbothies.org.uk>.

Advice from Mountaineering Scotland

Mountaineering Scotland is the representative body for climbers and walkers in Scotland. One of its primary concerns is the continued free access to the hills and crags. Information about stalking, bird restrictions, and general access issues can be obtained from Mountaineering Scotland.

Should any climber or walker encounter problems regarding access they should contact Mountaineering Scotland, whose current address is:

The Old Granary, West Mill Street, PERTH, PH1 5QP.   tel (01738 493 942). email <info@mountaineering.scot>, website <www.mountaineering.scot/>.

Some advice for those venturing into the hills can be found on the Mountaineering Scotland website
<www.mountaineering.scot/safety-and-skills>.

Minimal Impact Mountaineering Advice (MIMA)
A document about MIMA, can be downloaded from the Mountaineering Scotland website
<www.mountaineering.scot/assets/contentfiles/pdf/minimal-impact-brochure-091210-final.pdf>.

It covers the following issues:

Minimising Erosion
Reducing transport impacts
Supporting local communities
Reducing litter
Sanitation issues in the hills

Reducing nesting bird disturbance
Taking your dog into the hills
Camping specific issues
Climbing specific issues

Mountaineering Scotland Participation Statement
Mountaineering Scotland recognises that climbing and mountaineering are activities with a danger of personal injury or death. Participants in these activities should be aware of and accept these risks and be responsible for their own actions and involvement.

SAFETY

Participation

'Climbing and mountaineering are activities with a danger of personal injury or death. Participants in these activities should be aware of and accept these risks and be responsible for their own actions and involvement.'
UIAA participation statement

Liabilities

You are responsible for your own actions and should not hold landowners liable for an accident, even if it happens while climbing over a fence or dyke. It is up to the individual climber to assess the reliability of bolts, pegs, slings or old nuts, which over time may have become corroded and therefore fail.

Mountain Rescue

Contact the police, either by phone (999) or in person. Give concise information about the location and injuries of the casualty, and any assistance available at the accident site. It is often better to stay with the casualty but, in a party of two, one may have to leave to summon help. Leave the casualty warm and comfortable in a sheltered, well-marked place.

Equipment & Planning

Good navigation skills, equipment, clothing and planning can all help reduce the risk of accident. Mobile phones and GPS can help in communications and locating your position, but mobiles do not work in many mountain locations and both rely on batteries and electronics which can fail or be damaged. Consequently, they can never be a substitute for good navigation, first aid or general mountain skills.

Scrambling

Unroped scrambling is potentially one of the most hazardous of mountaineering activities. A simple slip or a single hold breaking off may have fatal consequences. Whether to use a rope for scrambling comes down to personal choice. If there are inexperienced or nervous members in the party then a rope should certainly be carried, and it should come out of the rucksack sooner rather than later. A rope might well prove useful in the case of retreat. The ability to abseil with a sling and karabiner could also be invaluable.

Rock Climbing

Two-thirds of climbing accidents are the result of a lengthy fall, due either to holds breaking or rockfall. About one-third are the result of planning errors – being too ambitious (trying a route that's too hard) or simply failing to judge how long a route will take and becoming benighted.

Maps

Various symbols are used on the maps in this guide to indicate different categories of summit:

▲	Munro
△	Munro Top
●	Corbett
○	Corbett Top
◆	Graham
◇	Graham Top
⊗	Other

Place names and map references have in general been taken from the OS 1:50,000 Landranger or 1:25,000 Explorer maps, though, after taking advice from Gaelic speakers, in some cases slightly different spellings have been used. The following Ordnance Survey and Harvey maps cover the area of this guide:

OS Landranger Map 23	North Skye
OS Landranger Map 32	South Skye

OS Explorer Map 407	Skye – Dunvegan
OS Explorer Map 408	Skye – Trotternish & The Storr
OS Explorer Map 409	Raasay, Rona & Scalpay
OS Explorer Map 410	Skye – Portree & Bracadale
OS Explorer Map 411	Skye – Cuillin Hills
OS Explorer Map 412	Skye – Sleat / Slèite

Harvey Superwalker	Skye: The Cuillin (1:25,000 and 1:12,500)
Harvey Superwalker	Skye: Storr & Trotternish (1:25,000)

Books

The following SMC and SMT publications may also be useful for hill walking, climbing and general mountain interest on the island:*Skye – The Cuillin*, *Skye – Sea-cliffs & Outcrops* (sister guides giving comprehensive coverage of all climbs on Skye), *The Islands of Scotland including Skye*, *The Munros*, *The Corbetts, The Grahams & the Donalds*, *Scottish Hill Names*, and *Hostile Habitats – Scotland's Mountain Environment*.

For more information and to order SMC and SMT publications, visit the SMC website <www.smc.org.uk>. See also p400.

TECHNICAL

Classification of Routes

There are difficulties in attempting to describe a mixture of walks, scrambles and climbs in the same guide. In order to make it obvious the type of outing involved, a logo is shown at the start of each route description. The scrambles and climbs are each further sub-divided into three levels of difficulty. All the routes are graded for **dry, summer conditions**. They will become much harder when it is damp or snowy. In winter they are much more serious undertakings, and appropriate winter mountaineering skills and equipment will be required.

WALKS

 No attempt has been made to classify walks, although some negotiate very rough ground, and ascend to high summits. Some may also take many hours to complete, and may require considerable navigational skills. What distinguishes walks from scrambles is that it should be possible to complete them without having to set hands on rock.

SCRAMBLES

At some point on a scramble the hands will need to be used for progress. A simple numerical grading system (1–3) is used to indicate the difficulty of a scramble. For those unfamiliar with scrambling, a rough guide might be to say that most hillwalkers should be fairly happy to tackle Grade 1 scrambles. However, those without climbing experience may well find that Grade 3 scrambles are too difficult or too frightening for them.

Grade 1: Easy Scrambles

Most hillgoers should find this grade of scramble reasonably straightforward. The hands will occasionally be required for progress, but the holds will normally be large, so the moves themselves will not be difficult. There may be some exposure, but usually it will not be too daunting.

Grade 2: Interesting Scrambles

Routes of this grade will normally require the hands to be used for more sustained sections. There may be considerable exposure. Some routes may have short technically difficult sections, while others may be easier but hard to escape from. Retreat may be quite difficult.

Grade 3: Advanced Scrambles

This grade of scramble may involve making thought-provoking moves on steep rock in very exposed situations. All but experienced climbers might prefer the reassurance of a rope in some places. In which case, a few slings, nuts and karabiners may prove useful for setting up belays. The route might be hard to escape from, and the ability to abseil could be useful if a retreat has to be made.

ROCK CLIMBS

 The rock climbs described in this guide are graded according to the standard adjectival system for summer climbs. Only routes in the three lowest grades are described. (The Easy grade is not recognised here.) Climbs are graded for their hardest move irrespective of length. Such routes will normally be climbed using standard rock climbing equipment.

Moderate

Climbs of this grade will normally make use of fairly obvious holds. However, there are likely to be tricky moves in exposed positions. The route could be sustained, and in a serious situation.

Difficult

Technical climbing skills are required here. There could be hard moves in very steep and serious situations. There might be long, exposed sections and protection might be hard to place.

Very Difficult

Routes of this grade call for a fairly high level of climbing skill. They may have quite small holds and be extremely exposed. Only a small number of outings of this grade are included in this guide. Most of them lie on the crest of the Cuillin main ridge.

Use of the rope

It goes without saying that a rope will only increase safety if at least one member of the party knows how to use it properly, and if it is put to use as soon as anybody needs it. Many parties decide to carry harnesses and a full rack of equipment for Difficult and Very Difficult climbs.

Left and Right

The terms left and right are used when facing the direction being described, i.e. facing a crag in ascent, and facing out in descent.

Diagrams

Most of the routes are shown on diagrams close to the relevant text. The route numbers in the text correspond to the route numbers shown on the diagrams. Walks and scrambles are marked as **dashed** lines – – – – , whilst climbs are shown by **dotted** lines · · · · · . A letter **D** indicates a relatively easy descent route, though it may involve some sections of easy scrambling.

Recommended Routes

A three star system has been used to indicate the 'quality' of a route. In the case of scrambles and climbs the stars generally refer to the quality of the activity itself, but the soundness of the rock, and the situation, sustainedness and escapability of the route all contribute to the quality rating.

AMENITIES

Travel to Skye

The Traveline Scotland website, among many others, gives general information about travel in Scotland: <www.travelinescotland.com/>.

Information about current incidents and roadworks in Scotland can be found on the Traffic Scotland website. See <http://trafficscotland.org/>.

Road

Skye has been connected to the mainland by a bridge at Kyle of Lochalsh since 1995. The very expensive toll on this bridge was removed completely at the end of 2004. The bridge is part of the A87 trunk road which begins on the mainland at Invergarry, and passes through Glen Shiel, before crossing onto Skye at Kyle of Lochalsh. It continues to Portree, and terminates at the ferry port of Uig in the north of Trotternish.

There is a 24 hour petrol station in Broadford. There are also petrol stations on the approach to Skye at Shiel Bridge, Inverinate and Kyle of Lochalsh.

Coach

Excellent coach services run twice daily from Glasgow via Fort William to Portree and Uig. A coach from Inverness also links with the Glasgow service at Invergarry. For details and online booking see <www.citylink.co.uk/>.

Rail

There are no railways on Skye, however, there are two extremely picturesque lines which terminate on the mainland opposite the island. One runs from Fort William to Mallaig, the other from Inverness via Plockton to Kyle of Lochalsh. Details of these services can be found at <www.scotrail.co.uk/>.

Ferry

There are two ferry crossings to Skye from the mainland. One of these operates (April–October) between Glenelg and Kylerhea. It is run by the Isle of Skye Ferry Community Interest Company. See <www.skyeferry.co.uk/>. This is one of the most scenic and certainly the most historic of all the approaches to the island. It is also the shortest crossing point. At one time drovers used to get their cattle to swim across here at slack water.

There is also an all-year-round service from Mallaig to Armadale operated by Caledonian MacBrayne. See <www.calmac.co.uk/>. This company also operates the following ferries between Skye and other islands: Uig and Tarbert (Harris), Uig and Lochmaddy (North Uist), and Sconser and Raasay.

Airport

There is an airstrip just south of Broadford (NG 693 245). There are no scheduled flights at present, but there is the possibility of private landings.

The Glenelg/Kylerhea Ferry   Photo: Clive Pearson

Travel within the Island

A number of bus services, operated by Stagecoach, run on the island.

54	Portree – Fiscavaig
55	Kyle of Lochalsh – Broadford – Elgol – Glasnakille
56	Portree – Lonmore – Glendale
57A	Portree – Staffin – Uig – Portree
57C	Portree – Uig – Staffin – Portree
59	Portree – Peinchorran
152	Portree – Ardvasar
155	Portree – Torrin

Accommodation

There are numerous hotels, guest houses and B&Bs scattered around the island. Many of these can be booked online at various websites, such as:

<www.booking.com>
.

Campsites

The most convenient campsite for the Cuillin is Glenbrittle Campsite, which is situated by the beach in Glen Brittle.

e-mail <glenbrittle@dunvegancastle.com>.

There are also campsites at Dunvegan, Borve, Staffin, Portree and Uig.

Climbing Huts

Glen Brittle Memorial Hut, (NG 412 216), BMC/MCofS.
See .
Coruisk Memorial Hut, (NG 487 197), Glasgow JMCS.
See <www.glasgowjmcs.org.uk/coruisk.php>.

SYHA Hostels

There are Youth Hostels on Skye at **Broadford**, **Glenbrittle**, and **Uig**.
There are also SYHA Hostels at Ratagan and on Raasay.
For details and online bookings see <www.syha.org.uk>.

Scottish Independent Hostels

Information about the independent hostels on Skye can be checked at
<www.hostel-scotland.co.uk>.

The following hostels are scattered across Skye:

Broadford Backpackers Hostel, Broadford, (NG 624 234), 38 beds,
   <www.hostel-scotland.co.uk/hostels/Broadford-Backpackers-Hostel.htm>.
Croft Bunkhouse, Bothies & Wigwams, Portnalong, (NG 348 353), 42 beds,
   .
Dun Caan Hostel, Kyleakin, (NG 754 264), 12 beds,
   .
Dun Flodigarry, Flodigarry, (NG 464 720), March–October, 40 beds,
   <http://flodigarry-hostel.scot//>.
Flora Macdonald Hostel, Kilmore, near Armadale, (NG 655 070), 24 beds,
   .
Portree Independent Hostel, Portree, (NG 481 435), 60 beds,
   .
Saucy Mary's Lodge, Kyleakin, 68 beds, .
Skye Backpackers, Kyleakin, (NG 750 263), 35 beds,
   <http://scotlandstophostels.com/skye/>.
Skye Basecamp, Broadford, (NG 647 232), 30 beds,
Skyewalker Hostel, Portnalong, (NG 346 348), 40 beds,
   .
Sligachan Bunkhouse, Sligachan, (NG 488 297), 20 beds,
Waterfront Bunkhouse, Carbost, (NG 379 317), 24 beds,
   .

VisitScotland Information Centres

There are local Tourist Information Centres, mostly seasonal, at:
   Broadford, Dunvegan and Portree.
There are also Information Centres at:
   Cluanie Inn, Kyle of Lochalsh, Mallaig and Tarbert.

Shops

Supermarkets are situated in Kyle of Lochalsh, Broadford and Portree.
There are also small outdoor shops in Harrapool (Walkers & Wellies), Portree
(Inside Out, and Island Outdoors) and Struan (Cioch Outdoor Clothing).

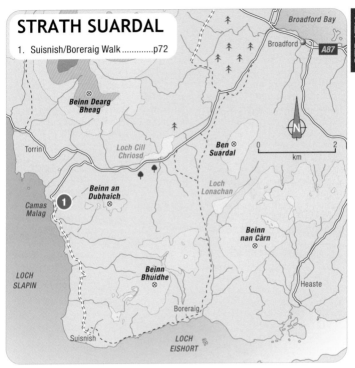

STRATH SUARDAL

1. Suisnish/Boreraig Walk p72

STRATH SUARDAL & STRATHAIRD

The south-eastern part of Skye, which is built mainly of Torridonian and Lewisian rocks, has its own distinctive character. It includes the large, but relatively low-lying, peninsula of Sleat, which is sometimes referred to as 'the garden of Skye'. There is pleasant walking on the hills overlooking Kylerhea, but otherwise this part of the island has limited attractions for the hillgoer.

The rocks change in character approaching Broadford, where Jurassic and Cambrian-Ordovician sediments predominate. All the outings in this chapter are approached along Strath Suardal by a single-track road that runs south-west from Broadford. This broad, open strath leads to the crofting township of Torrin, from where the road continues round the head of Loch Slapin and then runs across the peninsula of Strathaird to the tiny village of Elgol.

Strath Suardal

Map p71

The north side of Strath Suardal is dominated by the Eastern Red Hills which are described in the next chapter. The south side has a more gentle character and is very interesting geologically. Torridonian, Cambrian and Ordovician rocks are involved in several thrusts and the whole sequence is intruded by a large body of granite. Extensive outcrops of Ordovician limestone are cut by numerous dykes and riddled with short caves. Details of these caves can be found in *Caves of Skye* published by Grampian Speleological Group (1995).

The strath is famous for its marble quarries, one of which still operates at Torrin near Loch Slapin. The marble was formed where the limestone was affected by the heat spreading out from a large magma chamber which formed in the crust some 55 million years ago. This magma eventually cooled to create the Beinn an Dubhaich granite. As a result of this 'baking' the limestone underwent thermal metamorphism and recrystallised to form marble. The distinctive green and yellow streaks in 'Skye marble' are due to the presence of new minerals such as forsterite (altered to serpentine). Chert nodules within the limestone were also altered creating different new minerals at different distances from the granite.

In the early twentieth century a narrow-gauge railway was used to transport the marble from the quarry workings on the flank of Ben Suardal to a pier at Broadford. It was removed when the quarry closed in 1912. There is now a well constructed path along the line of this railway. It starts on the east side of the road about 1km from Broadford. There is parking space available on the opposite side of the road (NG 635 227). The path has links with two other paths which cross the road and descend to bridges over the River Broadford, one of which leads to Coire-chat-achan.

1 Suisnish and Boreraig 17km **
(NG 582 193) High Point 165m Map p71

This is a fairly long walk if the full circuit is completed as described, although it can be shortened by some 4km if a pickup can be arranged near Loch Cill Chriosd. The outing is of interest both historically and geologically. It visits the remains of two former communities, which were 'cleared' in the middle of the nineteenth century. The route crosses a great variety of rocks including shales and sandstones of Jurassic age as well as Ordovician limestones overthrust by ancient Torridonian strata. It also passes through some of the disused marble quarries at Kilchrist.

Approach

From Broadford follow the road along Strath Suardal until a little over 1km past Loch Cill Chriosd. Where the road to Torrin turns sharply right, take the less prominent left fork (NG 593 201) which carries straight on over a cattle-grid. Continue along the track to where the tarmac ends at a grassy area of raised beach by Camas Malag.

Looking east along the coast towards Boreraig

The Route
Follow the rough track heading south. Soon after cresting a slight rise the track swings left to cross a small stream – the Allt na Garbhlain. At this point it is worth making a small diversion on the downhill side of the track to examine the Camas Malag Caves. The top entrance of this little cave system can be found just a short distance down from the track (NG 584 187), where the Allt na Garbhlain flows off the Beinn an Dubhaich granite intrusion and immediately sinks underground. The stream resurges about 50 metres further downhill, where it is forced to cross an impervious dyke. It then plunges into a spectacular little pothole, before eventually resurging from the upper part of the nearby sea cliff and cascading onto the shore.

Many caves also occur in the glen of the Allt nan Leac slightly further south. These include the very sporting Uamh Cinn Ghlinn – the longest cave on Skye. The track soon passes onto Jurassic shales, and continues south with fine views across Loch Slapin to Blàbheinn and Strathaird. Eventually the track leads to the former settlement of Suisnish. There can be few more poignant reminders of just how brutal some of the clearances must have been. Archibald Geikie, the geologist, described the distress of the inhabitants as they left:

'When they set off once more, a cry of grief went up to heaven; the long plaintive wail, like a funeral coronach, was resumed; and, after the last of the emigrants had disappeared behind the hill, the sound seemed to re-echo through the whole wide valley of Strath in one prolonged note of desolation. The people were on their way to be shipped to Canada.'

Pass a derelict cottage with a corrugated roof and continue towards a modern farm building. Before reaching this turn sharp left and head uphill. Go through a gate and pick up a narrow path which contours round the hillside by a fence. Follow this along the cliff top below the craggy south face of Càrn Dearg, before eventually descending past outcrops of brown-weathered gabbro to the shore of Loch Eishort. A number of dykes and waterfalls stand out on the sizeable cliffs overlooking the shore. Eventually the cliffs recede and a small grassy headland overlooking the sea marks the site of an ancient hillfort (*Dùn Boreraig*). The first ruins of the community Boreraig are situated nearby. This grassy oasis must have harboured a community of a similar size to Suisnish. The area is interesting to explore, and ammonites can be found in rocks along the shore.

Look for a small 'standing stone' set back some distance from the sea. It is not especially conspicuous and looks more like a slabby headstone. It helps point to the path which climbs out of Boreraig through the bracken. As the path climbs northwards, waterfalls can be seen in the Allt na Peighinn to the east. Further on the path enters the Beinn nan Càrn native woodland enclosure which was established in 2000. At one point an outcrop of very distinctive conglomerate of Triassic age can be seen beside the path.

As the path nears its high point the scenery becomes rather more desolate. Once past Loch Lonachan, however, the situation changes quite quickly, and the path soon descends to better drained grassier terrain where limestone outcrops. In the spring delightful examples of mountain avens can be seen flowering in crevices (grykes) here. It is then a short distance to the spoil heaps of the old upper marble quarry workings.

It is possible to follow the obvious track northwards from here and pick up a very good path along the line of the former marble quarry railway which continues towards Broadford. After one kilometre a spur leads leftwards to a parking place beside the main road. However, the road can be gained slightly more quickly by taking the left fork at the upper quarry (NG 620 197), and heading in a westerly direction past further quarry workings towards the prominent ruined manse at Kilchrist (NG 615 200). The eastern end of the Beinn an Dubhaich granite intrusion is crossed before limestone is again encountered by the manse. There are a number of caves in the vicinity, as well as a 30 metres wide dyke which forms a raised ridge. An iron-rich mineral called magnetite was once mined here on a small scale. It formed in the limestone close to the boundary with the granite. These features deserve a separate visit, however, for it is only a short distance now to the road in Strath Suardal by Loch Cill Chriosd.

It is almost 4km along the tarmac road back to the start at Camas Malag.

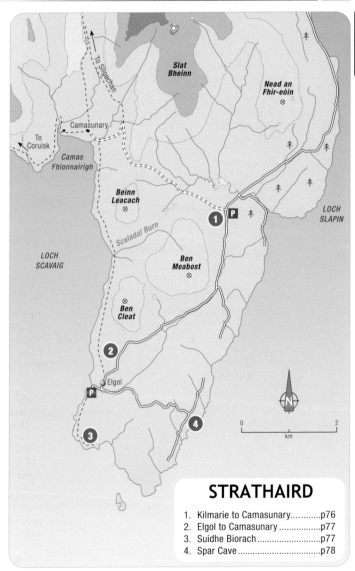

STRATHAIRD

1. Kilmarie to Camasunary............p76
2. Elgol to Camasunary p77
3. Suidhe Biorach p77
4. Spar Cave p78

Strathaird

Map p75

The peninsula of Strathaird is reached by following the road from Broadford along Strath Suardal to Torrin and then continuing north to pass around the head of Loch Slapin. There are superb views of Blàbheinn and Clach Glas on the last part of this route. The northern part of Strathaird is capped by a thick sequence of Palaeogene lavas, but further south the rocks are predominately sedimentary rocks of Jurassic age. The road eventually crosses over to the village of Elgol on the western side of the peninsula. It then descends very steeply to a car park overlooking a jetty and slipway with distant views of the Cuillin. It is possible to take boat trips into Coruisk from here.

Camasunary (more properly spelt Camas Fhionnairigh) is a pleasant broad sandy bay on the west side of Strathaird. It is well worth a visit in its own right, although it also makes a good base for outings on Sgùrr na Strì, Sgùrr Hain and Blàbheinn. It is a welcome stopping-off point on the walk into Coruisk via the Bad Step (Route 50) and also the walk north past Loch na Creitheach through to Sligachan (Route 48).

2 Kilmarie to Camasunary   4.5km (one way)

(NG 545 172)   High Point 189m   Map p75

This is the most direct route to Camasunary, but the least interesting. It follows a rough vehicular track throughout. The history of this track is steeped in controversy. It was constructed by the Territorial Army in the late 1960s as part of a package of measures dreamt up by Inverness County Council and the Inverness-shire Constabulary. The justification for this work was that it would facilitate the evacuation of injured climbers from Coruisk.

Vigorous opposition from the outdoor fraternity prevented blasting of the Bad Step (see Route 50), but suspension bridges were built across the River Scavaig at Coruisk and across the Abhainn Camas Fhionnairigh. These have long since disappeared.

Approach
Park on the east side of the Elgol road (NG 545 172) a short distance after the turning for Kilmarie.

The Route
Follow the track on the west side of the road for just over 2km to its high point near Am Màm (189m). From here on there are spectacular views of the Cuillin peaks. As the track swings to the north the southern flank of Blàbheinn becomes increasingly prominent. Then start to descend quite steeply via a hairpin bend. (A faint path which leads through to Sligachan cuts off on the right a short distance before the hairpin bend – see Route 48.) The track continues descending and peters out eventually near some private buildings.

An open bothy is situated at the western end of the bay. There are also plenty of opportunities for wild camping on excellent ground nearby. The next route offers a longer, but more interesting, route of return if transport can be arranged at Elgol.

3 Elgol to Camasunary   6km (one way)   *
(NG 520 138)   High Point 100m   Map p75

This route is much more enjoyable than it might appear from the map. It offers fine views of the Cuillin and leads to the sandy shore on the east side of the bay.

Approach
From the higher of the two car parks in Elgol walk back up the hill for 300 metres. A signpost marks the start of the route.

The Route
Follow a track past some houses, and then a path between fences to reach more open, grassy terrain. After about 700 metres the path descends leftwards for some distance. It then traverses the steeply sloping hillside below Ben Cleat, and continues under the craggy face of Càrn Mòr to reach flatter ground in Glen Scaladal.

Ford the Scaladal Burn, then head left and climb out of the glen by a narrow path which continues among trees, with exciting drops to the shore below at times. The angle eases after Rubha na h-Àirighe Bàine, and a further kilometre of easier walking leads to Camasunary. This fine bay has a big expanse of sand when the tide is out, in which case it may be easier to stay on the shore and paddle across the Abhainn nan Leac. Otherwise head for a bridge on the track from Kilmarie.

The main buildings at Camasunary are private property, but on the western side of the bay there is an open bothy – see the previous route.

4 Suidhe Biorach   3km   *
(NG 516 135)   High Point 30m   Map p75

This clifftop walk follows a faint path out along the headland to the south of Elgol. It passes some interesting geos and promontories, where some scrambling can be included if desired.

Approach
From the lower car park near the jetty in Elgol.

The Route
Pick up a path that heads south along the relatively flat clifftop. The first features of interest can be seen after 1km at Suidhe nan Eun. These include a sea-stack and a depression formed by a small landslip. It is possible to scramble down from here to a natural arch much frequented by seabirds. It is a short distance then to the headland of Suidhe Biorach (*rough seat*), from where there are fine views of Rum. Numerous rock climbs have been put up on the sandstone sea-cliffs here, although few are in the easier grades.

Just east of Suidhe Biorach there is a bouldery bay, which can be accessed at either end by scrambling at low tide. On the headland at the far eastern end of this bay is a cave where Bonnie Prince Charlie spent his final hours on Skye before sailing back to the mainland.

Return to Elgol by the same route.

5 Spar Cave   Grade 1 **
(NG 538 127)   Alt sea level   Map p75

This is only a short outing, but well worthwhile. It requires careful timing. The cave entrance is above high water mark, but it lies at the back of a deep cleft, which is only accessible for a short time at low tide. The cleft has been formed by the weathering out of a dyke in strongly cross-bedded, calcareous sandstone. Limy material seeping in from the neighbouring rocks has coated the floor and walls of the cave with deposits of spar (calcium carbonate). The best stalactite formations have not survived countless visits, but the cave is still a spectacular sight. Although the cave is quite short, a headtorch is essential.

Approach
From the upper car park in Elgol take the road which runs eastwards over the peninsula to the tiny community of Glasnakille. Turn right at the T-junction.

The Route
Leave the road about 150 metres after the T-junction, and descend through a field past a stone byre. Continue down a small grassy depression until near the cliff top. Go left for a short distance and then head right before spiralling down leftwards to gain the shore at the back of a rocky recess. Turn left and clamber along the coast over large boulders to the huge cleft. If your timing is right you should be able to traverse along a ledge at the base of the left wall and cross rather slippery seaweed-covered boulders to gain the floor of the cleft. The remains of a stone wall can be seen at the cave entrance.

Take the left fork at the entrance. The initial section is rather muddy, but soon leads to a beautiful staircase of sparkling calcium carbonate which offers some mild scrambling up its left-hand side – not as hard as it looks. There is a short level section halfway up. From the high point descend slightly to a long pool of crystal clear water which marks the end of the cave. Scott described this in his *Lord of the Isles*:

> Mermaid's alabaster grot,
> Who bathes her limbs in sunless well,
> Deep in Strathaird's enchanted cell.

The deep cleft on the coast near Glasnakille which gives access to Spar Cave

Lucy Williams examines the formations inside Spar Cave (Grade 1)

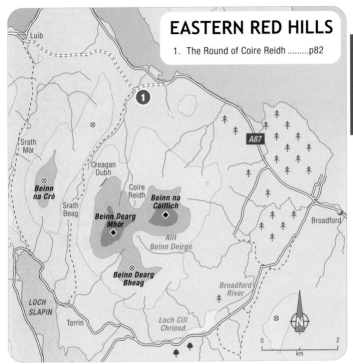

EASTERN RED HILLS

1. The Round of Coire Reidh p82

THE RED HILLS

The main road from Broadford to Sligachan skirts an impressive group of granite mountains known as the Red Hills. Although they appear more rounded and scree ridden than the Cuillin peaks, the Red Hills offer some surprisingly good walks as well as some minor scrambles. They are built from three different groups of granite intrusions.

The granites were all formed after the gabbros of the main Cuillin Complex. The first group of intrusions took place in the area around Strath na Creitheach and form the low hills of Meall Dearg and Ruadh Stac. The second group of intrusions forms the Western Red Hills and the third and youngest group forms the Eastern Red Hills. Although Marsco is built mainly from granite it has a small capping of gabbro on its summit ridge.

Eastern Red Hills

The scenery west of Broadford is dominated by the Eastern Red Hills. This group extends from Beinn na Caillich in the east to Glas Bheinn Mhòr which overlooks Loch Ainort in the west. Two deep glens, Srath Mòr and Srath Beag, cut through the hills from north to south. The route through Srath Beag involves greater ascent, but is rather more interesting, and much drier.

BEINN NA CAILLICH 732m

(NG 601 233) Map p81

Beinn na Caillich overlooks the town of Broadford and is the major mountain of the Eastern Red Hills group. It is the most conspicuous hill seen when travelling west from the bridge at Kyleakin. Welshman Thomas Pennant climbed to the summit in 1772 – one of the first recorded ascents of a mountain on the island. He wasn't the first though. He noted the presence of 'an artificial cairn of the most enormous size' on the summit.

6 Beinn na Caillich – The Round of Coire Reidh   11km **
(NG 603 266)   High Point 732m   Map p81

The mountain is commonly ascended from Strath Suardal, but the outing described is a very worthy alternative which approaches the mountain from its northern side.

Approach
Follow the main road beyond Broadford for some 5km, and park on a section of old road opposite the island of Scalpay just after a sharp left-hand bend.

The Route
Go through a gate and follow the track towards Luib for some 700 metres to where it crosses the Allt Strollamus. Leave the track and pick up a path on the west bank of this stream, which leads up to An Slugan – the high point on the route through Srath Beag. Follow this path as far as a stream junction, then head up the left-hand stream – the Allt na Teangaidh.

A prominent dark crag, Creagan Dubh, lies ahead. The aim is to reach the top of this feature. The easiest route is by a grassy runnel just to the left of the main north-east ridge. The latter can be gained by a heather terrace from the left and offers some easy (Grade 1) scrambling up slabs of baked basalt. The more adventurous may prefer to ascend a hidden gully on the right-hand side of the much steeper north face. It has a tricky exit (Grade 3).

Reach a small top (535m) above Creagan Dubh. On the slight descent from this top there is a dramatic change in the colour of the rocks as you pass onto granite. Pleasant easy walking over grass and boulders then leads to the broad summit of Beinn Dearg Mhòr (709m), from where there are extensive views to the south and west.

Turn left and descend north-eastwards, and then east along a slightly narrower ridge separating Coire Reidh from Coire Gorm. Then make the final ascent to the summit of Beinn na Caillich, which is graced by a trig point and a gigantic cairn. Just past the summit there is a splendid view down Coire Fearchair to Broadford.

Now turn left and descend the north-west ridge which overlooks Coire Seamraig. Try to stay near the right-hand edge where the going is slightly easier. Eventually head west-north-west, and make a descent on slabby rocks between two streams. Return along the Allt na Teangaidh as for the approach.

Western Red Hills

The Western Red Hills lie between Loch Ainort and Glen Sligachan. They form a rather irregular north–south chain and can be accessed either from the roadside to the east, or from Glen Sligachan to the west. The outings are described from north to south, rather than by the natural order of their starting points.

MEALL A' MHAOIL 284m

(NG 553 307)   Map p84

Although this is a fairly humble hill, there is a remarkably fine panorama from its summit. This makes it a rewarding goal in its own right.

7 Meall a' Mhaoil via the Allt Darach Gorge   Grade 3
(NG 553 320)   Alt sea level   Map p84

The Allt Darach gorge is cut in Torridonian sandstone. The rock is sound but rather slimy. The gorge approach is best done after a dry spell and is not recommended (and may not be possible) after wet weather.

Approach
Take the old road around the coast from the head of Loch Ainort, or join it from the other end near the golf club at Sconser. Park just east of the bridge over the Allt Darach.

The Route
Leave the road on the north-east side of the bridge and head down towards the sea. Turn into the mouth of the gorge and head upstream passing beneath the road bridge. A variety of techniques have to be employed on several tiny pitches in the early section of the gorge if feet are to be kept dry. It may be necessary to reposition small boulders in the stream bed to cross some of the pools.

The difficulties gradually ease and a long section of streamway is followed before the gorge eventually gives way to gentler slopes. Move onto the left-hand (eastern) flank of the stream and, when in sight of a lochan, head south-west to reach the summit. There are fine views of Rasaay and the Western Red Hills from the trig point. Head north-west across a broad col to visit Meall

WESTERN RED HILLS

1. Meall a' Mhaoil via Allt Darach Gorge......p83
2. Glàmaig, South-East Rib p85
3. Beinn Dearg Mhòr, North-East Ridge p86
4. The Beinn Deargs via Druim na Ruaige ...p87
5. Marsco, Fiaclan Dearg p88
6. Marsco, South-East Ridge p91
7. Coire na Seilg Slabs p93
8. Ruadh Stac, South Face p94
9. Meall Dearg, North Buttress.....................p95

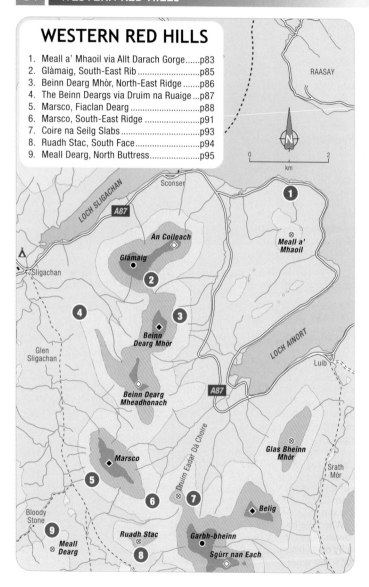

THE RED HILLS

Buidhe before descending ground on the west bank of the gorge to regain the road near the bridge.

GLÀMAIG 775m

(NG 513 300) Map p84

Glàmaig is the highest and most northerly of all the Red Hills. The mountain overlooks Sligachan and boasts an annual hill race, which was set up in 1988 partly to celebrate an extraordinary feat performed in 1899 by Ghurka Harkabir Thapa, who ran to the summit and back from the Sligachan Hotel in bare feet in just 55 minutes.

 8 South-East Rib Grade 2 or 3 *
(NG 518 293) Alt 415m Map p84

This outing takes a rather roundabout way to the summit. It is best combined with one of the next two routes in the guide. The scrambling is better than it looks, but can easily be avoided if necessary.

Start
The route as described starts from Bealach na Sgàirde, which can be reached by descending the north-west flank of Beinn Dearg Mhòr (Routes 9 or 10). Alternatively it can be approached either from Sligachan via Coire na Sgàirde, or from the east along the Allt Mòr Doire Mhic-uin.

The Route
The broad south-eastern flank of Glàmaig can be ascended from Bealach na Sgàirde without great difficulty. However, by seeking out a rocky rib a little to the right of the normal line, a more interesting ascent can be made. The rock is not granite as might be expected, but basalt heaved up and much altered by the granite intrusions.

From the bealach slant up rightwards over fine dark scree to a nose feature marking the start of a blocky rib. Move round to the right and back left to gain the crest of the rib above the nose. Ascend on good rock with some awkward step-ups. From the left-hand side of the rib make a steep crucial move rightwards (Grade 3) to stay on the crest. Easier options exist on the right.

Higher up move slightly left near the top of a short scree gully and move rightwards again to regain the rib. This gives pleasant scrambling, mainly Grade 2, with much variation possible. The rock is good on the whole, although slightly brittle in places. The best section starts at a mossy nose. From its right-hand side traverse hard left to reach the crest. The rocks above if taken direct are Grade 3.

When the rock peters out higher up, continue up a pleasant grassy ridge. Towards the top traverse hard right to reach a steep rock ridge with a small gully on its left. Move round to the right of this and follow an easy grass ramp for some distance until it fades out onto easier ground. Continue on grass heading slightly left to reach flatter ground. It is a short distance then to the summit cairn. Another cairn a little further on makes a better view point.

The route taken now will depend on your starting point, but a pleasant ridge can be followed, by the remains of an iron fence post, to the north-eastern top called An Coileach (673m). If returning to the start of the next route, descend the north-east ridge as far as the 300m level, then slant south-south-east to reach the road.

If returning to Sligachan you might try to emulate Harkabir Thapa's feat by striking directly down the west face – the present record to Sligachan from here is around 13 minutes! However a more sedate return can be made down a grassy slope to the west of the ascent route back to Bealach na Sgàirde from where a descent can be made via Coire na Sgàirde as for Route 10.

BEINN DEARG MHÒR 731m

(NG 520 285)   Map p84

This mountain lies immediately to the south of Glàmaig and is clearly seen from the main road when approaching from the east around the head of Loch Ainort. It is the higher of twin peaks which together form the largest massif in the Western Red Hills – the Beinn Deargs.

9 North-East Ridge   Grade 1
(NG 533 286)   *Alt 130m*   *Map p84*

This pleasant outing has the advantage that it starts at a height of 130m. The scrambling is enjoyable but fairly short-lived.

Approach
Park at the roadside just north of the highest point on the road between Broadford and Sligachan.

The Route
Cross a short section of boggy ground and then ascend a heather-covered slope. Short sections of fine scree lead to the start of some pleasant slabby ribs of sound granite. As the angle eases slightly the terrain changes to boulders and scree. The upper surface of the last glacier to form on this side of the mountain is marked by the change from moraine to scree and broken bedrock at about 350m – the approximate upper limit of vegetation cover.

Several sheep tracks cut across the ridge and contour around the hillside. Higher up there is much dwarf juniper and, where the ridge narrows slightly, there are further short sections of scrambling. Turn left at the top and soon reach the summit cairn. There are superb views down to Sligachan.

Continue down the north ridge to a tiny top, then zigzag carefully down unpleasantly steep scree on the north-west flank to Bealach na Sgàirde (*pass of the scree*), where there is a noticeable change in rock colour. Either turn right and descend beside the Allt Mòr Doire Mhic-uin to regain the road or, alternatively, continue onto Glàmaig (Route 8).

On the summit ridge of Beinn Dearg Mheadhonach looking north towards Glàmaig and Beinn Dearg Mhòr

10 The Beinn Deargs via Druim na Ruaige 10km *
(NG 486 298) High Point 731m Map p84

This is one of the most popular and straightforward circuits in the Red Hills. The views from the main crest are especially fine.

Approach
From the old bridge at Sligachan.

The Route
Follow the main path south along Glen Sligachan. Either fork left beside the Allt Daraich gorge or continue for some distance on the drier main path. Then head off towards the prominent nose at the north-western end of Sròn a' Bhealain. Ascend to this small grassy top and continue along the broad ridge of Druim na Ruaige. Climb scree to the long summit ridge of Beinn Dearg Mheadhonach.

Make a detour to the high point (651m) at the south-eastern end of the summit ridge before following the easy north ridge down to Bealach Mosgaraidh. Climb up the bouldery slope beyond to the main summit of Beinn Dearg Mhòr – a superb viewpoint.

Descend the north ridge to a tiny top (598m). Then zigzag carefully down very steep and rather unpleasant scree on its north-western flank to Bealach na Sgàirde. The great bulk of Glàmaig looms ahead.

Turn left and descend into Coire na Sgàirde. Pick up a traverse line on the left-hand flank which leads across to a ridge on the south side of the Allt Bealach na Sgàirde which gives easier walking. Continue as far as a prominent stream junction. Then, either cross the left-hand stream and head westward over very boggy ground to the path in Glen Sligachan, or cross the right-hand stream and follow the east bank of the Allt Daraich back to Sligachan.

MARSCO 736m

(NG 507 251) Map p84

Marsco, although not the highest, is arguably the finest of all the Red Hills. It is set apart from its neighbours and has a particularly striking profile when viewed from Sligachan. It offers the only rock climbing in the Red Hills. The most prominent buttress situated on its western flank is called Fiaclan Dearg (red tooth).

 11 Fiaclan Dearg – North-West Shoulder Grade 2 *
(NG 502 253) Alt 350m Map p84 Diagram p89

This route finds the easiest way to the summit of Fiaclan Dearg. There is some loose rock in places, but otherwise it makes an enjoyable scramble. The outing continues to the summit of Marsco.

Approach
Follow the path along Glen Sligachan for some 5km. When directly below Fiaclan Dearg head up the steep heathery hillside. This takes longer than expected. The going can be made slightly easier by hunting out occasional ribbons of granite slab.

The Route
From a slight bay on the left-hand side of the buttress slant leftwards up a broken rake. There is an awkward rock step fairly early on which forms the crux of the route. Continue slanting left and ascend a narrow rock ramp and a short slab to reach a grass patch. (The next route cuts right at this point.) Head left up easier ground for some distance to a grassy recess. Then slant left more steeply in a slightly more exposed position to reach the crest of the shoulder overlooking a deep gully containing the Allt Fiaclan Dearg.

Go up the shoulder easily to a rock band and then scramble pleasantly up rightwards by an obvious stepped weakness where a large block lies on a ledge. Zigzag up until the angle eases and soon reach the broad summit of Fiaclan Dearg. It is best to continue to the summit of Marsco from here.

Head up the bouldery slope above. Higher up the finer scree is slightly less pleasant, but eventually the angle relents and the crest is then followed rightwards to the summit. The best option from here is to descend the south-east ridge as far as a slight saddle and then cut down leftwards by a line of

THE RED HILLS

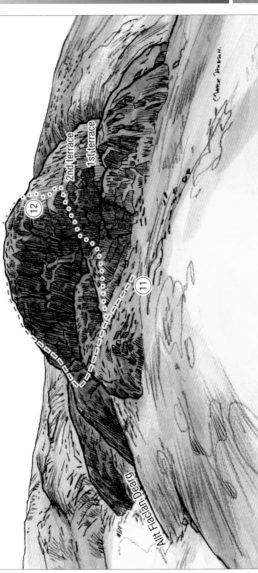

MARSCO
West Face - Fiaclan Dearg

11. North-West Shoulder   Grade 2 *
12. Odell's Route   Difficult *

2nd terrace

1st terrace

Allt Fiaclan Dearg

On the upper section of Odell's Route (Difficult)
Climber: Simon Fraser

fence posts to a broad shoulder forming the eastern side of Coire nan Laogh. Find a suitable place to cross the ravine containing the stream from the corrie, and continue more easily to Mam a' Phobuill. Descend by the north bank of the Allt na Measarroch and eventually rejoin the main path in Glen Sligachan.

12 Fiaclan Dearg – Odell's Route   Difficult   *
(NG 502 253)   *Alt 350*   *Map p84*   *Diagram p89*

This route was the very first rock climb made in the Red Hills. It was pioneered by Noel Odell in 1943 when he was carrying out a geological examination of the mountain. (Odell was on Everest in 1924 and made the last sighting of Mallory and Irvine.)

Approach
Approach along Glen Sligachan as for the previous route.

The Route
Slant leftwards to the grass patch as for Route 11. Then traverse hard right along a narrow rocky foot ledge (not a higher grassy one), which gradually becomes more difficult. A poor belay can be taken before climbing a damp groove and the slightly suspect rocks to its right. Then continue right more easily to reach a rising grassy ramp. Follow this hard right to gain The Shoulder – a commodious ledge with fine views to the south.

The rocks above look deceptively easy, but the next section provides the crux. Move rightwards initially then follow a series of short steep slabs slanting back left with one or two delicate moves. Continue more or less directly to easier ground. Move up slightly right into an alcove and fix a superb thread runner before continuing diagonally rightwards. Then climb up to the right of the buttress crest. Much easier climbing and then scrambling leads to the top of the buttress. Reach the summit of Marsco and return as for the previous route.

13 South-East Ridge   8km   **
(NG 518 243)   *High Point 736m*   *Map p84*

This is the most pleasant walking route to the summit of Marsco. There are magnificent panoramic views from the upper part of the route.

Approach
The shortest approach to this ridge is from the roadside south-west of Loch Ainort. Park near a bend where the road crosses the Allt Coire nam Bruadaran within sight of a fine waterfall. Ascend the Druim Eadar Dà Choire and cut off to the right before the high point to reach the broad bouldery bealach at the foot of the ridge. Longer but more aesthetically pleasing approaches can be made along the good path in Glen Sligachan. The first option is to fork off to the left after 3km and continue on a poorer path on the north side of the Allt na Measarroch to the Màm a' Phobuill. From there a slanting ascent of Coire nan Laogh leads to a dip on the ridge (as described in descent for Route 11). The other option is to continue much further up Glen Sligachan (some

Descending the south-east ridge of Marsco with Garbh-bheinn in the distance

6km) and follow the north bank of the Allt nam Fraoch-choire before ascending to the bealach at the start of the ridge. The latter option is little used but gives good views of the north face of Ruadh Stac en route.

The Route

There is a steep pull up from the bealach for some 300m before the ridge levels off at a small top. Descend easily just beyond this to a small grassy saddle, where a line of iron fence posts, which has been following the ridge, now cuts off down to the right into Coire nan Laogh. Continue up a broader section of ridge which gradually narrows as the top is approached. There can be few finer views from a hill of such modest stature. As well as the spectacular panorama of hills, a line of boulders can be seen on the right bank of the Allt Coire nam Bruadaran which is an old medial moraine.

To descend, either return to the saddle and head down Coire nan Laogh to Màm a' Phobuill and Sligachan as for Route 11, or go north from the summit and then pick a way down the steeper and less straightforward north-east flank to reach Màm a' Phobuill more directly. If returning to Loch Ainort from Màm a' Phobuill descend steeply at first in an easterly direction and follow the rather boggy north bank of the Allt Coire nam Bruadaran.

DRUIM EADAR DÀ CHOIRE 489m

(NG 525 244)   Map p84

This broad heathery ridge starts from the roadside near the head of Loch Ainort and rises to an undistinguished grassy summit linking Marsco with Garbh-bheinn. Immediately to the south-east of the summit a small dip on the ridge (429m) marks the transition from granite to much darker gabbro.

 14 Coire na Seilg Slabs   Grade 3   *

(NG 528 243)   Alt 300m   Map p84

This outing finds the best line up a sweep of glaciated granite slabs situated in the south-western corner of Coire na Seilg. The outing can easily be combined with a visit to Ruadh Stac – the next route described – or an ascent of Garbh-bheinn by its north ridge (Route 20).

Approach

Start from a bend where the A87 road crosses the Allt Coire nam Bruadaran south-west of Loch Ainort (NG 534 267). The slabs in question are situated about 2.5km from the road just below a dark gabbro crag called Creag Druim Eadar Dà Choire. Approach them by following the broad ridge leading to Druim Eadar Dà Choire. This is rather hard going to start with, but persevere and it gradually improves. Move slightly left to the eastern side of the crest and, just before reaching the first granite outcrop of Druim Eadar Dà Choire proper, slant leftwards off the ridge. Traverse south across the hillside to the obvious sweep of slabs. An alternative approach can be made along the Abhainn Ceann Loch Ainort.

THE RED HILLS

The Route

The route takes a more or less central line up the cleanest and driest strip of rock. After some pleasant introductory slabs a steep little overlap blocks the direct way ahead. This wall can be circumvented on either side; i) head for a point just a little to the left of the wall, and to the right of some overlapping slabs. Then climb steepish rock for a couple of moves before traversing hard right for some 8 metres to get established on the main strip of slabs, or ii) a slightly harder option is to ascend a small rock step then a short distance above make for a groove on the right-hand side of the wall. Then climb diagonally leftwards to gain the easier slabs above.

Ascend the slabs directly (Grade 2) with the difficulties easing very gradually as height is gained. Eventually when the slabs peter out ascend easier ground rightwards to emerge at a dip below the north ridge of Garbh-bheinn. The summit of Druim Eadar Dà Choire is just a short distance away to the right.

RUADH STAC 493m

(NG 514 233) Map p84

This lowly summit can be reached quite easily by walking across the west flank of Garbh-bheinn. It is well worth a visit. It gives unusual views of Blàbheinn and Clach Glas, as well as all the Cuillin.

15 South Face Grade 3

(NG 527 242) Alt 429m Map p84 Diagram p100

This route may appeal to those who relish more esoteric outings.

Approach

Start from the dip on the ridge (429m) just south-east of Druim Eadar Dà Choire, best reached by first completing the previous route.

Route

Descend only slightly on the western side of the dip, and then traverse southwards across the flank of Garbh-bheinn. Pick up a faint path in the scree and follow this until a short descent leads down to the bealach (337m) between Garbh-bheinn and Ruadh Stac. It is easy then to ascend the rounded summit plateau and continue to the highest point at its western end.

However, a more exciting and much more roundabout route to the summit is now described. Drop down slightly on the south side of the bealach between Garbh-bheinn and Ruadh Stac. Then make a long traverse across the southern flank of the hill following an animal track at about the 300m contour.

The ground becomes more craggy and much more serious (Grade 3) towards the western end. Then a crucial line has to be found down into and out of a very deep gully. After this the going gradually eases and it becomes possible to ascend to the crest of a broad ridge which leads back in a south-easterly direction to the summit. This is a fine vantage point offering splendid views down the glen to Camasunary.

As you return to the bealach between Ruadh Stac and Garbh-bheinn, look out for a faint path which takes a dogleg route across the head of Am Fraochchoire on the left. This makes a very convenient link to the broad bealach below the south-east ridge of Marsco (Route 13). From this bealach, either descend Coire nam Bruadaran and follow the extremely wet path along the Allt Coire nam Bruadaran, or traverse a long way right and descend the Druim Eadar Dà Choire.

MEALL DEARG 364m

(NG 493 230)   Map p84

This tiny hill is made from the first granite intrusion to 'invade' the earlier rocks of the Cuillin complex. The layered structures in the gabbro as well as the later cone-sheets all dip to a common focal point some 2–3km below this hill. So geologically speaking it is situated at the very heart of the Cuillin. Perhaps not surprisingly, there is a fine panoramic view from the summit.

 16 North Buttress   Grade 3
(NG 493 235)   Alt 180m   Map p84

Although the scrambling alone does not justify the long approach this is an enjoyable route and better than it looks. It could be used as an alternative way of gaining the Druim nam Ràmh ridge (Route 184).

Approach

From the old road bridge at Sligachan follow the path south along Glen Sligachan for just over 5km. Then head off rightwards towards Harta Corrie following a rather wet and indefinite path beside the River Sligachan.

Shortly before reaching the Bloody Stone, slant off leftwards and head for the steepest section of granite buttress on the northern flank of Meall Dearg.

Route

There is short wall at the start which can be avoided either to the right or left. After a short section of broken ground the rock becomes more continuous. The best option from here on is to deliberately hunt out the steepest line. The rock is generally excellent and gives surprisingly good scrambling. It starts to become more broken again as the angle gradually eases higher up. There are several conspicuous gabbro boulders lying on the granite bedrock. These are 'erratics' which were transported by ice to their present position. Continue easily to the summit.

Return to the foot of the route by descending ground to the east of the ascent route. Alternatively, head south along Druim Hain to join the path from Sligachan to Coruisk (Route 49). Another option is to cross undulating ground south-westwards over Meallan Dearg to gain the Druim nan Ràmh ridge at a sprawling top of around 500m.

CUILLIN OUTLIERS

1. Belig, South-East Ridge.............................p97
2. Garbh-bheinn, North Ridge p99
3. Sgùrr nan Each, North Buttress p103
4. Clach Glas, East Face........................p109
5. Clach Glas, West Face........................p114
6. Blàbheinn, Forked Pinnacle Ridge p117
7. Blàbheinn, North-East Face p122
8. Blàbheinn, Southern Buttresses........p131
9. Blàbheinn, South-West Buttress p135

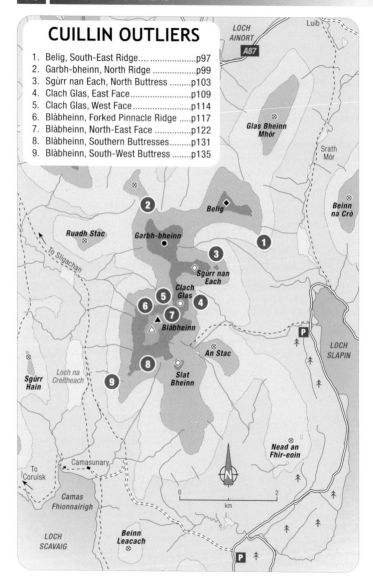

CUILLIN OUTLIERS

The chain of hills which extends from Belig southwards is built from very different rocks to Marsco and the other Red Hills. The dramatic change in colour of the rocks at the northern end of Garbh-bheinn is obvious even to the untrained eye. Garbh-bheinn, Clach Glas and mighty Blàbheinn are formed from the same gabbro intrusions as the Cuillin, and only an accident of erosion has separated them from the main Cuillin massif. For this reason this group is referred to as the Cuillin Outliers.

BELIG 702m

(NG 543 240)   Map p96

This fine hill has three rather different ridges which offer pleasant walking and some minor amounts of scrambling for those prepared to hunt it out. It is the grassiest hill of the Cuillin Outliers mainly because all the upper part of the mountain, including the summit, is built from basalt lavas. Gabbro occurs on its western flank, and an intrusive breccia on its northern ridge. An ascent of this hill can readily be combined with its bigger neighbour, Garbh-bheinn, to give enjoyable circuits from either Loch Slapin or Loch Ainort.

 17 South-East Ridge   5km   *
(NG 555 229)   Alt 60m   Map p96

A pleasant outing with grass underfoot for much of the way. It can be included as the first leg of an extended traverse of all the Cuillin Outliers.

Approach
Start from the head of Loch Slapin. Head across low ground near the mouth of Srath Mòr, ford the Allt Aigeinn and continue directly to the toe of the ridge.

The Route
The ridge steepens quite quickly and remains a stiff climb as far as the eastern shoulder, which gives a pleasant respite before the final section of narrower ridge leads more steeply again to the summit.

 18 North Ridge   Grade 2   *
(NG 542 249)   Alt 300m   Map p96

The area of broken crag at the start of the north ridge is frequently outflanked on the right, but if tackled more directly some interesting scrambling can be found.

Approach
Start from the A87 road around the head of Loch Ainort and set off along the Abhain Ceann Loch Ainort. Soon head off to the left on the rising ground between Coire na Seilg and Coire Choinnich.

One of the small buttresses on the South-West Ridge (Grade 1/2), Belig
Scrambler: Iain Thow

The Route
Aim for the steepest rocks guarding the base of the north ridge and zigzag up through these with interest staying to the right of a prominent gully. Break out onto the north ridge and continue without further difficulty to the summit.

19 South-West Ridge Grade 1/2 *
(NG 539 237) Alt 456m Map p96

Although this very broad ridge looks rather broken from a distance, the lower part of it is built of gabbro which offers some intermittent scrambling.

Approach
This route starts from Bealach na Beiste (456m) which can be gained from the corries on either side or via the north-east ridge of Garbh-bheinn (Route 21).

The Route
Much of this ridge consists of bouldery ground, but by deliberately aiming for several short ribs and buttresses some surprisingly pleasant scrambling can be pieced together. Eventually an old stone wall joins the crest from the left-hand side and this is then followed all the way to the summit.

GARBH-BHEINN 808m

(NG 531 232) Map p96

This hill is a prominent feature looking south from the head of Loch Ainort. Three ridges radiate from its summit, and each of them offers short sections of mild scrambling. Its traverse can be made the climax of two possible circuits which include the neighbouring peak of Belig. One circuit starts from the Loch Ainort side; the other starts from Loch Slapin and includes a traverse of Sgùrr nan Each.

20 North Ridge Grade 1/2 *
(NG 527 242) Alt 429m Map p96 Diagram p100

Once the start of the ridge is gained, this route takes a direct and very satisfying line to the summit.

Approach
From the road around Loch Ainort. Reach the dip at the foot of the north ridge, either by ascending the Druim Eadar Dà Choire ridge and traversing its grassy summit (489m), or by completing the scramble on the Coire na Seilg slabs (Route 14).

The Route
The initial section of ridge is fairly tame, and is marked by old fence posts, but the steeper middle section has slabby rocks with some scrambling interest. Ascend the crest where possible, thereby avoiding the worst of the scree further right. The ridge then eases slightly for some distance before a slight steepening leads to an abrupt left turn a short distance before the

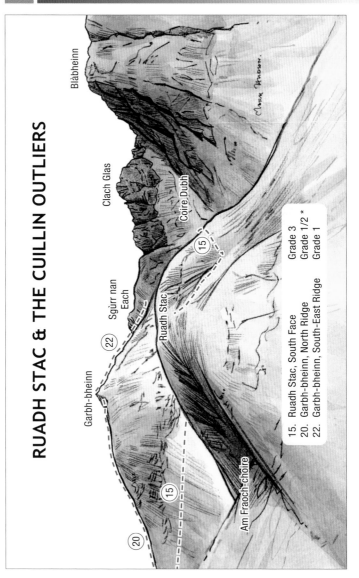

RUADH STAC & THE CUILLIN OUTLIERS

Blàbheinn

Clach Glas

Sgùrr nan Each

Garbh-bheinn

Coire Dubh

Ruadh Stac

Am Fraoch-choire

15. Ruadh Stac, South Face   Grade 3
20. Garbh-bheinn, North Ridge   Grade 1/2 *
22. Garbh-bheinn, South-East Ridge   Grade 1

summit – a delightful finish. There are superb views to the south of Clach Glas and Blàbheinn.

Either return the same way or continue by descending one of the next two routes.

21 North-East Ridge   Grade 1/2
(NG 539 237)   Alt 456m   Map p96

The natural way to complete this route is as part of a circuit with one of the neighbouring peaks.

Approach

This route starts from Bealach na Beiste (456m) which can be gained from the corries on either side or from the south-west ridge of Belig (Route 19).

The Route

From the broad flattening at Bealach na Beiste ascend a slight shoulder and continue up the bouldery slope above for some distance. The narrower upper section is more interesting, and gives some pleasant scrambling, either on or just left of the crest, before ending abruptly at the summit.

Depending on your destination, either descend the north ridge (Route 20) or the shorter south-east ridge (Route 22).

22 South-East Ridge   Grade 1
(NG 533 228)   Alt 636m   Map p96   Diagram p100

This is the shortest and easiest of Garbh-bheinn's three ridges. An easy section of ridge links it with the western end of Sgùrr nan Each.

Approach

The ridge is easiest to approach from the Loch Slapin side. Either complete one of the routes on Sgùrr nan Each (Route 23 or 24) or approach Coire a' Chàise by the path along the Allt na Dunaiche, and ascend the right fork at the top on very steep scree to Bealach Coire a' Chaise.

The Route

From the western end of Sgùrr nan Each descend an easy ridge in a north-westerly direction to a bealach. Follow the pleasant rocky ridge with no special difficulties directly to the summit.

From the summit, either descend by the north-east ridge which is a little tricky in its upper section, or go a short distance to the west and descend by the north ridge.

SGÙRR NAN EACH   720m

(NG 537 227)   Map p96

This top lies on a spur projecting eastwards from the ridge linking Garbh-bheinn and Clach Glas. It can be bypassed entirely on an easy scree slope. However, its traverse makes an interesting start to an ascent of either peak.

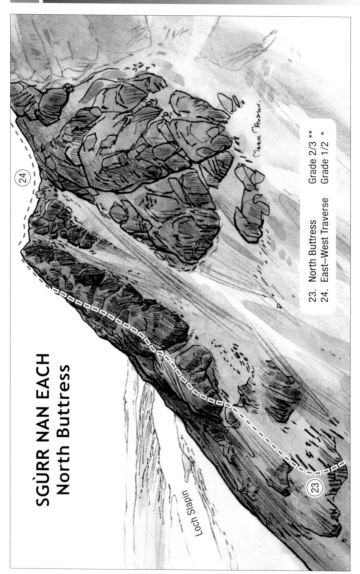

SGÙRR NAN EACH
North Buttress

Loch Slapin

23. North Buttress   Grade 2/3 **
24. East–West Traverse   Grade 1/2 *

23 North Buttress   Grade 2/3 **
(NG 541 231)   Alt 330m   Map p96   Diagram p102

This fine buttress is best seen from Bealach na Beiste. It was first ascended in 1898 by Harold Raeburn. He approached the route from Sligachan, and returned there via Clach Glas.

Approach
The more usual approach is from the head of Loch Slapin. Follow the north bank of the Allt Aigeinn past some delightful waterfalls.

The Route
Stay on the north bank until directly opposite the prominent buttress. Cross the stream and head up to the lowest tongue of slabby rock some distance below the buttress proper. This makes a delightful starter. Climb up onto it from the right and slant diagonally leftwards to the top. The rock is rough and covered with holds.

Continue on more broken rocks and scree for some distance, and eventually make directly for the start of the buttress. Either climb the very steep initial rocks directly, or continue up the slope to the right until it is possible to break left up a rib and then the groove on its right to reach the buttress crest. Zigzag up fairly easy ground to a grassy terrace below more continuous rocks. This is where the real fun starts.

Ascend the rocks on the left side of a left-slanting groove to a ledge. Continue up a steepish rib of rock with a black lichen-covered wall to the right. The rock is superb and furnished with large steps. Above a grassy ledge the rocks are less steep, until a short wall is reached. Slant right to find the easiest way up or climb a steep groove up the centre.

The angle then starts to ease slightly, and the next significant feature is a steep nose on a narrower section of ridge. Do not follow ledges on the right-hand side, but instead go left of the crest and made a couple of awkward step-ups on mossy ledges. Then ascend the left edge of a pleasant slab before regaining the crest on the right. The ridge pinches down to a slight neck. Outflank a small wall by its left-hand end, then continue more easily and finish on a small top (623m).

From the dip a little further to the west it is possible to return down the north flank by the obvious scree gully, but the best option now is to traverse Sgùrr nan Each as for Route 24.

24 East–West Traverse   Grade 1/2 *
(NG 546 219)   Alt 250m   Map p96   Diagram p102

This route makes a popular start to the traverse of Clach Glas. It is a varied outing with sensational views of the Cuillin at the western end.

Approach
Follow the normal approach path to Blàbheinn along the north bank of the Allt na Dunaiche as far as a flattening at 200m.

CUILLIN OUTLIERS

The Route

Head right and follow a rounded ridge leading to the south-east shoulder of Sgùrr nan Each. Some small outcrops high up give short sections of scrambling on a variety of rock types. Gain the eastern end of the summit ridge, and visit the small top above North Buttress. Then descend slightly to a dip, and continue up a broad grassy ridge for some distance. Then negotiate some rockier ground to reach the main summit. A rocky eminence between here and the western top gives some pleasant easy scrambling.

Go round to the left of a blocky pinnacle. A prominent slab sloping down to a dip can be bypassed on the left or downclimbed directly by a crack (crux). It is easier then to the small western top. Just beyond this top, a broad slope is reached overlooking Srath na Creitheach. There are superb views from here of Ruadh Stac and the whole Cuillin massif.

Now either continue onto Garbh-bheinn (Route 22), or traverse Clach Glas (Routes 25 & 26). However, it is also possible to descend steep scree immediately to the south from Bealach Coire a' Chàise into Coire a' Chàise.

CLACH GLAS 786m

(NG 534 221) Map p96

This spectacular and shapely peak is sometimes referred to as the 'Matterhorn of Skye'. Its summit is one of the most difficult to reach on the whole island. A traverse of the peak makes a superb outing. It is usually done from north to south, in which case strong parties will normally continue by making an ascent of Blàbheinn.

25 North Ridge Moderate ***

(NG 533 225) Alt 635m Map p96 Diagram p105

This outing is mainly scrambling, with very interesting route finding, chiefly on the right side of the crest. The final tower gives the crux, where a couple of pitches may justify a rope.

Approach

Approach along the path on the north bank of the Allt na Dunaiche, and where the ground levels off at about 200m head rightwards into Coire a' Chàise. At the head of the corrie fork left up steep scree and boulders to gain a low point on the ridge (635m) directly above Arch Gully on the west face.

The Route

Ascend a steep little wall out of the col, and scramble pleasantly up slabs and along a switchback crest. Climb down steeply into a gap on the Loch Slapin side, and then scramble up a short arête. Traverse slightly easier ground along ledges below the crest. Look out for two photogenic rock lumps with remarkable holes right through them situated up left on the crest itself.

From the bed of a gully make an awkward rightwards traverse beneath steep rocks. Continue more easily, traversing beneath a large pinnacle to gain

CLACH GLAS
North Ridge

Blàbheinn

27a

28

Black Cleft

25

30

25.	North Ridge	Moderate ***
27a.	Sid's Rake	Grade 2 *
28.	Ramp Route	Moderate **
30.	Pilkington's Route	Difficult *

Martin Moran.

a more prominent scree gully (above the Black Cleft) marking the start of the major difficulties.

Climb a slanting V-shaped chimney, bridging past some awkward bulges. Part way up, a possible alternative is to climb a steep crack in the right wall to a short ridge. Turn left to tackle the summit tower. This gives sustained Moderate climbing. Weave a way up in a sensational position with the difficulties gradually easing after 25m. Continue by bearing right to reach the superb rocky table top which constitutes the summit of the mountain.

There are magnificent vistas from the summit platform. The view to the south is dominated by the north-east face of Blàbheinn, the final goal for those attempting the full traverse.

The normal option from here is to descend the South Ridge – the next route described. This means initially reversing a feature called The Impostor – see Routes 26 & 30. It would also be possible to descend the east face via Sid's Rake (Route 27), although prior knowledge of that route would be a big advantage.

 ## 26 South Ridge Moderate **

(NG 533 218) Alt 695m Map p96 Diagram p107

This route starts from the bealach known as the Putting Green situated below the towering north-east face of Blàbheinn. The bealach itself is a small, grassy depression with several large boulders, but the obvious approaches to it from either side are up very unattractive scree slopes.

The route is here described in ascent, although it is more usually descended during a north–south traverse of the mountain. See p137 for a description of the full traverse of Clach Glas and Blàbheinn. Most of the steeper sections are tackled on the eastern or Loch Slapin side of the crest.

Approach

Those prepared for a hard slog will follow the good path on the north side of the Allt na Dunaiche and turn up into Coire Uaigneich until just below the east ridge of Blàbheinn. Then head off to the right away from the path. The initial ground is quite grassy but higher up it is all scree. There are faint paths in places to aid progress. Towards the top slant rightwards through more craggy ground to reach the Putting Green (695m).

The scree slope on the Coire Dubh or western side is slightly more pleasant, though few parties approach from this side.

The Route

Go along the ridge easily at first then descend on the left-hand side of the crest to enter a gap. Climb out the other side and slant rightwards following a brown cone-sheet onto the Slapin face. Ascend a slab to reach the highest point of a feature called the Bealach Tower. Cut diagonally leftwards over the crest at a narrow cleft and then shortly afterwards make an awkward descent to a gap the other side. Continue to a third gap marked by green rock with gullies on either side.

Ascend a sloping terrace on the east flank, below steep rocks, to reach a cleft. Climb this then slant leftwards up a slab. Follow a faint path curving round to a ledge below slabs and more broken rocks. Ascend these trending slightly right. From a ledge on the Slapin face gain a slab and ascend this back to the crest. After a tiny gap continue just left of the crest and soon reach a section of horizontal ridge formed by a cone-sheet. Go easily along this to the final steepening known as The Impostor (see Route 30). There are three options from here:

CLACH GLAS
South Ridge

CUILLIN OUTLIERS

Bealach
Tower

Garbh-bheinn

21.	North-East Ridge	Grade 1/2
22.	South-East Ridge	Grade 1
26.	South Ridge	Moderate **
30.	Pilkington's Route	Difficult *

The Impostor – the final section of the South Ridge (Moderate), Clach Glas
Scrambler: Iain Thow

a) The direct and most popular way climbs some slightly suspect rock for a couple of metres (crux) to gain the slab above. A recent rockfall here has not altered the grade, but the cracked rocks hereabouts may suffer further wear and tear. Continue up a slanting groove which soon eases and in a short distance reach the dramatic summit platform.

The next two alternatives are of similar grade to the classic way, but are on more reassuring rock. Both ascend the rocks on the east face a little to the north of The Impostor. They can be reached either by traversing delicately along the cone-sheet from the start of The Impostor, or more easily by descending a short distance on the east face to gain a grassy terrace running below the summit rocks – this is the finish of Sid's Rake (see Route 27).

b) The second option finishes up the same groove in the slab as The Impostor. Traverse northwards past The Impostor for 10m. Step up from the cone-sheet directly onto the summit slab and after just a couple of delicate moves on superb rock slant diagonally leftwards to regain the original route.

c) The third option ascends a prominent rift capped by a chockstone situated a further 10m northwards i.e. 20m beyond The Impostor. A groove leads from the grassy terrace up to the start of the rift. Either climb the rocks on the right-hand edge of the rift, or ascend the rift itself and climb out of it using footholds on the right wall and a good hold on the top of the chockstone. Ascend a mossy recess to arrive directly at the summit.

The natural continuation from the summit would be to descend the North Ridge (Route 25). However, this involves exposed and sustained down-climbing on the summit tower – harder and more intimidating than the climbing on the South Ridge. An easier alternative might be to reverse The Impostor and descend the upper section of Sid's Rake (Route 27). It would then be possible to regain the North Ridge below the summit tower by ascending the continuation of B Gully.

EAST FACE

The east face of Clach Glas is a striking feature seen from across Loch Slapin. It provides a couple of interesting routes with a real mountaineering feel about them.

27 Sid's Rake   Grade 2 * or 3 **
(NG 537 218)   Alt 450m   Map p96   Diagram p110

This is the original line on the face. It was first ascended by Sidney Williams in 1900. Dr and Mrs Inglis Clark had an epic descending this side of the mountain in a fierce storm in June 1901.

It should be borne in mind that descending The Impostor from the summit will involve some down-climbing at Moderate standard.

Approach
Follow the path on the north side of the Allt na Dunaiche. The route starts from a large terrace below the left-hand half of the face. To gain this terrace,

CLACH GLAS
East Face

Bealach Tower

Putting Green

Pinnacle Buttress

26

27b

27a

Rock Bridge

27

A Gully

Boulder Terrace

B Gully

28

26. South Ridge (The Impostor)   Moderate **
27. Sid's Rake
    a) Original Route   Grade 2 *
    b) Slapin the Face variation   Grade 3 **
28. Ramp Route   Moderate **

Mark Andsah.

either ascend scree further left and eventually slant back right, or find a way up rather tricky, damp slabs (Grade 3) between A and B Gullies, then traverse left across A Gully at the same level as the terrace. A gigantic boulder on this terrace offers an amusing scramble up its northern end.

The Route

Zigzag up the buttress left of A Gully on grass and rock until forced into a gully on the left. Ascend this for some distance and then climb out by its right wall to reach a sprawling juniper bush. An entertaining option now is to

On the 'Slapin the Face' variation of Sid's Rake (Grade 3), Clach Glas
Scrambler: Iain Thow

traverse rightwards across a slab to reach an amazing rock bridge which spans A Gully. Cross this to gain the buttress on the far side and scramble up slabby rocks before moving back left where the angle eases. Otherwise continue by re-entering the left-hand gully and following it to a shoulder above a gully which slants down to the right. There are two alternative routes from here:

a) **Original Route**   **Grade 2** (Moderate on the Impostor) *
Ascend the grassy gully on the left, and continue to the right of a rock rib. Reach a fine col left of a small tower. Then slant right up easier ground over soil and grass – much used by sheep – heading in the same direction as a prominent slot between the two upper pinnacles of Pinnacle Buttress on the opposite side of B Gully.

Cross a tiny shoulder with orange soil left of a rock boss, before joining B Gully. Ascend loose scree in the bed of B Gully until the angle eases slightly.

Continuing directly up B Gully leads to the top of the broad scree gully on the west face at the base of the summit tower (Route 25). However, it is more natural to stay on this face and follow a slanting grassy terrace leftwards. Slant down a short rock band to pick up a continuation of the grassy rake. Keep traversing left for some distance, staying well below the summit rocks. Eventually gain the horizontal arête just south of The Impostor. Finish up The Impostor or either of the two alternatives on the east face – see the previous route.

b) **'Slapin the Face' Variation**   **Grade 3** (Moderate on the Impostor) **
This is a much more interesting line. Instead of continuing up the grassy gully, break left up a broad V-shaped groove floored with boulders. Exit up the left-bounding rib and emerge onto easier ground. Continue traversing leftwards and then scramble up slabby rocks for some distance.

Traverse left and crawl under an enormous chockstone to reach a sloping terrace. Continue leftwards, and then head directly up a continuous section of rock before trending left again to a broken rock rib with a gully further left. Scramble up this rib, sticking to the crest as far as possible. Continue up rocks parallel to the right fork of the gully. Rejoin the original line at the arête just south of the Impostor. Finish as for the South Ridge (Route 26).

The simplest way off the mountain is to descend the original line of Sid's Rake.

28 Ramp Route   Moderate **
(NG 538 219)   Alt 300m   Map p96   Diagram p110
This varied route passes through some dramatic scenery. Only one pitch of Moderate grade should be encountered. Dr and Mrs Clark climbed a route in this vicinity in 1901.

Approach
Approach by the path on the north side of the Allt na Dunaiche.

Willie Jeffrey on the right-hand variation of Ramp Route (Moderate), Clach Glas

The Route

Ascend grass and heather right of B Gully to a grassy bay. Traverse left to reach the first reasonable rocks. Slant up leftwards at first, and then follow a delightful stretch of slabs intruded by numerous cone-sheets with good views of B Gully on the left. From a grassy terrace zigzag up a slightly steeper buttress (Grade 3), and then continue up more slabs to a second terrace.

Now slant rightwards up an obvious stony ramp. Head up and then back right to cross a steep gully, then continue diagonally rightwards up easier ground with steep rocks on the left. Ascend a short gully to reach the two main ramp features which characterise the route. Both features offer pitches of comparable difficulty but contrasting styles.

a) **The left-hand ramp** is situated at a slightly higher level below a spectacular vertical wall. It is separated from the right-hand ramp by a dyke gully. Reach the start of the ramp by scrambling awkwardly up left. The steep initial section is climbed on small incut holds where the rock may be damp.

b) **The right-hand ramp** is climbed by slanting right and ascending a narrow dyke. The crux is in a very exposed position where the dyke thins above a steep cone-sheet. Slightly easier rocks above then allow the left-hand ramp line to be joined.

Short rock bands continue to give interest before the going gradually eases. Then start to trend up leftwards, and bridge up a short rocky gully. Traverse left along the line of a cone-sheet and enter the upper reaches of B Gully. Continue traversing left and finish along a grassy terrace as for Sid's Rake.

WEST FACE

The west face of Clach Glas has slabby rocks with two main gullies either side of the steep summit tower. The climbs here are difficult to reach, but they offer worthwhile outings in a remote setting above Coire Dubh. This corrie is also known, appropriately, as the 'Lonely Corrie'. The best approach to the west face is from the Loch Slapin side. It is much further from Sligachan or Camasunary. The Loch Slapin approach is now described.

From a car park on the west side of Loch Slapin follow a good path on the north side of the Allt Dunaiche. At a height of 200m instead of turning left into Coire Uaigneich continue rightwards and eventually pick up a faint path which continues towards Coire a' Chàise. Stay on the right-hand side of the corrie and ascend the very steep scree in the right fork to gain the ridge at the western end of Sgùrr nan Each at a height of around 670m. This crossing point is known as **Bealach Coire a' Chàise**.

Go north-west for only a short distance before descending a long, easy scree slope which originates from the col (636m) between Garbh-bheinn and Sgùrr nan Each. Eventually curve leftwards and at about the 450m contour skirt below the lowest rocks just north of Arch Gully. Then ascend slightly to gain a boulder-strewn flattening in Coire Dubh below the west face of Clach Glas.

**CLACH CLAS
West Face**

Half-Crown
Pinnacle

Putting
Green

Bealach
Tower

Coire Dubh

Black
Cleft

Athain Gully

Arch
Gully

29. Athain Slab Route   Moderate **
30. Pilkington's Route   Difficult *

CUILLIN OUTLIERS

29 Athain Slab Route   200m   Moderate **
(NG 532 223)   Alt 600m   West facing   Map p96   Diagram p115

This route was first climbed by Hamish Brown and party in 1967. Although not an obvious line, it offers enjoyable climbing. It would make an unusual way of starting the North Ridge (Route 25).

Approach
Start to the right of Arch Gully (Moderate), at a narrow slabby ramp with a steep wall to its left which is undercut lower down.

The Route
Scramble up easy slabs, then climb two pitches of slabs to a rock step. From the right-hand side of this trend back left and continue more easily to a short, wide rock step. Move up by a large lump of brown rock set in a darker matrix, and follow easier-angled slabs to the base of a steep wall. (Possible escape route up a gully on the left.)

Move right slightly to two boulders on an edge overlooking Athain Gully. The wall above gives the crux. Zigzag up taking care with loose rock, then pull out onto slabs and continue to the base of another steep wall. Move up and round to the right, then follow a narrow glacis across a wall for two pitches. Turn left to reach easier ground. Clamber up rocks leftwards to reach the crest of the North Ridge.

30 Pilkington's Route   Difficult *
(NG 532 221)   Alt 600m   West facing   Map p96   Diagram p115

This is the route climbed by Charles Pilkington's party when they made the first ascent of Clach Glas in 1887. The main climbing difficulties in the initial section of gully are very short-lived, but sufficiently tricky to justify the grade.

Approach
At the mouth of the obvious gully on the right-hand half of the face.

The Route
Enter the gully and climb rocks mainly on the left to avoid trickles of water in the gully bed. Surmount a chockstone either on the right side on damp rock (crux), or on the left where the rock is drier but the holds less obvious. Continue up an easier section of gully until this becomes impracticable. Then traverse hard right along an obvious cleft to reach open slopes above.

Weave a way up slabs and broken rocks for some distance and eventually reach the horizontal arête just south of the Impostor. Pilkington described his party's ascent. '… *we found a knife edge of tremendous steepness coming down towards us. We put on the rope and nerved ourselves for the attack; we just had a look round the edge first, and seeing a piece of slanting rock, we crossed it, and, pulling ourselves out of the neck of a little gully, walked up the impostor in a few minutes.*'

The easiest way off from the summit is via Sid's Rake. Otherwise descend the South Ridge to the Putting Green.

BLÀBHEINN 928m

(NG 529 217) Map p96

Blàbheinn is a magnificent mountain – it is the highest of the Cuillin Outliers and the only Munro on the island outwith the Cuillin proper. It is a wonderful viewpoint for the whole of the Cuillin main ridge as well as all the Red Hills. Sheriff Nicolson regarded it as the finest mountain on Skye.

The mountain is most conveniently approached from Broadford in the east by a single-track road that runs along Strath Suardal to Torrin and then continues around the head of Loch Slapin. A good path leads along the north side of the Allt na Dunaiche to a flattening at a height of 200m. A rougher path climbs more steeply south-westwards up into Coire Uaigneich.

The routes are now described starting from the extensive north face overlooking Coire Dubh and working in a clockwise direction around the mountain.

NORTH FACE

The complex face at the northern end of the mountain was first explored in the late nineteenth century. The long approaches and the rather indefinite lines have ensured that since that time this side of the mountain has largely remained unpopular. However, on the right-hand half of the face lies one of the longest routes on the mountain – Forked Pinnacle Ridge.

A long scree gully, here named Pinnacle Gully, lies immediately to the right of Forked Pinnacle Ridge. This gully ends at a narrow shoulder two-thirds of the way up the face. The original route up Forked Pinnacle Ridge crosses this shoulder rightwards to finish up a very narrow ridge with a second gully, Summit Gully, immediately to its left.

For those returning to Sligachan a remarkably direct descent can be made from the summit by descending Summit Gully as far as the shoulder and then crossing over leftwards and continuing all the way down Pinnacle Gully.

31 Forked Pinnacle Ridge Moderate **

(NG 526 221) *Alt 500m   North-west facing   Map p96   Diagram p118*

Although this route is not always on the best of rock it finds a way through some impressive surroundings and gives a fine mountaineering day. The left-hand finish is preferred and this leads directly to the summit cairn.

It is a long way to the start of this route. Although it would certainly be possible to approach it from either Sligachan or Camasunary, the quickest options are from the Loch Slapin side. An approach via the Putting Green (695m) is perhaps the most direct but that via Bealach Coire a' Chàise (see p114) has the advantage of offering much better views of the very complex north face and a slightly lower crossing point on the intervening ridge.

Approach

Gain the boulder-strewn flattening in Coire Dubh as described for the West

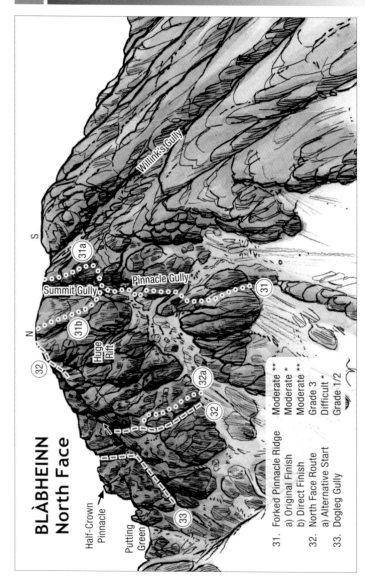

BLÀBHEINN
North Face

S

Willink's Gully

Pinnacle Gully

31a

Summit Gully

31

N

31b

32

Huge Rift

32a

32

33

Half-Crown Pinnacle

Putting Green

31. Forked Pinnacle Ridge   Moderate **
    a) Original Finish   Moderate *
    b) Direct Finish   Moderate **
32. North Face Route   Grade 3
    a) Alternative Start   Difficult *
33. Dogleg Gully   Grade 1/2

Face of Clach Glas (p114). Continue southwards across Coire Dubh towards the north face. Descend slightly to cross the main stream in the corrie near where it emerges from a gorge and is joined by a smaller stream originating from the north face directly above.

Slant rightwards over grassy ground, then scree for some distance to reach a steep leftward-leaning buttress. Skirt rightwards below the steep front face and continue around to the right of the lowest rocks. The first slabby face encountered on the right-hand side is just a little too difficult, so continue ascending further right to the next more amenable slabby face which has a grassy runnel backed by a steep wall on its right-hand side.

The Route
Climb the very pleasant slabs more or less directly. Where these finish cross easier ground to gain a second tier of slabs. Higher up seek out the best rock by traversing slightly left. Further delightful slabs continue for some distance. When the angle eases slightly instead of continuing straight ahead start to slant across to the right. Cross a small gully with scree and ascend the rocks on its right-hand side. A scree-filled cleft continues straight ahead, but traverese right across this to gain the slabby rocks below a large buttress.

Ascend to a prominent grassy ledge system which cuts right across the face. The steeper rocks above give sustained and absorbing climbing (crux) with

*Looking back at the summit of the first pinnacle on
Forked Pinnacle Ridge (Moderate), Blàbheinn*

the best way not always obvious. The rock has to be treated with care. At one point move onto the face on the right with a huge drop below to Pinnacle Gully. Eventually arrive at the summit of the first pinnacle.

Continue weaving a way up the crest of the ridge with easier ground to the left. Climb up between the two prongs of the forked pinnacle feature which gives the route its name. The ridge above is more straightforward, but the surroundings are impressive.

Eventually the ridge finishes at a narrow shoulder which marks the top of Pinnacle Gully on the right. On the left-hand side of the shoulder a more prominent gully, Summit Gully, continues directly ahead. There are two options from here – both of similar grade, but very different character.

a) Original Finish   Moderate   *

Goodeve, Walker and Inglis Clark were the first party to climb Forked Pinnacle Ridge in its entirety in April 1905. They finished up the ridge to the right of Summit Gully. To reach this ridge traverse rightwards from the shoulder to gain a ledge below a steep wall. Continue right to gain the more open slopes on the west flank. A large buttress directly above looks steep but gives good climbing up its right-hand side. Continue up the crest of the ridge. Cross a cleft with interest and higher up slant rightwards across a narrow scree gully to reach a very exposed arête with steep drops to Summit Gully on the left. Difficulties ease quite abruptly and the ridge peters out just a short distance south of the main summit by the top of Summit Gully.

b) Direct Finish   Moderate   **

This finish has a very different character. It was first ascended by Slingsby and Hastings in 1890, though they probably reached it via Pinnacle Gully. It takes a direct route up a huge, orange-brown, dolerite cone-sheet to the left of Summit Gully. It gives very sustained slab climbing and is fine in the dry, but is not recommended in damp conditions. Cross over scree in Summit Gully to reach the start of the slabs. Staying to the right of a gully which splits the slabs, climb by the easiest line finishing directly by the summit trig pillar.

 ### 32 North Face Route   Grade 3 or Difficult *

(NG 529 220)   Alt 550m   North facing   Map p96   Diagram p118

This route finds a devious way up the huge north face; much of it is on easy scree. A harder variation start involves Difficult rock climbing where a rope would be advisable. The route ascends a long easy scree bowl in the middle section of the face. There is some interesting route finding at the top and the route exits directly by the summit trig pillar.

Approach

Reach Coire Dubh as for the previous route and cross the main stream in the corrie just below where it emerges from a gorge. Find a way up ground to the left of a stream which drains from the face above. Pass to the right of a

Finishing North Face Route (Grade 3), Blàbheinn
Scrambler: Oliver Overstall

prominent buttress with a steep north face split by a ramp. Reach the foot of a leftward leaning slabby buttress. Diagonally rightwards from here there are prominent patches of green vegetation where water drains from a recess.

The Route

The normal route slants leftwards up fairly easy ground below and to the left of the slabby buttress. Continue in the same general line for a considerable distance slanting left to avoid a steep buttress. Cross a scree shoulder and head slightly right before continuing leftwards again.

a) Alternative Start   Difficult *

The slabby buttress gives enjoyable but very sustained climbing at Moderate standard before a leftward slanting line leads to a gully on the left. Awkward climbing up rocks on the right-hand side allows the gully to be gained (Difficult). Higher up climb out of the gully by its left wall and continue for some distance to reach a small col with a stumpy pinnacle overlooked by an intimidating wall. Descend the other side and climb down a short chimney to rejoin the normal route.

Keep slanting up leftwards until a vast scree bowl is reached. Ascend the rather tedious scree in this and eventually slant right to reach a prominent shoulder with superb views looking back to Clach Glas.

It is worth making a slight detour at this point. Around the face on the right (facing in) there is a prominent spiky pinnacle. Just before reaching the pinnacle drop down to the right and scramble under an enormous chockstone. Then turn left to reach an easy-angled platform on a ridge overlooking a stupendous rift. The ridge marks the top of a feature called Tower Buttress. The rift itself was first ascended by Sang and Burn in June 1923. Ronald Burn was the first person to complete 'everything' – i.e. all the Munros and tops – later that same year.

Return to the shoulder and scramble up a short distance to an obvious traverse line. Follow this a long way to the left before ascending again. Find a narrow horizontal ledge which leads back right to the edge of the buttress. Climb an awkward bulge in a very exposed position (Grade 3) to reach easier ground. Join a short section of arête and finish directly up easy rocks to the summit.

NORTH-EAST FACE

This face rears up above the Putting Green and bars easy access to Blàbheinn from Clach Glas. The most popular route weaves an intricate line up the face and is for climbers only. Two easier lines exist to the east and west, but both involve losing some height.

33 Dogleg Gully   Grade 1/2

(NG 532 217)   Alt 795m   North-facing   Map p96   Diagrams pp118 & 123.

This route is rarely used in ascent. However it offers a quick descent route into Coire Dubh so might be an option for parties heading back to Sligachan.

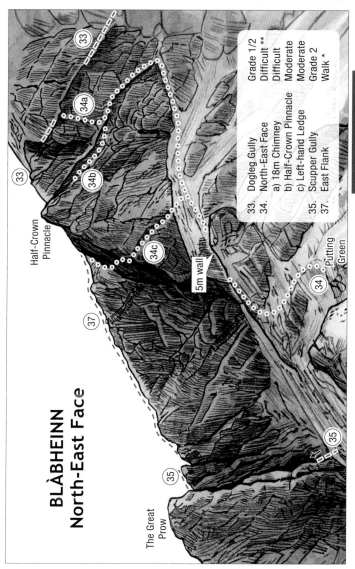

BLÀBHEINN
North-East Face

33.	Dogleg Gully	Grade 1/2
34.	North-East Face	Difficult **
	a) 18m Chimney	Difficult
	b) Half-Crown Pinnacle	Moderate
	c) Left-hand Ledge	Moderate
35.	Scupper Gully	Grade 2
37.	East Flank	Walk *

Half-Crown Pinnacle

5m wall

Putting Green

The Great Prow

It also offers the easiest way of reaching Clach Glas from Blàbheinn, though this entails 70m of reascent on scree to gain the Putting Green bealach. The route is therefore described in descent.

Approach
On the normal walking route up Blàbheinn (Route 37), at a height of about 795m, there is a small dip where the ridge turns away from the north-east face and rises in a south-westerly direction. This scree gully slants down in a north-westerly direction from this dip.

The Route
Descend steep scree and loose ground until another scree gully is reached, which originates from higher up the north face. Turn right and descend this, with some scrambling down slabby rock steps, to reach easier scree slopes below the Putting Green bealach.

To reach the South Ridge of Clach Glas (Route 26) ascend the obvious scree slope on the right directly to the Putting Green. It is also possible to join the ridge at one of the gaps by the Bealach Tower.

If descending Coire Dubh to Srath na Creitheach be aware that the main stream has cut a deep gorge in places. It is best to stay to the right of the stream in its upper reaches and then cross it leftwards at a flatter middle section around the 400m contour. However it is also possible to stay on the right bank at this point and head north for some distance before descending westwards again to a V at 200m where another large stream joins.

34 North-East Face   Difficult   **
(NG 533 218)   Alt 695m   North-east facing   Map96   Diagram p123
This route is technically the most difficult part of the Clach Glas–Blàbheinn traverse, although the situations (with one exception) are not as intimidating as on the final tower of Clach Glas.

Approach
Start from the Putting Green – a grassy hollow marking the bealach between Clach Glas and Blàbheinn. This bealach is normally approached along the ridge from Clach Glas, although it can also be reached by toilsome scree slopes on either side.

The Route
Follow a path leftwards at first, then curve back up right to a gap. Climb the steep 5m wall directly from the highest point of the gap (Difficult). The wall can also be climbed further left but with a more awkward exit. This is a nasty wall to do in reverse if travelling in the opposite direction.

From the top of the wall, walk up an easy scree slope. There are three ways up the face above. The first two options are reached by slanting right up a path in the scree, and traversing right to a scree chute. Ascend this leftwards to a sloping scree platform in a slight recess.

a) The 18m Chimney   Difficult
The classic way. Head up from the scree platform to a chimney with some

jammed chockstones. Ascend this and the wall to its right. Move right at the top and then gain the uppermost section of Dogleg Gully. Slant leftwards up this to join the east flank (Route 37) at a tiny dip on the crest (795m).

b) The Gap by the Half-Crown Pinnacle **Moderate**
Continue further left from the bottom of the 18m Chimney and descend slightly to gain a fairly loose broad gully leading up to a gap at the back of the Half-Crown Pinnacle. Make a couple of awkward moves down big chockstones from the gap (crux), and continue down a gully until it is possible to break right and join the east flank (Route 37).

c) The Left-hand Ledge **Moderate** – though it seems harder.
The scariest way; not an option for the faint-hearted, or those wearing big rucksacks. Instead of traversing right above the 5m wall make for an obvious leftward sloping ramp formed by a cone-sheet on the wall above. Follow this, then turn the corner and crawl painfully along a ledge of sharp rock. Cross an alcove above a horrifying drop (crux), and traverse left across a slightly easier gully to join the east flank (Route 37).

 35 Scupper Gully **Grade 2**
(NG 533 217) *Alt 650m* *North facing* *Map p96* *Diagram p123*
This offers a technically more straightforward way onto the east ridge, although it does involve some loss in height.

Approach
Descend awkward ground east of the Putting Green, or loose scree in a narrow gully below the 5m wall. (See Route 34.) Then slant rightwards down scree to reach the foot of a prominent gully immediately right of a soaring rock feature called the Great Prow. Do not confuse this gully with a forked gully immediately further right.

The Route
Ascend the rather loose gully easily at first. Bridge up a slightly more difficult section where it narrows. Shortly after, emerge from the gully and join the normal route up the east flank (Route 37).

EAST FACE

The east face of Blàbheinn is the aspect seen from Loch Slapin. The normal walking route to the summit ascends the east flank, starting to the left of a complex group of buttresses forming the toe of the east ridge. Further left, Great Gully leads directly to the gap between the twin summits.

36 East Ridge **Moderate** *
(NG 537 215) *Alt 450m* *East facing* *Map p96* *Diagrams pp126 & 128*
This route takes a very devious line up the right-hand buttress and pinnacles forming the toe of the east ridge. It is not a route to be underestimated. It was first climbed in 1900 by Sidney Williams, who took three days to work out the line.

BLÀBHEINN
East Ridge - North Face

36. East Ridge   Moderate *

Approach

Approach by the path on the north side of the Allt na Dunaiche. Turn left and continue up the steeper path leading to Coire Uaigneich. Slant right away from the path and head towards the base of the east ridge. Zigzag up fairly grassy ground, before traversing left along a ledge with good views of the scree fan below D Gully.

The Route

The key to the ascent of the first pinnacle is a dyke chimney running up the centre. Start by interesting scrambling up rocks to the right of a right-slanting break. Then slant right before cutting back left across steep grass and rocks to reach the dyke.

Climb up the dyke, which soon develops into a chimney. About three-quarters of the way up, it is possible to exit the chimney on the right. Exciting moves in an exposed position then lead to a grass ledge. Move well left of the dyke and climb slabby rocks to gain a broad grassy terrace below a rock band.

Climb up at the left-hand end of the rock band in an exposed position level with the fork in D Gully on the left. Continue with much scrambling to the summit of the first pinnacle.

Descend behind the pinnacle towards a tricky gap. Either climb down with care into the gap on the far side of a rocky boss or make a short abseil. A rather more long-winded option is to descend very steep grass in the right fork of D Gully to the base of a rock rib, then ascend an even steeper vegetated gully on the other side.

Continuing directly onto the second pinnacle is quite serious, so an easier option is now described. Descend the gully on the west side of the gap for a short distance. This is the top of Access Gully (Difficult), which has a large chockstone lower down. Climb the left wall mainly on grass to a slight recess.

The lines straight above are too difficult, so cut across right and descend a short scree chute with steep drops into Access Gully on the right. Ascend an obvious grassy groove rightwards, and make a difficult move out right at the top. Easier and more enjoyable scrambling now leads up leftwards for some distance. It is possible to visit the summits of the second and third pinnacles before crossing an earthy neck to reach the east flank route (Route 37).

37 East Flank 8km *

(NG 536 212)   Alt 440m   East Facing   Map p96   Diagram p128

This is the trade-route up the mountain. It is not a very inspiring line, but the upper section is rocky and offers unrivalled views.

Approach

Approach by the well constructed path on the north side of the Allt na Dunaiche. Slant leftwards and ascend more steeply on the north side of a stream to reach a delightful grassy alp in Coire Uaigneich.

The Route

Turn right and ascend the steep grassy hillside, by a rather indefinite line

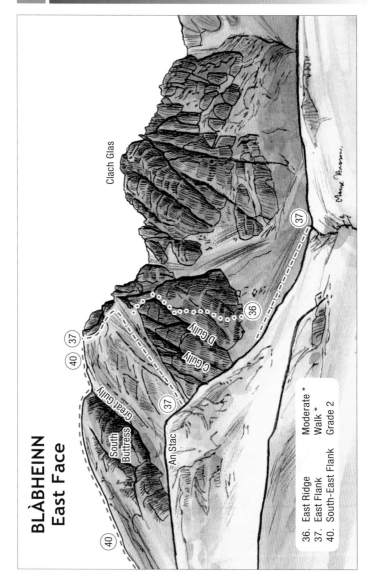

BLÀBHEINN
East Face

Clach Glas

South Buttress

Great Gully

An Stac

C Gully

D Gully

36. East Ridge   Moderate *
37. East Flank   Walk *
40. South-East Flank Grade 2

initially, but eventually trend right on stonier ground. Higher up, the top of the Great Prow can be seen on the right, and the ridge then slants left at a tiny dip (795m). Ascend rockier ground above, with several short sections of easy scrambling if taken directly. Then follow a stony path which twists up to the summit trig point. On a fine day the views of the Cuillin are superb.

A pleasant circuit can be made by descending the south-east flank (Route 40), but this involves a short section of Grade 2 scrambling out of a gap to reach the south top. A less agreeable alternative is to descend Great Gully (Grade 1) from the east side of the gap between the summits. Otherwise return by the same route.

38 Dyke Route   Moderate   **
(NG 534 214)   Alt 570m   Map p96   Diagram p130

This route offers a much more interesting and direct way of reaching the summit of Blàbheinn from Coire Uaigneich. The East Flank route heads rightwards in Coire Uaigneich to ascend a broad shoulder. This route takes a direct line up the right-hand side of a broad slabby face to the left of that shoulder. The face is probably best described as the Eastern Slabs.

Approach
Reach Coire Uaigneich as for the previous route. Ascend grass and slabs to a terrace below a narrow dyke which runs directly up the right-hand side of the face. A forked gully can be seen a little further to the right.

The Route
Climb the dyke itself initially, then make a high step up to gain the rocks just left of it. Continue with interest for some distance occasionally moving left or right to find the best holds. Move right to avoid a scree-covered ledge at the top and break out onto easier ground.

The dyke forms a broad recess at the start of the next main set of slabs. Ascend this and continue on pleasant slabs curving leftwards above a scab-like overlap to reach further scree. A prominent tower gives an exciting finale. Climb it mainly by its left edge taking care with some slightly scary horizontal flakes.

Follow easy ground and scree for some distance with occasional slabs. Join the East Flank route and reach the summit soon after.

39 Great Gully Slabs   Grade 2
(NG 532 213)   Alt 600m   East facing   Map p96

To the left of the Eastern Slabs and directly beneath a steep crag called South Buttress there is a broad scree slope. Higher up this slope a narrow gully, known as Great Gully, rises to the gap between the north and south summits. Great Gully itself is not a very attractive option in summer. However, the broad area of broken slabs to its right offers some slightly more pleasant scrambling. Much variation is possible, but a leftward-slanting line can be followed without undue difficulty.

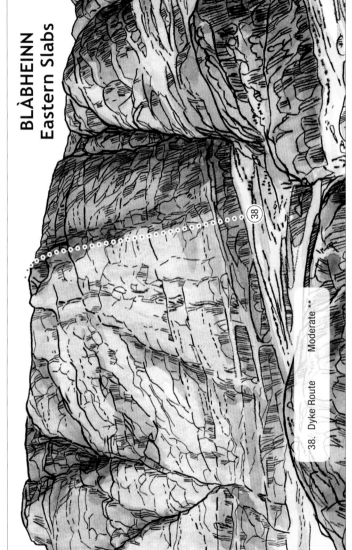

BLÀBHEINN
Eastern Slabs

38. Dyke Route .... Moderate **

40 South-East Flank   Grade 2

(NG 531 210)   Alt 615m   South-east facing   Map p96   Diagram p128

The route is described in descent, since this is probably how it is most often used. Only a short section of scrambling is involved.

The Route

From the main summit head off towards the south top situated 250 metres away, and descend easily into a gap. Then scramble directly up steep rock steps from the gap. Slightly easier ways can be found on the left-hand side, but they are rather looser. Continue easily to the south top (926m), which is only 2m lower than the main summit.

Continue over the summit and descend the south ridge for about 150 metres before slanting left to descend the south-east flank. Do not stray too far left where there are steep drops over South Buttress. The ground becomes loose and rather tiresome but eventually eases at a shoulder above the Abhainn nan Leac. Cut left and descend steeply on scree into the upper reaches of Coire Uaigneich to rejoin the ascent route. There is a prominent boulder in the floor of the corrie.

SOUTHERN BUTTRESSES

These buttresses lie on the eastern flank of the south ridge. They are best approached by a straightforward descent from the shoulder situated at the head of Coire Uaigneich (NG 532 210), and directly below the previous route. They offer a mixture of scrambling and fairly easy climbing and could be an attractive option when the upper part of the mountain is swathed in cloud.

An easy grassy rake slants up leftwards below the buttresses. This rake can be regained from the crest of the south ridge where it flattens off slightly at a height of about 630m. This means it is fairly easy to complete a number of the routes in a single visit. The buttresses are labelled from left to right, although they are described in the order they are normally approached.

Scott Muir and Nick Everett explored the four main buttresses in 2005. Iain Thow and Peter Duggan added B Minus Buttress in 2008.

41 D Buttress   Difficult   *

(NG 528 208)   Alt 540m   South-east facing   Map p96   Diagram p132

This is the broadest of the buttresses described. There is a prominent left-facing corner at the bottom which is hidden from view on the approach. (This is climbed by the direct start which is Severe.)

The Route

Start on the right-hand edge of the buttress and traverse left along an overhung ledge, then climb a rib right of a groove to ledges. Carry on slightly left then climb the right-hand edge of a slab, breaking through a steeper band by a weakness on the right. Traverse horizontally left on a grassy ledge, then go up to a steep wall and climb it with some difficulty at an obvious notch.

CUILLIN OUTLIERS

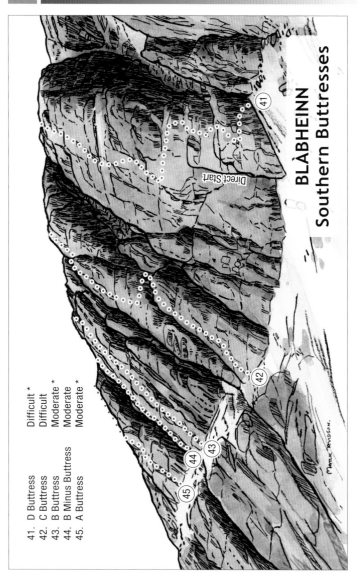

BLÀBHEINN
Southern Buttresses

Direct Start

41. D Buttress	Difficult	*
42. C Buttress	Difficult	
43. B Buttress	Moderate	*
44. B Minus Buttress	Moderate	
45. A Buttress	Moderate	*

Carry on up a groove and slabs above. Finish either up a prominent central crack – Difficult and very enjoyable – or easier to the right.

42 C Buttress   Difficult
(NG 527 208)   Alt 540m   Map p96   Diagram p132

Perhaps the route with the least character. Start on the left-hand corner of the buttress where the grass rake rises more steeply to the left.

The Route

Climb steeply at first then follow sustained Moderate slabs until the buttress pinches out between gullies. Either grovel up the slanting crack on the left or move up 10m higher and traverse left more easily. Stay on the buttress to its top, then climb steeply onto the buttress on the right. Go up this until it eventually breaks up into outcrops.

43 B Buttress   Moderate *
(NG 527 208)   Alt 570m   Map p96   Diagram p132

Ascend steeper ground to the left of C Buttress and continue leftwards on the grassy rake to the left-hand edge of the next buttress. Start at some blocks and climb quite sustained slabs with much choice of line.

44 B Minus Buttress   Moderate
(NG 526 208)   Alt 580m   Map p96   Diagram p132

Climb the thin rib in the gully on the left side of B Buttress. The most direct line has hard moves, but these are all avoidable.

45 A Buttress   Moderate or Difficult *
(NG 526 207)   Alt 600m   Map p96   Diagram p132

Perhaps the best route even though the shortest. Climbs the last buttress before the rake peters out.

Start at the central crack and follow rough slabs just left of this – sustained at Moderate. At the top a delightful thin crack provides an excellent finish and the hardest climbing (Difficult) but it is also avoidable.

The next route is the longest route on the mountain. It starts a kilometre north of Camasunary.

46 South Ridge   Grade 2 **
(NG 521 194)   Alt 105m   Map p96   Diagram p136

This outing is mainly an exhilarating walk up a remarkably long ridge. The hardest scrambling is the short descent into the gap beyond the south top to gain the main summit. Walkers may be content to go only as far as the south top.

Approach

The normal approach is from Camasunary, which is most easily reached by

*An autumn ascent of D Buttress (Difficult), Southern Buttresses, Blàbheinn
Climber: Peter Duggan*

Route 2. Cut off the track on the descent from Am Màm just short of a hairpin bend, and follow a path across two streams – the second of which is called the Abhainn nan Leac. Continue on the path for a further 150 metres to a slight shoulder peppered with boulders. The route slants off right from here. The path, which continues across the west flank, eventually joins the main path leading from Camasunary through to Sligachan (Route 48).

The Route
Ascend grassy ground towards a rocky toe at the base of the ridge. Bypass this on the right and follow the ridge above easily at first. The ridge then becomes more interesting. In several places the crest pinches down, and it is necessary to move slightly right to avoid the heads of gullies on the west face. Several rock steps offer some scrambling opportunities.

The ground becomes much stonier higher up. After a kink to the right there is a long slog up the final section of broad ridge leading to the south top. Beyond this, descend steep rock steps with care directly into a gap (crux), and soon reach the main summit. There are breathtaking views to the north and west.

Various options are available from here depending on your final destination. The simplest option is to return the same way. If continuing onto Clach Glas descend the first part of the East Flank Route (Route 37) as far as a tiny dip at 795m where the ridge changes direction. It is rather tricky descending any of the routes on the north-east face from here. Perhaps the quickest option is to descend a little further down the East Flank to a slight dip (715m) behind the Great Prow. Then descend Scupper Gully (Route 35) before reascending on scree to the Putting Green.

If returning to Camasunary it is possible to descend Dogleg Gully from the tiny dip already mentioned and so reach Coire Dubh (see Route 33). Eventually reach the path which leads south by Loch na Creitheach. Another option is to descend the south-east flank (Route 40) and return over the lochan strewn plateau of Slat Bheinn to the Am Màm track (Route 2).

Few will wish to repeat the feat of the Willink brothers in 1873, who descended the gully on the west side of the gap between the summits. They were stopped by a big drop and had to reclimb part of the gully before escaping to the north and eventually descending by a scree chute.

47 South-West Buttress Grade 3 *
(NG 517 201) Alt 95m Map p96 Diagram p136
This route may appeal to experienced scramblers wishing to add some spice to an ascent of the south ridge. It is at the upper limit of its grade, and requires good route-finding skills.

Approach
From Camasunary as for the previous route, but continue past the south ridge to gain a picturesque bealach to the east of a small top called An t-Sròn.

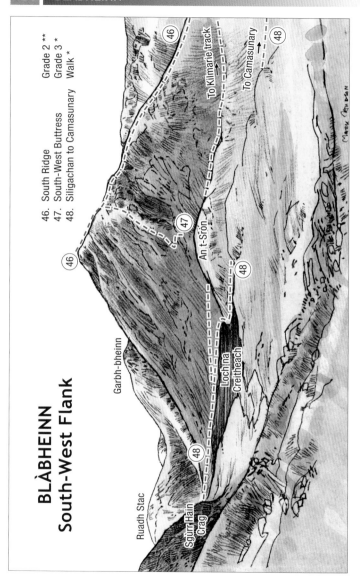

BLÀBHEINN
South-West Flank

46. South Ridge — Grade 2 **
47. South-West Buttress — Grade 3 *
48. Sligachan to Camasunary — Walk *

To Kilmarie track

To Camasunary

Garbh-bheinn

An t-Sròn

Loch na Creitheach

Ruadh Stac

Sgùrr Hain Crag

The Route

Head up the grassy hillside to the right of a stream, then trend left to gain a slight knoll. Descend slightly leftwards to reach an obvious sheep track. Follow this a long way left until below the lowest point of a rock outcrop. Zigzag up steepish rock on good holds, then slant right up slabby rocks. Climb a slab by a crack arising from a tiny recess, and continue right up a slabby ramp. Move up onto a higher slab and follow this rightwards to a grassy terrace with a steep wall above. Climb the wall and move left at the top onto a slab.

Head up mixed ground for some distance to a point overlooking an amphitheatre on the right. Then break back hard left across slabby rocks above a short wall, and below a bigger wall forming part of a knobble of rock above. Higher up, climb a rib right of a grassy groove, before slanting left towards a gully. Eventually climb a steep rounded rib immediately right of this gully (crux). Then continue up a broad scree slope above a chockstone in the gully.

From a slight bay left of a big wall, reach the crest of a rib on the left by cutting leftwards along a break on its right wall. Ascend the rib to a grassy ledge, then climb a short wall. Move right and climb part way up a slab before moving right to escape onto easier ground. Continue without further difficulty to the crest of the South Ridge (Route 46), which is joined at a height of 550m. It is still a long way to the summit.

Traverse of the Cuillin Outliers

This is a superb outing – one of the finest on the island. The standard outing, which involves the traverse of Clach Glas and the continuation onto Blàbheinn, requires good route-finding skills and climbing ability of at least Moderate standard. The normal way up Blàbheinn is Difficult.

A complete traverse of all the Cuillin Outliers makes a splendid expedition, but this is a fairly demanding option which will only appeal to those with a good level of fitness. Purists will first traverse Belig (Routes 17 and 19) and then Garbh-bheinn (Routes 21 and 22) before continuing onto Clach Glas. Scramblers may choose to ascend the North Buttress on Sgùrr nan Each (Route 23) and then complete the east to west traverse of that peak (Route 24) before starting Clach Glas.

When approaching from the west (for example when doing the Greater Traverse) the simplest option is to ascend the north side of Coire Dubh and gain the dip (636m) between Garbh-bheinn and Sgùrr nan Each. It is easy to make a detour from here to visit the summit of Garbh-bheinn via its south-east ridge.

The shortest option from the east is to ascend Coire a' Chàise and take the steep left-hand fork at the top to gain the start of the north ridge of Clach Glas at a dip on the ridge (approx 635m). This corresponds with the top of Arch Gully on the western or Sligachan face. The route over Clach Glas onto Blàbheinn is now described in detail starting from this dip.

Clach Glas – Blàbheinn Traverse **Difficult** *******
(NG 533 225) *Alt 635m* *Map p96* *Diagrams pp105, 107,110 & 123*

a) North Ridge of Clach Glas

Ascend a steep little wall out of the col, and scramble pleasantly up slabs and along a switchback crest. Climb down steeply into a gap on the Loch Slapin side, and then scramble up a short arête. Traverse slightly easier ground along ledges below the crest.

From the bed of a gully make an awkward rightwards traverse beneath steep rocks. Continue more easily, traversing beneath a large pinnacle to gain a more prominent scree gully marking the start of the major difficulties.

Climb a slanting V-shaped chimney, bridging past some awkward bulges. Part way up, a possible alternative is to climb a steep crack in the right wall to a short ridge. Turn left to tackle the summit tower. This gives sustained Moderate climbing (first crux). Weave a way up in a sensational position with the difficulties gradually easing after 25m. Continue by bearing right to reach the superb rocky table top which constitutes the summit.

b) Descent of the South Ridge of Clach Glas to the Putting Green

A short distance beyond the summit descend a shallow groove in a slab on the east side of the crest. This is the so-called Impostor. At the bottom of the slab it is necessary to face in for a couple of moves to climb down a steep and exposed rib. Reach a section of easier horizontal arête formed by a cone-sheet.

From the end of the arête descend the ridge just right of the crest until just after a tiny gap. Then descend slabs on the left-hand side of the crest and drop down to a ledge below. Follow a scree path, and then more broken rocks slanting slightly right. From a ledge, curve back left on a path to another slabby face on the Loch Slapin side. Descend this leftwards to a cleft. Climb down the cleft and then continue more easily down a sloping terrace.

Scramble down into a gap of green rock with gullies on either side. Ascend the other side more easily and then reach another gap. Make some awkward moves to escape out of this second gap, and continue towards the summit of a feature known as the **Bealach Tower** (approx 713m). Immediately before the highest point cut diagonally leftwards over the crest by a narrow cleft, and descend a slab on the Slapin side. Reach a brown cone-sheet and follow this back right to another gap, with a boulder jammed across the rift on the left. Scramble out of the gap on the right-hand side and continue more easily along a ridge to a grassy hollow with large boulders known as the **Putting Green** (approx 695m).

c) The North-East Face of Blàbheinn from the Putting Green

The north-east face of Blàbheinn can be tackled in a number of different ways. The two easier options – Dogleg Gully and Scupper Gully – both involve

The18m Chimney (Difficult), North-East Face, Blàbheinn
Climber: Lisa Hutchison   Photo: Roger Robb

losing a lot of height. (See Routes 33 and 35.) The classic and most direct option is to first climb a short wall (Difficult), after which there are three further variations. The classic way is now described.

From the Putting Green follow a path leftwards at first, then curve back up right to a gap. Climb the steep 5m wall (Difficult) directly from the highest point of the gap. The wall can also be climbed further left but this has a slightly more awkward exit.

Perhaps the most popular option now is to head for the 18m Chimney, (Route 34a, Difficult), but see also Routes 34b & 34c. Slant easily rightwards up a path in the scree, then traverse harder right to a scree chute. Ascend this leftwards to a sloping scree platform in a slight recess. Head up directly to an obvious chimney with some jammed chockstones. This gives the crux of the route and is graded Difficult, but it is not as scary as the summit tower on Clach Glas. The moves to get past the first chockstone are probably the hardest. Continue up the chimney and the wall to its right. Move right at the top to enter the upper reaches of Dogleg Gully. Follow this gully easily leftwards to join the east flank route where it changes direction at a tiny dip (795m). Continue easily at first. Then a rockier section gives some further scrambling before the final easy slopes lead to the trig pillar at the summit.

The normal descent is to return down the east flank (Route 37).

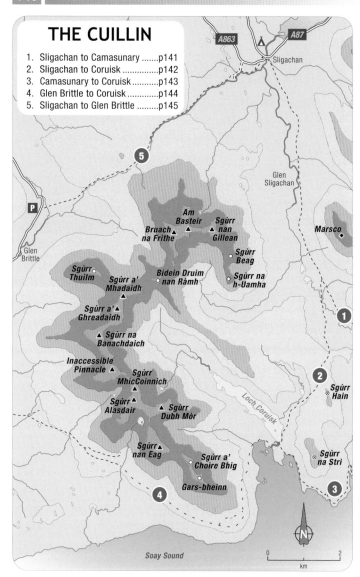

THE CUILLIN

1. Sligachan to Camasunary p141
2. Sligachan to Coruisk p142
3. Camasunary to Coruisk...........p143
4. Glen Brittle to Coruisk p144
5. Sligachan to Glen Brittle p145

A863   A87

Sligachan

Glen
Sligachan

Marsco

5

P

Glen
Brittle

Am
Basteir

Sgùrr
nan
Gillean

Bruach
na Frithe

Sgùrr
Beag

Sgùrr
Thuilm

Bidein Druim
nan Ràmh

Sgùrr na
h-Uamha

Sgùrr a'
Mhadaidh

Sgùrr a'
Ghreadaidh

Sgùrr na
Banachdaich

1

Inaccessible
Pinnacle

Sgùrr
MhicCoinnich

2

Sgùrr
Hain

Sgùrr
Alasdair

Sgùrr
Dubh Mòr

Loch Coruisk

Sgùrr
nan Eag

Sgùrr a'
Choire Bhig

Sgùrr
na Stri

Gars-bheinn

4

3

Soay Sound

N

0   2
km

CUILLIN APPROACHES

The Cuillin are the finest goup of mountains in Britain. No other massif is as rugged and rocky, or has such a long, sharp ridge crest, or is flanked by such dramatic corries. The Cuillin peaks are arranged in a 12km long arc, which is concave towards the east. Extending on the inside of this arc is a major lateral ridge, Druim nan Ràmh, with beautiful Loch Coruisk on its south-west side. More than 30 rock peaks protrude from the main spine and its subsidiary ridges, and these include 11 Munros. More than a dozen major corries flank the ridge.

The massif is built from a complex sequence of saucer-like bodies of gabbro, which are riddled by countless minor intrusions of basalt and dolerite. Evidence of fairly recent glacial activity is everywhere to be seen.

The Cuillin are situated in the district of Minginish, set back slightly to the south of Glen Drynoch. In cloudy conditions they are not as immediately apparent from the main road as the Red Hills. However, in clear weather they show a very striking jagged profile, which is readily recognisable from many mainland hills.

The origin of the name Cuillin is uncertain. Many of the hill names on the island are of Norse origin and the most likely derivation is from the Norse word *kiolen* meaning 'high rocks'.

The ridges and corries of the Cuillin are accessible from three main centres – **Sligachan** in the north, **Glen Brittle** in the west and **Coruisk** in the south. Both Sligachan and Glen Brittle can be reached by road. Coruisk is more remote and can only be reached on foot or by boat. The three main access centres are also linked by walking routes which can be used to circumvent the Cuillin. These are now described:

48 Sligachan to Camasunary   12.5km *
(NG 486 298)   High Point 90m   Map p140   Diagrams pp136, & 312

This route follows the long defile between the main Cuillin range and the hills immediately to the east i.e. the Western Red Hills and the Cuillin Outliers. Although it rises to a maximum height of only 90m at the halfway point, it is a fairly demanding outing. This is especially true if it is made part of a circuit with Routes 49 and 50.

Approach
Start from the old road bridge by the Sligachan Hotel.

The Route
Follow the path along Glen Sligachan for 3km, then cross the Allt na Measarroch and continue south past some big boulders with rowan trees. The path rises slightly as it continues below the impressive west face of Marsco. When the path starts to descend slightly, some 6km from Sligachan, take the left fork which continues below the south-west flank of Ruadh Stac to Loch an Athain. There are fine views of Clach Glas and Blàbheinn from here.

THE CUILLIN

Looking across the head of Loch Harport to the Cuillin

Walk along the flat floor of Srath na Creitheach and continue along the east side of Loch na Creitheach. Part way along this loch a path slants off on the left to cross a small bealach to the east of An t-Sròn. It eventually joins the track over Am Màm to the Broadford–Elgol road (see Route 2). However, the route to Camasunary stays beside the loch, and then continues south for just over a kilometre to reach the very welcome grassy haven by the beach.

49 Sligachan to Coruisk via Druim Hain   11.5km **
(NG 486 298)   High Point 317m   Map p140
This is the most straightforward of the walking routes into Coruisk, though it is still a long outing. It rises to a height of 317m on Druim Hain. The easiest way back is to return the same way.

Approach
Start from the old road bridge by the Sligachan Hotel.

The Route
Follow the path along Glen Sligachan for 3km, then cross the Allt na Measarroch and continue south past some big boulders with rowan trees. The path rises slightly as it continues below the impressive west face of Marsco. When the path starts to descend slightly, some 6km from Sligachan, take the right fork and head south across the floor of the glen. Then ascend steadily by a well-worn path for some distance and eventually reach the crest of

Druim Hain, from where there are dramatic views of the Cuillin. Volcanic breccia gives way to gabbro just as the crest is reached.

A popular option at this point is to slant across the west flank of Sgùrr Hain to an excellent viewpoint below Sgùrr na Strì (see Route 168). It gives magnificent views of Coruisk and most of the Cuillin. A short detour can also be made about halfway along this leg to visit Captain Maryon's Monument (GR 498 205). This well-constructed cairn lies some 50m below the path, at the spot where the captain lay dead for almost two years before his remains were discovered in 1948.

Otherwise drop down into Coire Riabhach, staying above the loch in its floor. The path becomes less obvious where the ground drops more steeply, and there are some awkward little sections of slab. Stay slightly left and eventually follow one of a number of paths all the way down to the shore of Loch Coruisk. Continue around a tiny bay to reach the stepping stones at the outlet from the loch.

 50 Camasunary to Coruisk via the Bad Step   Grade 1/2 **
(NG 510 187)   High Point 40m   Map p140   Diagram p315

The route from Camasunary around the coast to Coruisk is mainly a walk. It is only 4km in total distance, although it can seem longer when part of a bigger outing. The scrambling on the Bad Step is very short-lived, and not difficult if the correct line is taken.

Approach
The shortest approach to Camasunary starts from near Kilmarie on the Broadford–Elgol road (Route 2), but see also Routes 3 and 48. The bothy on the west side of the bay is a popular overnight base. It has several rooms and a concrete floor.

The Route
From the bothy, go west a short distance to the bank of the Abhainn Camas Fhionnairigh. It is usually necessary to walk upstream for about 250 metres to find a suitable crossing place above the tidal limit. (A crossing may not be possible in flood conditions.) Then walk back along the west bank and continue round the coast to Rubha Bàn. After a further kilometre, cut over a neck on the north side of a small knoll above Rubha Buidhe, and continue on a well-worn path below the west flank of Sgùrr na Stri. Eventually the ground becomes more rocky approaching the Bad Step. A prominent islet can be seen a short distance out in the loch at this point.

The best advice on the Bad Step is not to go too high. Follow a ledge to a slab which slopes down into the sea. Ascend a slanting crack, forming a natural gangway up the slab, until about halfway up. Then break left and soon reach a narrow shelf which leads horizontally left to much easier ground.

Continue around the edge of Loch nan Leachd without further difficulty and pass through a low gap between large rock masses. Arrive suddenly at the stepping stones by the mouth of Loch Coruisk – a dramatic sight.

Fay Wielochowska negotiates 'The Bad Step' above Loch nan Leachd en route from Camasunary to Coruisk Photo: Andrew Wielochowski

51 Glen Brittle to Coruisk via the coast   11km *
(NG 412 205)   High Point 315m   Map p140
The first part of this route is on a well-constructed path as far as the mouth of Coire a' Ghrunnda. The middle section as far as the southern flank of Gars-bheinn is also moderately worn because it is a popular approach route to the southern end of the Cuillin main ridge. The remaining section beyond Ulfhart Point is not so obvious, and requires good route-finding through some tricky terrain. It is something of a misnomer to describe this as a coastal route since for most of the way it lies some distance from the shore and more than 200m above sea level. Not a route to be underestimated.

Approach
Start from the campsite in Glen Brittle.

The Route
Head up the hillside, soon cross a track and after 800 metres take a right fork across a stream. Follow the path towards the base of Sròn na Cìche. At a prominent fork take the lower right-hand path, which eventually deteriorates in quality where it crosses the Allt Coire a' Ghrunnda well below the mouth of the corrie. Continue below the broad flank of Sgùrr nan Eag, and cross the

Allt Coire nan Laogh. Shortly after this, do not take the higher route that slants left up to the base of Gars-bheinn, instead keep traversing at the 225m level for a full kilometre, then slant gently uphill on grassy ground for some 300 metres.

There are two main ways of rounding the more broken ground on the south-east shoulder of Gars-bheinn. The upper way cuts the corner slightly by gaining and losing height. It slants up across a depression, and continues ascending the hillside to a shelf with a tiny lochan at a height of 315m. This lochan is the source of the Allt an Fhraoich. Continue for some 200 metres beyond the lochan, then make a gradual descent leftwards away from the stream. The lower route contours around the shoulder and eventually slants up beside the same stream before crossing it and heading in a northerly direction to join the other route.

Continue north at roughly the 280m level for a further 700 metres until almost directly above Eilean Reamhar in Loch Scavaig below. At this point it is possible to maintain height and continue northwards to gain a slightly higher, grassy terrace which eventually leads to An Garbh-choire (see p317). However, the way down to the coast now slants down steeply to the right on grass and heather. Halfway down it crosses over the Allt Coire a' Chruidh and then passes below a steep crag. Soon after this it rises slightly to cross a neck behind a small knoll (GR 481 192), before continuing down to the shore.

Cross a stream which descends from a grassy depression and shortly after cross the more impressive Allt a' Chaoich (Mad Burn). This stream can become impassable when in spate. Continue along the coast on awkward rock slabs (Grade 1), or use the shore when the tide is out, and soon reach the more open ground near the Coruisk Hut. Cross short sections of rock slab and head up a path to eventually reach the stepping stones over the River Scavaig, by the mouth of Loch Coruisk.

52 Sligachan to Glen Brittle via Bealach a' Mhàim   8km

(NG 479 297)   High Point 350m   Map p140

This walking route can be used to cross from Sligachan to Glen Brittle, although it is perhaps used more frequently to gain access to the northern Cuillin peaks.

Approach

Park in a layby some 700 metres west of the Sligachan Hotel. Follow a track leading to Allt Dearg Cottage, and cut off to the right on a path after 400m.

The Route

After skirting Allt Dearg Cottage the path follows the north bank of the Allt Dearg Mòr to Bealach a' Mhàim. It then descends a well-constructed path more steeply to Glen Brittle. After crossing the Allt an Fhamhair, it rises slightly to meet the Glen Brittle road, near to a small car park. It is a further 6km to the beach at Loch Brittle.

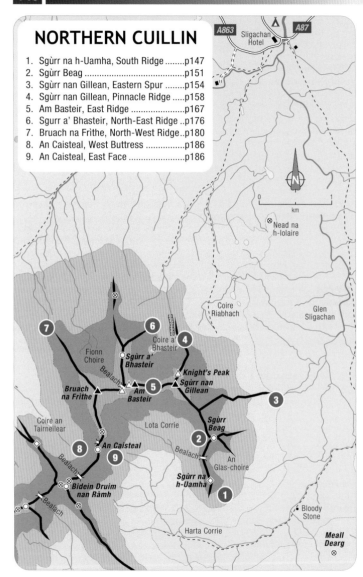

NORTHERN CUILLIN

1. Sgùrr na h-Uamha, South Ridge p147
2. Sgùrr Beag p151
3. Sgùrr nan Gillean, Eastern Spur p154
4. Sgùrr nan Gillean, Pinnacle Ridge p158
5. Am Basteir, East Ridge p167
6. Sgurr a' Bhasteir, North-East Ridge ..p176
7. Bruach na Frithe, North-West Ridge..p180
8. An Caisteal, West Buttress p186
9. An Caisteal, East Face p186

NORTHERN CUILLIN

The Northern Cuillin group is taken to extend from Sgùrr na h-Uamha to An Caisteal. It includes the shapely peak of Sgùrr nan Gillean as well as a prominent rock feature known as the Basteir Tooth. This part of the Cuillin is most readily accessible from Sligachan and the northern end of Glen Brittle.

There are three fairly easy crossing places on this section of ridge. The lowest, called Bealach Harta, lies close to Bidein Druim nan Ràmh. The most popular one, which links Fionn Choire with Lota Corrie, is called Bealach nan Lice, while Bealach a' Ghlas-choire links An Glas-choire with Lota Coire.

A slightly harder crossing can be made at Bealach a' Bhasteir between Coire a' Bhasteir and Lota Corrie. Although the northern side is easy – and well used – the southern or Lota Corrie side is rather more tricky and involves a short section of Grade 3 scrambling. It would also be possible to cross over at the deep gap north of An Caisteal. On the Coire an Tairneilear side there is a long but fairly straightforward steep scree slope. However, part way down the gully on the eastern side of this gap it is necessary to cross the left-hand (north) wall, Grade 2, to reach Lota Corrie.

The outings are now described starting with the the peak at the 'northern' end of the Cuillin main ridge called Sgùrr na h-Uamha.

SGÙRR NA H-UAMHA 736m

(NG 475 240) Map p146

This fascinating little peak is situated at the end of a southwards extension of the main ridge overlooking Harta Corrie. It is an extremely fine viewpoint. The easiest way off the summit by the north ridge is Moderate (Route 55).

53 South Ridge Grade 3 **
(NG 478 238)   Alt 500m   Map p146   Diagram p148

This route is in a remote setting and has some excellent rock. It was first ascended in 1896 by Naismith and Parker.

Approach

Follow the path along Glen Sligachan for almost 6km. During a dry spell it is possible to cross the River Sligachan and approach from An Glas-choire (see Route 54). Otherwise follow the left (south) bank of the river to the Bloody Stone. This huge boulder makes an entertaining diversion, and can be ascended by several lines. Cross the River Sligachan further on, and ascend the steep hillside left of a prominent stream to a terrace below the south-east face.

The Route

The first part of the route ascends rocks to the left of a faint gully which slants up to a shoulder on the south ridge proper. Zigzag up a slightly intimidating band of rough rock a little to the left of the gully line. Then follow very

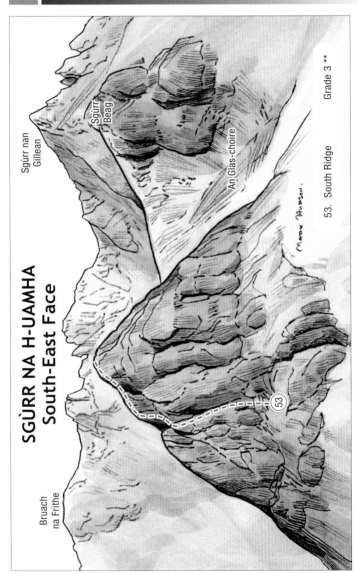

SGÙRR NA H-UAMHA
South-East Face

Bruach na Frithe

Sgùrr nan Gillean

Sgùrr Beag

An Glas-choire

53. South Ridge   Grade 3 **

pleasant slabby rocks parallel to the gully for some distance. The gully becomes better-defined higher up.

From the shoulder it would be possible to descend the other side to easier ground, but a steep rib above and slightly to the right gives sustained and sensational scrambling on rough rock. Ascend reddish rock with downward-sloping holds to a steeper section. Move up a little ramp on the left before traversing delicately back rightwards to the crest of the rib. Pass a slightly worrying section of rock with a cracked block. Then head diagonally right to an easier groove, which leads up to the crest of the ridge.

Walk up steep ground, weaving between blocks and ascending slabs. Move slightly right and scramble up delightful slabby rocks. Continue along the crest to the surprisingly broad top.

Traverse the summit and descend by the north ridge (Route 55).

 ### 54 North-East Face   Grade 3 or Moderate   *
(NG 478 241)   Alt 510m   Map p146   Diagram p150

This face was first climbed by Charles Pilkington, Horace Walker and James Heelis in 1887. Pilkington described their route as a 'capital scramble'. A harder variation can be taken on the upper section.

Approach

During a spell of dry weather the route can be approached by crossing the River Sligachan opposite Marsco. The floor of the glen is very boggy hereabouts. A prominent buttress at the foot of the slope (GR 487 245) has a pleasant scramble up its slabby left face. Cross over the Allt a' Ghlais-choire higher up, and continue to the foot of the north-east face. The start of the south ridge (Route 53) can be reached by traversing leftwards below the east face.

Alternatively, it is an easy matter to descend An Glas-choire from Bealach a' Ghlas-choire just south of Sgùrr Beag.

The Route

The route follows an obvious right-slanting break on a face that looks more north than north-east. Ascend a conspicuous slabby ramp, then continue up a left-slanting groove (sometimes wet). Instead of continuing up a broader section of gully, slant right up slabs. Make a thinner move up a tiny corner on light green rock, and then continue up very enjoyable slabs trending very slightly left. Stay on rocks to the right of boulders and scree.

The angle eases slightly as the gully on the left appears to swing to the right higher up. Ascend short slabby ribs and more broken ground, and eventually reach a scree terrace. Traverse right to find more slabby rock, and continue to a grassy terrace.

a) Original Finish   Grade 3

At this point Pilkington's party broke left across steep ground to gain the eastern flank. They then continued mainly on scree to the summit.

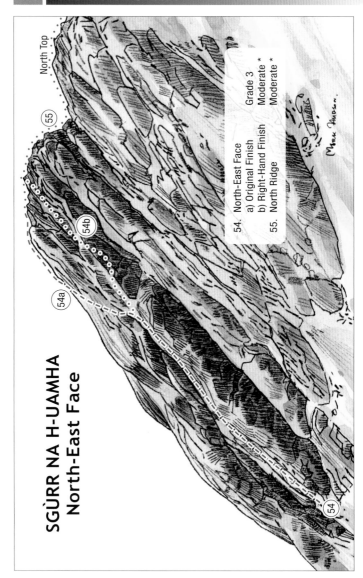

SGÙRR NA H-UAMHA
North-East Face

North Top

54. North-East Face
    a) Original Finish   Grade 3
    b) Right-Hand Finish   Moderate *
55. North Ridge   Moderate *

b) Right-hand Finish   Moderate   *

A more serious finish starts by slanting up right along the grassy terrace. (Purple flowers of devilsbit scabious are numerous here in late summer.) Follow narrow slabs continuing further right. Then step down into a gully in a much more exposed position. Make a few moves up the gully, then make a delicate move to get established on the slabby right wall. Ascend a crack heading away from the gully, and eventually reach a long rock band with an alcove to the left. Traverse to the right-hand end of the rock band.

The very exposed rocks above are sustained, and constitute the crux of the right-hand finish. Climb up a rib and continue up slabs just right of a dyke. Reach a ledge and step left onto the dyke where it leans back left slightly. Ascend the dyke for a short distance, then traverse back to slabs on the right by a juniper bush. Continue with less difficulty and join the crest a short distance north of the summit.

55 North Ridge   Moderate   *
(NG 475 243)   Alt 640m   Map p146   Diagram p150

This is the normal route used when bagging this peak from Sgùrr Beag. There is a relatively short section of Moderate rock, but it must also be negotiated in descent when returning from the summit. This is the route taken by Cundill and Hall when they made the first ascent of the peak in 1871.

Approach
From Bealach a' Ghlas-choire, which can easily be reached from the east or west side but is normally approached from Sgùrr Beag.

The Route
The ridge is fairly straightforward as far as a dip just beyond the small, rocky northern top. From the dip, traverse a grassy ledge on the west (Lota Corrie) side, and scramble up rocks and grass to reach a broad rock rib. Move into a grassy alcove on the left side of the crest, and ascend rightwards to a rib. Ascend this to gain a ledge below the steep final tier. Slant rightwards along the ledge, then climb a short steep wall (crux) to gain the summit ridge. Follow this more easily to the top. Return the same way.

SGÙRR BEAG 764m

(NG 476 245) Map p146

This minor top lies on the ridge linking Sgùrr na h-Uamha and Sgùrr nan Gillean. It is easily traversed from north to south. There is an unnamed corrie on the north side of the summit which offers a little-used but trouble-free way down to Glen Sligachan.

56 North–South Traverse   700m
(NG 474 249)   Alt 780m   Map p146
A pleasant but straightforward section of ridge .

NORTHERN CUILLIN

Approach

This traverse can easily be started either from the south-east ridge of Sgùrr nan Gillean or from Bealach a' Ghlas-choire.

The Route

Descend the continuation of the south-east ridge of Sgùrr nan Gillean beyond the point where the normal route from Sligachan (Route 58) gains the crest. This is a narrow rocky arête with very steep drops on the east side. From a dip a slight detour has to be made to the east to reach the summit. The broader and steeper south ridge is descended easily to Bealach a' Ghlas-choire.

SOUTH-EAST FLANK

There is a long tongue of rocky ground forming the south-east flank of Sgùrr Beag. This is guarded all round its base by an overlap formed by a cone-sheet. However, it is possible to traverse a wall on the south-west side rightwards (Grade 2) to gain the tongue. This gives pleasant easy scrambling. There are dramatic views looking north from a small top just before the summit.

SGÙRR NAN GILLEAN 964m

(NG 471 252) Map p146

This majestic peak is among the finest in the Cuillin. It has a commanding position at the northern end of the main ridge, and is an impressive sight from Sligachan. Three fine ridges, none of which is easy, lead to its summit.

57 South-East Ridge Grade 3 **

(NG 474 249) Alt 790m Map p146 Diagram p155

This is the easiest way up the mountain, but not a route to be underestimated. Route-finding can be a problem in poor visibility, and the crucial section is high up near the summit. This was the line followed by Professor James Forbes and Duncan MacIntyre when they made the first ascent of the peak in 1836.

Approach

Start a short distance west of the Sligachan Hotel.

The Route

Pick up a path which leads to a footbridge over the Allt Dearg Mòr. Cross this and shortly after head away from the river on a well constructed path. Eventually reach the north bank of the Allt Dearg Beag. Follow this stream for a short distance, then cross it by a narrow footbridge.

Follow a steeper path for a further kilometre to the crest of a broad shoulder. Descend slightly to cross Coire Riabhach, then climb out again more steeply on the south side. Continue on more bouldery ground, with Pinnacle Ridge prominent high up on the right. Curve up slightly rightwards on scree

The new bridge over the Allt Dearg Mòr near Sligachan, used to approach the South-East Ridge of Sgùrr nan Gillean and several other northern Cuillin peaks

to reach a steeper section of rockier ground. Break through this by slanting left up a broad cleft to reach a bouldery terrace. Zigzag up stony ground for some distance (junction with Route 57) to gain the crest of the south-east ridge.

Walk and clamber over blocks on the crest at first. Then continue over distinctive volcanic breccia with large brown blocks in it. Eventually take an easy line on the left side of the crest, and ascend a shallow gully. Exit from this by bridging out rightwards at the top to regain easier ground. Do not follow a ledge leading left, but move up into a short corner and ascend rightwards by means of flakes. Then continue up slabbier rocks, zigzagging up slightly right, until a short traverse hard right can be made to reach the crest.

Make an awkward and exposed step-up, and continue on the very narrow crest. Ascend delightful red-coloured slabs, and soon reach the final section of arête where the crest starts to level off. Cross a small but very exposed neck where the ridge pinches down, and shortly after reach the summit – one of the finest viewpoints in the Cuillin. The only problem now is that the easiest way down is back the same way.

58 Eastern Spur   Grade 2/3   **

(NG 485 251)   Alt 150m   Map p146   Diagram p155

This outing makes an entertaining alternative start to the normal route up the south-east ridge of the mountain (Route 57). It requires reasonably dry conditions for the approach across the River Sligachan.

Approach
Follow the path along Glen Sligachan for some 5km until directly below Fiaclan Dearg – the crag on the west face of Marsco. Head off over boggy ground at right-angles to the path, and cross the River Sligachan. Continue across the floor of the glen towards the right-hand of two buttresses situated either side of a stream.

The Route
The buttress on the right-hand side of the stream is known as Glen Sligachan Buttress. Move to the left-hand side of this buttress, and scramble up slabs of very rough rock coated in brown lichen. Weave a way up for some distance, and eventually break out onto more open ground with a stream visible below on the left.

Slant rightwards to gain a superb sweep of slabs – one of the best sections of the route. These are quite steep at first, but then continue for some distance at a very enjoyable angle. Eventually the broad crest of the spur is gained.

Continue with plenty of interest on the rounded crest. Some slabby sections are interrupted by short, steep noses, which are best taken direct. Eventually reach more bouldery ground, where a large crag comes into view above and slightly to the right.

Ascend boulders and short sections of scree heading for some right-slanting slabby rocks well to the left of the crag. Start from the left-hand end of a

SGÙRR NAN GILLEAN
Eastern Spur

57. South-East Ridge   Grade 3 **
58. Eastern Spur   Grade 2/3 **

Pinnacle Ridge

Glen
Sligachan
Buttress

57

57

58

58

Mark Penson.

ledge and ascend delightful slabs slanting rightwards. Head left at the top and finish on a boulder field where the normal route up the mountain is joined. There are good views of Pinnacle Ridge on the skyline to the right.

The simplest option from here is to descend Route 57 back to Sligachan. The preferred option, however, is to continue up the south-east ridge to the summit. Another option is to traverse Sgùrr Beag (Route 56) and visit Sgùrr na h-Uamha (Route 55).

NEAD NA H-IOLAIRE 229m

(NG 484 275) Map p146

This tiny hill is just over 2km from Sligachan. The main buttress on its craggy north-western flank has some climbing. Scrambling possibilities exist further left. A broad slabby buttress left of centre gives some rather heathery scrambling although steep rocks at the top have to be avoided on the right.

SGÙRR NAN GILLEAN 964m

(NG 471 252) Map p146

59 Riabhach Rib Moderate **
(NG 474 260) Alt 330m Map p146 Diagram p157

This route makes an interesting hors d'œuvre to an ascent of Pinnacle Ridge. It ascends an apron of slabs and then a delightfully sound rib at the back of Coire Riabhach. It is easily reached by a short diversion from the approach path to the south-east ridge (Route 57).

Approach
Follow the previous route as far as the broad shoulder some 3km from Sligachan. Descend slightly into Coire Riabhach, then leave the path and head towards some rightward-slanting slabby rocks immediately right of a tiny stream at the back of the corrie.

The Route
Ascend the pleasant slabs, then head leftwards on easier ground towards an obvious rib feature left of a gully. Climb this superb rock buttress in a fine position finishing all too soon at a broad terrace. There are a number of rock climbs on the steeper rocks above, but keep trending a long way right on a broad terrace. Follow a slightly narrower ledge to gain Pinnacle Ridge a short distance above the normal start.

60 Basteir Gorge – Cooper's Gully Moderate *
(NG 470 263) Alt 430m Map p146

The Allt Dearg Beag flows out of Coire a' Bhasteir through the Basteir Gorge. This spectacular ravine was first ascended in its entirety by Hastings,

SGÙRR NAN GILLEAN
North Face

61 1st Pinnacle

61

59

59

59. Riabhach Rib   Moderate **
61. Pinnacle Ridge   Difficult ***

MARK BANDSON.

Hopkinson and Slingsby (Alpine Club) in 1890, but they had to swim across a 10-metre-long pool. The following route visits the main part of the gorge, but escapes by the left wall without entailing any aquatic antics. It was possibly first ascended by C.H. Cooper in 1913, though a dry exit from the gorge was reported in 1893. It is best done during a spell of dry weather, when it can be used as an alternative approach to Pinnacle Ridge (Route 61).

Approach
From Sligachan, follow the path to the Allt Dearg Beag as for the previous route but, instead of crossing the narrow bridge, stay on the north bank and follow it all the way to the mouth of the gorge.

The Route
Enter the gorge and make progress easily at first. Then ascend a chockstone, and traverse along a ramp on the right wall to avoid a tiny pool. Further minor difficulties, usually taken on the right, lead to a long pool where the AC party took to the water.

*In the early section of the Basteir Gorge
on the approach to Cooper's Gully (Moderate)*

Now walk back along the gorge from this pool for about 30 metres and look for a gully on the east wall, i.e. on the left when heading upstream. Make a slightly awkward move to enter the gully, and ascend it fairly easily at first. When it gets a bit steeper and wetter, make a ticklish traverse across the right wall, and move further round into a more exposed position. Make a tricky move up by the edge of a block (crux) and re-enter the gully briefly before transferring to some slabby rocks on the right-hand side. These continue pleasantly for some distance before giving way to easy ground. Move up slightly left to gain a broad slabby toe leading to the start of Pinnacle Ridge.

 ### 61 Pinnacle Ridge   Difficult ***
(NG 472 258)   Alt 600m   Map p146   Diagram p159
This is the north ridge of the mountain. It is a popular outing with some sensational situations, although not always on the best of rock. The normal way of tackling the crucial descent of the third pinnacle is to make a scary 25m abseil from the summit, although it can be down-climbed at Difficult. It is also possible to avoid this manoeuvre altogether by traversing across the east face lower down.

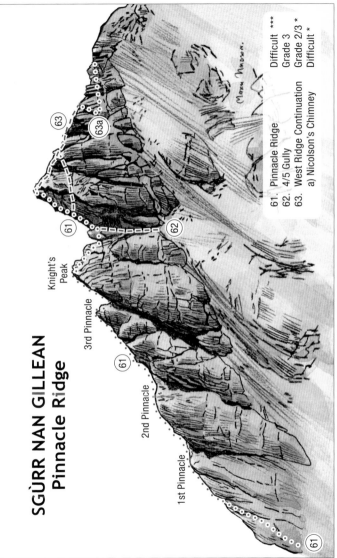

SGÙRR NAN GILLEAN
Pinnacle Ridge

1st Pinnacle

2nd Pinnacle

3rd Pinnacle

Knight's Peak

61. Pinnacle Ridge   Difficult ***
62. 4/5 Gully   Grade 3
63. West Ridge Continuation Grade 2/3 *
    a) Nicolson's Chimney   Difficult *

Peter Duggan scrambles up Knight's Peak,
Pinnacle Ridge (Difficult), Sgùrr nan Gillean

The ridge was first climbed by the Charles Pilkington, Horace Walker and James Heelis in 1887, but only after Pilkington had failed on his first attempt.

Approach

From Sligachan, follow Route 57 as far as the high point on the path just north of Coire Riabhach. Then head in a south-westerly direction up a broad shoulder, following traces of a path at first.

After 1km the shoulder becomes more rocky and better defined. The Basteir Gorge lies immediately to the west. Make directly for the steeper rocks forming the base of the first pinnacle. A faint path slants rightwards across scree at this point, and skirts all the way below Pinnacle Ridge. It eventually leads to the start of the west ridge (Route 63) and Bealach a' Bhasteir.

The Route

Slant left on well-worn ground, easily at first, then ascend a grassy groove and broken rocks. Move slightly further left and cross slabs to reach another grassy groove. Continue slightly leftwards to a ledge in a more exposed position with good views of Coire Riabhach.

Slant back right along a rake to regain the crest of the buttress. Continue slightly right again and ascend a groove. Cut back hard left along a ledge, then climb a steep nose by a narrow dyke (Grade 3). Continue more easily then, at a short horizontal section, cross over to the right-hand side of the crest. Ascend a block and a groove to regain the crest. Then follow a pleasant arête, and continue for some distance with a gully on the right. Move slightly left and eventually reach flatter ground marking the top of the first pinnacle.

Turn right and soon pass the top of a prominent gully dividing the first and second pinnacles. By heading slightly left, it is no more than walking to the dip between the second and third pinnacles. Otherwise slant hard right over slabs, and hunt out a little scrambling to gain the broad summit of the second pinnacle.

Ascend scree to where the rocks steepen at the start of the third pinnacle proper. Scramble up a small gully and pass to the right of a minor pinnacle. There are two options from here:

a) **Traverse of the Third Pinnacle   Moderate with a 22m abseil** **

Trend slightly right and scramble up broken ground to reach a steep groove on the right-hand side of the crest. Climb this with one awkward move, then continue with less difficulty to the dramatic summit. A good thread belay slightly to the left allows an exciting abseil to be made into a narrow gully. This leads down to the gap before Knight's Peak. Experienced climbers may prefer to down-climb from the summit at Difficult standard (by either the left or right-hand arête), but this is probably more time-consuming.

b) **Traverse of the East Face   Grade 3** *

A short distance above the minor pinnacle break left onto the east face. Cross slabs fairly easily at first. Then, after some orange-stained rock, stay high and ascend knobbly rock. Continue quite delicately across slabs to reach easier ground. Do not follow a grassy ledge, but descend slightly to enter a gully which is followed to the gap before Knight's Peak. Drop down 2m to a ledge on the west side.

To ascend Knight's Peak, follow an obvious ledge leading right. Stride boldly across two gaps in the ledge. Continue past a big block and round a corner to a stony ledge. Now cut back leftwards for some distance and pass an awkward nose to a point where there are good views to the east. Ascend a groove slanting back slightly right to reach the summit of Knight's Peak. This is marked by twin tops of very similar height. The south-eastern top is rather harder to ascend.

The descent from Knight's Peak gives quite sustained scrambling, and requires good route-finding. Follow a ledge on the south side slanting down to the left, and cross a tiny gap to reach a shoulder. Drop down right slightly, then slant back leftwards to a gap (876m). (A Difficult 5m chimney on the east side of this gap offers a possible escape route. It can be downclimbed to reach an easy scree slope on the eastern flank. It is quite awkward in ascent.)

Traverse below a sizeable pinnacle on the Coire a' Bhasteir side and reach a higher gap marking the start of the fifth and final pinnacle. Now climb a slab directly out of the gap by using a very high foothold under an overlap and stretching up high for a good handhold (crux). It is also possible to climb the rocks a short distance down and right from the gap, but this is slightly more sustained. Move slightly left and climb a steep rib to easier ground.

Climb up an obvious chimney/recess on the left-hand side of the crest with an awkward move to surmount a block. An easy ledge system now leads to the right. The normal way on from here is to climb a slightly intimidating section of rock, slightly left to start with then more or less directly. Eventually join the west ridge near a rock tower which features a 'window'. The easiest option, however, is to follow the ledge horizontally a long way round to the right and join the west ridge at a lower level where it is composed of distinctive concrete-like rock. Continue up the west ridge to the summit.

62 Knight's Peak via 4/5 Gully   Grade 3
(NG 470 254)   Alt 780m   Map p146   Diagram p159

This gully offers perhaps the easiest way of reaching the summit of Knight's Peak. However, it is a hard scramble – at the upper limit of its grade. It is not recommended as a descent route. The preferred option is to finish up Sgùrr nan Gillean, but this is slightly harder.

Knight's Peak was first listed as a Munro Top in the 1997 edition of Munro's Tables. It is one of the hardest of all the Munro Tops to reach, though not as hard as the nearby Basteir Tooth. Its height was confirmed by the OS in 2006 as 915m.

Approach
Follow the previous route to the base of the first pinnacle. Then ascend a faint path – at times on very steep scree – to reach the prominent scree fan emanating from the gully between Knight's Peak and the main summit rocks.

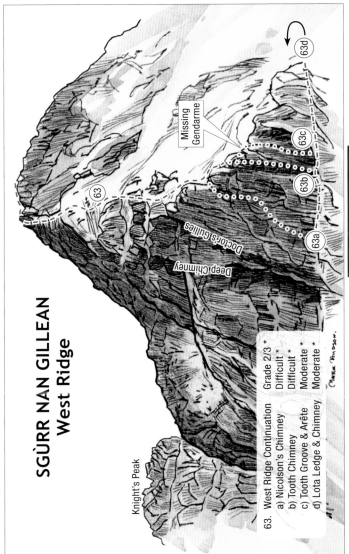

SGÙRR NAN GILLEAN
West Ridge

Knight's Peak

Deep Chimney

Doctor's Gullies

Missing Gendarme

63

63a

63b

63c

63d

63. West Ridge Continuation   Grade 2/3 *
a) Nicolson's Chimney   Difficult *
b) Tooth Chimney   Difficult *
c) Tooth Groove & Arête   Moderate *
d) Lota Ledge & Chimney   Moderate *

The Route
A large chockstone blocks the gully low down. Teeter past this by a leftwards traverse (first crux). Then scramble up rocks mainly on the left side of the gully. Take the right fork of the gully, and bridge up this with sustained interest (second crux) to slightly easier ground. Traverse left below a pinnacle to reach a gap. Slant diagonally leftwards along a break, then head back right to a shoulder. Cross a small exposed gap and slant left to the crest by the twin tops. An ascent of both tops would seem mandatory!

WEST RIDGE

The west ridge of the mountain forms part of the main Cuillin ridge. It is guarded at its base by a section of steep rock which can only be ascended by climbing. The rest of the ridge is a pleasant scramble.

The four routes described can be approached from Bealach a' Bhasteir, either by ascending scree in Coire a' Bhasteir or along the ridge from Am Basteir (Route 65). The first three routes are reached by walking along an obvious ledge on the Coire a' Bhasteir side.

 ### 63a West Ridge: Nicolson's Chimney   Difficult *
(NG 469 253)   Alt 865m   Map p146   Diagram p163

The main chimney feature, which characterises this route, is quite short but smooth-walled. It is marginally easier to slither down than climb up. It was first descended by Alexander Nicolson in 1865. He was also in the party that made the first ascent 14 years later.

Approach
Follow the ledge leftwards for 50 metres to a prominent alcove with a gully below. Then continue around the next corner on a much narrower continuation of the ledge. It is also possible to take a lower line on scree immediately below the first tier of rock.

The Route
Either scramble up directly to the foot of the chimney/groove or start slightly further left near twin gullies (Doctor's Gully Left and Right) and slant rightwards along a slabby break more easily.

Climb the rather smooth tube-like chimney with some difficulty. Move right on a shelf at the top to join the crest of the west ridge a short distance above the finish of the next two routes.

 ### 63b West Ridge: Tooth Chimney   Difficult *
(NG 469 252)   Alt 865m   Map p146   Diagram p163

This classic chimney offers a steep and very direct climb to the crest of the west ridge beyond the remains of the Tooth (or Gendarme). Although technically slightly harder than the next route, it is more enclosed and so feels less frightening. The first recorded ascent was by W.M. MacKenzie in 1956, although it had probably been climbed earlier.

Approach
Follow the ledge leftwards for some 50 metres to the obvious recess.

The Route
At the back of the recess on the left there is a prominent chimney. This is climbed direct in one pitch. The main difficulty is using back and foot to get past a chockstone. It finishes on the crest immediately above the rickety arête of the next route.

 63c West Ridge: Tooth Groove & Arête   Moderate   *
(NG 469 252)   Alt 865m   Map p146   Diagram p163

This is possibly the easiest way up the west ridge. However, the crucial section of arête on which the Tooth (or Gendarme) used to sit has very steep drops on either side and is still an intimidating obstacle.

Approach
Follow the ledge leftwards to where it broadens. This point is marked by two boulders, and is just short of the recess of the previous route.

The Route
Ascend the right-hand of two parallel groove/crack lines which merge together higher up, like an inverted tuning fork. Continue up the single groove to reach the crest of the arête. Make some delicate moves in a very exposed position to pass the stub of the former Tooth. Continue on rather better holds, and pass the top of Tooth Chimney. Soon reach easier ground where Nicolson's Chimney joins the crest.

 63d West Ridge: Lota Ledge & Chimney   Moderate   *
(NG 469 252)   Alt 865m   Map p146

This fourth option lies on the face overlooking Lota Corrie.

Approach
From Bealach a' Bhasteir instead of following the obvious ledge leftwards cut round to the right of the rocks forming the toe of the ridge.

The Route
Follow a ledge horizontally rightwards with increasing difficulty directly below a steep wall. (The former Tooth once sat on the crest of this wall.) Go across a right-angled corner on much smaller holds and continue rightwards until it is possible to ascend a chimney. This has one awkward step in it, but the angle eases soon after. Continue up leftwards on slightly looser ground to gain the crest of the ridge where the other routes also finish.

 63 West Ridge Continuation   Grade 2/3   *
(NG 470 252)   Alt 885m   Map p146   Diagram p163

The remainder of the west ridge is no more than scrambling. A fairly long but straightforward section of ridge leads to some rather more delicate scrambling on curious concrete-like rock – a volcanic pipe – just left of the

NORTHERN CUILLIN

crest. Shortly after this reach a tower marked by a window which offers an amusing through route. From a small gap at the back of the tower traverse along the right-hand side of the ridge. Regain the crest and soon after reach the small platform marking the summit.

Alexander Nicolson wrote an account of his traverse of Sgùrr nan Gillean in 1865 using a quill fashioned from an eagle's feather which he found on the summit. The carpet of moss which he described there has long gone, but this spot remains a superb viewpoint.

The easiest descent is by the south-east ridge (Route 57). However, confident scramblers may prefer to return down the west ridge as it is marginally quicker to reach Sligachan by descending Coire a' Bhasteir.

64 South Face   Grade 3 (or Difficult) *
(NG 471 248) Alt 550m   Map p146

The broad south face of Sgùrr nan Gillean overlooks Lota Corrie. It lies between the west and south-east ridges of the mountain. There are no distinctive lines here, but the route described gives an unusual and interesting outing.

Approach

This face is rather awkward to reach. Any one of the three bealachs which link with Lota Corrie can be used to approach it. All involve a significant loss of height before the base of the face is reached. Perhaps the most straightforward approach is from Bealach na Lice (890m), but this involves the biggest height loss. A slightly shorter but more difficult approach can be made from Bealach a' Bhasteir (833m). A third option via Bealach a' Ghlas-choire (640m) gives the least height loss but the longest approach. It would also be possible to gain the base of the face by ascending Harta Corrie and continuing up into Lota Corrie by rocks on the right-hand side of the main stream.

Start from the back of the corrie between two streams at about 550m where there is a broad slabby toe to the face. Alternatively traverse in higher up along any one of a number of easy grass ledges.

The Route

The lower section consists of a series of slabby buttresses which give pleasant but fairly easy scrambling. This section eventually finishes at a grassy terrace below a steeper rock band. There is a large scree-filled recess to the left at this point with a steep drop to it from the left-hand end of the terrace.

The rock band can be climbed direct at Difficult grade starting just right of the steepest section. A couple of delicate moves allow a good jug to be reached. A swing right can then be made to gain a leftward leaning slabby ramp. This is followed until some steeper moves soon lead to easier ground.

It is more in keeping with the general standard of the outing to avoid this rock band by descending very slightly to the right and then continuing diagonally up right until it is relatively easy to cut back left above the rock band. Continue traversing leftwards for quite some distance until the ledge system peters out with steep drops to the recess on the left.

Scramble up through slightly more amenable rocks to reach a bigger leftward-leaning terrace. This can be followed to easy ground further left but instead swing right at a flake below an overhang to gain leftward-slanting slabs. Then head diagonally right below a steepening and soon reach easy ground.

Ascend scree and easy ground for some distance. Climb a fairly prominent cracked wall right of centre. This is quite fun, and thereafter much variation is possible. One option is to traverse a long way left to the west ridge, but it is more natural to continue straight up turning difficulties on the right. Eventually join the south-east ridge fairly high up. Follow this to the summit.

SGÙRR COIRE AN LOBHTA

(NG 469 252)

At the base of the west ridge of Sgùrr nan Gillean, a short spur juts out southwards into Lota Corrie. This minor top on the spur can easily be reached by clambering along a short section of ridge.

AM BASTEIR 934m

(NG 465 252) Map p146

This fine peak presents a very steep north wall to Coire a' Bhasteir. Its western end is guarded by a spectacular pinnacle known as the Basteir Tooth. The distinctive profile of this feature can be recognised from afar. The easiest route to the summit is by way of the east ridge, but a recent rockfall has created a 'Bad Step' part-way up.

 65 East Ridge Grade 2 or Difficult/Very Difficult *
(NG 468 252) Alt 833m Map p146 Diagram p168

The direct route along the crest is now much harder than it used to be. An easier option, which skirts the difficulties on the Lota Corrie side, requires careful route-finding. There are no easy ways off from the western end of the peak.

Approach
Reach Bealach a' Bhasteir either by ascending scree in Coire a' Bhasteir or by following Route 70 below the north wall of Am Basteir.

The Route
Ascend the ridge easily until it starts to steepen slightly.

a) Left-hand Variation Grade 2 *
Look for a faint path on the left-hand side of the crest which leads to an orange-brown slab. Ascend the slab then cut horizontally leftwards for some

NORTHERN CUILLIN

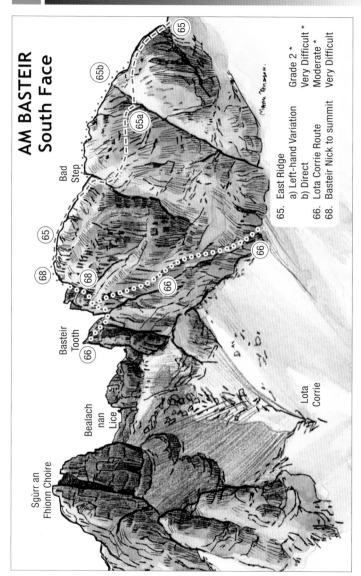

AM BASTEIR
South Face

Bad Step

Basteir Tooth

Bealach nan Lice

Sgùrr an Fhionn Choire

Lota Corrie

65. East Ridge   Grade 2 *
    a) Left-hand Variation   Very Difficult *
    b) Direct
66. Lota Corrie Route   Moderate *
68. Basteir Nick to summit   Very Difficult

distance. Continue round in a slightly exposed position and eventually cross a wall to join a ramp of purple-stained rock. Go up this more easily and soon reach the gap just beyond the Bad Step.

b) **Direct Route   Difficult or Very Difficult ***

Instead of leaving the ridge on the left, continue pleasantly up the crest. Some enjoyable scrambling in a fine position eventually leads to a narrow section of ridge and an abrupt drop. Although this is quite short it is very exposed and graded Very Difficult (possibly harder for those with a short reach). Only confident climbers will decide to down-climb this step.

By returning a short distance from this Bad Step, however, it is possible to climb down the wall on the Lota Corrie side. This is rather tricky but no harder than Difficult if the correct way is found. Slant down leftwards (looking down) on small holds, and eventually step onto a tiny nose. Then climb down to the right (again looking down) to reach sloping ground at the base of the wall. Walk up a short distance to reach the gap just beyond the Bad Step.

Both routes rejoin at this point. Continue more easily to the airy summit. Scramblers will now have to return the same way. It is much more straightforward climbing up the Bad Step on the return, otherwise follow the easier variation right of the crest.

66 Lota Corrie Route   Moderate *
(NG 467 251)   Alt 760m   Map p146   Diagram p168

The Basteir Tooth was first visited – from Am Basteir – by Collie and King in 1887. This climb was discovered by Collie and Mackenzie the following year. The route follows a slanting weakness across the south face of Am Basteir. It offers an easier alternative to Naismith's Route on the Tooth. However, the continuation onto Am Basteir is significantly harder (see Route 68).

Approach

The normal approach is made from Bealach nan Lice – an easy pass on the main ridge – which can be reached either from Fionn Choire or Coire a' Bhasteir. There is a prominent rock spike on the north-east side of this bealach on the Lota Corrie side. Keep descending into Lota Corrie by a faint path in the scree to reach the lowest rocks of the south face. Do not be tempted to join the route any sooner, as this significantly increases the grade of the climb.

This same place can also be reached by scrambling down into Lota Corrie from Bealach a' Bhasteir. Slant down diagonally leftwards at first. When the rocks start to steepen cut back rightwards and eventually find a way down to the scree slope below. Head rightwards to reach the lowest rocks of the south face.

The Route

Now turning to look uphill, head up to an obvious leftwards-leaning ramp/gully feature which has an outcrop of light-coloured intrusion near its mouth. Ascend the gully on scree and continue up a narrower groove above. Transfer to the left edge and then step down slightly and continue in the same

Peter Duggan ascending the initial gully of
Lota Corrie Route (Moderate), Am Basteir

direction with a steep drop on the left for a short section. Ascend by some small chockstones, then avoid a bigger one by rocks to the left. It is possible to continue up the gully line but, by moving slightly left, a fine slab can be climbed in a fairly exposed position. Then move up rightwards to regain the original line. Continue until a high step up to the right allows a move left onto a boulder in a cleft.

Above are twin grooves separated by a steep boss. Start up the right-hand groove, then step hard left and follow the left-hand groove. From a grassy recess make a stride out left and ascend a slabby rib to reach easier ground.

The route to the summit of Am Basteir (Route 67) climbs a gully above and slightly right. Instead, follow an obvious traverse line leftwards and descend a short cleft to reach the Nick before the Basteir Tooth. Ascend a pleasant slab to reach the highest point of the Tooth (916m). There is a spectacular drop on the other side.

There are no easy ways off from here. Either descend from the Basteir Nick by abseiling down King's Cave Chimney (Route 69) or return up the short cleft and ascend Am Basteir as for Route 68.

67 Naismith's Route, Basteir Tooth   Very Difficult   ***
(NG 465 252)   Alt 890m   Map p146   Diagram p172

This is the most intimidating route on the Cuillin main ridge. It has been the undoing of many tired climbers making a south–north traverse. It gives a sensational climb, and avoids the considerable height loss suffered by the popular alternatives (Routes 66 and 70). It leads directly to the summit of the Basteir Tooth.

The route was first climbed by Naismith and Mackay in 1898. Naismith inspected the upper section on a rope prior to his ascent.

Approach
From Bealach nan Lice (890m), either descend a short distance into Lota Corrie, or scramble along the crest of a ridge immediately to the north.

The Route
Gain a ledge, either from directly below or by a rightwards traverse. Ascend to a higher ledge and traverse along it to the right. Climb a steep wall slightly leftwards (first crux) to gain a more accommodating chimney crack. Ascend this, then traverse right and make a tricky mantelshelf onto a ledge (second crux). Finish on the huge slab which leads easily to the summit of the Tooth.

68 Basteir Nick to Am Basteir   Very Difficult
(NG 465 252)   Alt 895m   Map p146   Diagrams pp168 & 172

It is a simple matter to ascend the broad slab to the summit of the Tooth from the top of Naismith's Route or from the Lota Corrie Route via the Basteir Nick. The drop on the west side of the summit is sensational.

The continuation onto the summit of Am Basteir, however, is far from straightforward. The most obvious way is very strenuous.

AM BASTEIR

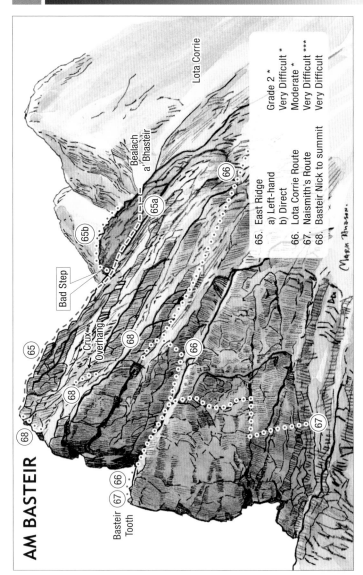

Lota Corrie

Bealach a'Bhasteir

Bad Step

Crux Overhang

Basteir Tooth

65. East Ridge   Grade 2 *
  a) Left-hand
  b) Direct   Very Difficult *
66. Lota Corrie Route   Moderate *
67. Naismith's Route   Very Difficult ***
68. Basteir Nick to summit   Very Difficult

Mike Brownlow abseiling down King's Cave Chimney, Am Basteir
Photo: Nick Carter

**AM BASTEIR
North Face**

69. King's Cave Chimney Difficult + Abseil Walk
70. Base of North Wall Walk

Basteir Tooth

Basteir Nick

tunnel

Abseil

69

Bealach
nan Lice

70

69

Bealach a'
Bhasteir

70

Approach
From the Basteir Nick between the Basteir Tooth and Am Basteir.

The Route
Scramble up a short cleft to reach a rightwards traverse line. Follow this round to a gully which cuts back left. Ascend the gully, staying just to the right of a dyke. A short section of easier ground leads to a fiercesome rock band.

  The most popular option from here is to climb an overhanging niche and pull up rightwards (hard) to gain a continuation of the gully. A less strenuous but more sustained option is to climb the wall further right and make a long step left to enter the gully. Other options climb the right wall lower down but they are not as obvious and no easier. (A cone-sheet which leads leftwards below this crucial rock band only leads to an even more difficult groove.)

  Continue up the gully more easily. (It is possible to abseil this section when descending from the summit by placing a tape over a boss of rock high on the left wall – looking down). A short but enjoyable section of steep scrambling leads to the summit. The usual descent is by the east ridge (Route 65).

69 King's Cave Chimney   Difficult with a 25m abseil
(NG 465 252)   Alt 895m   Map p146   Diagram p174

The route described offers perhaps the most convenient way of descending from the Basteir Tooth. It was the scene of an epic ascent in 1889, and was originally known as Basteir Nick Gully.

Approach
From the Basteir Nick between the Basteir Tooth and Am Basteir.

The Route
Head away from the Lota Corrie side and descend a broad rift with boulders. Find a small hole on the right and climb down a narrow spiral-shaped tunnel. Make a very awkward final step down (crux) to reach the floor of a cave below a massive chockstone. Abseil 25m to the foot of the gully using a very long thread belay.

70 Base of the North Wall   500m
(NG 464 252)   Alt 890m   Map p146   Diagram p174

This is the easiest option for scramblers wishing to reach the east ridge of Am Basteir when travelling north along the main ridge. It is just a walk but involves a significant height loss.

Approach
Start from Bealach nan Lice (890m) below a boss of rock (896m) .

The Route
Descend a well-worn path in the scree on the north side of the boss of rock. Cross below the mouth of King's Cave Chimney and continue below the imposing north face of Am Basteir. Drop down over 100m before re-ascending scree and broken ground to reach Bealach a' Bhasteir (833m).

SGÙRR A' BHASTEIR 898m

(NG 464 257) Map p146

This peak is the high point on the ridge dividing Coire a' Bhasteir and Fionn Choire. A traverse of the summit makes a fine outing and offers unrivalled views of the Pinnacle Ridge of Sgùrr nan Gillean. The approach by the north-east ridge is preferred – the north-north-west ridge being slightly looser and less pleasant in its lower section.

71 Traverse by the North-East Ridge   Grade 1/2 **
(NG 470 262) Alt 460m   Map p146 Diagram p177

This route is a good choice for newcomers to the Cuillin with limited scrambling experience. It offers some mild scrambling with superb views, and can easily be combined with Bruach na Frìthe.

Approach
From Sligachan, follow the path along the west bank of the Allt Dearg Beag towards the Basteir Gorge (as for Route 41).

The Route
Ascend a worn route over stony ground and slabby rocks, some distance above the west side of the gorge. The floor of Coire a' Bhasteir and its tiny lochan can be reached by continuing in a southerly direction. Instead, when the path levels off (some distance before a massive overhang which makes a good shelter), head right up a broad ridge on slabs and grass.

Follow the ridge – with plenty of opportunities for scrambling – to a slight shoulder. Continue up pleasant slabby rocks to reach a narrow neck, where a gully plunges down into Coire a' Bhasteir on the left. (The guide John Mackenzie had a fall from the top pitch of this gully before making the first ascent in 1902.)

The going is then little more than walking for some distance. From the junction with the north-north-west ridge, head south along a very fine arête to the summit.

Continue beyond the summit, with steep drops on either side, until the ridge broadens and there are excellent views of the Basteir Tooth. The boss of rock marking Bealach nan Lice lies straight ahead.

There are several options at this point. The easiest option is to descend Fionn Choire on the right. A rather rougher but more direct descent can be made down Coire a' Bhasteir on the left. (At the bottom it is better to exit from the corrie by moving right onto the slabby toe of rock on the eastern side of the Basteir Gorge.) However, it is also easy to include an ascent of Bruach na Frìthe and Sgùrr an Fhionn Choire before descending as described.

72 North Face   Grade 3
(NG 466 262) Alt 510m   Map p146 Diagram p177

This route can be used as a direct start to a traverse of Sgùrr a' Bhasteir, but

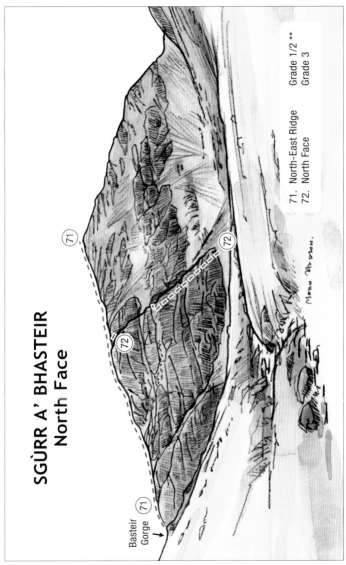

SGÙRR A' BHASTEIR
North Face

Basteir Gorge 71

71

72

72

71. North-East Ridge   Grade 1/2 **
72. North Face   Grade 3

NORTHERN CUILLIN

it is for experienced scramblers only. It climbs the open face to the left of a prominent leftward-slanting gully, and finishes up a hidden subsidiary gully. Loose scree in the latter requires careful handling – not a route for big parties.

Approach
Follow the path along the Allt Dearg Beag (as for the previous route) and, some distance before the Basteir Gorge, head right to an open grassy corrie below the north face. Start at the rocks a little to the left of the central gully.

The Route
Weave a way up the steep initial section. As height is gained, the rock lies back slightly and its quality improves. Eventually reach a grassy terrace below a much steeper upper section. There are good views from the right-hand end of the terrace into the central gully.

Start some 10 metres left of the edge overlooking the gully and ascend a narrow gully/groove just right of some stacked blocks. Move slightly right to a grassy ledge, then continue up a groove to reach a more prominent gully slanting up to the left. Ascend this on its left side initially. Ignore a grassy break which cuts across the right-hand wall.

Continue up the bed of the gully on sections of loose scree with occasional bridging. Surmount a small chockstone on its left-hand side. Then climb up past a bigger chockstone on the right wall. Higher up, some devious moves allow a tricky exit to be made along a ledge on the left wall. Finish up a rib just left of the scree-filled gully to reach easy ground. The previous route is joined at the shoulder on the north-east ridge.

SGÙRR AN FHIONN CHOIRE 935m

(NG 464 252) Map p146

This little peak can be skirted altogether on its north side, but it is a splendid viewpoint and makes a worthwhile traverse. It is of similar height to Am Basteir and offers fine views of the Basteir Tooth.

 73 Traverse by West Ridge and North Face   Grade 2/3 *
(NG 462 252)   Alt 903m   Map p146
The west ridge can be ascended by staying on the crest when heading east from Bruach na Frithe. The main difficulties are at a steep step. A descent of the north face is easily achieved by means of a gully (barely Grade 1), which leads directly to Bealach nan Lice.

BRUACH NA FRÌTHE 958m

(NG 460 251) Map p146

The summit of Bruach na Frìthe marks a change in direction of the Cuillin main ridge from north–south to east–west. It is a superb viewpoint and boasts

NORTHERN CUILLIN

Traversing late snow below Sgùrr an Fhionn Choire with Am Basteir behind
Photo: Andrew Wielochowski

the only triangulation pillar in the Cuillin. It is one of the few Cuillin summits accessible to the walker. Professor Forbes made the first recorded ascent with Duncan MacIntyre in 1845.

 74 East Ridge via Fionn Choire   12km   *
(NG 462 252)   Alt 903m   Map p146   Diagram p181

Although this outing ascends one of the tamest corries in the Cuillin, it crosses some very rough ground. The east ridge itself is quite short and not at all exposed. The featureless nature of the terrain can cause navigation problems in poor visibility.

Approach

Approach Fionn Choire by the path to Bealach a' Mhàim (Route 52). The Glen Brittle start is marginally shorter.

The Route

Head up into the open corrie for some 2km. Various paths converge as height is gained. Numerous boulders floor the corrie, and the ascent follows the general line of a stream. A small mossy spring at a height of some 820m is one of the highest sources of drinking water in the Cuillin – a fact worth knowing in scorching weather.

Steeper scree in the upper section of the corrie leads directly to Bealach nan Lice. Skirt to the right below Sgùrr an Fhionn Choire on a well-worn path and reach a dip on the ridge marking the start of the east ridge proper. Continue along the broader crest on bouldery ground. Move slightly left to reach the summit.

A more adventurous return to Sligachan can be made via Coire a' Bhasteir (as for Route 71). Otherwise return by the outward route.

 75 North-West Ridge   Grade 2   **
(NG 448 267)   Alt 360m   Map p146   Diagram p181

This very long ridge makes a fine outing. It has better views than the previous route and takes a more direct line to the summit.

Approach

The shortest approach starts from Glen Brittle by the path to Bealach a' Mhàim (Route 52). Leave the path at its high point near a lochan.

The Route

Slant leftwards along a narrow stony path to gain the broad grassy crest. Continue just left of the crest overlooking a broad bowl with numerous streams. Pass an outcrop of breccia marking a volcanic vent. Then ascend a much steeper scree slope to reach a narrower section of ridge where an alternative approach from Sligachan also joins the crest.

Follow the almost level ridge to a steeper section where the scrambling begins. The rock is largely basalt and can be slippery in damp conditions. Several ledges lead off rightwards. Indeed the whole outing is just a walk if

THE NORTHERN CUILLIN
Bruach na Frìthe & Fionn Choire

74. East Ridge   Walk *
75. North-West Ridge Grade 2 **
76. South Ridge   Grade 2 *

faint paths are followed on the right-hand side of the crest. However, by staying on the crest some enjoyable scrambling can be found. Maintain position by moving left from time to time, but be wary of steep drops on the left-hand side. Pass the top of the only climb on the mountain (North Chimney) and reach the summit with its triangulation pillar soon after. The easiest descent from this very fine viewpoint is by the east ridge (Route 74), but confident scramblers may prefer to reverse the next route and descend Coire an Tairneilear.

 76 South Ridge via Sgùrr na Bàirnich Grade 2 *
(NG 461 245)   Alt 764m   Map p146   Diagram p181

This long rocky ridge has only short sections of scrambling. Sgùrr na Bàirnich (860m) is a minor top at the southern end of the ridge. The route starts from a deep gap on the main ridge which is reached by a long scree gully from Coire an Tairneilear. A more interesting approach can be made by completing a route on An Caisteal first and then descending that peak's north ridge (Route 77), but this involves steep down-climbing of Moderate standard.

Approach
From a small car park in Glen Brittle descend the path on the east side of the road, take a right fork and eventually continue along the north bank of the Allt Coire an Tairneilear. A picturesque section of this stream – with cascades, several deep potholes and a natural rock arch – is known as The Fairy Pools.

An alternative approach from Sligachan follows an old path heading south from Bealach a' Mhàim. The start is rather indistinct but it then slants across the west flank of Bruach na Frìthe all the way to the Allt Coire an Tairneilear.

There are two routes into Coire an Tairneilear. One climbs steep, loose ground on the left (north) bank of the stream to reach a high traverse path; the other takes a more undulating line on the south bank. The latter route is perhaps more enjoyable in descent.

From the floor of the corrie, slant slightly left and ascend a long, broad gully on rather tedious scree. In the upper section, move left and then back right. Finish up a much narrower section of gully to gain the gap below the steep north wall of An Caisteal.

The Route
Clamber out of the gap and zigzag up rocks and a stony path on the left, before slanting back right to the crest. Continue to where an orange-brown dyke crosses the crest. A short, steep wall on the north side gives a Difficult climb, but this is easily avoided by skirting round to the right. Continue more easily to the summit of Sgùrr na Bàirnich (named by Harker, the geologist).

There is a short section of scrambling on the descent from the north end of this top. Then follow a long section of rocky ridge interspersed with short sections of scrambling. The final difficulty entails crossing a small gap. Enter this from the left-hand side of the crest, go round the back of a knobble of rock, and traverse right across a slab. Continue more easily to the summit.

*Peter Duggan on the steep wall at the
start of the north ridge of An Caisteal*

AN CAISTEAL 830m

(NG 460 244) Map p146

This rocky peak has a very narrow north–south summit ridge with steep flanks either side. There are several long climbs on its eastern face.

77 North Ridge Moderate *

(NG 461 245) Alt 764m Map p146 Diagrams pp185 & 188

Only a short, steep section at the bottom of this route is of Moderate grade. On a south–north traverse of the main ridge this gives a rather tricky descent.

Approach

Reach the deep gash on the main ridge between Sgùrr na Bàirnich and An Caisteal, either by ascending the long scree gully from Coire an Tairneilear as for the previous route or, better, by traversing Bruach na Frìthe.

The Route

Climb the rather intimidating wall directly above the gap. It is steep but the holds are good. Traverse a short distance to the right, then ascend a short corner. Scramble up leftwards and reach slabby rocks, with an impressive wall further left. Ascend the slabs and gain a short section of horizontal ridge. Then turn left and shortly after slant up right to reach the airy summit.

78 South Ridge Grade 2 **

(NG 458 240) Alt 760m Map p146 Diagrams pp185 & 188

This splendid ridge becomes increasingly exposed as height is gained. Further interest is provided by three narrow gaps.

Approach

Reach the floor of Coire an Tairneilear as for Route 76. Then slant slightly right and scramble up a slabby rock tongue between two forks of a stream – the right fork lies in a small gorge.

Head up the scree shoot above and slant rightwards to gain another scree slope which leads up to one of the lowest points (760m) on the main ridge, a short distance north of Bealach Harta.

The Route

The first feature on the ridge is a minor eminence here named **An Turaid** *(the turret)*. At its southern end it is guarded by a steep nose. This can be ascended directly by a steep groove (Grade 3). However, it can also be skirted altogether by easier scrambling on either side – usually the right.

Continue along the crest more easily. Eventually reach the first of three gaps. This is crossed easily by ledges on the Tairneilear side. A short distance further on a second gap is negotiated in similar fashion. The ridge becomes increasingly exposed approaching the third and most spectacular gap. Either make a bold stride across it or descend a slab on the right-hand (east) side to gain the base of the gap. The summit is reached soon after.

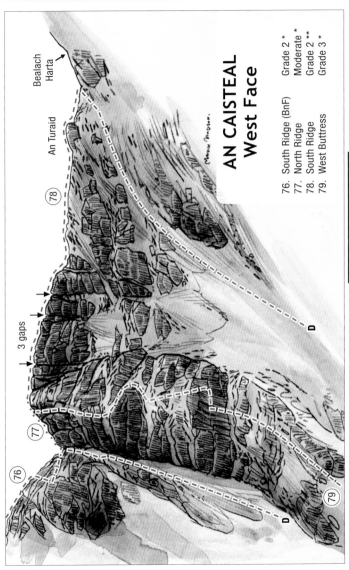

Bealach Harta

An Turaid

AN CAISTEAL
West Face

76. South Ridge (BnF)   Grade 2 *
77. North Ridge   Moderate *
78. South Ridge   Grade 2 **
79. West Buttress   Grade 3 *

3 gaps

NORTHERN CUILLIN

The tricky descent by the north ridge starts from the left (west) side of the crest. Continuing directly north leads to a spectacular drop.

 79 West Buttress   Grade 3   *
(NG 458 245)   Alt 560m   Map p146   Diagram p185

This prominent buttress lies directly below the summit. It gives a surprisingly straightforward outing. The only difficult scrambling is on the first major rock band, which has excellent rock.

Approach

Approach Coire an Tairneilear as for Route 76, and ascend broken ground directly to the foot of the buttress.

The Route

Head for the first slabby rock band. Start just right of centre and scramble up 5m, then traverse left along an obvious weakness. Break back right and scramble up to a steep wall. Traverse right along a narrow ledge to reach a dyke which slants very slightly left. Ascend this steeply on good holds until a stride right can be made to gain a cone-sheet which leads right to easier ground.

Continue via a minor outcrop to a much steeper rock band. This can be climbed direct (Very Difficult), but it is better to walk right along its base and then slant a long way back left up an easy break to reach the buttress crest.

Three closely-spaced dykes cut through the next rock outcrop. Climb the central one and move slightly left. Continue up steep but sound rock to a ledge. Then move left again and break out onto slabbier rocks. Scramble up an easy rib with slabs to the right and scree to the left.

Eventually reach a small shoulder with a good view of a prominent chimney/gully on the left side of the buttress crest some distance above. Move right and ascend easier rocks. Then weave a way up slightly steeper and more broken rocks. Climb a rib and reach a slight dip marking the top of a gully on the left side of the crest.

Follow an obvious grassy ledge to the right, then cut back left on slightly unpleasant ground. The way ahead looks rather intimidating. Either climb the steep rocks directly, or follow easier rock steps further right. Eventually join the crest of the north ridge by a runnel of brown scree. Turn right and soon reach the summit.

EAST FACE

The east face of An Caisteal is split into three separate buttresses by two long gullies – South Gully on the left and North Gully on the right. Another deep gully (unnamed), further right again, forms the right-hand border of the face. Although the climbs described include long sections of scrambling, they are fairly serious undertakings. The normal approach from Sligachan up Harta Corrie takes three hours. The combination of a lengthy approach, and quite tricky route-finding on a big face, means there is plenty of scope for epics.

Bouldering on The Bloody Stone in Harta Corrie

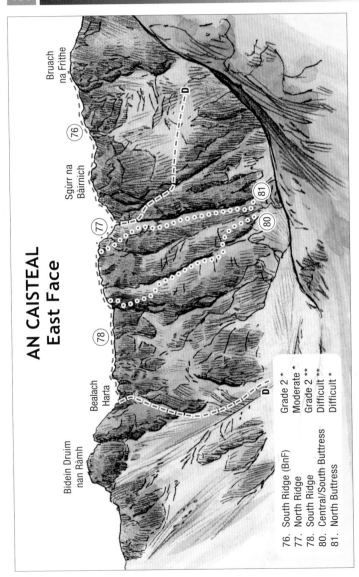

AN CAISTEAL
East Face

Bruach na Frithe

Sgurr na Bàirnich

Bidein Druim nan Ràmh

Bealach Harta

76. South Ridge (BnF)   Grade 2 *
77. North Ridge   Moderate *
78. South Ridge   Grade 2 **
80. Central/South Buttress Difficult **
81. North Buttress   Difficult *

80 Central–South Buttress   Difficult ** *
(NG 465 241) Alt 390m   Map p146   Diagram p188

South Buttress was first climbed by McLaren and Shadbolt in 1911. The same pair had made the first continuous traverse of the Cuillin main ridge some three months earlier. The entry pitch they used to gain the crest of South Buttress starts some distance up South Gully just below a great barrier pitch. It climbs out of the gully by the left wall (looking up) and then descends a long, narrow ramp slanting all the way back down the wall before traversing round onto the front face. A later direct start (done in 1946) avoids this long descent pitch by climbing a very intimidating wall at the mouth of South Gully using a suspect flake. Neither of these two starts is at all attractive!

The lower section of Central Buttress on the other hand has some delightful slab climbing on immaculate rock. It was first ascended by an SMC party led by Harold Raeburn in April 1905 – the first route to be done on this face. Raeburn put on klettershue to tackle the delicate slabs low down. The middle section of Central Buttress, however, is rather broken and easy-angled. The best combination hereabouts starts up Central Buttress, then crosses South Gully and finishes up South Buttress. This is now described.

Approach
Follow the path along Glen Sligachan for 5.5km. Then head off to the right and pick up a faint path on the east bank of the River Sligachan. Follow this for a further kilometre to the Bloody Stone. This massive boulder is worth a few minutes diversion.

Continue along what is now the south bank of the river and eventually ascend rising ground to reach the upper section of Harta Corrie. Cross undulating terrain then head up to the obvious tongue of slabs situated below and to the right of South Gully.

The Route
Scramble up the delightful slabs fairly easily at first. They gradually get harder and after a slightly steeper section a groove leads to an impressive sweep of slabs slanting leftwards below steeper rocks. This is the 'Kletterschue Pitch'.

Climb leftwards up the slabs until there are good views of South Gully on the left. At this point Raeburn ascended a rather intimidating steep groove and ramp before eventually moving rightwards back to the crest of Central Buttress. However, better climbing can be found by continuing the traverse leftwards – across a rather tricky wall of suspect rock – to reach the bed of South Gully.

Continue traversing leftwards and ascend an awkward small scoop on the opposite wall of the gully. Then traverse a long grassy ledge leftwards around onto the crest of South Buttress. Pleasant scrambling ensues for some distance. Then climb a steep nose directly to gain a superb stretch of slab.

There is much scope for variation above this. The tendency is for the lines to lead rightwards away from the crest with steep drops to South Gully further right. It is important to cut back left towards the buttress crest where possible.

The buttress gradually tapers as height is gained. Eventually a long section of scrambling leads to a very narrow arête with a horrifying drop on the left-hand side. Follow this with interest, then start up a broad slabby gully just right of the crest. Do not follow this as it ends in a big drop. Instead, after a few metres, break out rightwards and cross an alcove to gain the crest of the right-hand buttress. Further scrambling up this for some distance leads to the crest of the south ridge. Follow that route and soon gain the summit.

The easiest way off is to return down the south ridge of An Caisteal and descend from Bealach Harta. To return to Harta Corrie enter a slanting scree gully a short distance south of the lowest point on the ridge. Alternatively descend into Coire an Tairneilear and return to Sligachan via Bealach a' Mhàim. However, the most enjoyable way of returning to Sligachan is probably to descend the north ridge (Route 77), traverse Bruach na Frìthe (Routes 76 and 74) and descend either Fionn Choire or Coire a' Bhasteir.

After making the first ascent of Central Buttress in 1905, Raeburn's party started down the gully on the east side of the gash between An Caisteal and Sgùrr na Bàirnich. They moved left where it widens and descended beside a rock wall. Just above the point where the gully steepens dramatically they traversed a ledge on the left-hand wall – narrow in places (Grade 2) – for about 100 metres before descending mixed ground to the floor of Lota Corrie.

81 North Buttress   Difficult   *
(NG 465 242)   Alt 370m   Map p146   Diagram p188

This remarkably long route (15 pitches totalling over 600m) was first climbed by Ted Wrangham in 1953. Apart from a fierce entry pitch, which is hard for its grade, the route is mainly an enjoyable mixture of scrambling and Moderate climbing on sound slabby rock. It is easier than its neighbour.

Approach
Approach from Sligachan as for the previous route.

The Route
The buttress is bounded on the left by North Gully and on the right by a much deeper unnamed gully. Scramble up to the steep rocks close to North Gully. Climb up until a leftward traverse (crux) leads round and up to a good ledge overlooking North Gully. Break back right onto the crest and follow easy slabs for some distance.

When North Gully peters out, continue up a grassy ramp trending slightly right. Slant back left and then head up more or less directly to reach a steeper wall of angular rock. Climb this by slanting first right and then left. Continue past a green rock scar and eventually reach a grassy terrace.

Break through the steeper rocks above by slanting from left to right and continue to a short arête. Climb a groove on the left side of the tower above and then move back right at the top. Continue up a rib, then scramble up scree and a grassy gully to finish on the ridge very close to the summit. (See the previous route for options from here.)

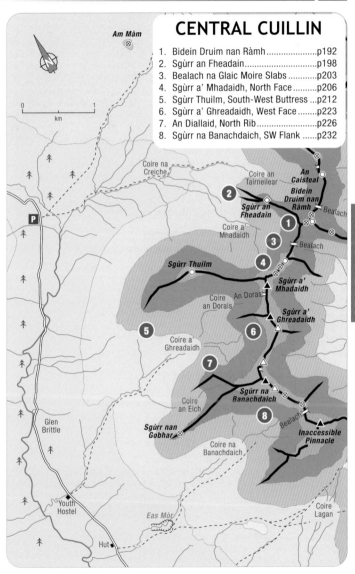

CENTRAL CUILLIN

1. Bidein Druim nan Ràmh.....................p192
2. Sgùrr an Fheadain.............................p198
3. Bealach na Glaic Moire Slabs p203
4. Sgùrr a' Mhadaidh, North Face..........p206
5. Sgùrr Thuilm, South-West Buttress ...p212
6. Sgùrr a' Ghreadaidh, West Face p223
7. An Diallaid, North Rib.......................p226
8. Sgùrr na Banachdaich, SW Flank p232

CENTRAL CUILLIN

CENTRAL CUILLIN

The Central Cuillin group is here taken to extend from Bidein Druim nan Ràmh to Sgùrr na Banachdaich. This part of the Cuillin is most readily accessible from Glen Brittle.

The major peak of the group is Sgùrr a' Ghreadaidh. This magnificent mountain crowns one of the most committing sections on the main ridge. It gives a superb traverse with magnificent views. In contrast Sgùrr na Banachdaich further south, though boasting a fine south-east ridge, is one of the easiest Cuillin summits to reach. The four tops of Sgùrr a' Mhadaidh to the north are significantly harder to cross. However, the main difficulties on this section are the lowly but complex three tops of Bidein Druim nan Ràmh.

Three contrasting ridges on the western side of the range – Sgùrr nan Gobhar, Sgùrr Thuilm and Sgùrr an Fheadain – offer very different options for approaching the main ridge. There are only two easy crossing places over the main ridge proper – Bealach Coire na Banachdaich (851m) and Bealach na Glaic Moire (760m). They both lead to the head of Coir'-uisg.

BIDEIN DRUIM NAN RÀMH 869m

(NG 456 239) Map p191

The triple peaks of Bidein Druim nan Ràmh hold a commanding position where two major side ridges lead off from the main ridge. The traverse of all three peaks constitutes one of the more formidable sections on the main ridge. The individual peaks can be reached by scrambling routes, but a complete traverse of all three involves intricate route finding and Difficult climbing. It is possible to skirt below the peaks on the northern side on scree, although the best way at the western end is not obvious in poor visibility.

82 North Peak Grade 2 * or 3 **
(NG 458 240) Alt 760m Map p191 Diagrams pp193 & 194

This little peak (852m) is a worthy goal although its summit can be avoided. It was first ascended by Naismith in 1880.

Approach
It is best ascended from Bealach Harta, see Route 78.

a) **North-East Ridge Grade 2 ***
Start a short distance above Bealach Harta just left of some large boulders. Ascend broken slabs for some distance. Much variation is possible. Scramble up a steeper rock band near the right edge. Pleasant slabs and easier ground soon lead to the summit. There is a steep drop on the south-west side.

b) **South Flank Grade 2**
From the central/north gap the easiest option is to follow a ledge which curves round the right-hand (southern) side of the peak to join the north-east ridge some distance below the summit.

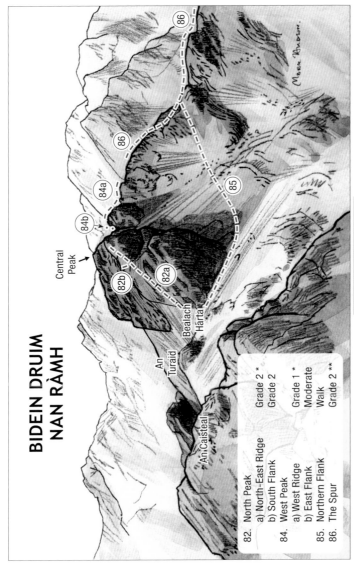

BIDEIN DRUIM
NAN RÀMH

CENTRAL CUILLIN

Meall Rudha

86

86

84a

84b

85

Central
Peak →

82b

82a

An
Turaid

Bealach
Hàrta

An Caisteal

82.	North Peak	
	a) North-East Ridge	Grade 2 *
	b) South Flank	Grade 2
84.	West Peak	
	a) West Ridge	Grade 1 *
	b) East Flank	Moderate
85.	Northern Flank	Walk
86.	The Spur	Grade 2 **

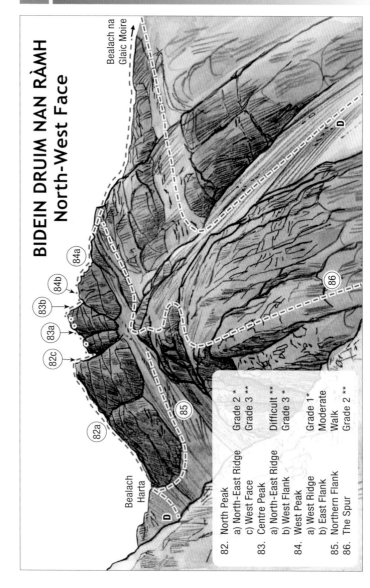

BIDEIN DRUIM NAN RÀMH
North-West Face

Bealach na Glaic Moire

Bealach Harta

82.	North Peak	
	a) North-East Ridge	Grade 2 *
	c) West Face	Grade 3 **
83.	Centre Peak	
	a) North-East Ridge	Difficult **
	b) West Flank	Grade 3 *
84.	West Peak	
	a) West Ridge	Grade 1*
	b) East Flank	Moderate
85.	Northern Flank	Walk
86.	The Spur	Grade 2 **

c) **West Face   Grade 3 ****

A harder and much more direct alternative from the gap is to follow a narrow ledge which spirals up leftwards along a cone-sheet. Then climb much steeper rocks on the west face (Grade 3) to finish right by the summit.

83 Central Peak   Grade 3 * or Difficult **

W/C Gap Alt 826m; C/N Gap Alt 823m   Map p191   Diagram p194

This is the highest (869m) and most difficult of the three peaks. It was first climbed by Lawrence Pilkington, Hulton and Walker in 1883.

a) **North-East Ridge   Difficult ****

This side of the peak is the most testing part of the traverse. A steep face rears up from the gap below the North Peak. Avoid this by a short overhanging wall further left. This is climbed by making a very long step left from a slab, using handholds at full stretch (crux) – rather stiff for Difficult. Slant further up left up rock steps before cutting back hard right on easier slabs. (Many parties abseil this section in descent.)

Move round to the right of a tiny top and reach a small gap. Traverse left slightly and climb Moderate slabs via a small overlap and a crevice. At the top, cross to the right side of a crest. (Many parties also abseil this section in descent.) Now follow a ledge leftwards more easily to cracked blocks forming the summit. There are fine views from the tiny summit.

b) **West Flank   Grade 3 ***

From the gigantic boulder called the 'Bridge Rock' in the west/central gap move up a short distance then traverse right on a narrow ledge, descending very slightly at first. When the angle above relents slightly climb up again. Cut back hard left on a ledge, and ascend a prominent dyke chimney (crux).

Move slightly left then trend right. Ascend a crack between two blocks to reach the summit. The easiest descent from here is to return the same way.

CENTRAL CUILLIN

84 West Peak   Grade 1 * or Moderate

(NG 455 239)   Alt 815m   Map p191   Diagram p194

This is the least interesting of the three peaks. Its summit is a massive boss (847m) sitting on a cone-sheet.

Approach

From Bealach na Glaic Moire (see p203) follow an easy section of broad ridge as far as a steepening. Then either traverse left for some distance to join the ridge from Sgùrr an Fheadain (Route 86), or ascend a basalt staircase more directly to a broad shoulder with fine views.

a) **West Ridge   Grade 1 ***

From the broad shoulder follow the crest of the ridge easily at first. Eventually scramble up an obvious orange-coloured dyke just left of the crest – the upper basalt staircase. The boss forming the very summit of the peak gives a short scramble, but the only way off is by descending the same way. The continuation to the Central Peak descends slabs immediately to the south.

Peter Duggan ascends the upper 'basalt staircase' on the West Ridge (Grade 1), West Peak, Bidein Druim nan Ràmh

*Peter Duggan tackles the crux moves above the Bridge Rock on
the East Flank (Moderate) of the West Peak, Bidein Druim nan Ràmh*

b) East Flank Moderate
Start from the enormous jammed boulder in the west/central gap called the Bridge Rock. Make some awkward moves out of the gap on poor handholds (hard in descent). Continue up slabs and pass to the left of the summit boss to reach easy ground.

85 Northern Flank 700m
(NG 455 241) Alt 750m Map p191 Diagrams pp193 & 194
It is possible to avoid the intricacies of this triple peak by cutting round scree and broken rocks on its northern flank.

Approach
Start from either Bealach na Glaic Moire on the west side or Bealach Harta on the east. The way is easier to find when travelling west from Bealach Harta.

The Route
From Bealach na Glaic Moire follow the broad ridge easily in a north-easterly direction. On meeting steeper ground traverse round leftwards to reach the crest of the ridge from Sgùrr an Fheadain (780m).

Descend the ridge to a slight neck (750m). Then turn sharp right and slant down across a scree slope. Gullies can be seen above leading to the gaps between the triple peaks. (Both main gullies can be ascended without undue difficulty, though the scree in the west/central gully is very loose.) Continue across the scree slop descending to a low point of 720m. Then continue below the steep north wall and ascend to regain the ridge at Bealach Harta.

SGÙRR AN FHEADAIN 688m

(NG 452 245) Map p191

This peak lies on a side ridge which divides Coire an Tairneilear and Coire a' Mhadaidh. It takes its name from a prominent gully, Waterpipe Gully, which cleaves the ridge at its north-western end. This dogleg gully is a conspicuous feature when descending the road into Glen Brittle.

86 The Spur Grade 2 **
(NG 450 250) Alt 300m Map p191 Diagram p199
This outing has some grand situations, although the rock on the crest could be better. Climbers may wish to combine this route with a traverse of Bidein Druim nan Ràmh.

Approach
Begin from a small car park in Glen Brittle and start down the path to Sligachan (Route 52), but after a short distance take the right fork which descends to the floor of the glen. Follow the path all the way up to Coire na Creiche (as for Route 76). Continue to where the old path from Bealach a' Mhaim crosses the Allt Coire an Tairneilear. Take this fainter path to the right and soon head up to the slabby rocks forming the left-hand toe of the ridge.

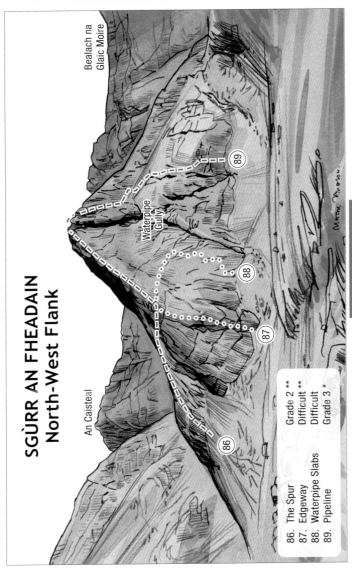

SGÙRR AN FHEADAIN
North-West Flank

An Caisteal

Bealach na
Glaic Moire

Waterpipe
Gully

86. The Spur   Grade 2 **
87. Edgeway   Difficult **
88. Waterpipe Slabs Difficult
89. Pipeline   Grade 3 *

The Route

Scramble pleasantly up sound rock with numerous cone-sheets. Reach a broad terrace, then head hard right on a path across the scree. Ascend near a prominent rowan tree to gain the crest of the north-west ridge.

Follow the crest of the ridge more or less directly. Short sections of scrambling give interest from time to time. The upper section of Waterpipe Gully can be seen on the right higher up. Eventually the ridge starts to ease off slightly. There are fine views of the imposing north-east face of Sgùrr a' Mhadaidh from the summit.

Move onto the right-hand side of the ridge to descend from the summit and scramble down slightly broken rocks to a dip in the ridge. There are ways off from here into the corries on either side. However, it is preferable to continue along a most enjoyable stretch of ridge.

From a small neck it is possible to traverse hard left on scree beneath Bidein Druim nan Ràmh and ascend to Bealach Harta. Otherwise ascend an easier crest trending slightly right to reach the main ridge.

It is only a short distance up the ridge to the West Peak of Bidein Druim nan Ràmh. If the traverse of that peak is too daunting, scramble down rocks to the right and continue more easily to Bealach na Glaic Moire. Then descend into Coire a' Mhadaidh (see Route 90).

87 Edgeway   Difficult   **
(NG 449 249)   Alt 300m   Map p191   Diagram p199

This route makes a superb direct start to the previous route. It is on magnificently rough rock. It was first climbed by Clive Rowland in 1980.

Approach

Approach from Glen Brittle as for the previous route. A more direct line can be taken across the moor from a bend in the river. Head for the rocks well left of Waterpipe Gully. Start at the foot of a faint gully on the front of the buttress, known as Spur Gully, which has a mossy wall to its right.

The Route

Scramble up rocks slightly right of the gully/groove line to reach the left-hand end of a grassy terrace. Move left and climb a steep groove to reach a ledge below a rightward slanting crack. Slant up left along a cone-sheet to reach a recess with several rowan trees. Climb slightly steeper rocks immediately right of the narrow gully, using a foothold in the gully at one point.

The rocks then lean back slightly and a more interesting section of the gully can be seen slanting left above. Do not try to force a way up straight ahead. Instead, traverse part-way along a ledge to the right and feel around for good holds on an overhanging wall. Climb this (crux) and continue delicately up slabs. Slant right to rock with white veining, and shortly after reach a ledge with a groove above.

Traverse left a short distance and climb a slab, then move back right, before slanting left up a groove. Continue more easily to join the previous route.

CENTRAL CUILLIN

*Peter Duggan on The Spur (Grade 2), visiting the summit of
Sgùrr an Fheadain, with Bidein Druim nan Ràmh in the distance*

88 Waterpipe Slabs   Difficult
(NG 449 249)   Alt 300m   Map p191   Diagram p199

This climb finds a way up the rather complex ground immediately left of Waterpipe Gully. The original route hereabouts was graded Hard Severe, but with good route-finding a significantly easier way can be found.

Approach

Start at an apron of slabs to the right of a large vertical wall and a short distance left of Waterpipe Gully.

The Route

Climb the slabs moving to the left edge near the top and so gain a grass ledge. Traverse hard right below a steep wall and descend slightly to reach a groove with a crack at the back. Ascend the groove with interest and continue to slightly easier ground. Climb up a chimney/groove and at the top make a very delicate traverse right (crux). Go round the corner and make an awkward step down to gain a prominent slab. Make some very delicate moves up the slab and traverse right at the top. Continue up grooves, and bridge up a steeper section before the climbing gradually eases.

Ascend slabs rightwards and continue up a grassy ramp to a slight crest. Descend slightly until a prominent grassy ramp can be found slanting back left. Start up this until the way on looks too hard, then traverse horizontally left and follow a parallel ramp-line trending left to the crest of the buttress.

89 Pipeline   Grade 3   *
(NG 448 246)   Alt 310m   Map p191   Diagram p199

This route finds a way up the rocks to the right of Waterpipe Gully. The upper section is fairly committing and requires good route-finding skills. It is at the upper limit of its grade.

Approach

Approach from Glen Brittle by the path to Coire na Creiche. Cross the main river near a bend, and head directly for Waterpipe Gully. Move across to the rock apron on the right-hand side of the gully. Start halfway between a central weakness and the right-hand end.

The Route

Scramble up pleasant slabs for some distance. Slant left from a grassy groove to find a more interesting way up steeper rocks. Continue more easily. Scramble up slabby rocks trending slightly left.

Ascend a dyke staircase through a slightly steeper section. When this becomes grassy, continue for a short distance before traversing out left. Follow a cone-sheet further left and reach the crest of a rib with a grassy gully on its left-hand side. Scramble up this very pleasant rib for some distance. At the top, avoid a block by moving round onto the left-hand flank overlooking the gully. Soon break out onto an extensive scree slope.

The upper section of the route is harder and more serious. Those having second thoughts can escape rightwards at this point. Head up and slightly left to a broad shoulder. Ascend a grassy weakness leading right. This narrows slightly at one point. Then make a very long traverse left in a much more serious position. Weave a way up to reach an alcove with a big slabby wall (wet?) on its left-hand side. Move right and pull up onto a blocky rib. Move right again into a recess and from a chockstone make a tricky step up to reach an easier gully above. Jink back left onto the rib. Weave to and fro to find the best way.

At another alcove climb a big step on the left and stride up and right to exit. Follow a left-slanting weakness rather than a chossy dyke/gully on the right. Leave it by stepping up and left. Continue over big blocks which lead back to the right-hand gully line. Climb a very awkward steep final runnel on its right-hand side.

Easier scrambling and walking for some distance leads to a minor top above Waterpipe Gully. Reach the summit of Sgùrr an Fheadain shortly after and continue as for Route 86.

BEALACH NA GLAIC MOIRE SLABS

CENTRAL CUILLIN

(NG 451 241) Map p191

At the head of Coire a' Mhadaidh there is an easy pass over to Coruisk called Bealach na Glaic Moire (760m). Directly below this pass on the Glen Brittle side there are some impressive slabs split by three gullies. The normal way to Bealach na Glaic Moire ascends loose scree to the left of these slabs, then cuts a long way right above the slabs on a slanting terrace. However, the three main sections of slab all offer more direct and interesting ways of reaching the bealach.

 90 North Buttress   Grade 2   *
(NG 451 241)   Alt 520m   Map p191   Diagram p204

The narrow left-hand slab is bounded on its right by North Gully. A narrow chimney (Stag Gully) splits the left-hand half of the buttress.

Approach

Approach from Glen Brittle as for the previous route. To reach Coire a' Mhadaidh, ascend a shallow scoop with a stream some distance to the right of Waterpipe Gully. Slant right and break out onto a broad shoulder. (This is a much easier route than one further right by a gorge.) Then follow a faint path which slants up left towards the scree slope left of the slabs.

The Route

The lower rocks of the buttress are fairly easy-angled, and some debris lies on ledges. When the rocks steepen, trend slightly right towards North Gully. Then cut back left to the buttress crest. Follow this, with much variation possible, to a prominent terrace.

Slant hard right along the terrace for 250 metres to reach Bealach na Glaic

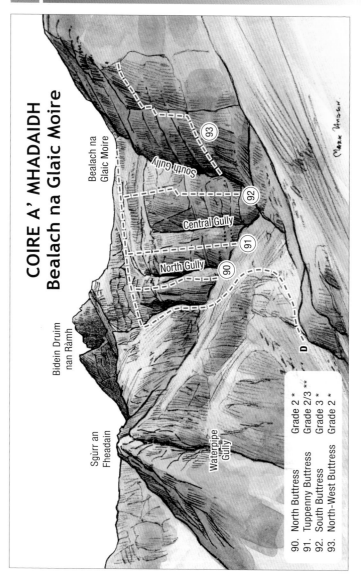

COIRE A' MHADAIDH
Bealach na Glaic Moire

Bidein Druim nan Ràmh

Sgùrr an Fheadain

Bealach na Glaic Moire

South Gully

Central Gully

North Gully

Waterpipe Gully

90. North Buttress   Grade 2 *
91. Tuppenny Buttress   Grade 2/3 **
92. South Buttress   Grade 3 *
93. North-West Buttress   Grade 2 *

Moire, which has superb views down to Loch Coruisk. When returning along the terrace be sure to continue all the way to the angle by the Sgùrr an Fheadain ridge before scrambling down to reach the scree gully which leads into Coire a' Mhadaidh.

91 Tuppenny Buttress Grade 2/3 **
(NG 451 241) Alt 500m Map p191 Diagram p204

This is the central buttress, bounded by North Gully on the left and Central Gully on the right. It gives a most enjoyable scramble. In 1997 Willie Jeffrey found two King George V pennies part-way up this route. They were half buried in grit on a minuscule ledge. One was dated 1915 – the same year that Bishop, Fraser and Hirst made an attempt on Central Gully.

Approach
Approach from Glen Brittle as for the previous route. Ascend sharp scree and grass to the foot of the buttress.

The Route
Follow easy slabs to a grass terrace. Scramble up the steeper slabs above, weaving to and fro to find the easiest line. Sometimes dyke staircases offer the best way through steeper sections. The angle gradually eases as height is gained. Eventually join the terrace leading to Bealach na Glaic Moire.

92 South Buttress Grade 3 *
(NG 450 240) Alt 500m Map p191 Diagram p204

This is the longest and broadest of the three buttresses. The route is low in its grade and open to much variation. It is bounded on the right by South Gully, one of the best Severe gullies in the Cuillin.

Approach
Approach from Glen Brittle as for Route 90. Follow the stream up the floor of the corrie towards South Gully.

The Route
Scramble up a small wedge of slabby steps just to the left of the mouth of South Gully. Then continue up slabs to a sloping grassy terrace. Just to the right at this point there is a gigantic pointed block in the bed of South Gully.

There are various ways on from here. A slabby buttress, slightly to the right and quite close to South Gully, gives some enjoyable scrambling. Cross grass and scramble up rocks at the right-hand end of an extensive rock band. Move left onto a broad section of easier ground below the main section of buttress.

Weave a way up keeping a central position on the buttress. Large slabby blocks lie on the buttress further right. Reach a tiny grass ledge near a small muddy alcove with a distinctive green rear wall. Move up slightly right and follow a small grassy ledge rightwards.

A delightful section of padding, just to the left of a dyke, gives some of the best scrambling on the route. Move right, over a much narrower section

CENTRAL CUILLIN

of the dyke, and ascend to the right of a block. Follow a dyke and the rocks to its left. Then continue more easily to a terrace.

Move slightly right to find a way through the steep final tier. Trend right to reach Bealach na Glaic Moire.

SGÙRR A' MHADAIDH 918m

(NG 446 235) Map p191

This magnificent mountain has four tops on its summit ridge. The highest is the fourth or western top which runs off at a right-angle to the other three. The complex north face is dark and forbidding. It is crossed by several major slanting breaks formed by cone-sheets. Left of centre it harbours a huge scree-filled recess known as the Amphitheatre.

93 North-West Buttress & the Upper Rakes   Grade 2   *
(NG 450 240)   Alt 500m   Map p191   Diagram p207

The impressive tower-like buttress to the left of the Amphitheatre is known as North-West Buttress. It was first ascended by Collie in 1896, but it gives a rather disappointing climb (Very Difficult). However, various scrambling routes can be fashioned up the face hereabouts.

It should be borne in mind that continuing along the summit ridge from the tops of the various finishes may involve some Difficult climbing (see Route 95). They offer possible escape routes off the ridge.

Approach
Start from upper Glen Brittle, and reach Coire a' Mhadaidh by the depression to the right of Waterpipe Gully as for the previous route.

The Route
There is a gully on the left-hand side of North-West Buttress. This route starts up a buttress to the left of this gully. Follow the base of a big slabby face leftwards to the mouth of South Gully. Ascend a grassy groove just right of, and parallel to, the start of South Gully. Then scramble hard right up a slabby break to reach the crest of the buttress. Ascend the buttress on excellent rock, with scrambling to suit all tastes. Then, at a steeper section, move into the bouldery gully on the right.

a) **Left-hand Rake   Grade 1/2**

This is the least interesting way. Continue up the gully, and scramble up a groove right of the main gully to reach a shoulder below a more open scree slope. Ignore the first scree ledge which cuts rightwards to the crest of North-West Buttress. (It leads to a tricky Difficult nose.) Instead ascend scree for some distance, then cut hard right along the next scree shelf. This leads across the easy upper section of North-West Buttress and continues across the face to join the crest of the main ridge between the first and second tops.

b) **Upper Rake – Superior Finish   Grade 2   ***

Instead of continuing up the gully, slant right on steep scree to gain a narrow

SGÙRR A' MHADAIDH
North Face

93. North-West Buttress — Grade 1/2
    a) Left-hand Rake — Grade 2 *
    b) Upper Rake – Superior Finish — Grade 1
    c) Upper Rake – Standard Finish — Moderate **
94. Foxes' Rake — Difficult **
95. Traverse of the Four Tops
97. North-West Ridge — Grade 2/3 **

rake which leads round onto the crest of North-West Buttress. This is a very fine viewpoint. Directly above is the tower-like section which gives the crux of the North-West Buttress climb. (It was first climbed direct at Very Difficult standard by W.W. King in 1901.)

Go round the crest of the buttress and continue to a small shoulder. Then make a slanting descent, in a spectacular position, to reach the floor of the Amphitheatre. The start of the Upper Rake is on the opposite wall. It is possible to reach this point by ascending the Amphitheatre from directly below. (Scramble up the left-hand side of a rock band at its base – well above the start of Foxes' Rake.)

Make a steep move to get established on the Upper Rake, then continue round to the right more easily. Soon emerge onto a huge scree-covered terrace.

Curve round to the left and head for a gully breaching the rocks above. Ascend this, circumventing chockstones on the left wall. Ascend a rib on the left, and a short distance above head hard right along a narrow rake. Finish on the summit of the third top.

c) Upper Rake – Standard Finish   Grade 1
Instead of heading for the gully breaching the upper rocks, trend rightwards up loose and tedious scree for some distance. Emerge on the ridge at the dip between the third top and the main summit.

94 Foxes' Rake   Moderate   **
(NG 449 237)   Alt 640m   Map p191   Diagram p207

This is a superb way to the summit of Sgùrr a' Mhadaidh. It is a better outing than the Upper Rake, but harder. Although most of the route is scrambling, the crucial section is quite sustained and justifies the climbing grade. It would be difficult to reverse. The route is a natural drainage line, and is best avoided after wet weather. It was first ascended by Raeburn, Fraser & Russell in 1898.

Approach
Cross the stream in the floor of Coire a' Mhadaidh and ascend grass and slabs trending away from the stream. Head for the scree slope below the Amphitheatre. Ascend rocks left of the main gully then cross rightwards. Eventually reach a fairly obvious rightward-sloping glacis which leads onto the start of the route.

The Route
The initial section is mainly walking. Continue on clean easy-angled slabs – scarred in places by falling rocks. Reach a platform where a wall of rock blocks the line of the rake.

The next section is the crux. Move right and slant back left. Ascend a runnel, where the rocks are often wet. Climb up steeper rocks, then traverse right with sustained interest.

Continue right on easier slabby rocks, along a broader section of rake, for some distance. Eventually reach a slight shoulder.

It is possible to follow a much narrower continuation of the rake from here, but this ends on a very rickety arête. Instead, traverse horizontally a long way left, and scramble up slabby rocks to the right of a prominent chimney. Zigzag up for some distance and finish at a small step on the north-west ridge.

There is a nose of steep rock on the ridge above. Move to the right of this and at the first opportunity ascend the right-hand flank to regain the crest. Continue rightwards along the ridge and foot-traverse a cracked block to reach the summit of Sgùrr a' Mhadaidh.

The easiest way off is to descend the west face (Route 98) or the more popular south-west ridge to An Doras (Route 99). Climbers will prefer to traverse the four tops (Route 95) or descend the north-west ridge (Route 97).

95 Traverse of the Four Tops   Difficult ** *(NG 446 235)   Alt 918m   Map p191   Diagrams pp207 & 210*

The traverse of the complex summit ridge of Sgùrr a' Mhadaidh is one of the more demanding sections on the main ridge. It is best done from west to east (i.e. from fourth to first top), thereby allowing the difficult sections to be taken in ascent. The crux of the outing is a short climb on the western end of the second top.

Approach
The route is described starting from the fourth or main western summit. This is most usually reached by the south-west ridge from An Doras (Route 99).

The Route
Go north along the narrow crest until the ridge takes a dramatic turn to the east at a broad tower where the north-west ridge also joins. From a deep notch climb a steep wall (7m) to the top of the tower. Descend on the far side more easily. After another notch turn right and scramble down a long rib to the gap before the third top. There are excellent views of Coruisk from here. In dry conditions it is possible to cut the corner and avoid the tower by descending delicate slabs on the right-hand side of the crest. Cross a small gully and climb a short wall to gain the rib used by the normal way. This short-cut is harder than the normal way and unlikely to be any quicker.

The steep nose of the third top rears up from a dip in the ridge. There are two options here – both of Moderate grade. The popular way is to descend slightly to the right and then ascend slabby grooves on the right-hand flank back to the crest. However, confident climbers may prefer to scramble straight up from the dip and make a couple of steep moves just right of the crest. Then traverse across to the right. The difficulties then quickly ease and the summit of the third top is soon gained (894m).

A straightforward descent from the third top leads to a dip below a very steep wall guarding the second top. This marks the crux of the traverse and cannot be avoided. Start by moving to the left then slant back rightwards. Climb the steep final rocks directly by a couple of Difficult moves. Then continue more easily to the summit of the second top (887m).

SGÙRR A' MHADAIDH

Sgùrr nan Gillean

Bruach na Frithe

Coire an Uaigneis

Bealach na Glaic Moire

1st Top

2nd Top

3rd Top

Main Summit

An Doras

95. The Four Tops   Difficult **
99. South-West Ridge Grade 2/3 *

Peter Duggan approaches the crux moves on the south-west face of the Second Top (Difficult), Sgùrr a' Mhadaidh

From the summit descend easily at first before reaching a deep gully where a narrow dyke crosses the ridge. Move over to the right before cutting back left to gain the bed of the gully. Then ascend a steep wall on the other side. A short distance along the ridge there is a good bivouac ledge where the uppermost rake joins the crest (see previous route). Continue pleasantly to the summit of the first top (896m).

A relatively straightforward descent from the first (and last!) top leads down to a steep final band of overlapping slabs. Climb down these slanting diagonally leftwards. Then cut to the left side of the crest and follow an easy scree path down to the broad flattening of Bealach na Glaic Moire.

SGÙRR THUILM 879m

(NG 438 242) Map p191

The scree-ridden peak of Sgùrr Thuilm is linked by a delightful narrow ridge to the very fine north-west ridge of Sgùrr a' Mhadaidh.

 96 Traverse via Black Slab   Grade 3 or Moderate   *
(NG 429 237)   Alt 390m   Map p191   Diagram p213

Although it is possible to ascend the south-western flank of this hill without the need for scrambling it is more entertaining to start by scaling the crag at its base – called South-West Buttress.

Approach
An approach is normally made by the path to Coire a' Ghreadaidh from the Youth Hostel in Glen Brittle. However, a shorter, more direct line can be taken from higher up Glen Brittle by ascending the steep grassy hillside from a car park by the road bridge over the River Brittle (GR 417 246).

The easier-angled left-hand face of the crag is known as Black Slab.

The Route
Black Slab is open to variation and two different starts can be used. A prominent left-facing ramp/groove is a useful landmark near the start.

The easiest way starts just to the right of a heathery recess. Slant diagonally rightwards across a fairly clean section of slab to reach the top of the groove.

a) Direct Start   Moderate   *
A slightly harder and better option starts a short distance to the right at a shallow alcove. Climb sound rock on good holds to gain the bottom of the main groove feature and follow this to join the easier start.

Continue more or less directly. Pass a long headwall at its left-hand end and soon gain easier but slightly looser ground.

Ascend the long slope above for several hundred metres to the fine summit of Sgùrr Thuilm. Scramble down the delightful south-east ridge (Grade 1) to the dip at the start of the north-west ridge of Sgùrr a' Mhadaidh. Although it is possible to escape into the corries on either side, the next route makes a natural continuation.

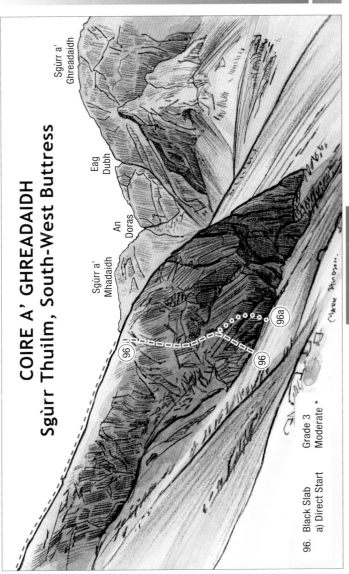

COIRE A' GHREADAIDH
Sgùrr Thuilm, South-West Buttress

Sgùrr a' Ghreadaidh

Eag Dubh

An Doras

Sgùrr a' Mhadaidh

96. Black Slab   Grade 3
a) Direct Start   Moderate *

Andrew Wielochowski on the Slab Variation (Moderate),
North-West (Thuilm) Ridge, Sgùrr a' Mhadaidh

SGÙRR A' MHADAIDH   918m

(NG 446 235)   Map p191

97   North-West (Thuilm) Ridge   Grade 2/3   **
(NG 443 237)   Alt 747m   Map p191   Diagram pp207, 216 & 218

Despite the rather devious approaches, this ridge gives a very enjoyable route to the main summit of Sgùrr a' Mhadaidh.

Approach
The previous route gives the best approach, but a popular alternative is to gain the upper left-hand lobe of Coire a' Ghreadaidh – called Coire an Dorais – then traverse scree leftwards from below An Doras. The start can also be reached from the Coire a' Mhadaidh side.

The Route
Scramble up the crest of the ridge following the natural line. Eventually reach a large slab situated on the left side of a prominent wide chimney.

**a) Slab Variation   Moderate **

Traverse rightwards across the slab. This feels a little intimidating although the rock is excellent. Then scramble up easier grooves for some distance.

    An alternative way, more in keeping with the general standard of the outing, moves left to the buttress edge a little earlier. Cross over to the left-hand side of the crest for a short section and ascend slightly awkward rocks past a recess before returning to the right-hand side.

    The remainder of the ridge is fairly straightforward apart from one steep step on the crest. Eventually the impressive indent of Deep Gash Gully can be viewed on the left-hand side of the crest. Reach a small flattening which marks the exit from Foxes' Rake (Route 94). Move slightly right and scramble up by a chimney/groove, then slant rightwards on ledges to the summit. Cross a cracked block on the crest to reach the summit cairn.

98   West Face   Grade 1/2
(NG 444 235)   Alt 670m   Map p191   Diagram p218

This face lies between the North-West Ridge of Sgùrr a' Mhadaidh and the scree gully that leads to An Doras. It may not be a very attractive line of ascent, but it offers the easiest way off the mountain.

Approach
Reach Coire an Dorais by the path from the Youth Hostel in Glen Brittle. Instead of continuing up the scree gully to An Doras itself, head left in the direction of the dip on the Thuilm ridge.

The Route
Ascend scree leftwards until it is possible to find an easy way back right to gain a higher scree slope. Then slant a long way left at first on scree. Continue on broken rocks to gain the easy upper section of the North-West Ridge.

SGÙRR A' MHADAIDH

93.   NW Buttress
    b) Upper Rake – Superior Finish   Grade 2 *
96.   South-East Ridge, Sgùrr Thuilm   Grade 1 *
97.   North-West Ridge   Grade 2/3 **
    a) Slab Variation   Moderate **
99.   South-West Ridge   Grade 2/3 *

99 South-West Ridge via An Doras   Grade 2/3 *
(NG 446 234) Alt 847m   Map p191   Diagram pp216 &218

This is the standard way for Munro-baggers to conquer the peak.

Approach

Leave the road directly opposite the Glen Brittle Youth Hostel and follow a path up the south bank of the Allt a' Choire Ghreadaidh. This stream has a gorge in its lower reaches and a delightful waterslide higher up.

To reach Coire an Dorais slant up left following a scenic section of tributary stream by its steep west bank. Then head east and cross a slabby rise before following the bed of a gully. When the stream disappears, ascend boulders and scree trending slightly left. Then scramble easily up scree and slabby rocks in a gully to reach An Doras *(the door)*. This dip is the lowest point on the main ridge between Sgùrr a' Mhadaidh and Sgùrr a' Ghreadaidh.

The Route

The main difficulty on this route is the short section of scrambling out of the north side of An Doras. Fairly straightforward, pleasant scrambling then leads to the inclined slab forming the summit. The easiest way down from here is to descend the previous route (Route 98). Confident scramblers may prefer to descend the North-West Ridge (Route 97) and traverse Sgùrr Thuilm.

SGÙRR A' GHREADAIDH 973m

(NG 445 231) Map p191

This majestic mountain dominates the head of Coire Uisge. Its superb summit ridge forms one of the most impressive and committing parts of the Cuillin main ridge. It includes a tricky section of arête linking the south top with the main summit. A subsidiary peak, called Sgùrr Eadar da Choire, lies on its western flank.

The summit is most easily gained from the north by either An Doras (847m) or the slightly higher cleft called Eag Dubh (881m). Neither of these two gaps can be regarded as passes over the main ridge. Both are readily accessible from the west, but the gullies on the east (Coruisk) side involve at least Moderate and Difficult pitches respectively.

In Ashley Abraham's book *Rock Climbing in Skye* the first ascent of this peak is credited to John Mackenzie and Wilberforce Newton Tribe in 1870 when they were aged 14 and 15 respectively. No other source has come to light to support this claim, so it is perhaps debatable.

100 North-North-East Ridge Grade 2 * or 3 *
(NG 446 234) Alt 847m   Map p192   Diagram p218

This is the easiest way to reach the main north summit. Although most of the route is straightforward the wall out of An Doras is quite intimidating, particularly in descent. A very deep cleft a little further to the south called

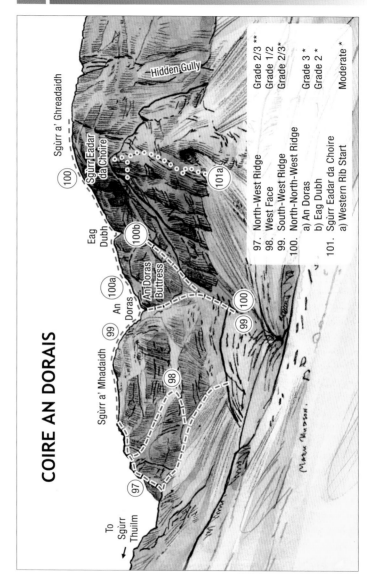

COIRE AN DORAIS

To Sgùrr Thuilim

Sgùrr a' Mhadaidh

An Doras

Eag Dubh

Sgùrr Eadar da Chòire

Sgùrr a' Ghreadaidh

Hidden Gully

97. North-West Ridge — Grade 2/3 **
98. West Face — Grade 1/2
99. South-West Ridge — Grade 2/3 *
100. North-North-West Ridge
   a) An Doras — Grade 3 *
   b) Eag Dubh — Grade 2 *
101. Sgùrr Eadar da Chòire
   a) Western Rib Start — Moderate *

Eag Dubh offers an alternative option. For those nervous about reversing the moves into An Dorus perhaps the best combination is to go up from An Dorus and descend by Eag Dubh. Both options are described.

Approach

Start from the Youth Hostel in Glen Brittle as for the previous route. From the floor of Coire an Dorais ascend by a stream on the right-hand side of the corrie. Continue up a bouldery depression making for a prominent scree gully which slants slightly left to An Doras – the low point on the skyline.

The Route

a) **An Doras**   **Grade 3**   *

The trade route. Ascend the scree gully by a well-worn route. The tricky south wall of An Doras is best climbed a short distance down from the gap on the Glen Brittle side. Ascend a ramp slanting leftwards to reach the top of the wall. Other ways can also be found, but all of them are hard to do in reverse. Cut over the crest by a dyke and ascend some slabs on the Coruisk side. Soon reach the dip of Eag Dubh, which has an impressive narrow cleft on the Glen Brittle side.

b) **Eag Dubh**   **Grade 2**   *

This feature is well named. The cleft itself has huge steep walls on either side and is a sombre place. It gives a very different experience to An Doras.

Instead of taking the obvious scree gully which slants slightly leftwards to An Doras, make for an obvious break to the right of a large buttress (An Doras Buttress). Ascend fairly steeply up scree and broken ground. Continue up the bed of the narrow cleft above – mainly on scree with only minor rock steps.

Once at the gap descend slightly on the Coruisk side, and then slant back right up slabs. It is easy then for some distance. A large wall marks the start of a feature called 'The Wart'. This can be outflanked with surprising ease on the right, and the main north summit is reached soon after. This is the highest of the central Cuillin summits and a wonderful viewpoint for the whole ridge.

The continuation across to the south top and down the south ridge (Route 102) is quite sustained and committing, and there are no easy ways off until Sgùrr na Banachdaich is reached. So the simplest descent is to return the same way. Confident scramblers may prefer to regain Coire an Dorais by reversing the top part of the next route instead.

101 West Flank via Sgùrr Eadar da Choire   Grade 3

(NG 444 234)   Alt 700m   Map p191   Diagram pp218 & 220

The small peak of Sgùrr Eadar da Choire is linked to the upper rocks of Sgùrr a' Ghreadaidh by a very sharp arête. This separates Coire an Dorais from the main part of Coire a' Ghreadaidh.

The most direct approach ascends a blocky rib (Moderate) on the west face a short distance to the left of a prominent cave/recess. The normal start continues beyond the west face and slants up a terrace on the north flank. The top part of the route can also be gained from the bottom of Eag Dubh.

CENTRAL CUILLIN

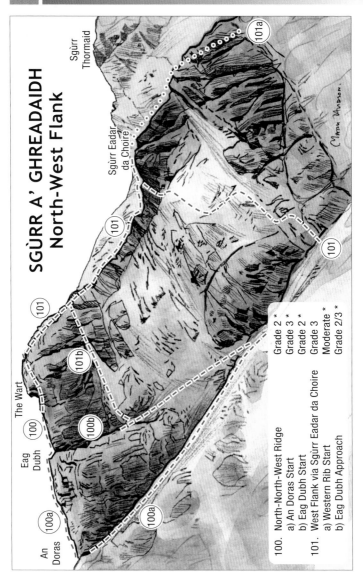

SGÙRR A' GHREADAIDH
North-West Flank

Sgùrr Thormaid

Sgùrr Eadar da Choire

The Wart

Eag Dubh

An Doras

100. North-North-West Ridge — Grade 2 *
    a) An Doras Start — Grade 3 *
    b) Eag Dubh Start — Grade 2 *
101. West Flank via Sgùrr Eadar da Choire — Grade 3
    a) Western Rib Start — Moderate *
    b) Eag Dubh Approach — Grade 2/3 *

Approach
Start from the Youth Hostel in Glen Brittle as for Route 99. Either head up to the cave at the base of the west face for the much harder direct start or continue round by the stream into Coire an Dorais proper.

The Route
Ascend a bouldery gully as if heading for the scree gully to An Doras. Go past a narrow right-trending rake. Just before a craggy wall develops on the south side of the gully, zigzag up broken rocks to reach a scree terrace parallel to the rake. Ascend this a short distance, then cut up left to a higher slope. Scramble up through a rock step then trend right over boulders quite easily for some distance. Ascend a recess to a gain the ridge, then turn right and soon reach the twin tops forming the summit of Sgùrr Eadar da Choire.

Return from the summit and continue along the ridge. Staying on the arête proves fairly nerve-racking. Some big blocks seem rather suspect and the situations are exciting. (The whole ridge can be avoided without difficulty on the left flank if necessary.) Take two minor tops as directly as possible, but pass to the right of a gendarme. The ridge eases slightly before it joins with the upper part of the face.

The start of the final section is marked by a cone-sheet which slants up from left to right. Move right and ascend a gully formed by a dyke for 7m, then use the rocks mainly on the left side. Exit from the gully and continue more easily. Zigzag for some distance and join the summit ridge at the southern end of The Wart. Turn right and soon reach the summit.

a) Western Rib Start   Moderate   *
(NG 441 233)   Alt 650m   Map p191   Diagram pp218 & 220
A more direct approach to the summit of Sgùrr Eadar da Choire can be made up the western face. A number of different lines are possible. However, much of the rock is poor, and the way described is perhaps the best option.

Near the right-hand end of the face there is a prominent cave/recess and a short distance further left there is a blocky rib with a gully immediately to its left. The initial rocks are a little steep so bypass these on the right-hand side. Ascend a narrow dyke for a short distance until it is possible to move leftwards onto the crest of the rib. Follow this with interest, weaving to and fro to find the easiest way. Cross a surprising slabby recess. Continue by keeping to the crest where possible. Reach more broken ground with a steeper section of ridge above. By heading right at this point it is possible to reach a terrace which slopes down into Coire a' Ghreadaidh near Hidden Gully.

The way on to the summit of Sgùrr Eadar da Choire is a little intimidating and if the rock is also found a little unnerving it is possible to traverse leftwards at this point to join the normal start.

b) Eag Dubh Approach   Grade 2/3   *
The final part of the route can be reached, perhaps more enjoyably(!), by following an easy rake rightwards from the foot of Eag Dubh. The traverse is little more than walking. The upper part of the face – described above – gives pleasant scrambling (Grade 2/3).

Looking over the Three Teeth to the twin summits of Sgùrr a' Ghreadaidh

102 South Ridge via Sgùrr Thormaid   Grade 3 ***
(NG 440 226)   Alt 888m   Map p191   Diagram p224

The traverse of this ridge is one of the finest outings in the Cuillin, especially when it is made part of a round of Coire a' Ghreadaidh. It is exposed and committing, and has sensational views. The scrambling is sustained but not unduly difficult. The hardest part is the section linking the two summits.

Approach

Although the route as described starts from Bealach Thormaid, the only easy way of gaining this dip on the ridge from the Glen Brittle side is by first traversing the summit of Sgùrr na Banachdaich (see Route 107). A much harder alternative is to ascend Route 105. An easy scree slope gives access via a forked gully on the Coruisk side.

The Route

The first section from Bealach Thormaid follows the south ridge of Sgùrr Thormaid. It is a common mistake to go too far left part-way up this section and end up above a huge drop on the west face. From the bealach negotiate some minor pinnacles mainly on the left, but after this it is important to take a direct line up steeper rocks on the crest slightly over to the right. Continue up the ridge, and soon reach the summit of Sgùrr Thormaid (*Norman's Peak*). This attractive little peak (926m) was named in honour of Norman Collie.

Descend pleasant slabs just right of the crest. A short distance further on an extended group of pinnacles – **The Three Teeth** – can be ascended or traversed by short climbs of Difficult/Very Difficult standard. The simplest option, however, is to dodge this section by following a faint path on the right-hand (Coruisk) flank across rightward-sloping slabs. A short ascent at the end regains the crest. The Teeth can also be avoided without any great difficulty on the left (Glen Brittle) side.

Continue down the ridge to a broad dip at the start of the south-west ridge of Sgùrr a' Ghreadaidh. There are no easy ways of reaching this dip from the adjoining corries. There are good bivouac places here.

Follow the ridge, which becomes narrower and more exposed as height is gained. The scrambling is absorbing and the views superb. Eventually reach the south top (970m). The continuation to the main summit gives the trickiest part of the route. Descend an exposed section of arête to a dip, then ascend the other side slightly more easily. A steep nose can be taken direct or avoided by ledges on the left. Reach the main summit soon after.

The normal way on from here is to descend the north-north-east ridge past The Wart to An Doras (Route 100).

103 Diagonal Buttress   Grade 2 **
(NG 443 230)   Alt 700m   Map p191   Diagram p224

The main central section of Coire a' Ghreadaidh is one of the grandest corries in the Cuillin. Despite there being large areas of rock, with the exception of Hidden Gully Buttress, there are no distinguished rock climbs here.

CENTRAL CUILLIN

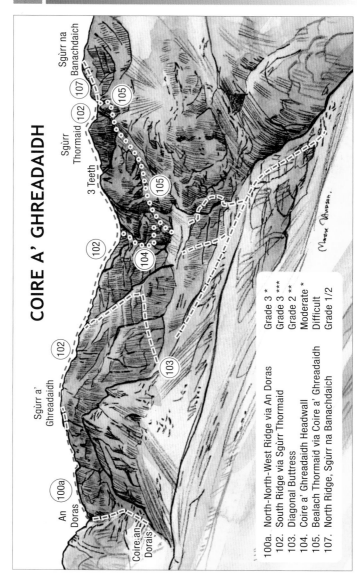

COIRE A' GHREADAIDH

Sgùrr a'
Ghreadaidh

An
Doras

Coire an
Dorais

Sgùrr
Thormaid

3 Teeth

Sgùrr na
Banachdaich

100a. North-North-West Ridge via An Doras — Grade 3 *
102. South Ridge via Sgùrr Thormaid — Grade 3 ***
103. Diagonal Buttress — Grade 2 **
104. Coire a' Ghreadaidh Headwall — Moderate *
105. Bealach Thormaid via Coire a' Ghreadaidh — Difficult
107. North Ridge, Sgùrr na Banachdaich — Grade 1/2

This route finds a surprisingly straightforward way up the big western face of the mountain. The continuation over the south top and main summit is slightly harder (Route 102). It can be combined with the north-north-west ridge (Route 100) to give an unusual and interesting traverse of the mountain.

Approach
From the Youth Hostel in Glen Brittle follow the path on the south side of the Allt a' Choire Ghreadaidh. The main corrie has three distinct levels. The lowest level is overlooked on its south side by the north-west face of An Diallaid (714m). Here the stream from Coire an Dorais joins with the stream from the main corrie.

Access to the middle level is up delightful slabs to the right of a stream and left of a deep gorge. Then slant left at first, before heading straight up to the left-hand side of the uppermost level of the corrie.

The route starts quite close to Hidden Gully Buttress (Very Difficult) at the left-hand end of the face. It then slants a long way right to gain the broad buttress situated immediately to the left of Diagonal Gully. This left-slanting, boulder-filled gully is guarded at the bottom by an extremely slippery scoop.

The Route
A long, narrow ledge formed by a cone-sheet offers the easiest way of gaining Diagonal Buttress. Follow the ledge easily at first. There is a slightly awkward step at one point, then cross a small recess marking the line of Vanishing Gully. Continue rightwards on a grassy ledge and eventually head upwards to break onto the crest of Diagonal Buttress.

Pleasant scrambling ensues for some distance up the broad crest of the buttress. There are some slightly steeper rock bands but generally it is relatively easy scrambling. The angle gradually eases and the ground becomes more broken. There are good views of the upper section of Diagonal Gully on the right, but this soon starts to peter out.

Much variation is possible high up, but continue easily in the same line until a short section of steeper crag is reached. Cross this from left to right and then shortly after gain the crest of the south ridge. Follow the ridge to the south top and continue to the main summit as for the previous route.

104 Coire a' Ghreadaidh Headwall   Moderate   *
(NG 441 228)   Alt 670m   Map p191   Diagram p224

This is not a very notable route, but it gives an excuse to visit a magnificent corrie. It is not a rock climb as such, although it does involve some Moderate moves and some difficult route finding.

Approach
Gain the middle level in the corrie as for the previous route. There are then three different ways of reaching the centre of the uppermost level. The easiest is to slant left for some distance up slabby rocks, before slanting back right. The most direct way is to ascend a steep tier of rock by a dyke just right of a

CENTRAL CUILLIN

stream. The third and most difficult option is to start further right and find a way up rocks to the right of a stream in a small gorge. Part-way up, cut hard left over the stream along a fairly obvious break.

The route starts on an apron of slabs right of centre. Diagonal Gully lies a little further to the left.

The Route
The slabs are best ascended starting from the bottom left-hand side and trending up right. The easiest line is not obvious and is likely to be Grade 3 with sections of Moderate. At the top, join a grassy terrace slanting up to the right.

Now cut hard left along a fairly obvious ledge and cross a small gully. Ascend rocks trending slightly left, then zigzag up easier ground for some distance. Either surmount a more difficult section by a chockstone, or avoid it on the left and then slant slightly right. Eventually trend slightly left and emerge at the broad dip between Sgùrr a' Ghreadaidh and Sgùrr Thormaid.

105 Bealach Thormaid via Coire a' Ghreadaidh   Difficult
(NG 441 228)   Alt 670m   Map p191   Diagram p224

This is not a particularly inviting way of reaching Bealach Thormaid but, like the previous route, it gives an excuse to visit this very impressive corrie. The main difficulties are concentrated in the final section of gully just below Bealach Thormaid itself.

Approach
Reach the apron of slabs in the uppermost level of Coire a' Ghreadaidh as for the previous route.

The Route
Start on the left, and find a way up the slabs as for the previous route. Then follow the obvious terrace slanting up to the right for some distance. Ascend steep, unstable scree towards the base of a very steep rock face. Then slant right slightly more easily below the face. Turn a corner and pass below a tiny cave. Continue traversing right and eventually reach a scree gully. A rib of rock separates a narrower chimney section on the left from the main gully on the right.

Ascend this right-hand gully easily at first. Where it gets narrower, bridge up on nightmarish, shattered rock and eventually exit by the left wall. Continue more easily to the narrow dip marking Bealach Thormaid (888m). A gully drops down the other side to Coruisk, and the rocks of Sgùrr na Banachdaich rise immediately to the south. Turn left to reach Sgùrr Thormaid (see Route 102).

106 An Diallaid: North Rib   Grade 2/3   **
(NG 434 231)   Alt 450m   Map p191   Diagram p227

This splendid rib gives an interesting way of approaching the middle level of Coire a' Ghreadaidh. The rock is mostly very good.

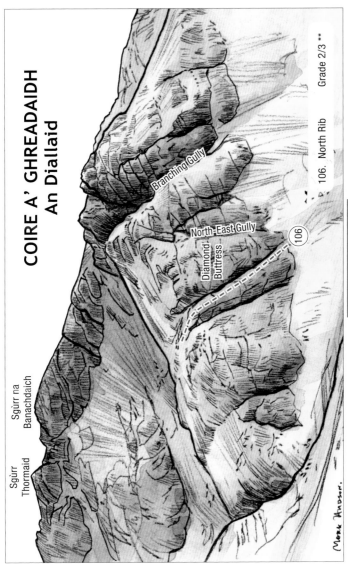

COIRE A' GHREADAIDH
An Diallaid

Sgùrr Thormaid

Sgùrr na Banachdaich

Branching Gully

North-East Gully

Diamond Buttress

106

106. North Rib   Grade 2/3 **

Approach
From the Youth Hostel in Glen Brittle follow the path on the south side of the Allt a' Choire Ghreadaidh to the lower level of Coire a' Ghreadaidh. Walk right to reach the foot of a well-defined rib more or less in the centre of the slabby north-west face of An Diallaid. It has a dyke gully just to its right.

The Route
Follow the rib as directly as possible staying fairly close to the gully on the right. Make a couple of moves almost in the gully at one point. Eventually traverse left for 6 metres away from the gully, and ascend big steps on the right side of a narrow runnel with clumps of grass. Bands of more angular, broken rock have to be treated carefully.

A slightly harder section involves first making a step up left onto a good foothold, with much more shattered rock further left. Then step back right onto a higher foot-ledge. Continue for some distance with the angle gradually easing. There is a fair amount of debris lying on the final section.

Traverse across for some distance to the middle level of Coire a' Ghreadaidh. Another option is to turn right and head uphill and weave a way through more difficult rocks (Moderate) to gain the eastern top of the three bumps forming the summit of An Diallaid (714m).

SGÙRR NA BANACHDAICH 965m

(NG 440 224) Map p191
The summit of Sgùrr na Banachdaich is a very fine viewpoint and the easiest summit on the main ridge accessible from Glen Brittle. The mountain's best feature is its south ridge. Its western ridge, which ends in a small top called Sgùrr nan Gobhar, is also worthwhile. It is the most westerly of all Munros.

107 North Ridge Grade 1/2
(NG 440 226) Alt 888m Map p191
This route has no special merit and is used merely as a link between Sgùrr Thormaid and Sgùrr na Banachdaich. It is perhaps more usually taken in descent.

Approach
Reach Bealach Thormaid by traversing Sgùrr a' Ghreadaidh from An Doras (reverse route 102). Route 105 is a less inspiring option.

The Route
The normal way is to ascend loose scree, boulders and broken rocks on the right-hand side of the crest. Weave to and fro to find the easiest way. It is possible, however, to find some much more enjoyable scrambling by cutting back left to the crest after the initial section of steep rock. At the top move slightly right to join the well-worn uppermost section of the west flank route.

Continue easily to the summit. There is a sheer drop down the east face

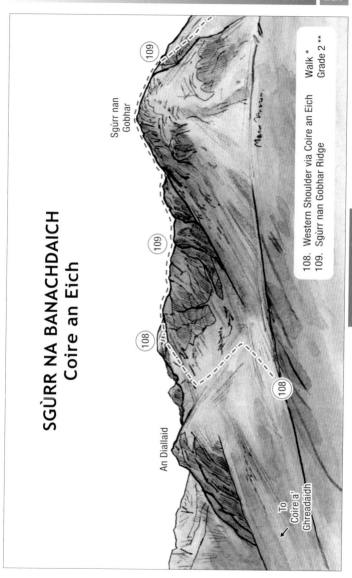

SGÙRR NA BANACHDAICH
Coire an Eich

Sgùrr nan Gobhar

An Diallaid

Main Pinnon

To
Coire a'
Ghreadaidh

108. Western Shoulder via Coire an Eich   Walk *
109. Sgùrr nan Gobhar Ridge   Grade 2 **

CENTRAL CUILLIN

with superb views of the great basin of Coruisk below. The Inaccessible Pinnacle can be seen peeking over the summit of Sgùrr Dearg to the south. The easiest descent is by the next route.

108 Western Shoulder via Coire an Eich   7km   *
(NG 423 231)   Alt 215m   Map p191   Diagram p229

This is the easiest route to a major summit in the Cuillin. However, it ascends very steep scree and is far from an easy walk. The terrain above Coire an Eich can be very confusing in bad visibility. The walk is worthwhile for the dramatic views from the summit.

Approach
From the Youth Hostel in Glen Brittle, follow the path on the south bank of the Allt a' Choire Ghreadaidh.

The Route
The scree bowl of Coire an Eich lies on the north side of the Sgùrr nan Gobhar ridge. Leave the main path to Coire a' Ghreadaidh by turning sharp right and following the west bank of the stream from Coire an Eich. It is possible to leave the main path somewhat earlier and take a more direct line across the hillside, but this is easier to see in descent.

Eventually cross over to the left (north) bank of the Allt Coire an Eich and ascend a worn route up steep scree. A more interesting option is to trend further left and ascend to An Diallaid *(the saddle)* on the northern side of Coire an Eich. The ridge here has three little bumps with steep drops to the north and excellent views across Coire a' Ghreadaidh.

Continue up the ridge and/or the corrie and slant right on bouldery ground to gain a slight flattening at the eastern end of the Sgùrr nan Gobhar ridge. Then zigzag up the broad western shoulder on easy scree and minor rock steps for some distance. Trend slightly right towards the top to reach the summit. The spectacular views from here are the outing's chief reward. The whole Coruisk basin is backed by the Druim nan Ràmh ridge.

The only option for walkers now is to return the same way. Care is needed to find the way into the top of Coire an Eich in bad visibility. It is very easy to start down the Sgùrr nan Gobhar ridge, or even head into Coire na Banachdaich, by mistake.

109 Sgùrr nan Gobhar Ridge   Grade 2   **
(NG 423 221)   Alt 350m   Map p191   Diagram p229

A delightful ridge links the little top of Sgùrr nan Gobhar (630m) with the western shoulder of Sgùrr na Banachdaich. It makes a most enjoyable outing and has fine views of Coire na Banachdaich. It is described in ascent, although it is perhaps more enjoyable in descent because of the tiresome ground at the steep western end.

Approach
The start of this route is equidistant from the Youth Hostel and the Memorial

*Peter Duggan on the easy middle section of the
South-West Flank (Grade 3), Sgùrr na Banachdaich*

Hut in Glen Brittle. The approach from the Memorial Hut is probably more popular, because it is possible to make use of a faint path on the north side of Eas Mòr – a huge hollow with a spectacular waterfall.

The Route

A prominent orange-brown dyke cleaves the western flank of Sgùrr nan Gobhar. The normal line of ascent is up unpleasantly steep scree and loose ground to the right (south) of this gully. However, the gully itself can be ascended in part and makes a reasonable scramble.

Once the fine little summit has been gained the going is very much more enjoyable. The initial section is mainly walking, although the ridge is quite narrow at times. The ascent is enlivened higher up by several sections of pleasant scrambling up steps on the crest. Eventually the ridge merges with the much broader western shoulder of the previous route. This is then followed easily to the summit.

 110 South-West Flank   Grade 3   *
(NG 437 220)   Alt 600m   Map p191   Diagram p239

This is a rarely visited part of Coire na Banachdaich. The route described finds a devious way up the complex ground to the left (north) of Banachdaich Gully.

Approach

Start near the Memorial Hut in Glen Brittle and follow the path into Coire na Banachdaich as described for the next route. After passing below Window Buttress (Route 114), instead of heading over to the right to avoid the broad rock band at the back of the corrie, continue towards the large stream in the corrie floor. Cross this and head for the steep rocks well to the left of Banachdaich Gully. Slant leftwards until a deep recess is found facing down the corrie.

The Route

The start is quite difficult and the route finding not obvious. Ascend the rocks on the right-hand side of the recess where they face across the corrie. Make a steep rising traverse to the right. This is quite sustained. Eventually break across rightwards on better rock where water trickles down the face.

The line continues to make a rising traverse rightwards for quite some distance. The aim is to reach a horizontal traverse-ledge some distance away which seems to lead into Banachdaich Gully. Once the ledge is gained go only a short distance to the right beyond an imposing black wall. Then ascend slightly more amenable rocks trending slightly left at first. These are quite sustained. Then continue fairly directly. Eventually ascend a short chimney on the right side of a gully and soon break out onto easier ground. Ascend scree for some distance. Trend slightly right to reach the main ridge near Bealach Coire na Banachdaich.

The next route makes a natural continuation.

*Peter Duggan ascends the Centre Top
on the south ridge of Sgùrr na Banachdaich*

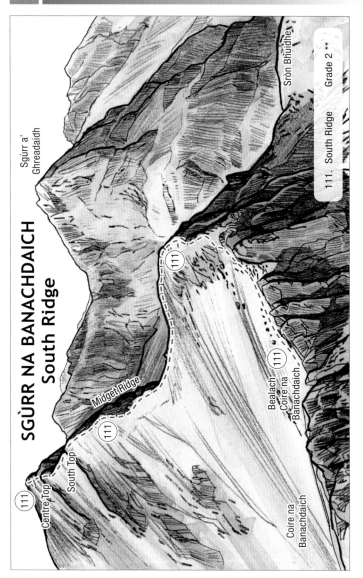

SGÙRR NA BANACHDAICH
South Ridge

Sgùrr a' Ghreadaidh

Sròn Bhuidhe

111. South Ridge   Grade 2 **

Midget Ridge

Centre Top

South Top

Bealach
Coire na
Banachdaich

Coire na
Banachdaich

111 South Ridge   Grade 2 **
(NG 442 217)   Alt 851m   Map p191   Diagram p234

This very enjoyable outing traverses three tops before reaching the main northern summit. It has steep drops on the right but generally less exposed ground to the left. It can easily be combined with the previous route or made part of a round of Coire na Banachdaich. The ridge arises from Bealach Coire na Banachdaich, an important pass over the main ridge between Glen Brittle and Coruisk. The approach to this bealach from Glen Brittle is now described.

Approach
Start immediately south of the Memorial Hut in Glen Brittle by some stone sheep fanks and follow a path which leads away from the road. After a few hundred metres cross the Allt Coire na Banachdaich by a footbridge and ascend the grassy hillside to the rim of Eas Mòr.

Continue around the rim of this impressive chasm. Do not follow the path straight ahead which goes to Coire Lagan. Instead go left round the eastern end of Eas Mòr, and pick up a good path on the south side of the Allt Coire na Banachdaich. Eventually reach the open lower part of Coire na Banachdaich. Continue on more stony ground and occasional slabs.

Bealach Coire na Banachdaich (851m) is the lowest point on the skyline at the head of the corrie. However, the direct route to it is blocked by a broad band of steep slabs split by the prominent gash of Banachdaich Gully. The route now zigzags up (to the left of a gorge) to pass the right-hand end of this rock band by an easy scree gully (see diagram on page 240). A more interesting line can be taken up the slabs immediately to the left of this gully. The slabs to the right of Banachdaich Gully offer an alternative approach for more experienced scramblers. See Route 112 described in the next section.

The normal way then slants back a long way left on scree. At one point it is necessary to descend very slightly, otherwise the tendency is to scramble up loose ground towards the north ridge of Sgùrr Dearg. Then ascend slightly steeper scree to the bealach, which is notable for its orange soil. A gully leads down to a broad scree slope on the Coruisk side. There is large knobble of rock just north of the bealach with a similar scree gully on the other side.

The Route
The first part of the ridge leads over an easy top (878m) above the shoulder of Sròn Bhuidhe. Ledges on the Coire na Banachdaich side offer the easiest options, but the best scrambling, and the best views, are on the crest itself. Pleasant scrambling then leads over the very narrow South Top (917m).

A popular option next is to traverse narrow ledges across the west face of the Centre Top. However, a more direct line is preferable, and probably no more time-consuming. Traverse the high point (942m), and scramble down very steeply, slightly on the west side, to the final dip.

Ascend some sharp rocks then slant easily up a cone-sheet showing conspicuous spheroidal weathering. Continue without difficulty to the main north summit.

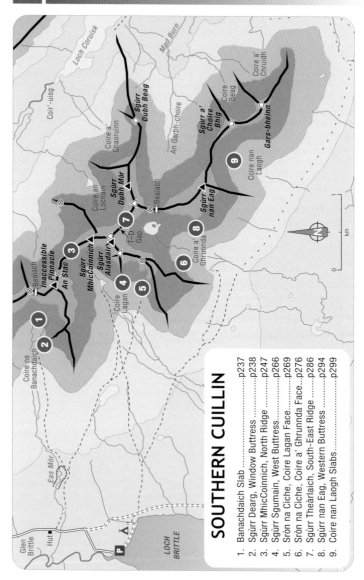

SOUTHERN CUILLIN

1. Banachdaich Slab p237
2. Sgùrr Dearg, Window Buttress p238
3. Sgùrr MhicCoinnich, North Ridge p247
4. Sgùrr Sgumain, West Buttress p266
5. Sròn na Cìche, Coire Lagan Face..........p269
6. Sròn na Cìche, Coire a' Ghrunnda Face ..p276
7. Sgùrr Thèarlaich, South-East Ridge p286
8. Sgùrr nan Eag, Western Buttress p294
9. Coire nan Laogh Slabs p299

SOUTHERN CUILLIN

The Southern Cuillin group is here taken to include all the peaks from Sgùrr Dearg to Gars-bheinn. These include the two highest Cuillin summits – Sgùrr Alasdair and the Inaccessible Pinnacle of Sgùrr Dearg. Four contrasting corries lie on the south-west side of the main ridge. Coire Lagan has some of the best climbing in the Cuillin. Its neighbour, Coire a' Ghrunnda, has vast areas of bare rock in its floor. Both contain beautiful lochans in their upper tiers.

The easiest way over the main ridge is by Bealach Coire na Banachdaich at the northern end of the group. Other crossings can be made, in increasing order of difficulty, at Bealach a' Gharbh-choire, Bealach Coire an Lochain, Bealach MhicCoinnich and Bealach Coire Lagan.

This part of the Cuillin is most readily accessible from the lower end of Glen Brittle.

SGÙRR DEARG   978m

(NG 443 215) Map p236

This lofty peak would not attract as much attention as it does but for an extraordinary fin of rock, known as the Inaccessible Pinnacle, that springs from the east side of its summit ridge. A complex ridge drops down further east over An Stac to the rim of Coire Lagan. The impressive and forbidding north face overlooks the scree descent from Bealach Coire na Banachdaich to Coruisk.

Although the Inaccessible Pinnacle is out of bounds to all but rock climbers, the summit of Sgùrr Dearg itself is an easier objective. Its north-west flank is little more than a very rough walk, and its south-western ridge is a relatively easy scramble.

The next three outings all start from Coire na Banachdaich.

112 Banachdaich Slab   Grade 3   **

(NG 439 218)   Alt 630m   Map p236   Diagram p239

This route just qualifies as belonging to Sgùrr Dearg. It can be used as a more interesting approach to Bealach Coire na Banachdaich. It is sustained, at the upper limit of its grade, and is not recommended after wet weather.

Approach
From the Memorial Hut, take the path up into Coire na Banachdaich as for the previous route. Head for the rocks immediately to the right of Banachdaich Gully. This gully gives a Very Difficult climb, best done after a dry spell. (It was first climbed by Gibbs, King & Mackenzie in 1898.)

The Route
Ascend a recess just right of the gully, then scramble pleasantly up a right-facing corner/groove formed by a dyke. Slant diagonally right across slabs. Make a tricky step up to the right of a rock pedestal in a tiny recess. Step

SOUTHERN CUILLIN

right and break up onto slabs. Move right and down slightly on a grassy ledge. Then climb up and stretch for a good hold to allow a move back left onto a ledge above. Traverse left some distance, step between some big blocks and ascend to a tiny alcove and juniper bush, with a slightly steeper wall above. Go to the right-hand end of a ledge and step up onto a slab. Slant slightly left by a narrow dyke and continue with further interest to a grassy terrace.

Traverse hard right along the terrace and ascend a broad dyke forming a gully. This a fairly sustained for some distance and leads to a good ledge. Move right and make one steep move left of a nose. Then either cross slabs leftwards or carry straight on up, and soon emerge onto big boulders. Continue directly to join the traverse line leading left on the normal route to Bealach Coire na Banachdaich.

 ### 113 North-West Flank   Grade 1
(NG 442 217)   Alt 851m   Map p236   Diagram p240

This is one of the least interesting sections of the main ridge. Apart from some mild scrambling out of Bealach Coire na Banachdaich, this route is mainly a slog up steep scree. However, there are fine views looking back north. In descent it is important to go more west than north from the summit.

Approach
Ascend to Bealach Coire na Banachdaich as for Route 111.

The Route
Just short of the actual bealach, scramble up steep rocks on the right to gain the crest of the ridge. Soon reach a narrower section of ridge with good views across the precipitous north face. Continue to the start of a broad scree slope. Zigzag up the rather tedious scree for some distance and eventually reach the long horizontal crest forming the summit. The Inaccessible Pinnacle is close by. This is a good place to watch the antics of climbers on the West Ridge (Route 119).

The south-west ridge of Sgùrr Dearg (Route 115) offers a more interesting descent. It is only slightly more difficult than the route up.

 ### 114 Window Buttress   Difficult **
(NG 436 216)   Alt 580m   Map p236   Diagrams pp239 & 240

This prominent buttress is situated at a height of 600m on the south side of Coire na Banachdaich. It has enjoyable climbing and some varied situations. It is a popular climb to do on the way up to the Inaccessible Pinnacle. It was first done by Norman Collie in 1906.

Approach
Follow the path into Coire na Banachdaich as for Route 111. Scramble up an obvious broad sweep of slabs directly to the foot of the buttress.

The Route
From the lowest rocks, climb up first slightly right, then left on good holds.

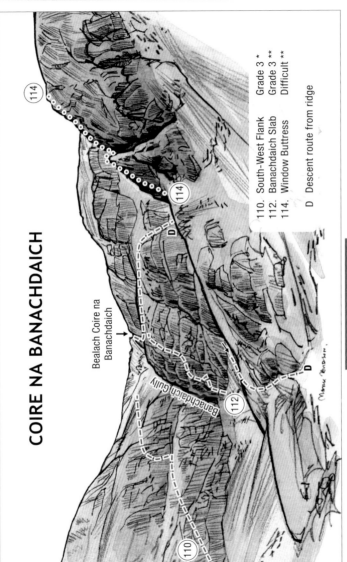

COIRE NA BANACHDAICH

Bealach Coire na Banachdaich

Banachdaich Gully

110. South-West Flank   Grade 3 *
112. Banachdaich Slab   Grade 3 **
114. Window Buttress   Difficult **

D   Descent route from ridge

SOUTHERN CUILLIN

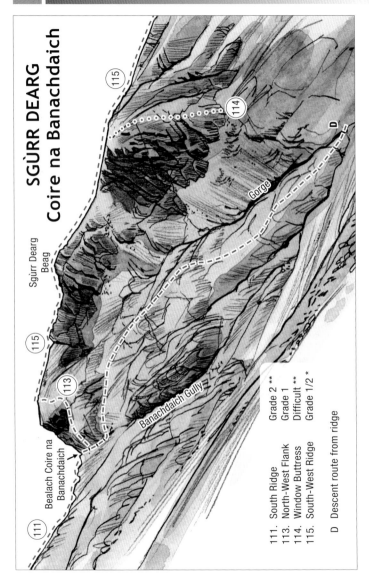

SGÙRR DEARG
Coire na Banachdaich

115

114

113

115

111

D

Gorge

Sgùrr Dearg Beag

Bealach Coire na Banachdaich

Banachdaich Gully

111. South Ridge   Grade 2 **
113. North-West Flank   Grade 1
114. Window Buttress   Difficult **
115. South-West Ridge   Grade 1/2 *

D   Descent route from ridge

Move right to a parallel groove and after a couple of steep moves follow a left-slanting line more easily to reach a large ledge.

Climb the very steep right-facing corner above (crux). A little higher, move right and climb a short wall by a prominent crack to gain a stretch of slabs. Eventually trend right to reach the nose of stacked blocks leaning against the face which gives the route its name.

Direct routes up to **The Window** itself are rather difficult, so traverse left and ascend an obvious groove to a stony ledge. Continue to the crest of the buttress. There is a gully on the other side leading to a neck, but the best option here is to stay on the crest and make some steep moves to ascend a pinnacle and so reach the highest point.

Drop down easily into the neck. Climb up sound rocks the other side (Moderate), going first right and then back left. Continue up short blocky corners and slabs. Then ascend a bouldery ridge for some distance. Emerge onto an extensive scree shoulder below Sgùrr Dearg Beag.

115 South-West Ridge via Sgùrr Dearg Beag   Grade 1/2   *

(NG 429 213)   Alt 380m   Map p236   Diagram p240

This is probably the best of the easy ways to the summit of Sgùrr Dearg. However, it is hard work ascending the long scree slope of Sròn Dearg. This is rewarded by superb views across Coire Lagan.

Approach

The outing can be started either from the Memorial Hut or from the campsite by the beach. The path to Coire Lagan from the campsite is slightly better. It heads uphill from the toilet block and crosses over a rough track soon after. Stay on the left-hand path where the route to Coire a' Ghrunnda forks right across a stream.

The Route

Starting just to the east of Loch an Fhir-bhallaich, choose any convenient line up the trying scree of Sròn Dearg. A popular option is to follow a brown dyke. Eventually the angle eases slightly and the scree becomes more stable. Reach a slight flattening at 800m. Then ascend steeper ground on scree, boulders and big blocks to gain the minor summit of Sgùrr Dearg Beag (927m).

The remaining ridge, which curves leftwards to the summit of Sgùrr Dearg, is narrower and rocky. There are short sections of interesting scrambling on the crest, or easier ledges first on the right side and later on the left. The dramatic sight of the Inaccessible Pinnacle marks the climax to the ascent.

116 South Flank – Central Buttress   Grade 3

(NG 443 212)   Alt 730m   Map p236   Diagram p242

This is not the most inspiring of lines, but it offers experienced scramblers a more taxing route onto Sgùrr Dearg than the previous outing. It takes full advantage of the good path into Coire Lagan.

SOUTHERN CUILLIN

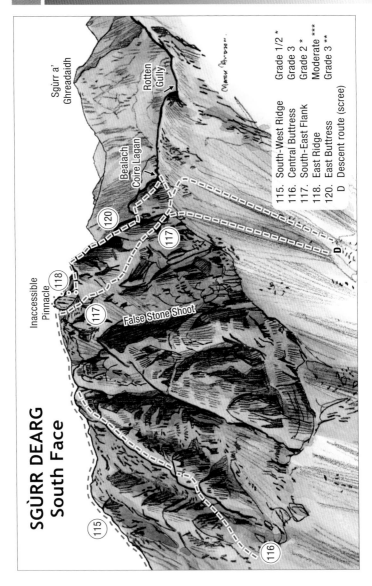

SGÙRR DEARG
South Face

Sgùrr a' Ghreadaidh

Rotten Gully

Bealach Coire Lagan

Inaccessible Pinnacle

False Stone Shoot

115. South-West Ridge — Grade 1/2 *
116. Central Buttress — Grade 3
117. South-East Flank — Grade 2 *
118. East Ridge — Moderate ***
120. East Buttress — Grade 3 **
D   Descent route (scree)

Approach

From the campsite by the beach in Glen Brittle. Take the path to Coire Lagan as for the previous route. Stay on the path east of Loch an Fhir-bhallaich, and continue past a distinctive pointed boulder known as the **Matterhorn Block**. Eventually ascend slabs and looser ground above to reach the beautiful lochan in the ice-scooped basin of upper Coire Lagan.

The Route

Turn and face Sgùrr Dearg. To the right is the prominent climbing crag called South Buttress. (This has two Difficult routes – Baly's Route, which starts up the left-bounding gully, and East Corner, which takes the right-hand edge.) Central Buttress is a rather indefinite ridge straight above with a scree gully to its left. Further left again is another rather indefinite buttress. Move slightly left and weave a way up excellent slabs to more broken ground below the left-hand buttress.

Ascend scree for some distance, then start to slant diagonally right towards a steep crag forming the lower section of Central Buttress. This is too difficult so avoid it by moving round it on the left-hand side. Tackle the next section more directly on very steep rock. The route-finding is interesting and care is required with loose blocks. Continue up the rickety ridge, which becomes less definite as height is gained. Eventually join the previous route near the crest of the south-west ridge. Turn right and follow the rocky ridge to the summit.

 117 South-East Flank Grade 2 *

(NG 446 214) Alt 820m Map p236 Diagram p242

This is the easiest way of reaching Sgùrr Dearg when traversing the main ridge northwards. It takes the line of a prominent cone-sheet which skirts below the south face of An Stac. It is not at all exposed. In descent it is important to cut left over a small shoulder marked by big boulders, thereby avoiding a 'false stone-shoot' which ends in a steep drop over broken rocks. The route is low in its grade.

Approach

This route starts from Bealach Coire Lagan. This dip on the main ridge can be gained from the floor of upper Coire Lagan (reached as for the previous route), but it involves making an unpleasant ascent of the An Stac screes. A slightly better approach can be made by hard scrambling up rocky ribs further right – to the left of the lowest point on the rim of the corrie. (Rotten Gully lies on the Coruisk side.) Then traverse a broad top and descend slightly to reach the bealach. It is possible to pick a way down steep ground on the Coruisk side of the bealach, but this is not a recommendable pass over the ridge.

The Route

From the bealach, descend broken rocks on the Coire Lagan side, then follow an obvious path on scree slanting up left. Continue in the same line by scrambling easily up slabs and stones. Eventually go through a gap by big

SOUTHERN CUILLIN

boulders, and turn slightly right. After a short distance it is important to scramble up to a higher, parallel ramp. Continue along this until the Inaccessible Pinnacle comes into full view. Slant up a broad slabby shelf, scattered with stones, to reach the horizontal crest marking the summit of Sgùrr Dearg.

INACCESSIBLE PINNACLE 986m

(NG 444 215) Map p236

This amazing fin of rock outstrips Sgùrr Dearg by 8m and must therefore be regarded as the true summit of the mountain – much to the discomfort of many a Munro-bagger, including Sir Hugh himself. The pinnacle itself is a slice of tholeitte sheet which was originally sandwiched between two dykes. It rests on a dipping cone-sheet. It is the hardest mountain summit to attain in all the British Isles.

Since a lightning strike destroyed the highest mass of rock in 2007 the huge westernmost block, known as the Bolster Stone, has become the highest point.

118 East Ridge Moderate ***
(NG 444 215) Alt 930m Map p236 Diagram p242

This sensational climb has good holds, but also exceptional exposure – a wonderful combination if you like that sort of thing. It was first climbed by the Pilkington brothers in 1880. Few today will approach this climb as they did from Sligachan via Coruisk. If you don't like queuing, it is best to avoid this route on the last weekend of May (Spring Bank Holiday, except Scotland).

Approach
Reach the summit of Sgùrr Dearg by any one of the preceding five routes (Routes 113–17). Descend stone-covered slabs on the south side of the Pinnacle and gain an extensive platform below the start of the ridge.

The Route
Climb up the south flank by a short, easy pitch, and take a stance on the left just below the crest. Gain the crest and follow this on good holds to a slightly steeper section which constitutes the crux. The difficulties are short-lived, but the exposure is considerable. Continue more easily to a good ledge beside large blocks at the summit.

The normal practice is to descend by abseiling 20m down the West Ridge. Move down a sloping slab to reach a thread belay (steel cable) at the base of the Bolster Stone.

119 West Ridge Very Difficult *
(NG 443 215) Alt 965m Map p236

The route up the short end of the Inaccessible Pinnacle is steeper, and the climbing more technical, than that on the East Ridge. It has become somewhat polished, and the start is quite tricky. It was first climbed by Stocker and Parker in 1886.

Approach
Drop down just a short distance from the summit of Sgùrr Dearg.

The Route
Some rock has fallen off the base of the West Ridge, and the route now starts up steep rocks on the left (north) face. Climb up to a sloping ledge, trending left, then move delicately up right. Continue more easily up ledges trending right to gain the sloping slab below the Bolster Stone. Either abseil back down or, if there is no traffic, climb down the East Ridge.

AN STAC 954m

(NG 444 215) Map p236

This is a minor top on the east ridge of Sgùrr Dearg below the Inaccessible Pinnacle. It throws down an impressive buttress towards Bealach Coire Lagan, and an even more impressive face to the north. It seems to have acquired its name by mistake. (The Inaccessible Pinnacle was originally called An Stac.) John Mackenzie suggested that the top be called Sgùrr na Cailleach.

The summit can be reached by a simple scramble from the foot of the East Ridge of the Inaccessible Pinnacle. It is well worth a short detour from the South-East Flank (Route 117) to take in the unusual views of the Inaccessible Pinnacle from this top.

 **120 East Buttress Grade 3 ** **
(NG 446 214) Alt 820m Map p236 Diagram p246
This is the preferred way up An Stac for confident scramblers. The route becomes increasingly exposed as height is gained. Gibson, Morse and Wicks descended this way in 1892. They were unaware of the easier option below the south face. It is at the upper limit of its grade.

Approach
Reach Bealach Coire Lagan as for Route 117.

The Route
Slant up a left-trending ramp on the Coire Lagan side of a peaklet immediately west of the bealach. Reach a col with a broad scree-filled recess to the left (possible escape route) and steep drops to the right (north). The buttress proper now rises above.

Start a short distance down from the col on the Coire Lagan side. Scramble left up steps and grooves. Follow a rickety staircase slightly left instead of a groove on the right. Zigzag up a stony path to a shoulder with even steeper drops to the right. Cut back left and scramble up the narrowing arête with continuous interest to a ledge.

Follow the ledge to the right and ascend a slightly steeper groove, then cut

SOUTHERN CUILLIN

AN STAC
South-East Face

117. South-East Flank   Grade 2 *
120. East Buttress   Grade 3 **
121. An Stac Chimney   Moderate *

back hard left on a glacis and spiral round to the summit. It is also possible to continue along the ledge system to the right, but there is a horrifying drop on the right-hand side. It is then necessary to backtrack slightly to reach the summit. An easy scramble descent from the summit leads down to the dip before the Inaccessible Pinnacle.

 121 An Stac Chimney   Moderate   *

(NG 445 214)   Alt 840m   Map p236   Diagram p246

This prominent chimney cleaves the east face to the left of the previous route. It was first climbed by Goggs and Russell in 1908.

Approach

From Bealach Coire Lagan. Follow the first part of the South-East Flank route (Route 117) until a short distance past the broad scree recess.

The Route

Scramble up a broad stone-filled groove, then a rib and slabs, to the foot of the chimney. The first part of the chimney is easy to enter. Most climbers should be able to go under one chockstone, and possibly also a second, but the chimney then becomes too narrow. The crux is climbing up exposed rocks on the right wall. Move in and out of the chimney above and eventually join the East Buttress route just before the rightward-leading ledge. Finish as for that route.

SGÙRR MHICCOINNICH 948m

(NG 450 210) Map p236

The west face of this peak forms the impressive headwall of Coire Lagan. Cutting across this face some 30m below the summit is one of the most useful cone-sheet ledges in the Cuillin. The mountain's finest feature is its north ridge. The peak is named in honour of John Mackenzie, who was in the party (Pilkington, Walker, Heelis & Mackenzie) that made the first ascent in 1887.

122 North Ridge   Grade 2   **

(NG 447 213)   Alt 804m   Map p236   Diagrams pp248 & 252

This is a very fine ridge and, despite there being basalt on the upper section, it makes a most enjoyable scramble. The top section is narrow and exposed. This is the route taken by Charles Pilkington and his party on the first ascent.

Approach

Gain Bealach Coire Lagan as for Route 117.

The Route

From the bealach, traverse a plateau-like top and descend easily rightwards to the lowest point on the corrie rim. The ridge proper rises above. The scrambling is interesting without being unduly difficult. Weave a way up small paths and clamber up blocks and grooves. Eventually reach the crest and

SOUTHERN CUILLIN

SGÙRR MHICCOINNICH
West Face

122. North Ridge   Grade 2 **
123. West Buttress   Difficult **
124. Hart's Ledge   Grade 2 **
125. King's Chimney   Very Difficult **

D   Descent route

follow this fairly easily at first. About two-thirds of the way along the crest look for the exit of Hart's Ledge on the Coire Lagan side. There is a slight rise on the crest immediately after this. The remainder of the ridge to the summit is narrow and delightfully exposed.

The southern end of the mountain, just beyond the summit, plunges steeply to Bealach MhicCoinnich. The only practicable way for scramblers to reach this bealach is to return down the north ridge and follow Hart's Ledge (Route 124) across the west face. Otherwise return down the north ridge.

123 West Buttress   Difficult **
(NG 448 210)   Alt 690m   Map p236   Diagrams pp248 & 252

This enjoyable route takes a direct line to the summit from Coire Lagan. It is mainly hard scrambling with interesting route-finding. There are a couple of climbing pitches, one below and the other above Hart's Ledge. It was first ascended by the Abraham brothers in 1906.

Approach
Reach the lochan in upper Coire Lagan as for Route 116. Start at the back of the corrie, a little to the left of the prominent scree fan forming the bottom section of the Great Stone Shoot.

The Route
At the base of the buttress there is a crag with a dark, wet left-hand wall. A start can be made either side of this crag. The left-hand option involves some tricky scrambling to reach a small neck at the back of the crag. The right-hand option is more straightforward, but entails a detour to the right across slabs and back left to the same neck.

Scramble up for some distance staying right of the crest. When the rocks start to steepen make some harder moves to break up left onto the crest. Ascend a rib until it peters out on a broader section of ridge. A grassy ledge leads rightwards off the buttress at this point. Zigzag up a short distance, then cut hard left along a horizontal traverse line, with one awkward step onto a brown slab. Break up left, then follow a rightward-slanting rake. Cut back left along a slabby groove to the centre of the buttress. Go left or right of the next rock band. The rock is somewhat mossy in places. Take a direct line up a short wall of sounder rock. Stay slightly right of the crest and weave a way up through tiny buttresses. Make some pleasant moves up a short groove with a block in it.

A choice of lines can be taken at a steepening. Going left involves an awkward move pulling up the right-hand side of a block. Eventually slant easily up right on looser ground. At a steep nose, traverse right and ascend small ledges to emerge on easier ground. Ascend some slabs to reach a steep groove with a good flake belay at the base of its right wall. Climb the corner groove on good rock, then move hard right and pull onto a ramp which slants back left. Take a belay on Hart's Ledge below another corner groove.

Climb the corner for a short distance then traverse right until it is possible to make some steep moves to gain easier rocks. Continue to a good belay.

Move slightly right and take a direct line to the summit. The easiest descent is by the north ridge.

124 Hart's Ledge (Collie's Ledge)   Grade 2 **

(NG 450 210)   Alt 892m   Map p236   Diagrams pp248 & 252

This remarkable ledge gives access to the north ridge of the mountain from Bealach MhicCoinnich. It was discovered by the Irish climber Henry Hart with John Mackenzie in 1887. It is commonly known as Collie's Ledge, but Collie did not team up to do it with John Mackenzie until a year later, so the credit should really go to Hart.

Approach

Reach the lochan in upper Coire Lagan as for Route 116. The approach to Bealach MhicCoinnich starts up the Great Stone Shoot in the upper right-hand corner of the corrie. Ascend the very loose scree forming the lower half of this shoot, then, when a rock wall starts to appear directly ahead, traverse diagonally left across more stable ground. Head for a dark brown rock rib. Traverse left across this and ascend a gully the other side. Weave to and fro to find the easiest line. Higher up, find a way to break rightwards through a steeper section by interesting scrambling on good holds (Grade 2). Continue on slightly easier ground to gain the bealach.

The approach from the Coruisk side is normally made via Coire an Lochain. Ascend an easy scree gully at first, then scramble up a short section of slabs. Make further awkward moves to exit at the top (Grade 2/3).

The Route

Hart's Ledge is a fairly obvious feature slanting up the west face from the bealach. From a terrace just on the east side of the bealach, trend slightly right on slabby ledges to a tiny recess with some scree. Ascend a steep groove by making a very high step up with the right foot. Move back left above to get established on the ledge proper. After this crux section the scrambling is fairly easy, though quite exposed at times. Stay below a steeper break which rises to the base of King's Chimney (see next route). Continue across the crest of West Buttress and round a corner in a fine position.

The way on is obvious. It is mainly exposed walking, with several short sections of scrambling where the ledge fades temporarily. One or two moves involve slight descents. Eventually ascend with surprising ease onto the crest of the north ridge.

125 King's Chimney   Very Difficult **

(NG 450 210)   Alt 900m   Map p236   Diagram p248

This is the most enjoyable climb of its grade on the main ridge, and all the better for being easier than it looks. The footholds are quite small though, so it feels harder in bendy boots. It allows a direct line to be taken from Bealach MhicCoinnich to the summit of the mountain. It was first climbed by King, Douglas and Naismith in 1898.

On Hart's Ledge (Grade 2) heading towards Bealach MhicCoinnich, with the pointed summit of Sgùrr Theàrlaich behind. Scrambler: Peter Duggan

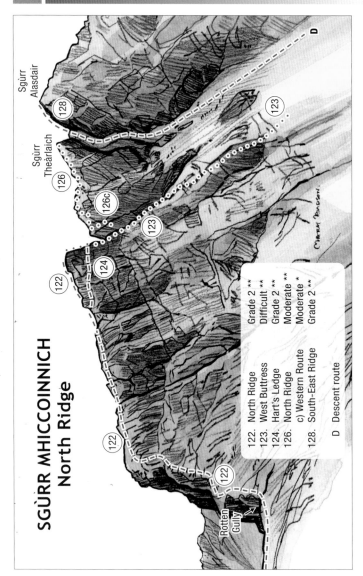

SGÙRR MHICCOINNICH
North Ridge

Sgùrr Alasdair

Sgùrr Thearlaich

Rotten Gully

122.	North Ridge	Grade 2 **
123.	West Buttress	Difficult **
124.	Hart's Ledge	Grade 2 **
126.	North Ridge	Moderate **
	c) Western Route	Moderate *
128.	South-East Ridge	Grade 2 **
D	Descent route	

Approach
Gain Bealach MhicCoinnich as for the previous route.

The Route
Follow the first part of Hart's Ledge, then ascend a higher, leftwards-rising break on slightly dubious rock to reach the base of the prominent corner. Ascend the corner on good holds. There is a helpful chockstone in the corner crack. Eventually traverse out right in a fine position beneath an overhang to reach a good ledge. Climb slabs to reach a terrace at the top – a delightful viewpoint. Continue easily up the ridge to the summit.

SGÙRR THEÀRLAICH   978m

(NG 450 207) Map p236

This is the eastern top of Sgùrr Alasdair. The traverse of this summit is one of the most demanding sections of the main ridge. The mountain's south-east ridge is split by the notorious Theàrlaich–Dubh Gap (see Route 150), and its north ridge plunges steeply to Bealach MhicCoinnich. It can be ascended with least difficulty from near the top of the Great Stone Shoot. The peak was first climbed by Charles Pilkington and Horace Walker in 1887. It is named (Charles's Peak) in honour of Pilkington.

126 North Ridge   Moderate or Very Difficult **
(NG 450 210) Alt 892m   Map p236   Diagrams pp252 & 329

This is quite a taxing part of the main ridge, especially when tackled, as it usually is, in descent. The main north ridge itself is delightful, but the steep rocks at the start above Bealach MhicCoinnich are very tricky and route-finding is not easy on first acquaintance. Three different ways of overcoming this section can be used. Each option has its advocates, but none is easy. The second two options visit a commodious high platform at the end of the north ridge.

Approach
Gain Bealach MhicCoinnich as for Route 124.

The Route

a) **Eastern Traverse   Moderate **
This is the most straightforward way of ascending the ridge from Bealach MhicCoinnich. However, in descent the crux step is exposed and rather intimidating. The route traverses the Coruisk side of the ridge.

From the bealach skirt the first rocks by descending slightly on the east side. Scramble up to an obvious ledge (upper bealach) and follow this some way leftwards descending very slightly. Just before it ends at a drop climb up rocks slanting left to a grassy ledge. Continue traversing leftwards on an easy ledge until it ends. The rock step above is the crux. Climb a greasy crack/groove or the rocks immediately to the left of it. Gain another ledge

A party descends the short chimney towards the bottom of the Western Route (Moderate) at the north end of the North Ridge of Sgùrr Theàrlaich

Descending the North Ridge (Moderate) from the summit of Sgurr Theàrlaich
Scrambler: Peter Duggan

and follow this leftwards. Scramble up a short distance to a higher ledge system and follow this round the corner. Continue more easily to join the crest of the main north ridge just beyond a commodious platform.

b) **East Wall & Slab   Very Difficult   ***

This is the hardest option. Some of the situations are exciting. It finishes up a very exposed slab on small but positive holds.

From the higher ledge above the bealach move left a short way until the steep rocks overlooking the ledge can be climbed by a steep groove. Gain a crucial traverse line leading back right. Continue up slabs and small steps trending slightly left to reach the halfway platform. Turn left and go to the back of the platform. (The next option goes hard right on slabs at this point beneath a dark wall.) Go left slightly and clamber through a cleft.

The final section ascends an amazing roof-like section of slabs. This gives delightful climbing on adequate holds (Difficult), but in a very exposed position. Finish on a commodious platform also visited by the next start.

c) **Western Route   Moderate   ***

This is perhaps the most popular option, but it takes a very roundabout route. Start on the Coire Lagan side of the bealach. Descend a short way until it is possible to traverse left, across curious rubbly rock, to a short chimney/groove immediately to the left of a small rock pillar. Ascend the chimney and then slant back leftwards on rather loose ground to a sizeable platform at half-height, also gained by the previous start. Continue to the back of the platform/ridge then (instead of going left to a cleft) pass behind a large boulder and follow a sharp rightwards traverse across delicate slabs beneath a very steep wall. It is best to stay high where possible. Soon reach a small ledge on the right-hand edge. Then head straight up a short rock rib and pass through a small slot between rocks to gain a commodious platform.

All three starts join at a narrow gap on the crest of the north ridge, where a gully falls steeply into the Great Stone Shoot. Negotiate the gap and follow a ledge on the left-hand side of the crest and soon reach another gap. The remainder of the ridge is very pleasant, with much of the crest being formed by a cone-sheet dipping to the east. There are fine views to the south from the summit. Sgùrr Alasdair, the highest peak on the island, is not far away to the west. The next route offers the easiest descent.

 127 South Ridge via the Great Stone Shoot   Grade 3   *
(NG 451 207)   Alt 920m   Map p236   Diagram p288

The south ridge of Sgùrr Theàrlaich forms the natural continuation of the south-east ridge from the Theàrlaich–Dubh gap (Route 150). However, it can also be gained by ascending the Great Stone Shoot or by traversing Sgùrr Alasdair.

Approach

The easiest way to gain this ridge is by ascending the Great Stone Shoot from Coire Lagan as described for the next route.

Looking down the south ridge of Sgùrr Theàrlaich (Grade 3)
Scrambler: Peter Duggan

The Route

The saddle at the top of the Great Stone Shoot (955m) has a short but rather steep wall on its eastern side. The south ridge can be gained by a number of rather strenuous little climbs directly up this wall. However, a more reasonable option is to descend on the Coire a' Ghrunnda side by a stony path until it is possible to walk easily left onto the ridge. Do not descend too far, because the ground falls away steeply below.

Scramble up onto the crest, moving onto the right-hand side where it narrows. A sizeable section of the crest has fallen off in recent times and the rock has to be treated with care. Steady scrambling leads to the fine summit. The neighbouring peak of Sgùrr Alasdair has a domineering presence on the other side of the Great Stone Shoot.

The continuation by the north ridge involves very awkward down-climbing at Moderate grade (see the previous route), so the easiest option from here is to return to the top of the Great Stone Shoot.

SGÙRR ALASDAIR 992m

(NG 450 207) Map p236

The highest mountain on Skye has a shapely summit, which is set apart slightly to the west of the main ridge. It lies on an important subsidiary ridge which includes Sgùrr Sgumain and Sròn na Cìche. It can be ascended with least difficulty via the Great Stone Shoot from Coire Lagan. On a traverse of the main ridge it is standard practice to make the short detour required to take in the wonderful views from its summit. The mountain is named after Sheriff Alexander Nicolson who first ascended the peak with A. Macrae in 1873.

 128 South-East Ridge   Grade 2   **
(NG 450 207)   Alt 955m   Map p236   Diagrams pp259, 288 & 290

This short rocky ridge gives the easiest route to the summit. It starts from the stony saddle at the top of the Great Stone Shoot at a height of 955m.

Approach

Follow the path from the campsite by the beach in Glen Brittle to upper Coire Lagan. Go round the left-hand side of the lochan, then slant right to where an obvious scree fan descends to the corrie floor. The lower part of the Great Stone Shoot consists of unstable scree and is very hard work to ascend. A slightly easier line can be found to the left of the main fan where the bouldery ground is more stable.

The upper half of the shoot is enclosed by rock walls, and the ground underfoot is badly eroded. Care is required where bedrock is exposed and some big boulders are undermined. Be aware also that, because the shoot is gently curved, it may not be possible to see other parties below. The saddle at the top of the shoot is a welcome sight.

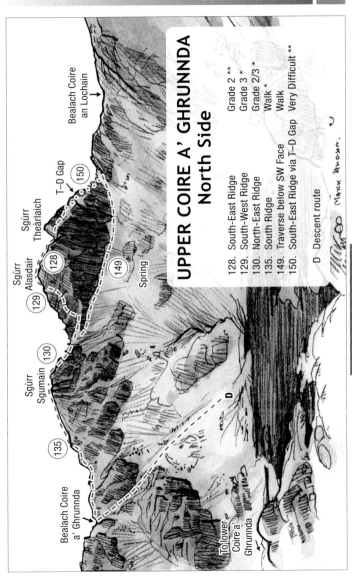

UPPER COIRE A' GHRUNNDA
North Side

128.	South-East Ridge	Grade 2 **
129.	South-West Ridge	Grade 3 *
130.	North-East Ridge	Grade 2/3 *
135.	South Ridge	Walk *
149.	Traverse below SW Face	Walk
150.	South-East Ridge via T–D Gap	Very Difficult **

D   Descent route

The crux chimney on the south-west ridge of Sgùrr Alasdair (Grade 3)
Scrambler: Peter Duggan

The Route

The ridge looks intimidating but, once embarked on, it proves fairly straightforward. The rock is largely basalt, but the way is well-worn and there are adequate holds. Follow slabby rocks and small rock steps close to the crest. The right-hand side is rather exposed in the lower section. The views from the summit are exceptional, and many parties linger here secure in the knowledge that the Great Stone Shoot offers a rapid descent route. Note that there is no way down the Coire a' Ghrunnda side from the saddle at the bottom of the ridge.

 129 South-West Ridge   Grade 3   *
(NG 449 207)   Alt 921m   Map p236   Diagrams pp259 & 288

This ridge offers a more interesting route to the summit than the previous one. It starts from Bealach Sgumain – a dip in the ridge between Sgùrr Sgumain and Sgùrr Alasdair. A nasty little wall at the start of the ridge, known as the Bad Step, is rarely done because it can be avoided by a relatively straightforward chimney some distance further right. It has become quite popular to ascend this ridge instead of negotiating the Theàrlaich–Dubh gap.

Approach

The ridge crest by Bealach Sgumain is marked by several troll-like pinnacles. The scree on the Coire Lagan side of the bealach is unpleasantly steep and is not recommended in either ascent or descent. The Coire a' Ghrunnda side is also largely scree, but again this is not an attractive approach route. There are two more pleasant options; one is to traverse Sgùrr Sgumain (see the next route), the other is to follow a path in the scree below the south-west face of Sgùrr Theàrlaich from Bealach Coire an Lochain (see Route 149).

The Route

Ignore the obvious difficulties posed by the steep rocks near the crest. Instead follow a ledge further right which descends slightly to reach the base of a chimney. Scramble up the chimney itself to start with. Then climb up the left wall (crux), before exiting on the right. Above this the scrambling is fairly sustained for some distance. Slant left and right to find the easiest way. Much variation is possible and the rock is rather broken in places. Eventually move back left to the crest and follow this in a fine position to the summit. The normal descent is by the previous route.

SGÙRR SGUMAIN 947m

(NG 448 206) Map p236

This peak lies on the ridge between Sròn na Cìche and Sgùrr Alasdair. It makes an enjoyable traverse en route to the major summit. It has a dramatic north-west face and an extensive west buttress. The easiest way to its summit is by the south ridge from Bealach Coire a' Ghrunnda. This bealach can be reached by the Sgumain Stone Shoot from Coire Lagan.

SOUTHERN CUILLIN

130 North-East Ridge   Grade 2/3 *
(NG 449 207)   Alt 921m   Map p236   Diagram p259

This short, narrow ridge starts from Bealach Sgumain. It is probably done more often in descent when linking the peak with Sgùrr Alasdair.

Start

The most pleasant way of reaching Bealach Sgumain is by Route 149 from Bealach Coire an Lochain. (See also Route 129).

The Route

From the bealach, follow ledges mainly on the Coire a' Ghrunnda side. The scrambling is quite interesting and there are one or two more awkward moves. There is a small top, with a tiny window feature, just before the much broader main summit is reached. The views northwards are especially fine. It is a simple matter to descend the south ridge (Route 135) to Bealach Coire a' Ghrunnda.

131 North Ridge   Moderate **
(NG 447 208)   Alt 730m   Map p236   Diagram p263

Although this route does not appear very striking from below, it is in fact a most enjoyable excursion with interesting route-finding. The rock is somewhat suspect, but not unpleasantly so. The route has much scrambling and is fairly easy for its grade. It is best done on a summer evening when the ridge catches the sun.

The steep nose at the bottom is too difficult to take direct. It is possible to head up directly behind the lochan (as for the next route) and join the ridge from the right-hand side behind the initial bastion. However a gully which once allowed easy access has become more difficult through wear. There are other ways further right, but none of them is easy. The simplest option is to join the ridge from the other side.

Approach

Reach upper Coire Lagan (as for Route 116), go round the lochan and head up the first part of the Great Stone Shoot staying over to the right-hand side. Eventually reach a level where it is easy to follow a ledge horizontally rightwards to join the ridge crest behind the difficult nose at the bottom.

The Route

Weave a way up the crest mainly on big blocks on the right-hand side. This gives very enjoyable scrambling. Then an easier section leads to a prominent rock band which gives the main difficulties of the ascent. The direct way is too difficult, so traverse hard left to the foot of the leftmost arête. (It is possible to walk off leftwards here.)

Climb up steep rocks on good holds slanting slightly right. Make a move right at one point to a good foot-ledge, and slant right past a mossy alcove above. From a scree shelf continue slanting right to gain a broken groove which lies back slightly.

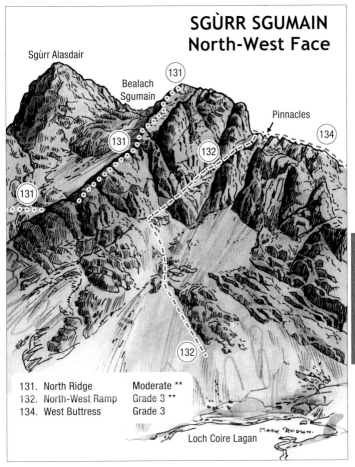

**SGÙRR SGUMAIN
North-West Face**

Sgùrr Alasdair

Bealach
Sgumain

Pinnacles

131. North Ridge   Moderate **
132. North-West Ramp   Grade 3 **
134. West Buttress   Grade 3

Loch Coire Lagan

SOUTHERN CUILLIN

Ascend by the scree-filled groove using the rocks mainly on its right-hand side. Then follow a more definite rib on the right. When the groove starts to peter out, ascend flakes leading slightly left towards a dyke. Stay on the right side of the dyke on pleasant rocks. Eventually step left across a narrow gully and slant diagonally left to where the rocks are more amenable. When the pinnacles in Bealach Sgumain come into sight, slant right on more broken rocks. Frankland's Gully is visible further right.

Towards the top, do not go round a corner on the right but instead ascend an enjoyable rib slanting slightly left. Break out onto easy ground and soon reach the commodious summit. There are superb views to the south.

The easiest option now is to descend the south ridge to Bealach Coire a' Ghrunnda (Route 135). However, the best combination is to traverse the summit, descend Route 130 and ascend the south-west ridge of Sgùrr Alasdair (Route 129).

 132 North-West Ramp   Grade 3   **
(NG 446 208)   Alt 660m   Map p236   Diagram p263

This route crosses an impressive face and has some spectacular situations. The first recorded ascent was by J.S. Napier, R.G. Napier and J.H. Bell in 1896.

Approach
Reach upper Coire Lagan as for Route 116 and go round to the opposite side of the lochan.

The Route
Ascend a fairly stable scree slope slanting left below rock outcrops. Scramble up slabs and grooves, where water trickles down, to reach a higher scree slope. Slant left and head for the start of the obvious ramp feature that slants rightwards below the huge face.

Follow a grassy ledge easily to the start of the slabby ramp. Ascend the slabs right of the corner, weaving to and fro to find the easiest and cleanest line. Move back closer to the corner, then reach a small alcove with wet rock to the left and a steeper wall to the right. Scramble up the alcove on small square-cut holds trending slightly left (crux). Break out onto easier slabs. Eventually trend a long way right to a flat, gritty ledge.

Move left and follow a faint ramp/weakness. Curve leftwards at first then go back right. Ascend an awkward block and continue on rough blocks to the crest of a ridge (West Buttress). Follow the last section of the ridge left to an impressive final tower. A small window is visible on the skyline high above. Traverse a long way right, with surprising ease, along a prominent horizontal ledge. Reach the south ridge of Sgùrr Sgumain, a short distance uphill from Bealach Coire a' Ghrunnda. Either descend by the Sgumain Stone Shoot or continue easily to the summit of Sgùrr Sgumain.

 133 Lochan Traverse   Moderate   **
(NG 444 207)   Alt 560m   Map p236   Diagram p265

There is a prominent break crossing the rocks which form the lower part of the West Buttress of Sgùrr Sgumain. It marks an inward-dipping contact between two different types of gabbro (dark brown above and lighter brown below). This route traverses along the break. It is best done from left to right i.e. from upper Coire Lagan to the Sgumain Stone Shoot. Although most of the route is scrambling there are some awkward moves on the first half of the traverse which just justify the climbing grade.

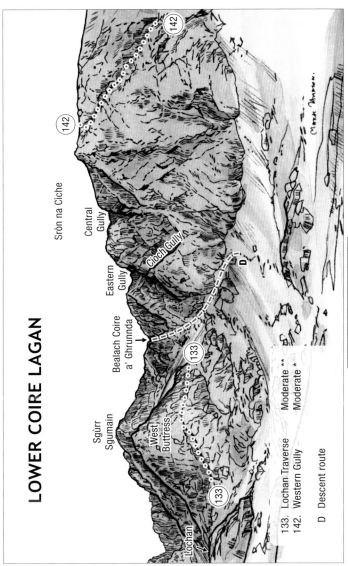

LOWER COIRE LAGAN

Sgùrr Sgumain

Sròn na Ciche

Central Gully

Eastern Gully

Cioch Gully

Bealach Coire a' Ghrunnda

West Buttress

Lochan

D

133

142

133. Lochan Traverse — Moderate **
142. Western Gully — Moderate *

D Descent route

Approach

From upper Coire Lagan, cross wonderfully ice-sculpted rocks on the right-hand (west) side of Loch Coire Lagan. Descend slightly to reach the start of the fairly obvious traverse line above an apron of steep slabs.

The Route

The start of the route is usually wet and constitutes the crux. Make some steep moves up and left to get established on the break proper. Move out of the fault by a drippy wall and traverse across delightfully rough, sound slabs. At a steeper section, make an awkward bridging move to pull up past a boulder in a slightly more exposed position.

An easier ledge is then followed to a rift with boulders. There is some vegetation in the break, and then a steeper section is reached with an overhanging left wall and damp rock. One or two tricky moves give access to a more secure rift. Then step up onto a boulder to reach more straightforward scrambling. The traverse line then starts to flatten out and an easier section is followed for some distance. There are occasional juniper bushes, and further right there are fine views of the Cioch on Sròn na Cìche. After the high point of the traverse there is one further section of scrambling by a small gap, but after that it is mainly walking to reach the Sgumain Stone Shoot.

 134 West Buttress   Grade 3
(NG 444 205)   Alt 600m   Map p236   Diagrams pp263 & 267

There are a number of climbs on the main face of West Buttress that looks out over Coire Lagan. This route avoids the lower section of the buttress altogether on the right, and gains the crest where the angle begins to ease. However, some rickety pinnacles high up involve Difficult climbing, so an escape is suggested down the south flank. This is a rather artificial line, and the rock is worrying on the crest. Worthwhile only for the unusual views across Coire Lagan.

Approach

Follow the path from the camp site to Coire Lagan. A short distance beyond Loch an Fhir-bhallaich (and before the Matterhorn block), take a less distinct right fork, and follow this across two streams towards the north face of Sròn na Cìche. Do not go up to the foot of the face, but slant left and find a way up scree, big blocks and rock outcrops to gain the main Sgumain Stone Shoot. Ascend this until above the level of the Lochan Traverse (Route 133).

The Route

There are several places on the first part of the route where it is easy to escape rightwards and rejoin the stone shoot. Slant left across fairly easy ground at first. A slab with a dyke running up it has a chockstone 4m above a corner. Squeeze up under this on the left. Continue up scree, ascend a groove and move left along a thick cone-sheet. Where the terrace pinches out break right to more broken ground. Go up rocks to the right of some chockstones to more scree. Cut hard left below a grassy alcove, and ascend a shallow recess with

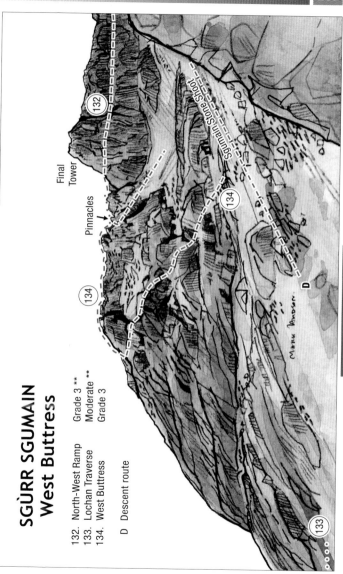

SGÙRR SGUMAIN
West Buttress

132. North-West Ramp   Grade 3 **
133. Lochan Traverse   Moderate **
134. West Buttress   Grade 3

D   Descent route

a groove above. Break right and step up by a juniper bush onto a slab, then pass round a blocky pinnacle on its right-hand side.

Slant diagonally leftwards up slabs and grassy grooves below steeper rocks forming the tower-like crest of the buttress. Go further left and scramble up rocks to the left of a dyke. Make a tricky move left onto a slabby ledge. There are now views of the northern flank. Do not break back right to the crest until beyond the first mass of rock. Then follow the crest as closely as possible.

The shattered nature of the rock detracts from the fine position. There are excellent views of both Sgùrr MhicCoinnich and Sròn na Cìche. At one point make a reverse à cheval move to descend a sharp arête. Shortly after this the crest becomes even more tricky, and it is left to climbers to fnd a way past some tottering pinnacles. Instead, pick a way down the right-hand flank, slanting right at first with some care, to gain an easier scree slope which merges with the Sgumain Stone Shoot lower down.

135 South Ridge 8km *
(NG 448 204) Alt 840m   Map p236   Diagram p259

Some very rough ground has to be ascended to reach the start of this ridge at Bealach Coire a' Ghrunnda (840m). The summit is a fine viewpoint, but walkers will have to return from it the same way.

Approach

The most direct approach to the start of this ridge is by the Sgumain Stone Shoot from Coire Lagan (see previous route). The terrain is hard going, but fairly well-worn once the main shoot is reached. The face of Sròn na Cìche is an impressive sight to the right and, high up the slope, a rocky ridge known as Ladies' Pinnacle stands out on the left. An alternative approach is to traverse Sròn na Cìche (Route 143).

The Route

A prominent brown-orange peridotite dyke crosses the crest near the bealach and, shortly above this, gabbro gives way to a large intrusive sheet of grey tholeiite (here an amygdaloidal breccia). This rock forms an obvious capping to the summit of Sgùrr Sgumain. Ascend the ridge without any great difficulty to the broad summit.

SRÒN NA CÌCHE 859m

(NG 447 203) Map p236

The long, wedge-like spur of Sròn na Cìche separates Coire Lagan from Coire a' Ghrunnda. On its northern and south-eastern flanks it has some of the best climbing on offer in the Cuillin. The Coire Lagan face is particularly impressive, being a full kilometre wide and 300m high. This superb precipice is the preserve of rock climbers. Not surprisingly, the routes described here have a fairly serious air about them. An extraordinary boss of rock, known as the Cioch, protrudes from the middle of the face. Most climbers will have an ambition to reach the summit platform of this unique piece of rock architecture.

The flank which overlooks Coire a' Ghrunnda faces south-east, and seems slightly more friendly. It has two sizeable buttresses, with some very enjoyable climbs. The south-western flank, by contrast, is a broad scree and boulder slope of no great interest. The summit itself is not distinguished but it links, via Bealach Coire a' Ghrunnda, with Sgùrr Sgumain.

COIRE LAGAN FACE

The huge north-north-west face of Sròn na Cìche is split by two major leftward-slanting gullies – Eastern and Central Gullies – into three main sections, Eastern Buttress on the left, Central or Cioch Buttress in the middle, and Western Buttress to the right. Most of the routes described here are on Cioch Buttress. It is possible to reach the Terrace below the Cioch itself by two different routes which involve only scrambling, but otherwise this side of the mountain is for climbers only. The face is in shadow until late in the day.

 136 Collie's Route, The Cioch   Moderate **
(NG 445 204)   Alt 640m   Map p236   Diagram p270

This climb was pioneered by Collie and Mackenzie when they made the first ascent of the Cioch in 1906. It takes a very devious route, but has plenty of atmosphere. The outing as described finishes by ascending the upper section of Eastern Gully to reach the summit of Sròn na Cìche.

Approach

Approach the face of Sròn na Cìche as for Route 134. Ascend steep scree and broken ground to reach the foot of the face near the centre of Cioch Buttress. Then slant left below the face and cross a deep scoop in the scree. This was gouged out by a major rockfall in April 1999. Ascend debris with care to reach an obvious traverse line where a cone-sheet slants right. The start is harder than it used to be, but is still little more than Grade 2 scrambling.

The Route

Traverse delicately right and soon reach a more comfortable shelf. Continue right into the boulder-filled break of Eastern Gully. Make a tricky rightwards traverse across a slab – below a steep, wet wall. Move round onto the Terrace below the spectacular Cioch Slab. All the ways onto the Cioch from here involve rock climbing.

This route follows the first obvious crack slanting left up the Cioch Slab. It looks quite intimidating from below. However, the climbing is not technically difficult, although the drop into Eastern Gully on the left adds some spice. Where the rocks start to steepen, do not go straight up, but look for a ledge leading round to the left onto the wall of Eastern Gully. Ascend a section of dyke and continue traversing left across the wall until it is possible to reach the floor of the gully. Go a short distance up the gully, then traverse right

SOUTHERN CUILLIN

THE CIOCH & CIOCH SLAB

136. Collie's Route, The Cioch   Moderate **
137. Arrow Route   Very Difficult ***
138. Cioch Slab Corner   Difficult **
139. South-West Face, The Cioch   Moderate **
140. Cioch Gully & SW Chimney   Grade 3 **

across slabs. Follow a break leading right and, after a short delicate section, descend a more secure rift known as the Shelf. Continue down the exposed right-hand crest to reach the neck behind the Cioch.

A bold step up from the neck soon leads to easier rocks and the amazing summit platform (718m). An alternative option from the neck is to traverse slightly left along a ledge and ascend a chimney. This is possibly a touch harder but less exposed.

After enjoying the vistas from the top, some tricky moves have to be reversed to get back down to the neck. (An abseil can be arranged from a rock boss on the Coire Lagan side of the summit platform.) Follow the Shelf all the way back to Eastern Gully. It is possible to descend Eastern Gully, but this involves an abseil.

A more entertaining option is to continue up Eastern Gully. An athletic wriggle to get past a big chockstone on the left-hand side is followed by an awkward little traverse on the left wall. Higher up take the right fork. Emerge on the south-west flank of Sròn na Cìche and continue without difficulty to the summit. If nothing more ambitious is planned, an easy descent can be made down the Sgumain Stone Shoot from Bealach Coire a' Ghrunnda.

137 Arrow Route   Very Difficult   ***
(NG 444 203)   Alt 670m   Map p236   Diagram p270

This climb finds a way up the middle of Cioch Slab on wonderfully sound, dimpled rock – Cuillin gabbro at its best. It is not over-endowed with protection, but modern rock slippers make it a less harrowing lead than it once was. It was first by climbed by Jerry Wright in 1928 and graded Severe.

Approach
Reach the Terrace below the Cioch Slab by either Route 136 or 140.

The Route
Start directly below Cioch Slab Corner and follow a left-slanting crack to a stance by a small niche with a flake belay. Then climb boldly up, slanting slightly left, on perfect rock. Towards the top, trend right up a shallow ramp to reach the Shelf. A superb pitch.

138 Cioch Slab Corner   Difficult   **
(NG 444 203)   Alt 670m   Map p236   Diagram p270

This is a direct and very enjoyable way of reaching the Cioch from the Terrace. It is well protected and on delightful rock.

Approach
Reach the Terrace below the Cioch Slab by either Route 136 or 140.

The Route
Climb the introductory slab and the obvious corner above in two pitches – the second being the crux. At one point it is necessary to leave the corner and climb the steep slab on the left. Finish on the neck behind the Cioch. Reach the summit platform as for Collie's Route.

Looking straight down on the Cioch from the top of Sròn na Cìche.
A party is sitting on the Cioch and a climber is leading Arrow Route.

139 South-West Face, The Cioch   Moderate   **

(NG 444 203)   Alt 675m   Map p236   Diagram p270)

Although this route is not as spectacular as the ones on Cioch Slab, it catches more of the sun. A prominent crack slanting across the back face of the Cioch is the key to the climb.

Approach
Reach the Terrace below the Cioch Slab by either Route 136 or 140.

The Route
Continue slanting right up the Terrace beyond Cioch Slab Corner. Make a foot-traverse across a short wall to reach a continuation of the Terrace. Slanting right from here leads round a corner towards Cioch Gully. Instead head up to a slight recess in the rocks above, which form the western nose of the Cioch.

Gain the recess by slanting left up a slab, then climb rightwards by a sharp-edged crack. Step down slightly and make a tricky move to get established in a very prominent crack which slants across the slabby face forming the back of the Cioch (visible in the photo on page 272). Follow this crack with interest to the ledge by the chimney which gives access to the summit of the Cioch.

140 Cioch Gully & South-West Chimney   Grade 3 **
(NG 443 203) Alt 550m   Map p236   Diagram p274

This is a very enjoyable way of reaching the Terrace below the Cioch, though only climbers will be able to progress any further up the face. Collie used this route as a way of descending from the Terrace. When combined with the previous route, it offers climbers a quick way of approaching the routes on Cioch Upper Buttress.

Approach
Approach the face of Sròn na Cìche as for Route 134. Ascend steep scree and broken ground to reach the foot of the face near the centre of Cioch Buttress.

The Route
To the right of a steep buttress there is a slabby gully where water trickles down. Start by scrambling up this by the rocks on the left side. Then transfer to the right and weave a way up pleasant slabs to reach easier ground. Join the main line of Cioch Gully and slant leftwards along this. A break on the right leads up to the Amphitheatre (see next route). At this point Cioch Gully becomes more difficult.

Scramble pleasantly up the gully at first. Move onto the rocks to the left of the gully, then trend back right. Follow a rib and rake to the left, then ascend a crack in a steeper section of slab to gain a platform with boulders by an alcove.

At a point where a chockstone can be seen in the steeper gully above, follow a prominent break which slants left away from Cioch Gully. Ascend a mossy groove, surmount a chockstone and enter a chimney/rift. Thrutch up the chimney (easier with a small rucksack), and break out onto a ledge on the front face of Cioch Buttress.

Traverse left a short way along the ledge and as soon as possible make an awkward step up to get established on a beautiful section of slab (crux). Continue up the slab in a fine position, and eventually reach bouldery ground below the western nose of the Cioch. The Terrace below Cioch Slab can be gained by descending slightly to the left and foot traversing a short wall. However, the natural continuation from here is to climb the nose directly above as for the previous route.

141 Amphitheatre Arête   Difficult **
(NG 443 203) Alt 550m   Map p236   Diagram p274

This route ascends a long slabby rib up an impressive section of face on Western Buttress. It is a very enjoyable route with plenty of atmosphere. The main difficulties are short-lived, and the climb is low in its grade. It was first ascended by Norman Collie in 1907.

Approach
Approach the face of Sròn na Cìche as for the previous route. Start at a slabby gully where water trickles down.

SOUTHERN CUILLIN

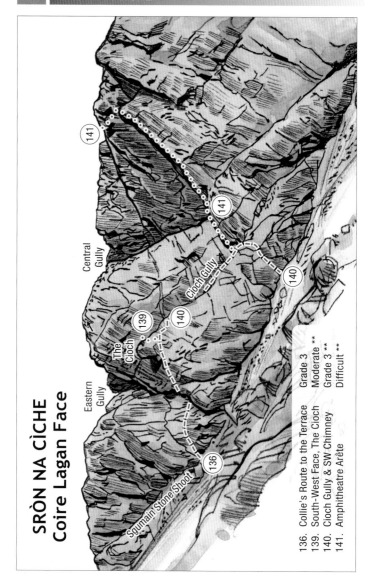

SRÒN NA CÌCHE
Coire Lagan Face

136. Collie's Route to the Terrace   Grade 3
139. South-West Face, The Cioch   Moderate **
140. Cioch Gully & SW Chimney   Grade 3 **
141. Amphitheatre Arête   Difficult **

The Route
Scramble up to the main part of Cioch Gully as for the previous route. Leave Cioch Gully by climbing up slabs and grooves on the right. The easiest line is not obvious, and the rock is often wet. It is best not to stay in the left-hand corner. Some delicate padding on damp slabs (first crux) leads to easier ground where Central Gully cuts across the face. A broad recess in the face above is known as the Amphitheatre.

Do not continue straight up, where the rocks are often wet, but instead traverse hard right along a ledge. Ascend slabs for some 6m to easier-angled rocks, then continue traversing right to reach a ledge at the start of the broad rib or arête which is the main feature of the route. Climb easily up the arête on pleasant rock for some distance.

Eventually the arête starts to curve leftwards as a gully develops on the right. Do not follow a ledge horizontally left below steep rocks; instead move right and climb steep steps up a nose (second crux). Continue to an alcove with intimidating rocks above. Trend up left and then traverse right across a wall by a narrow ledge. Reach a break cutting back left and follow this to easier ground. The extensive summit plateau is nearby.

There is a prominent pinnacle (The Finger) to the left of where the route finishes. It is sitting on a ledge which is a continuation of the same cone-sheet forming the Cioch Terrace. Either descend boulders and scree on the south-west flank or continue to the summit of Sròn na Cìche (see Route 143).

142 Western Gully   Moderate *   (NG 440 202)   Alt 520m   Map p236   Diagram p265
This gully lies at the far right-hand end of Western Buttress. It offers a different kind of outing to the main face climbs, and has very fine seaward views. The route as described was first ascended by Collie and Mackenzie in 1906.

Start
Follow the path to Lower Coire Lagan as for Route 134. Once across the Allt Coire Lagan bear right and head directly towards the base of Western Gully (see diagram on Page 265). Ascend scree and slabs to the mouth of the gully.

The Route
A dyke marks the line of the gully. The initial section is rather steep so scramble up rocks to the left of the gully itself. (The direct route up the gully was climbed by Guy Barlow soon after the first ascent.) Weave a way up the left-bounding buttress for some distance. Interesting scrambling alternates with minor pitches of climbing up steeper rock steps. Eventually it becomes more attractive to traverse rightwards into the gully.

There are several short pitches in the gully with some tricky moves by chockstones. The crux pitch finishes with a delicate traverse across the right wall to regain the bed of the gully.

The gully now starts to lie back, and there are only minor pitches before the gully forks. The main gully is filled with scree, so follow the more interesting right fork and then break out onto the south-west flank of Sròn na Cìche. Either descend scree and boulders to join the path from Coire a' Ghrunnda or traverse the summit as for the next route.

143 Traverse by South-West Flank 7km
(NG 436 195) Alt 300m Map p236

The broad south-west flank is the easiest, but least inspiring, route to the summit of Sròn na Cìche. It does, however, offer a convenient descent route from the neighbouring face climbs, and there are fine views of Rum and Canna from its upper reaches.

Approach
Follow the path from the campsite in Glen Brittle as for Coire Lagan, but take a right fork across a stream after 800 metres. The path, which has been much improved of late, eventually crosses the Allt Coire Lagan. Shortly after this, two parallel paths cross the toe of Sròn na Cìche. The lower path leads to Gars-bheinn and continues as an intermittent feature around the coast to Coruisk. The upper path is used to reach Coire a' Ghrunnda and also the start of this route.

The Route
Leave the upper path and head up between small crags to a broad slope of scree and boulders. Ascend this rather tedious ground for some distance. The angle starts to ease at about the 750m level. Continue over bouldery ground and pass indents in the left-hand rim of the plateau marking the two forks of Eastern Gully. A walk of little more than one hundred metres then leads to the summit.

Soon after the highest point a steep drop cuts across the slope, so it is necessary to move right and find a way back left down slabby steps. It is only a short distance then to Bealach Coire a' Ghrunnda. An easy descent can then be made down the Sgumain Stone Shoot into Coire Lagan. However, it is a simple matter to visit the summit of Sgùrr Sgumain first by using Route 135. A more adventurous return can be made via Coire a' Ghrunnda (see the diagram on page 259).

COIRE A' GHRUNNDA FACE

Coire a' Ghrunnda itself is arguably the rockiest of all the Cuillin corries. It is a magnificent example of glacial sculpturing. Three levels of superb boiler-plate slabs form the floor of the lower corrie, and much of the rock basin in the upper corrie is occupied by Loch Coire a' Ghrunnda – at 697m, the highest body of water in the Cuillin. A visit to Coire a' Ghrunnda alone is very rewarding. However, the easiest way to the upper corrie requires good route-finding as well as some scrambling ability.

The south-east face of Sròn na Cìche, which overlooks Coire a' Ghrunnda, has two main sections of crag separated by a broad, wet gully. The left-hand

Looking up Coire a' Ghrunnda

section, known as South Crag, is very impressive and has excellent climbing. Two rakes cut across this crag from right to left. The right-hand section of the face, known as North Crag, is quite complex and consists of two buttresses – Stack Buttress and Slab Buttress – divided by North Crag Gully.

All the routes described on this face were first climbed by Steeple and Barlow in 1920. The routes on South Crag are described first.

144 Stony Rake   Grade 1   *
(NG 446 195)   Alt 550m   Map p236   Diagram p279

This route is not a particularly worthwhile outing in its own right, but it offers a possible descent route from the climbs on South Crag, or a different way home from Coire a' Ghrunnda. It finishes on the broad shoulder of Sròn na Cìche.

Approach

Follow the path from the campsite in Glen Brittle as described for Route 143. A little way after crossing the Allt Coire Lagan, follow the left fork of the path which climbs uphill past a prominent boulder. Contour across the toe of Sròn na Cìche for one kilometre.

There are two ways into Coire a' Ghrunnda. The higher route is more convenient for approaching South Crag. It breaks off to the left below a steep rock wall. Ascend an earthy gully quite steeply, with a rock wall on the left, to reach a slight flattening marked by a boggy hollow. Then ascend stony ground for some distance to gain a broad terrace below the prominent rock face of South Crag.

The Route
Slant rightwards up a weakness to gain a much narrower terrace at the foot of the main face. From the left end of this terrace ascend the obvious leftward-slanting rake formed by a cone-sheet. Short sections of easy scrambling lead to a more open section of face. The continuation of the rake is mainly walking on much grassier terrain. Eventually break out onto the south-western flank of Sròn na Cìche. Descend diagonally across the slope in a westward direction to rejoin the approach path.

145 Central Buttress   Difficult ***
(NG 446 197)   Alt 550m   Map p236   Diagram p279

This is one of the most enjoyable routes of its grade in the Cuillin. It has several pitches of delightful, open climbing on good rock. A slightly scrappy pitch above Pinnacle Rake is more than compensated for by sensational climbing on the final tower.

Approach
As for the previous route.

The Route
From a slight alcove above the start of Stony Rake, climb along a narrow, leftward-slanting intrusion above and parallel to the rake. Reach a feature called the Horizontal Ledge which extends some distance across the face. Good thread belay by huge block. The next pitch starts just left of a small projecting rib, some 3 metres to the left of the gully/groove climbed by Trap Dyke Route (Difficult). Climb a ragged crack with white veining, and weave a way up on superb rock trending slightly left. Sustained climbing by narrow dykes with very little protection leads to a stance below slightly steeper rocks.

Continue up a dyke trending slightly right at first, then cut back left to the centre of the buttress. Make an awkward step up, then take a fairly direct line up a groove with some pleasant bridging. Take a stance just below a cone-sheet which slants up leftwards below steeper rocks. Go left along the cone-sheet to the left edge of the buttress, where there are good views into a gully (Green Recess Chimneys). Climb up the left edge in a fine position. Stay on the arête apart from a couple of moves on the left-hand side. The angle gradually eases as height is gained. A stance can be taken just below Pinnacle Rake to avoid problems with rope drag.

Cross a slight neck to reach Pinnacle Rake just left of one of the two spectacular pinnacles after which it is named. Continue directly above and head for a prominent tower with gullies on either side. Start at the bottom right-hand side of the tower and step left onto its front face. Traverse left on

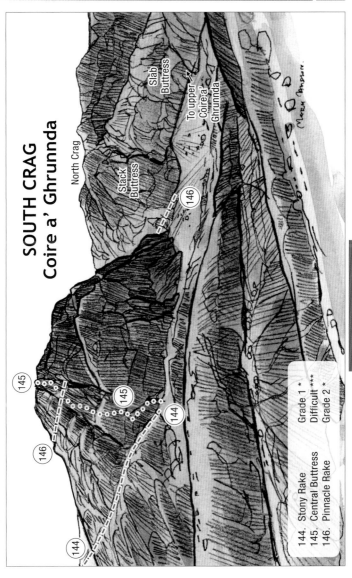

SOUTH CRAG
Coire a' Ghrunnda

North Crag

Slab Buttress

To upper Coire a' Ghrunnda

Stack Buttress

Malin Inglis.

144. Stony Rake   Grade 1 *
145. Central Buttress   Difficult ***
146. Pinnacle Rake   Grade 2 *

On the top pitch of Central Buttress (Difficult)
Climber: Peter Duggan

small foot-ledges to reach the centre of the face. Move up slightly then traverse hard right to near the right edge, before moving up and then returning to a central position. Climb up very steeply on jutting blocks and flakes in a fine position (crux). The climbing gradually eases above. Eventually reach a fine stance on a ledge. A further short pitch leads to the top.

To return to the foot of the face, descend the south-west flank of Sròn na Ciche as far as a sharp leftward bend in its south-eastern rim. It should then be possible to identify the upper grassy section of Stony Rake (Route 144). Descend the rake to the start of the route.

146 Pinnacle Rake   Grade 2   *
(NG 447 199)   Alt 630m   Map p236   Diagrams pp279 & 283

This rake crosses the upper part of South Crag from right to left. It is difficult to identify from below, and is best seen from the base of Stack Buttress or when descending from upper Coire a' Ghrunnda. It is more difficult than Stony Rake and harder to follow, but like that route it offers an alternative way home from Coire a' Ghrunnda.

Approach
Approach as for Route 144. Go past the base of South Crag and slant right to just beyond where water drains from the gully dividing North and South Crags. A short section of leftward-leaning brown slab marks the best access point to the rake.

The Route
A striking pinnacle, which resembles an owl, stands out on the skyline to the left of the rake. Ascend the short slab, then traverse left across damp and slightly broken rocks to eventually gain the obvious break to the right of the owl-like pinnacle. The ground gradually steepens and becomes unpleasantly loose. Pick a way up rather shattered rock with care (crux) and bridge up a groove on the left. Soon gain an easier and more grassy section. Continue by a small rowan tree and, shortly after, go over boulders beside a second, finger-like pinnacle. The Central Buttress climb (Route 145) crosses the rake near here.

Turn a slight corner and traverse across a recess marking the upper part of Green Recess Chimneys. The rake now appears to peter out. By descending a grassy groove for a short distance it is possible to pick up the line of a cone-sheet which is the key to the final section of the route. Follow this with interest around several corners and eventually emerge on the south-west flank of Sròn na Ciche. Descend that slope to regain the approach path.

147 Stack Buttress Direct   Difficult   **
(NG 447 199)   Alt 630m   Map p236   Diagram p283

This very enjoyable route offers a remarkably different style of climbing to Central Buttress. It has very interesting route-finding, and is quite hard for the grade.

Approach

Approach as for Route 144, then continue beyond South Crag. Stack Buttress is set back slightly and starts at a higher level.

It is also possible to approach by the lower route into Coire a' Ghrunnda. Slant left up veined slabs to reach a fault that runs along the base of a prominent rock band. Follow this a long way right until a short easy scramble leads to bouldery ground directly below Stack Buttress. (See diagram p279.)

The climb starts near the centre of the buttress (well to the left of North Crag Gully) below a rightward-slanting diagonal crack/break.

The Route

Climb up to the break and follow it over some awkward jutting blocks. Go horizontally right to a stance below a sloping roof. Move further right and climb over some slightly suspect flakes. Then break back up left for some distance and traverse horizontally left to a stance.

Make some steep moves up a slight depression, and pull up onto a large slabby ramp overlooking North Crag Gully. Follow the ramp left for a short distance then break right, across a wall, and shortly after reach another ramp. Follow this up left to a stance.

The bulging wall above proves rather difficult. With careful footwork it is possible to use some excellent handholds above and slightly left. Soon reach a grassy rake which is followed easily up to the left. Continue up a slab to a commodious terrace.

The slabby wall above is the south face of a tapered tower known as The Stack. Start by slanting very slightly left up a gully/groove then, at the first opportunity, traverse right onto the face. The standard way is to then climb directly up a crack. However, after climbing up slightly, it is possible to traverse delicately right again and then continue fairly directly to the crest of The Stack – a superb pitch.

Weave a way up left with fine views of upper Coire a' Ghrunnda. Finish up a rightward sweep of easy slabs. Either traverse over the summit of Sròn na Ciche or descend its south-west flank (Route 143).

 148 Slab Buttress Grade 3 **
(NG 447 199) Alt 630m Map p236 Diagram p283

This is an interesting meander up a big face, with several harder options available to climbers. The rock is generally very good.

Approach

Approach as for the previous route. Slab Buttress lies immediately to the right of Stack Buttress. The route to upper Coire a' Ghrunnda ascends a broad gully which slants below the base of the buttress.

The Route

The superb slabs forming the lower part of the buttress can be ascended by climbers. However, an easier option starts further left near the bottom of North Crag Gully, and this is now described.

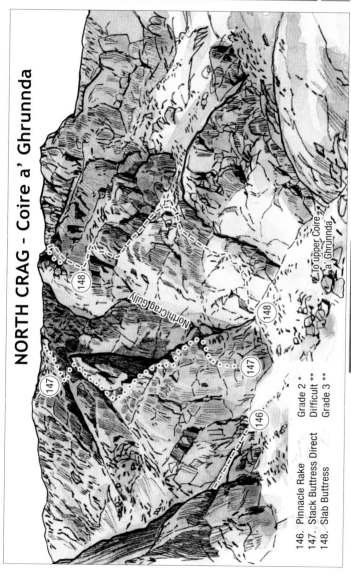

NORTH CRAG - Coire a' Ghrunnda

North Crag Gully

To upper Coire a' Ghrunnda

SOUTHERN CUILLIN

146. Pinnacle Rake   Grade 2 *
147. Stack Buttress Direct   Difficult **
148. Slab Buttress   Grade 3 **

Slab Buttress (Grade 3), Coire a' Ghrunnda
Scrambler: Andrew Wielochowski

Go up by the stream which issues from North Crag Gully. A short distance below the mouth of the gully, find a way onto the right-hand wall by a dyke. Move right round a corner, then traverse easily along a grassy terrace some distance to the right. Before reaching the end of the terrace, move up to a higher rock ledge. Traverse right and use a deep dimple for the left hand to ascend a steeper section by a dyke. Break back leftwards on rock which gradually gets easier as height is gained. Clamber carefully past some loose blocks, then move left from an alcove and follow a dyke trending slightly right. Eventually reach a point overlooking a damp chimney/gully on the right. Move back left and step up onto fine slabs. Follow these to easier ground.

Reach a big slanting terrace where an easy escape is available off to the right. Continue up fairly easy rocks in the same general direction, and eventually reach another big slanting terrace. This time the rocks directly ahead are too steep, so go right and ascend coarse scree. Then cut back hard left up the higher of two sloping rock shelves. From the top of the shelf there are views across into North Crag Gully.

The next tier gives very sustained scrambling. Go back down the shelf a short distance. Ascend a broken groove to the right of a more prominent groove near a corner. Then move left to gain the left-hand groove. Follow this on slightly slimy rock for a short distance, then traverse right and follow an arête to the right of a slab. Move right along a crack-line and ascend to a ledge. Traverse left and ascend a crack behind a huge block to reach a sloping grassy terrace.

Ascend a prominent slab by moving left and scrambling pleasantly up a rightward-trending break. Reach another terrace and follow this up left. There is a prominent tower directly above with a right-slanting slabby corner on its right-hand side. The corner is delightful but not as easy as it looks (Difficult). The scrambling option goes up the slabs slightly further to the right. Then, from an easy terrace, traverse back hard left. Soon reach the bouldery plateau of Sròn na Cìche.

The top of Eastern Gully in Coire Lagan lies directly across the slope. It is a simple matter to visit the summit of Sròn na Cìche. Then either descend the Sgumain Stone Shoot (see Route 143) or return down the South-West Flank.

SGÙRR THEÀRLAICH 978m

(NG 450 207) Map p236

This peak was described earlier, along with the peaks surrounding Coire Lagan (see p253–8). However, its south-east ridge is described here because it overlooks Coire a' Ghrunnda. This ridge is cleaved by one of the most formidable obstacles on the Cuillin main ridge – the Theàrlaich–Dubh Gap.

Fortunately there are easier options for non-climbers. See the next route and Route 175 in the Coruisk section.

SOUTHERN CUILLIN

149 Traverse below the South-West Face 450m
(NG 451 206) Alt 870m Map p236 Diagram pp288 & 290

This route has become quite a popular way of avoiding the Theàrlaich–Dubh Gap. However, the natural continuation to the summit of Sgùrr Alasdair is a Grade 3 scramble.

Approach

The route starts from Bealach Coire an Lochain. It is most likely to be approached along the main ridge. See Route 150 for a description of how to approach Bealach Coire an Lochain from Coire a' Ghrunnda.

The Route

From Bealach Coire an Lochain follow the south-east ridge for a short distance, and traverse over a very minor rise. Then find a way off the left-hand side of the ridge. See the diagram on page 288. Pick up a faint path which crosses the scree fan below the Theàrlaich–Dubh Gap. (The gully which leads directly up to the gap is mainly a loose scramble with a short section of Moderate.)

Follow the path close to a rock wall on the right without any difficulty. Towards the upper end it curves gently left and then ascends scree to the right of a cave. Continuing directly above leads to Bealach Sgumain. The normal route up the south-west ridge of Sgùrr Alasdair follows a ledge to the right, a short distance below the bealach itself (see Route 129).

150 South-East Ridge via the Theàrlaich–Dubh Gap Very Difficult (with an abseil) ** *(NG 452 205) Alt 855m Map p236 Diagram p288*

This is one of the hardest obstacles on the Cuillin main ridge traverse. Only Naismith's Route on the Basteir Tooth is of a similar standard. The problem of the gap was first solved by Collie and King when they scaled both its walls on the same day in 1889.

Approach

Although this route is normally reached along the main ridge, the approach from Coire a' Ghrunnda is described for completeness. Follow either of the two routes up the left-hand side of Coire a' Ghrunnda (see Route 147) to the base of Slab Buttress. Gain the upper corrie by first slanting up a broad gully below Stack Buttress. Then scramble up rocks well left of the stream which drains Loch Coire a' Ghrunnda. (When descending this way be sure not to follow the line of the stream.) Then clamber over boulders and traverse across rough ground to where the stream leaves the loch.

Slant up rough ground on the left-hand side of the loch. Pass a delightful spring with green vegetation – one of the highest sources of water in the Cuillin. Then either ascend the obvious scree gully direct to the T–D Gap (with a short section of scrambling) or slant diagonally rightwards to reach the crest of the main ridge. To reach Bealach Coire an Lochain continue rightwards (south-east) along the ridge weaving between enormous blocks.

An unknown climber on the long pitch out of the T–D Gap (Very Difficult)
Photo: Nick Carter

The Route
Follow the crest of the ridge and pass to the left of a minor boss of rock. Then climb up a section of much steeper rock, trending slightly left at first, to arrive at the lip of the gap. The normal practice is then to abseil some 10m down the south-east wall directly into the gap. In ascent this wall gives a very steep climb of Very Difficult/Severe standard. The best line is just to the left of centre when looking up.

The climb up the north-west side of the gap is longer (25m) but slightly easier than the one on the other side. In perfect conditions it may seem easy for its grade. However, it is rather polished and becomes extremely treacherous in the wet. The lower section is a steep chimney/crack with an awkward jamming move halfway up which is easier with a rock boot on one foot and a big boot on the other! The upper section follows a slightly less steep groove. Scramble pleasantly up the remainder of the ridge until it is possible to slant left and ascend easily on scree to the saddle at the top of the Great Stone Shoot. It is normal then to make a detour to the summit of Sgùrr Alasdair (Route 128).

It is an easy matter to rejoin the ridge in the same place. Then continue up the south ridge to the summit of Sgùrr Theàrlaich (See Route 127).

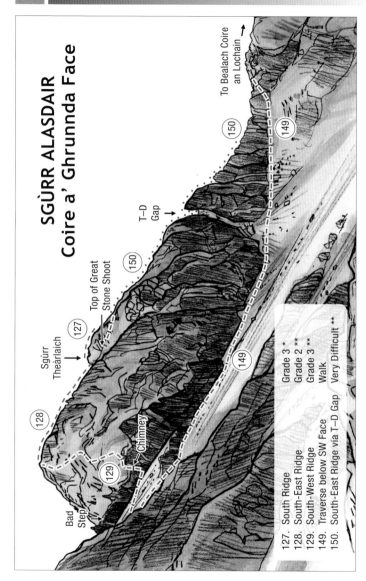

SGÙRR ALASDAIR
Coire a' Ghrunnda Face

Sgùrr Theàrlaich

Top of Great Stone Shoot

Chimney

Bad Step

T–D Gap

To Bealach Coire an Lochain

127. South Ridge — Grade 3 *
128. South-East Ridge — Grade 2 **
129. South-West Ridge — Grade 3 **
149. Traverse below SW Face — Walk
150. South-East Ridge via T–D Gap — Very Difficult **

SGÙRR DUBH NA DÀ BHEINN 938m

(NG 455 204) Map p236

This shapely peak is composed of peridotite – a rock which is even rougher than gabbro. The three ridges radiating from the summit separate three spectacular corries. On a traverse of the main ridge it is now common practice to make a detour from this summit to visit Sgùrr Dubh Mòr – a Munro.

151 North-West Ridge   Grade 1
(NG 452 205)   Alt 855m   Map p236   Diagram p293
This is the easiest of the mountain's three ridges.

Approach
Approach Bealach Coire an Lochain as for the previous route. This bealach can also be reached without undue difficulty from the Coire an Lochain side.

The Route
Fairly straightforward walking and some easy scrambling soon lead to the summit of this peak. It is an excellent viewpoint.

152 East Ridge to Sgùrr Dubh Mòr   Grade 2 or 3 *
(NG 455 204)   Alt 938m   Map p236   Diagram p293
Since this route is frequently used to visit Sgùrr Dubh Mòr from the main ridge, it is described starting from Sgùrr Dubh na Dà Bheinn.

The Route
From the summit, scramble down the fairly narrow east ridge without great difficulty to a low point at 886m. Pass some sizeable pinnacles on the right side, or take them more directly to add extra interest.

The south-west spur of Sgùrr Dubh Mòr rises ahead. Weave a way up ledges starting on the right (Grade 2), or climb more directly up steep walls in a spectacular position (at least Grade 3). The summit lies a short distance along the chisel-like crest. Return the same way. See also the Dubh Slabs (Route 172).

153 South Ridge   Grade 2 **
(NG 454 202)   Alt 803m   Map p236   Diagram p293
This ridge gives an enjoyable scramble. It is characterised by massive blocks of rough rock.

Approach
The dip on the north side of Caisteal a' Gharbh-choire can be reached by ascending rough ground from either of the neighbouring corries. From the Coire a' Ghrunnda side finish by scrabbling under a huge leaning block.

The Route
Clamber up huge blocks close to the crest but generally just on the Coire a'

SOUTHERN CUILLIN

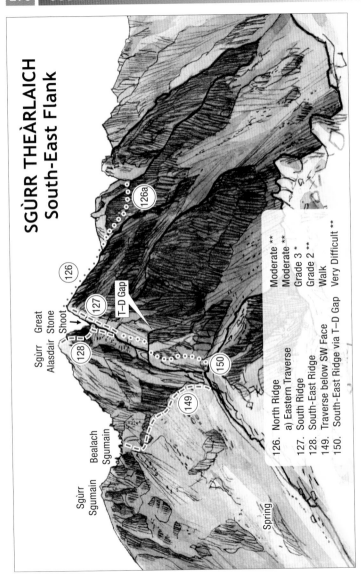

SGÙRR THEÀRLAICH
South-East Flank

T–D Gap

Sgùrr Alasdair

Great Stone Shoot

Sgùrr Sgumain

Bealach Sgumain

Spring

126.	North Ridge	Moderate **
	a) Eastern Traverse	Moderate **
127.	South Ridge	Grade 3 *
128.	South-East Ridge	Grade 2 **
149.	Traverse below SW Face	Walk
150.	South-East Ridge via T–D Gap	Very Difficult **

Ghrunnda side. Much variation is possible. At one point move left along a good ledge and then back right to a nose. Continue for some distance with the angle gradually easing. Curve rightwards to reach the summit.

CAISTEAL A' GHARBH-CHOIRE 828m

(NG 454 202) Map p236

To the east of Loch Coire a' Ghrunnda there is a pass over to Coruisk called **Bealach a' Gharbh-choire** (797m). An impressive rock bastion, called Caisteal a' Gharbh-choire, is situated in the bealach. The feature is well named *(castle of the rough corrie)*. It is built from extremely rough peridotite. Its distinctive profile can be recognised even from the landing stage in Loch na Cuilce by the Coruisk Hut.

   The summit is accessible only to climbers. The whole mass can be bypassed most easily by a path on the east side. When crossing to Coruisk, the best option is to gain the ridge at the southern end of Caisteal a' Gharbh-choire, skirt round by this path on the east side and then descend into An Garbh-choire from the northern end.

 154 North-East Ridge   Difficult *
(NG 454 202) Alt 803m   Map p236   Diagram p293

This route was climbed by Naismith and Arthur in 1912, when they traversed the peak from north to south. Confident climbers can descend this way, though it should not be confused with the overhanging northern end, which is sometimes abseiled. The north-west end gives a route of similar grade.

Approach
From the dip at the northern end of Caisteal a' Gharbh-choire, move down very slightly left onto the An Garbh-choire side.

The Route
Climb steeply up the rather indefinite ridge for some 8m, then continue with slightly less difficulty. Slant right to gain the summit crest. The highest point is towards the southern end. Descend by the south ridge or west face as described for the next route.

 155 South Ridge & West Face   Moderate **
(NG 454 201) Alt 797m   Map p236   Diagram p293

This combination gives a most enjoyable way of traversing this fine little peak. The grade would be harder but for the superbly adhesive quality of the rock.

Approach
Start from Bealach a' Gharbh-choire at the southern end of Caisteal a' Gharbh-choire. There are big blocks set in the rock hereabouts.

The Route
Scramble up the crest to where it steepens. Climb amazing rock in a superb

position. The easiest line lies slightly left of the crest. From the summit continue down the crest then climb down the middle of the west face. Scramble around the north-western side and ascend loose ground to the tunnel by the leaning block.

SGÙRR NAN EAG 924m

(NG 457 195) Map p236

This bulky mountain is the most southerly Munro in the Cuillin. There are superb views from its 400-metre-long and almost level summit ridge. It has a steep face to the north overlooking An Garbh-choire, and a broad and fairly uninteresting south-western flank. It is normally traversed by its east and north ridges.

 156 North Ridge Grade 1 or 2 **
(NG 454 201) Alt 797m Map p236 Diagram p293

This is the usual way of bagging the peak from Glen Brittle. The easiest way has only mild scrambling and is well worn.

Approach

Approach Coire a' Ghrunnda as described for Routes 143/144. Either ascend the left-hand side of the lower corrie by the fault along the base of the rock band or by the higher terrace which slants below the base of South Crag. Continue past Slab Buttress and scramble up rocks some distance left of the stream which spills from Loch Coire a' Ghrunnda. Once in the upper corrie, walk round the south side of the loch and slant up rough ground to one of the two possible starts.

An alternative approach can be taken up the superb slabby floor of the lower corrie. Scramble up a cleft formed by a wide dyke close to the west flank of Sgùrr nan Eag. When this becomes too hard traverse left along a terrace and find a way through the rock band above to gain the upper corrie.

The Route

a) **Ridge Crest Grade 2 ****

The best scrambling line starts from Bealach a' Gharbh-choire and follows the crest as closely as possible. From the south side of the loch scramble up extremely rough ground to reach the bealach. The rock at the start is peridotite with conspicuous fragments in it, but this soon gives way to gabbro. The middle section has slightly more awkward route-finding over big blocks. Higher up, where the crest coincides with a cone-sheet, the going is easier.

b) **Right-hand Flank Grade 1**

The easier option starts by slanting up rightwards on broken ground some distance below Bealach a' Gharbh-choire. Follow scree paths with only minor sections of scrambling to the right of the crest. Join the route up the ridge where the angle starts to ease some distance before the summit.

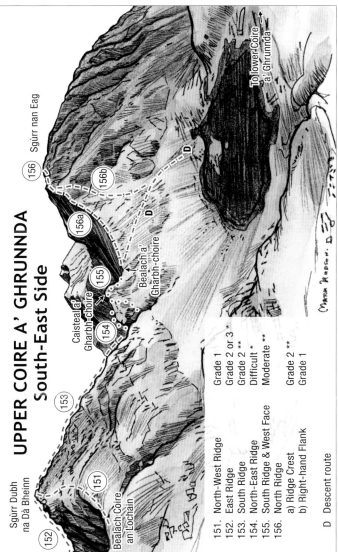

UPPER COIRE A' GHRUNNDA
South-East Side

Sgùrr Dubh na Dà Bheinn

Sgùrr nan Eag

Caisteal a' Gharbh-choire

Bealach a' Gharbh-choire

Bealach Coire an Lochain

To lower Coire a' Ghrunnda

151. North-West Ridge — Grade 1
152. East Ridge — Grade 2 or 3 *
153. South Ridge — Grade 2 **
154. North-East Ridge — Difficult *
155. South Ridge & West Face — Moderate **
156. North Ridge
   a) Ridge Crest — Grade 2 **
   b) Right-hand Flank — Grade 1

D Descent route

SOUTHERN CUILLIN

A minor top is crossed just before the long summit ridge is reached. There are several rocky eminences on the crest, the second of which has a steep drop at the far end. The third one is marginally the highest.

The continuation to Gars-bheinn at the far end of the ridge presents no difficulties (see Routes 159 and 162–4). It is possible to avoid Sgùrr nan Eag on the return by using one of Harker's short cuts. This starts from the dip in the ridge (774m) between Sgùrr a' Choire Bhig and Sgùrr nan Eag. Drop down only a short distance on the north side into An Garbh-choire. Then traverse across the north-east flank of Sgùrr nan Eag. The main difficulty involves crossing a slab at the start which may be wet. Then continue below the gash of The Chasm – a classic Very Difficult climb. After that, pick a way carefully over very rough boulders for some distance. The line more or less contours the slope, with only a slight rise towards the end to reach Bealach a' Gharbh-choire (797m).

157   Western Buttress   Difficult   **
(NG 452 196)   Alt 720m   Map p236   Diagrams pp295 & 297

There is much rock on the west face of Sgùrr nan Eag but very little climbing. The buttresses are generally too broken and chaotic. The only distinctive feature is the curving line of Western Buttress which lies high up in the middle of the face. The start is rather awkward to reach, but once established on the route it gives a mixture of scrambling and climbing with some tricky route-finding. The rock is excellent on the harder sections – all in all, a fine mountaineering excursion.

Approach
It is possible to descend diagonally rightwards from high up in Coire a' Ghrunnda to gain the start. The most pleasant approach, however, is to follow the lower section of the next outing and then make a long rising leftwards traverse along a prominent ledge system – see diagram p297.

The Route
There are some confusing bosses of rock at the bottom with several steep corners and chimneys. The best way onto the crest of the buttress is to avoid this section on the left-hand side. Scramble up rock steps and easier ground then follow a rising rightwards line up grooves and a ledge system with a massive block. Continue rightwards up a boulder-filled rift and then ascend a slightly steeper section to gain the crest of the buttress.

Go to the right-hand end of a short wall and climb back up left. Follow a narrower section of ridge with stacked blocks. (An obvious ledge, which crosses the slope on the right-hand side of the buttress, can be followed all the way right to a hidden gully at the top of the next route.)

Continue up the ridge for some distance and climb up a steeper section. At one point use a narrow dyke for the left foot. Ascend just right of the crest and then follow the ridge without great difficulty up to a ledge.

This is where the fun starts. Above there is a wall with a ledge at half-height

SGÙRR NAN EAG
Coire a' Ghrunnda

157.	Western Buttress	Difficult **
158.	WSW Flank	Grade 2/3 *

(158)

Escape to Route 158

(157)

MARK HUDSON

SOUTHERN CUILLIN

and a right-facing corner on the left. Go slightly right round a corner then swing up leftwards from a handjam to gain the right-hand end of the ledge. Traverse left past a spike-like boulder. The last couple of moves into the corner are awkward. One very inelegant way is to sit down facing out and stretch the right leg across to the corner!

Climb up the corner to a good ledge. Move right and climb up to the foot of a left-trending crack. Follow this and soon arrive on a large terrace.

The wall above is too hard, so go to the right-hand end of the terrace, climb down a short groove and make a delicate traverse to the right. There is a broad recess on the right, but it is too steep at this point. So climb up steep cracked rocks until it is possible to step right to a ledge. Continue up the broad recess – not as easy as it looks. Make a series of awkward step-ups, moving slightly left at the top.

Break out onto easy ground. Continue to a prominent wall with crazy-paving rock. Climb up the right-hand end by twin cracks and so reach the top of the wall. Traverse left along a ledge and scramble up a short corner to reach easy ground. Follow an easy slope covered with giant boulders to the most western top on the summit ridge. Finish as for the previous route.

 158 West-South-West Flank   Grade 2/3 *
(NG 450 194)   Alt 450m   Map p236   Diagram p297

This scramble takes an interesting route up Sgùrr nan Eag which is more direct than the standard route via the north ridge. A rib overlooking a hidden gully offers an enjoyable finish.

Approach
Use the normal approach to Coire a' Ghrunnda (see Route 144) but, instead of ascending the gully by the rock wall, continue rightwards into the mouth of the corrie. Then head right and drop down slightly to cross the stream in the floor of the corrie.

The Route
A leftward-slanting grassy gully cuts through the steep rock band at the base of the face. It is difficult to see from below. Approach it by scrambling pleasantly up some introductory slabs. The biggest slab below the rock band is ascended by following a cone-sheet slanting right. High up this, make an awkward move to break back left onto an easier section of slab. Then slant leftwards onto easier ground.

The grassy gully lies immediately to the right of two massive stacked blocks and a squat pillar with a hole between them. Ascend the gully without difficulty and then slant hard left on a very narrow grassy ledge for some distance. Scramble up short rock steps to reach easier-angled ground, where a broad terrace slants leftwards across the face.

Walk up to a rock band which lies a short distance to the right of a gully. Pull up to gain a cone-sheet slanting right, and follow this to reach a grassy ledge below another rock band. There is a scoop to the right of a steeper section of wall. Gain the scoop and slant delicately left to reach a crack with a good finger slot. Continue to a more continuous sweep of slabs.

Ascend this by a prominent rightward-slanting cone-sheet for some distance. Slant back left along a cracked weakness, then follow another cone-sheet slanting right. Break up through slabs more directly, then move left again. (A narrow but easy ledge system can be followed a long way up leftwards at this point to reach the start of the previous route.)

Weave to and fro more easily for some distance. Slant right along another cone-sheet to reach a scree slope. Go hard right and ascend stepped rocks

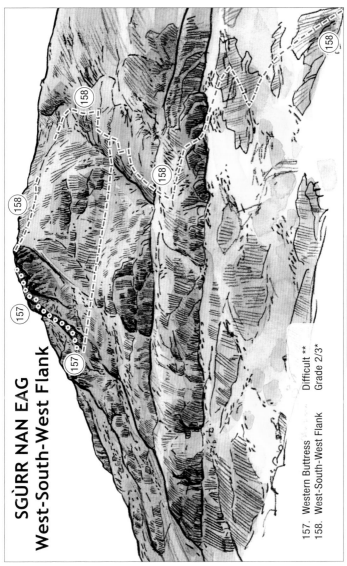

SGÙRR NAN EAG
West-South-West Flank

157. Western Buttress   Difficult **
158. West-South-West Flank   Grade 2/3*

SOUTHERN CUILLIN

West-South-West Flank (Grade 2/3), Sgùrr nan Eag
Scrambler: George Archibald

pleasantly back left. Follow a grassy rake slanting right and, when it levels off slightly, break diagonally left. Ascend the rocks to the right of a grassy runnel, and then weave to and fro on easier ground. Scramble up steps of rock with vertical banding, a short distance right of where water trickles down.

The water originates from a hidden gully which slants a long way left further up the face. The next objective is reaching the bed of this gully. In dry conditions it is possible to move left and scramble steeply up a drainage line to gain the gully. Otherwise continue directly to eventually reach the edge of the south-west flank. From there it is also possible to drop down a short distance and cross a rounded, bouldery rib and descend a prominent grassy rake to reach the bed of the gully.

Scramble up the gully for some distance over boulders, slabs and small chockstones until the bed of the gully changes to fine grey scree. Then cut back left on fairly easy ledges across the left wall of the gully. Ascend back right to gain the crest of the rib which overlooks the gully. Continue up the delightful crest with very enjoyable scrambling up short walls and blocky noses with good holds. The angle gradually eases and the route passes the finish of the previous route. Continue to the summit as for the previous route.

 159 East Ridge   Grade 1
(NG 461 194)   Alt 774m   Map p236   Diagram p303

This is a straightforward section of the main ridge which is normally ascended as part of a traverse from Gars-bheinn. It is therefore described starting from the dip between Sgùrr a' Choire Bhig and Sgùrr nan Eag. See also the next two routes.

The Route
There are short sections of very easy scrambling early on, but the upper section is just a steep walk on scree. Interest can be added by looking for some holes on the Coire nan Laogh side of the crest about two-thirds of the way up the ridge. They mark the exit from a Very Difficult climb called The Chasm. The climb starts on the An Garbh-choire side (see Route 156). After a very tricky entry pitch, it turns into a most unusual subterranean excursion. It was largely filled with snow and ice when it was first climbed by Steeple and Barlow in 1915. They returned in 1919 with Doughty to make the first summer ascent.

COIRE NAN LAOGH

(NG 460 190) Map p236

This quiet corrie is rarely visited. The main feature in the centre of the corrie is a broad band of steep slabs, which can only be ascended by climbing. However, easier scrambling routes can be found up either side. There are comfortable bivouac sites in the upper part of the corrie not far below the bealach (774m) between Sgùrr nan Eag and Sgùrr a' Choire Bhig, so this makes a good starting place for a traverse of the main ridge. The route up the right-hand side of the corrie is certainly more pleasant than the scree slope on the south-west flank of Gars-bheinn.

The main rockband which spans the corrie is split by two prominent gullies – Central Gully on the left and East Gully on the right. They were both climbed by Herford and Laycock in 1912. Herford found fame on the Central Buttress of Scafell two years later, although he was killed shortly after in the First World War. Laycock – a gritstone expert of his day – was very enthusiastic about Central Gully in a Fell & Rock Climbing Club Journal; *"… a remarkable place, of the most romantic, and a very worthy climb. I would almost say it is unique within my experience."* The gully starts with a tunnel pitch under a giant chockstone, and this is followed by an overhanging chockstone which is circumvented by a severe pitch up either wall.

 ### 160 Western Slabs Grade 2/3 *
(NG 460 191) Alt 600m Map p236 Diagram p301

This route wanders up slabs to the left of the steep rock band in the centre of the corrie. It finishes on the lower part of the east ridge of Sgùrr nan Eag.

Approach
Follow the path from the campsite in Glen Brittle as for Route 143. Stay on the lower or right-hand path across the base of Sròn na Ciche and eventually cross the Allt Coire a' Ghrunnda some distance below Coire a' Ghrunnda itself. Continue on the path for a further kilometre then slant left up the hillside and follow the stream up into Coire nan Laogh. Stags may be seen and heard here during the rutting season.

The lower floor of the corrie is largely heather-covered, but some small rock bands of almost flint-like basalt give short sections of scrambling. Central Gully has a conspicuous chockstone part-way up. Slant left from a grassy terrace to reach the mouth of this gully.

The Route
Scramble diagonally left up surprisingly awkward slabs. Traverse right into a groove, and ascend this for two or three moves, before breaking back left onto the slabs. Follow these to a big terrace. Head up to a rock band and pull up steeply at the left-hand end of a long flake. Traverse right along a foot-ledge and climb up by a tiny dyke. Continue more easily, then slant a long way left along a scree terrace.

A key feature on the next section of the route is a leftward-leaning gully/groove. The scramble goes up rocks a little further left. Slant left up a grassy cleft heading towards the groove, but then traverse left along an intrusion to reach a ledge with a small juniper bush. Now weave a way up slabs trending slightly right (crux) in the general direction of a boulder on the skyline above. Join a faint buttress, which lies to the left of the groove, and follow this pleasantly for some distance. Ascend a short wall from a recess with junipers.

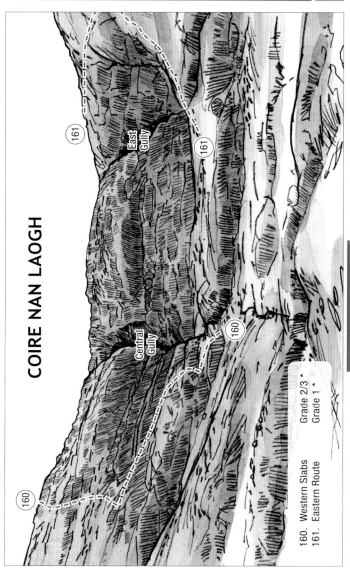

COIRE NAN LAOGH

East Gully

Central Gully

161

160

160. Western Slabs   Grade 2/3 *
161. Eastern Route   Grade 1 *

When the groove on the right starts to peter out, slant right across slabs and soon reach easier ground. Continue up easy slabs, staying slightly left rather than following bouldery ground further right. Reach a rock band with a long roof and slant right with surprising ease to gain a good ledge. Traverse right past a steep wall then ascend a corner to reach easier slabs and soon break left to a grassy ledge. Scramble over an overlap by trending slightly right. Take a direct line up slabs then follow an enjoyable leftward-trending slabby ramp. Break back right and soon join the lower section of the east ridge.

161 Eastern Route   Grade 1   *
(NG 461 191)   Alt 600m   Map p236   Diagram p301

This route is mainly a walk if the easiest line is taken. The best way is hard to find in descent.

Approach

There is a short but awkward rockband above the first grass terrace which can be tackled either by a) ascending the lower reaches of Central Gully then escaping up a corner on the right wall, b) by slanting rightwards in the middle (hardest) or c) by a gully on the right. Start not far from the bottom of East Gully.

The Route

Slant rightwards and zigzag up steepish ground before breaking a long way back left more easily. Follow a slanting terrace with some pleasant grassy bivouac sites before eventually gaining the main ridge at the bealach between Sgùrr nan Eag and Sgùrr a' Choire Bhig.

It is possible to avoid the ascent of Sgurr na Eag by traversing across to Bealach a' Gharbh-choire as described for Route 156 on p294.

SGÙRR A' CHOIRE BHIG 875m

(NG 465 191) Map p236

This peak is frequently hurried over early in the morning by parties starting a traverse of the main ridge. However, its shapely summit warrants a more leisurely treatment. It offers excellent views and can be traversed without difficulty by its south and north-west ridges.

The mountain's finest feature is its north-east ridge, which is described later in the Coruisk chapter (see Route 171). There is also a fine cliff on the Coruisk side of the north-west ridge. There is scope for further exploration here.

162 North-West Ridge   500m   *
(NG 461 194)   Alt 774m   Map p236   Diagram p303

The usual way to approach the start of this ridge would be to first traverse Sgùrr nan Eag (see Routes 156 & 159). The previous route offers a possible alternative.

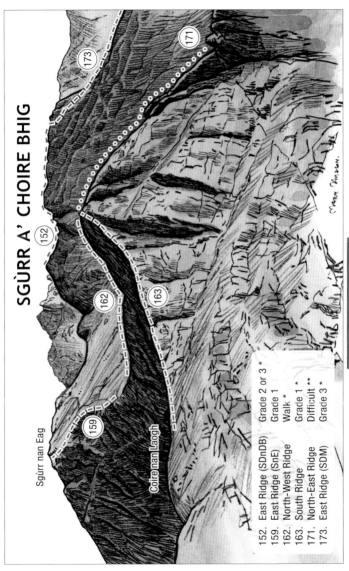

SGÙRR A' CHOIRE BHIG

Sgùrr nan Eag

Coire nan Laogh

152. East Ridge (SDnDB)   Grade 2 or 3 *
159. East Ridge (SnE)   Grade 1
162. North-West Ridge   Walk *
163. South Ridge   Grade 1 *
171. North-East Ridge   Difficult **
173. East Ridge (SDM)   Grade 3 *

SOUTHERN CUILLIN

GARS-BHEINN

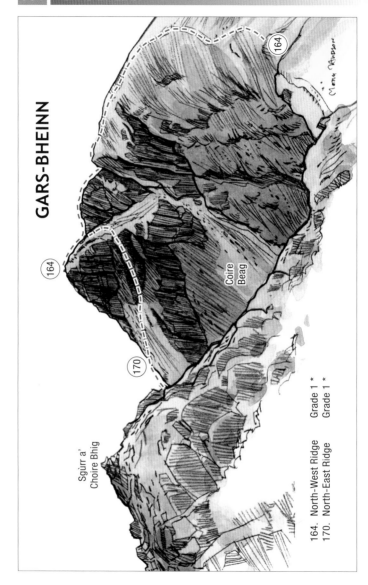

164. North-West Ridge   Grade 1 *
170. North-East Ridge   Grade 1 *

The Route
From the dip between Sgùrr nan Eag and Sgùrr a' Choire Bhig ascend the ridge to a broad flat section of whale-back slabs and boulders. This is a better place to bivouac before tackling the main ridge than the more cramped locations around the summit of Gars-bheinn.

Continue pleasantly up the ridge. Although the upper section narrows dramatically, it is no more than walking. From the summit there are fine views of Gars-bheinn, as well as Sgùrr Dubh Beag and Sgùrr Dubh Mòr on the other side of An Garbh-choire.

 163 South Ridge   Grade 1   *
(NG 465 189)   *Alt 835m   Map p236   Diagram p303*

This short, rocky ridge is the natural continuation from the north-west ridge of Gars-bheinn – see the next route described.

The Route
Follow the narrow ridge crest with only short sections of very mild scrambling up short steps early on. Reach the summit abruptly. Continue by descending the previous route.

GARS-BHEINN 895m

(NG 468 187)   Map p236

The most southerly mountain on the Cuillin main ridge is a fine peak with magnificent views. On a clear day most of the main ridge can be seen, as well as many mainland mountains such as Ben Nevis. Unfortunately, the normal approach from Glen Brittle involves the ascent of 500m of purgatorial scree on the mountain's south-west flank. Some rather more pleasant approaches are described in the Coruisk chapter.

 164 North-West Ridge   Grade 1   *
(NG 465 189)   *Alt 835m   Map p236   Diagram p304*

The ridge itself is pleasant enough, but the approach from the Glen Brittle side is hard going. Two minor tops before the main summit can cause confusion in bad visibility.

Approach
Follow the path from the campsite in Glen Brittle as for Route 143. Take the lower path across the base of Sròn na Cìche, and continue for a further 2km – crossing the streams from Coire a' Ghrunnda and Coire nan Laogh on the way. Ascend the steep south-west flank on loose scree and rubble. Fine views of Soay and Rum offer some distraction from the tedium. The ridge crest is normally gained (with great relief) midway between the dip below Sgùrr a' Choire Bhig and the summit of Gars-bheinn.

SOUTHERN CUILLIN

The Route
Walk along the pleasant grassy crest over the first minor top. Pass the top of a narrow scree-filled gully which lies on the north or Coire Beag side of the ridge. Traverse a second top and scramble down to a dip before the main summit. (Another branch of the scree gully leads down into Coire Beag from here.) Easy scrambling on steeper ground leads up to the fine summit. Superb views can be obtained of Loch Scavaig by walking a short distance down the south-east ridge.

RUBHA AN DÙNAIN

(NG 387 161)

Before describing the routes which are approached from the Coruisk side of the Cuillin, it is convenient to mention here some low-level outings from Glen Brittle. **The Fairy Pools** in Coire na Creiche, and the spectacular waterfall of **Eas Mòr** below Coire na Banachdaich, have already been referred to (see Routes 76 and 111 respectively). They both make enjoyable short walks. The easy hills above the forest on the west side of Glen Brittle are also worthwhile and offer unusual views of the Cuillin. One delightful outing, however, deserves a separate description.

165 Rubha an Dùnain   13km **
(NG 413 204)   High Point 75m
The headland of Rubha an Dùnain lies to the south of the Glen Brittle camp-site between Loch Brittle and Soay Sound. It harbours several fascinating sites of historical and archaeological significance. The walk is fairly long, and allowance should also be made for dallying at the various localities of interest. The most useful map for this outing is the OS Explorer Map 411.

Approach
Park near the beach and walk along a track through the campsite. Go through a gate behind the toilet block.

The Route
There are two options on the first part of this walk. Either turn right and follow a gently undulating footpath near to the shore, or go uphill a short distance (pass to the left of some water storage tanks) and join a vehicular track which takes a higher route parallel to the path. Taking the path on the way out and the track on the way back makes a good combination.

   After 1.5km the route crosses the Allt Coire Lagan. This stream may be a problem to cross when in spate, in which case a small wooden footbridge situated halfway between the path and the track may offer the best solution. Continue for some distance until the track peters out by a stream.

   Carry on in the same direction and take the left fork which slants gradually uphill. Pass by a small lochan and go to the left of a small top called Creag Mhòr (120m). From the southern end of this rocky knoll there are good views

Loch na h-Àirde

of the way ahead. A wide dyke, which cuts all the way across the headland, has formed a linear depression known as Slochd Dubh *(black ditch)*. Drop down and slant leftwards across this feature, heading in the direction of Rum. Go through a wall and continue in the same general direction across fairly featureless ground. Eventually descend slightly to a hollow where the remains of a building and an enclosure can be seen. This is Rhundunan, a former home of the MacAskills.

Now start to slant right, in the direction of Canna, and find a way through the high bracken towards Loch na h-Àirde. This loch is only a very short distance above sea level. Go left along its shore and continue along the east side of its outlet channel. This was deepened at some time in the past to allow boats to be brought up to the safe anchorage inside. Still on the east side of the stream, ascend to a small promontory where the remains of an Iron Age dun can be inspected.

Then cross the stream and go round the western tip of Rubha an Dùnain and, on the return, visit the north side of Loch na h-Àirde. A chambered cairn is situated very close to the loch on the east side of a wall. It is hard to see until close up to it. When it was excavated in the 1930s the remains of six adults and fragments of Beaker pottery were found.

Return by a more northerly path with fine views of the Cuillin in the distance. After crossing the end of Slochd Dubh, skirt left below Creag Mhòr to eventually rejoin the path or track used on the approach.

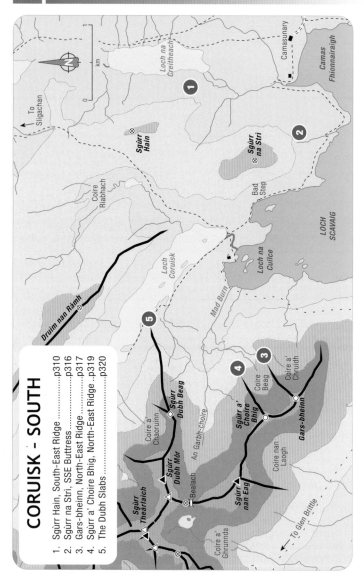

CORUISK – SOUTH

1. Sgùrr Hain, South-East Ridge p310
2. Sgùrr na Stri, SSE Buttress p316
3. Gars-bheinn, North-East Ridge p317
4. Sgùrr a' Choire Bhig, North-East Ridge ..p319
5. The Dubh Slabs p320

Loch na Crèitheach

Camasunary

Camas Fhionnairaigh

Sgùrr Hain

Sgùrr na Stri

To Sligachan

Coire Riabhach

Bad Step

LOCH SCAVAIG

Loch Coruisk

Loch na Cuilce

Druim nan Ràmh

Mad Burn

Sgùrr Dubh Beag

Sgùrr Dubh Mòr

Coire Beag

Coire a' Chruidh

Sgùrr a' Choire Bhig

Gars-bheinn

Coire a' Chaoruinn

An Garbh-choire

Coire nan Laogh

Bealach

Sgùrr nan Eag

Sgùrr Thearlaich

Coire a' Ghrunnda

To Glen Brittle

CORUISK

The great hollow known as Coruisk lies in the heart of the Cuillin. It is enclosed by the southern and central sections of the Cuillin main ridge, and the long side ridge of Druim nan Ràmh. Lying in the floor of this huge corrie is Loch Coruisk – a 2.5 kilometre-long freshwater loch, the ice-scooped floor of which lies over 30m below sea level. Coruisk is the anglicised version of Coir'-uisg, (or more formally Coire Uisge) which means water corrie. The term 'Coir'-uisg' tends to be associated with that part of the corrie upstream of Loch Coruisk. Whereas the term 'Coruisk' is used rather more loosely to refer to the whole basin which contains Loch Coruisk, and also the area around its outflow into Loch na Cuilce at the head of Loch Scavaig.

The water draining out of Loch Coruisk flows along the River Scavaig for only 400 metres before it spills down slabs into the sea. There is an important crossing point over the River Scavaig at its outflow from Loch Coruisk, but the stepping stones there can quickly become submerged in spate conditions.

The Coruisk Memorial Hut is situated below a long crag near the mouth of the River Scavaig. It is a private hut and is kept locked when not in use. There is plenty of scope for camping on slightly boggy ground nearby. However, on occasions when wind is funnelled into this area, conditions can become very difficult for camping.

Coruisk was first described in rapturous terms early in the nineteenth century by MacCulloch the geologist. It has attracted sightseers ever since. Among the early visitors were several artists and poets – such as Scott, Daniell and Turner – who tried, with mixed success, to portray the awesome grandeur of the scenery.

There is certainly a special atmosphere about this part of the Cuillin, although it may be hard to appreciate when thick cloud obscures all the tops and heavy rain transforms all the streams into white, foaming torrents. In good weather, however, this is one of the finest mountain locations in the country, and its delights can only be enjoyed properly at first hand.

Sailing into Loch na Cuilce in fine weather is one of the best possible ways of experiencing this part of the Cuillin. In the summer months there are busy boat services between Elgol and the little landing stage in Loch na Cuilce. Most of the trips allow visitors ashore for only an hour or so, but some sailings allow for lengthier landings. See for example: <www.aquaxplore.co.uk/>, <www.bellajane.co.uk/>, and <www.mistyisleboattrips.co.uk/>. Boats can also be chartered from Arisaig and Mallaig.

It is also feasible to reach Coruisk by crossing the main ridge from several places in Glen Brittle – the three main options being via:

Bealach na Glaic Moire (760m)	*p203 / Diagrams pp204 & 332*
Bealach Coire na Banachdaich (851m)	*p235 / Diagram p240*
Bealach a' Gharbh-choire (797m)	*p291 / Diagrams pp293 & 318.*

Crossing the stepping stones at the mouth of Loch Coruisk

In addition, there are three low-level approaches on foot from Sligachan in the north, Camasunary in the east and Glen Brittle in the west. These approaches were fully described in the introductory Cuillin section (Routes 49, 50, and 51 on pp142–5).

The various outings are now described starting in the east and then working in a clockwise direction around the Coruisk basin.

SGÙRR HAIN 420m

(NG 503 210) Map p308

The summit of this rocky hill is often bypassed to the west on the path from Sligachan to Coruisk (Route 49). However, it is well worth diverting from Druim Hain to pay it a visit. The extraordinary panoramic view from the summit includes the whole Cuillin range as well as Blàbheinn and Marsco. The next two routes offer interesting approaches from the Camasunary side.

 166 South-East Ridge   Grade 1 *
(NG 508 202)   Alt 120m   Map p308   Diagrams pp311 & 312
For those based at Camasunary this makes an excellent little outing. The

THE CUILLIN FROM ELGOL

166. South-East Ridge — Grade 1 *
169. South-South-East Buttress — Grade 2/3 **
184. Druim nan Ràmh — Grade 2 or Difficult **

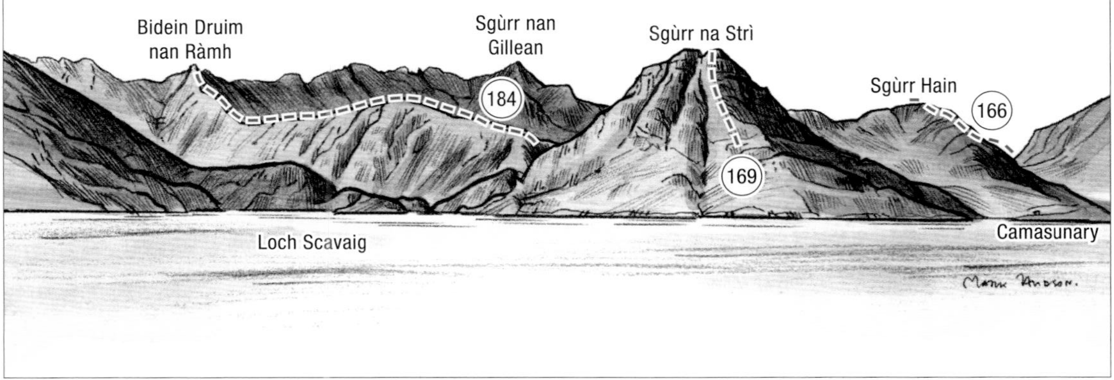

Bidein Druim nan Ràmh

Sgùrr nan Gillean

Sgùrr na Stri

Sgùrr Hain

Loch Scavaig

Camasunary

CORUISK

SGÙRR HAIN
East Face

48. Sligachan to Camasunary   Walk *
166. South-East Ridge   Grade 1 *
167. South-East Slabs   Moderate *

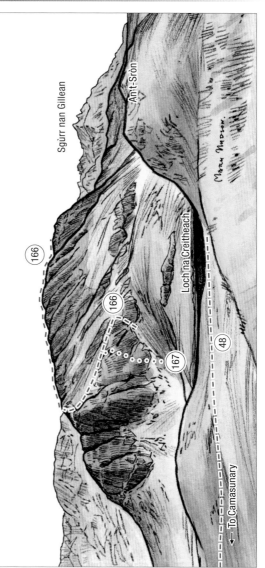

Sgùrr nan Gillean

Àn t-Sròn

Màrh Midich.

Loch na Crèitheach

To Camasunary

scrambling does not amount to much, but the views from the summit ridge are exceptional.

Approach
Follow the east bank of the Abhainn Camas Fhionnairigh upstream. Pass some pleasant slabs in the stream bed, and eventually cross a fork of the stream by some stepping stones. Follow the left fork for a short distance, then cross that as well by stepping stones. Go past an impressive crag with two buttresses, and continue beyond its more slabby right-hand wing.

The Route
Slant rightwards up a grassy ramp, staying to the left of a broad slabby nose. Move left to join a grassy ramp slanting left below a rock band. Make a very long rising traverse left along the ramp. Eventually ascend a short rib to reach the crest of the ridge above the main right-hand buttress. This point can also be reached more steeply from the corrie to the west.

Turn right and ascend the crest on delightful slabby rocks. There are some very minor rock bands but the main interest is the ever-improving view. The first top has a tiny lochan just below it, but the highest point lies 250 metres away across a slight dip. The views from the main summit are stupendous. A straightforward descent by the north ridge leads to the path over Druim Hain (Route 49). By traversing back across the west flank of Sgùrr Hain it is possible to cross the ridge and descend a nameless corrie to the starting point.

 167 South-East Slabs   Moderate   *
(NG 508 202)   Alt 110m   Map p308   Diagram p312

The ice-smoothed slabs forming the right-hand wing of the crag mentioned in the previous route offer a more serious direct start. They are quite sustained and good route-finding is required if harder ground is to be avoided.

The Route
Start centrally and scramble up some introductory slabs to a break. Continue up steeper slabs by a short rightward-slanting crack. Reach a narrow leftward slanting dyke which is followed to another one that slants back right. Cross a slanting grassy ramp and follow big steps up a dyke. Reach a fairly large and steeply-sloping heathery terrace.

Slant leftwards at first then go straight up and back diagonally right. Exposure starts to become more noticeable. Go to the left of an alcove and after a delightful section of brown slabs head for a grassy depression to the right of an overlap. Eventually join the grassy ramp of the previous route.

SGÙRR NA STRÌ 494m

(NG 499 193) Map p308

This lowly but rugged peak is well seen from Elgol. It has twin tops of similar height, separated by a long trench-like depression. The western top offers breathtaking views of Loch Coruisk.

CORUISK

Loch Coruisk and the Cuillin viewed from Sgùrr na Strì
Photo: Scott Muir

168 North Ridge   12km (from Sligachan) *
(NG 500 213)   Alt 322m   Map p308

The most straightforward way of ascending this peak is to divert from Druim Hain en route from Sligachan to Coruisk.

Approach

When approaching from Sligachan (Route 49), follow the path which carries straight on from the crest of Druim Hain. If starting from Loch Coruisk, follow the path from the stepping stones towards Druim Hain and cut back along a broad ramp on the north-west flank.

The Route

Traverse across the west flank of Sgùrr Hain and gain the crest of the north ridge a short distance after a minor rounded summit. Some paths trending round to the right just lead to viewing points for Loch Coruisk. Instead, hold the highest ground and eventually reach the fine western top. Fragments of a crashed jet aircraft can be found hereabouts. It is worth visiting the eastern top, which lies 100 metres away on the other side of the trench-like depression. The easiest descent is to return the same way. See the next route for a description of a descent route to Camasunary.

CAMASUNARY & SGÙRR NA STRÌ

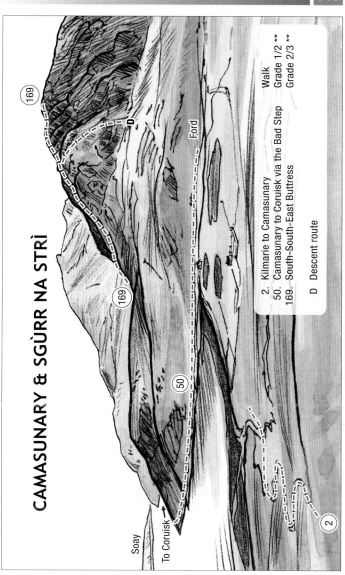

Soay

To Coruisk

169

169

50

Ford

D

2

2. Kilmarie to Camasunary	Walk	
50. Camasunary to Coruisk via the Bad Step	Grade 1/2 **	
169. South-South-East Buttress	Grade 2/3 **	
D Descent route		

CORUISK

169 South-South-East Buttress   Grade 2/3 **

(NG 504 186)   Alt 150m   Map p308   Diagrams pp311 & 315

There is a prominent gully on the southern flank of the peak, which is a continuation of the depression that splits the summit. This route ascends the buttress on the right-hand side of the gully. It gives a very fine scramble on excellent rock, and is open to much variation.

Approach

The easiest way to identify the buttress is from the coast path between Camasunary and Coruisk (Route 50) just north-west of Rubha Bàn, where a stream from the gully reaches the coast. The route starts at a height of 150m by a prominent slab, which rises from a broad, grassy saddle just west of a lochan.

The Route

Ascend the delightful slab, moving right to a crack high up. Then continue more easily for some distance to the start of the buttress proper. Scramble up slabs to the right of a grassy groove and gain a ledge. Follow steps up a steep rock rib on the left side of a recess.

Ascend a broad leftward-trending dyke as far as a cone-sheet, then follow very pleasant slabs on the right for some distance. Move back left into the dyke for a short stretch, then scramble up slabs of very rough rock to a recess with big boulders. Follow the slabby crest trending left. Step up from a boulder on the right and make some interesting moves left to ascend the left-hand end of an overhanging wall. From a platform of stripy rock, go to the left-hand end of the wall, then slant right up a broken ramp.

Trend left up slabby rocks to reach a steeper section of buttress, which provides the crux. Starting on the left-hand side, make an awkward move up, then step delicately left onto a slab. Move slightly left again and break up through to easier ground. Slant back right to stay on the crest. Ascend sound rocks two metres right of a small overhang. From a terrace, some more fun can be had by finding a way up a small headwall via a recess. Then traverse four metres right along a cone-sheet and ascend some tricky slabs on the right side of a left-slanting gully. Either step out left from the top of an alcove, or ascend the rib on the left more easily. Climb to the top of a flake/block and pull onto a wall. Step left, move up, then back right before continuing straight up to another terrace. Follow easier rocks and a broad, undulating ridge to the eastern summit, from where there are excellent views of Blàbheinn and Camasunary.

Slant left to find a way down into the central depression and soon gain the western top. After enjoying the wonderful views, it is possible to descend to Loch Coruisk by slanting off left from the north ridge in the vicinity of Captain Maryon's Monument. Descend a grassy depression with a stream to join the path from Druim Hain.

To descend to Camasunary, enter the depression between the summits and follow the gully in a southerly direction until it steepens and becomes choked with large boulders. (The gully marks the line of a light-coloured vein rather than the more usual dolerite dyke.) Then exit the gully on the left-hand side and cross over the crest of the buttress – previously ascended – by a terrace. Descend a slanting grassy rake fairly steeply down the south-eastern flank of the hill. Eventually head east over less steep grassy ground to where the Abhainn Camas Fhionnairigh can be forded.

AN GARBH-CHOIRE

Map p308

This corrie is situated between the southern Cuillin peaks and the long ridge of the Dubhs. The name is apt; it is the roughest corrie in the Cuillin. The floor in the upper part of An Garbh-choire is covered with a jumble of extremely rough, giant boulders of peridotite. Great care is needed when clambering over and between these extraordinary blocks. It would be easy to break a leg here. Caisteal a' Gharbh-choire forms a distinctive profile at the head of the corrie where there is a crossing place into Coire a' Ghrunnda.

An Garbh-choire is most usually approached from the Coruisk side by a grassy depression and stream immediately south of the Mad Burn. It can also be approached by more open ground from halfway along the southern side of Loch Coruisk, or even from the Glen Brittle coastal path (see p144).

When descending from Bealach a' Gharbh-choire cross the ridge on the south side of Caisteal a' Gharbh-choire and then skirt below this feature by a path on the east side to the gap at the north end. Then turn right to descend An Garbh-choire staying slightly closer to the Sgùrr Dubh Mòr side in the upper part of the corrie.

GARS-BHEINN 895m

(NG 468 187) Map p308

The most southerly peak on the main ridge can be attained in a number of ways from Coruisk. Fairly careful route-finding is needed to reach the fine south-east ridge via Coire a' Chruidh. It is also possible to ascend Coire Beag and gain the north-west ridge by either one of two scree gullies. A third and more direct option is now described.

170 North-East Ridge   Grade 1   *

(NG 472 191)   Alt 500m   Map p308   Diagrams pp304 & 318

The ridge is fairly straightforward apart from a steep section early on which is easily avoided on the right. A narrow shelf is used to outflank the fearsome summit headwall. The route was ascended by Sidney Williams and John Mackenzie in 1896.

Approach

Go along the coast from the Coruisk Hut and cross the Mad Burn. Ascend the

CORUISK

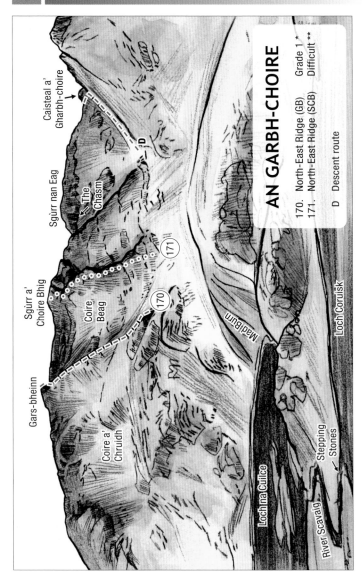

AN GARBH-CHOIRE

170. North-East Ridge (GB) Grade 1 *
171. North-East Ridge (SCB) Difficult **

D Descent route

next grassy depression with a stream and eventually reach the broad and rather featureless lower level of An Garbh-choire. Head up to the left passing small outcrops and boulders of the distinctive peridotite rock which characterises this corrie.

The Route

Ascend a long stretch of hillside to a narrow nose forming the left-hand side of Coire Beag at the 600m level. This can be taken directly or outflanked more easily on the right. Continue up the fairly narrow crest to a level section. Ascend the much broader crest without difficulty for some distance. A small pinnacle, with a capping of luxurious moss on its summit, is passed easily to the right. Continue on broken basaltic rocks and scree.

At the very steep rocks below the summit, traverse right and descend ever so slightly. Look for a narrow shelf below a rock band on the right flank (see diagram on p304). Follow this round to a gully with boulders leading left to a dip on the crest just west of the summit. Easy scrambling leads to the top.

It is possible to descend by easy scree gullies back into Coire Beag from either of the two dips on the ridge a short distance west of the summit.

SGÙRR A' CHOIRE BHIG 875m

(NG 465 191) Map p308

This peak has a cap of brittle basalt, but most of the northern side is excellent gabbro. The finest feature of this peak is its north-east ridge. It offers a challenging and varied route direct to the summit from An Garbh-choire.

171 North-East Ridge Difficult **
(NG 471 195)   Alt 370m   Map p308   Diagrams pp303 & 318

The lower part of this ridge has some delightful slabs reminiscent of the Dubh Slabs on the other side of the corrie. Higher up it changes character, however, and there are some short sections of climbing on the steeper parts of the upper ridge. It is much harder than its neighbour. It was probably first ascended by Sidney Williams in 1896.

Approach

Gain the lower level of An Garbh-choire as described for the previous route. Slant up slightly right towards the sweep of slabs forming the right-hand border of Coire Beag.

The Route

The superbly rough slabs give very enjoyable scrambling and can be ascended by any number of lines. There is a prominent curving overlap on the right-hand side of the crest at about half-height. Then follow more broken ground without great difficulty to a steeper rock band, with an outward-dipping cone-sheet at its base, which blocks the direct line up the ridge. Do not be tempted to follow slanting ledges on the left flank. Instead, traverse a short distance

CORUISK

to the right and ascend a gully/chimney by a chockstone until it is possible to climb out on the right-hand rib. Higher up where the ridge becomes much narrower, some stumpy pinnacles are taken on the right-hand side of the crest. Ascend some short steps and arrive at a final rock band which blocks the way. Again the secret is to move over to the right and ascend a rocky gully/alcove. Climb out by the left wall and continue on more broken rocks to the shapely summit.

The quickest descent off the summit is via Coire Beag as described for the previous route. Alternatively, scramble down into An Garbh-choire from the dip between Sgùrr a' Choire Bhig and Sgùrr nan Eag, staying left at first.

SGÙRR DUBH BEAG 733m

(NG 465 204) Map p308

A magnificent sweep of slabs falls from this summit to Loch Coruisk. This route has one of the most continuous outcrops of rock in Britain.

 172 The Dubh Slabs Moderate *
(NG 477 207) Alt 50m Map p308 Diagram p322

The unique combination of easy climbing on immaculate slabs, a superb setting, a scary abseil and a Munro tick, makes this arguably the finest outing of its grade in the country. An ascent of Sgùrr Dubh Mòr and Sgùrr Dubh na Dà Bheinn (though not the Dubh Slabs!) by two past presidents of the SMC inspired a much quoted piece of verse:

> *Said Maylard to Solly one day in Glen Brittle,*
> * 'All serious climbing, I vote, is a bore;*
> *Just for once, I Dubh Beag you'll agree to do little,*
> * And, as less we can't do, let's go straight to Dubh Mòr.'*
>
> *So now when they seek but a day's relaxation,*
> * With no thought in the world but of viewing the views,*
> *And regarding the mountains in mute adoration,*
> * They call it not 'climbing', but 'doing the Dubhs'.*

Those of more modest climbing ability may not find some parts of the outing quite as relaxing as this poem suggests. The abseil from the summit of Sgùrr Dubh Beag is certainly far from straightforward, and the continuation onto Sgùrr Dubh Mòr also has its moments. This is not a good route to choose for a first abseil. Fortunately there is an alternative way which avoids the abseil, although it begins more than 100 metres lower down the route. This latter option was used until Douglas, Lamont and Rennie made the first direct descent by abseil from the summit in 1896.

Approach
Follow a path on the south side of Loch Coruisk over ice-smoothed slabs and

CORUISK

On the immaculate Dubh Slabs (Moderate)
Scrambler: George Archibald

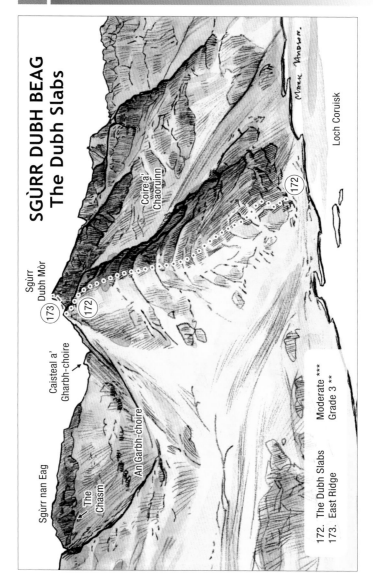

SGÙRR DUBH BEAG
The Dubh Slabs

Sgùrr nan Eag

The Chasm

An Garbh-choire

Caisteal a' Gharbh-choire

Sgùrr Dubh Mòr

Coire a' Chaoruinn

Mhic Mhoire

Loch Coruisk

Moderate ***
Grade 3 **

172. The Dubh Slabs
173. East Ridge

some boggier ground until directly below the slabs. An approach can also be made by descending An Garbh-choire, either from Bealach a' Gharbh-choire or from the so-called coast path from Glen Brittle (Route 51). From the lower level of the corrie, descend a broad depression with a stream, on the south side of the slabs, to reach an area peppered by tiny lochans close to Loch Coruisk.

The Route

The slabs extend for well over one kilometre at an average angle of almost 30°, from just above the shore of Loch Coruisk to the summit of Sgùrr Dubh Beag. The hardest unavoidable section is getting established on the main sweep of slabs at the bottom. Ascend a grassy gully immediately to the right of a toe of steep slabs, and emerge on a broad platform with good views down Loch Coruisk.

Turn right to face a wall of steeper rock, then move to the left-hand end of the ledge and follow widely-spaced steps up leftwards from a leaning block. After some awkward moves trend slightly right and soon reach the crest of the ridge where the difficulties quickly ease.

A prominent rock band rises above a grassy terrace. Either move left and weave a way up steep rocks in a rather exposed position, or ascend slabs more easily at the right-hand end of the rock band. After this, the slabs can be climbed almost anywhere for some considerable distance. It is only rarely that hands are needed for lengthy sections. Occasional grassy depressions running across the crest give ample opportunities to take in the magnificent views. In one or two places slanting grassy gullies on the left flank offer escape routes into An Garbh-choire.

A stretch of excellent slabs higher up has a slanting grassy gully on its right-hand side. From the lush grassy depression above this, ascend slightly steeper slabs to the left of a more lichenous section. Then follow more broken rocks with boulders for some distance. A splendid crack up a short clean slab gives the last scrambling before the delightful summit of Sgùrr Dubh Beag is reached.

Many find the abseil down the west side of Sgùrr Dubh Beag the crux of the outing. A slightly dubious anchor from a lower ledge has been replaced by a more secure but higher one, so it is now almost 30m to reach the deck. The take-off over the steep part is rather awkward and two sections are completely free. A short distance further down the ridge it is necessary to face in to descend a tricky rock step.

The option which avoids the abseil starts some 120 metres before the summit. It descends an easy gully on the left (south) for a short distance, and then picks a way easily round broken rocks to reach a broad ramp line. This leads up diagonally, parallel to the ridge. It comes out just by the final descent after the abseil, at the dip on the ridge leading to Sgùrr Dubh Mòr.

At this point it is worth knowing that there is an escape route from the north side of this dip down Coire a' Chaoruinn. Most parties, however, will choose to continue via the next route onto Sgùrr Dubh Mòr.

Peter Reynolds abseils from the summit of Sgùrr Dubh Beag (Route 172)
Photo: Mike Dixon

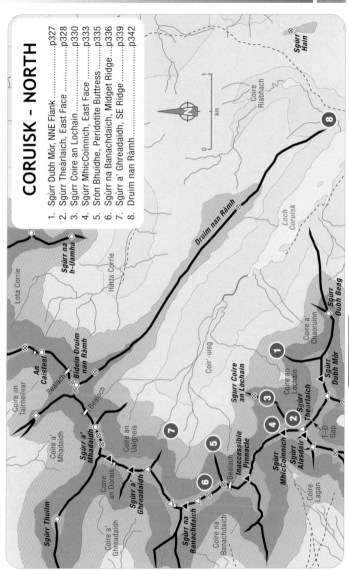

CORUISK - NORTH

1. Sgùrr Dubh Mòr, NNE Flank......p327
2. Sgùrr Thearlaich, East Face p328
3. Sgùrr Coire an Lochain......p330
4. Sgùrr MhicCoinnich, East Face p333
5. Sròn Bhuidhe, Peridotite Buttress p335
6. Sgùrr na Banachdaich, Midget Ridge...p336
7. Sgùrr a' Ghreadaidh, SE Ridge p339
8. Druim nan Ràmh......p342

CORUISK

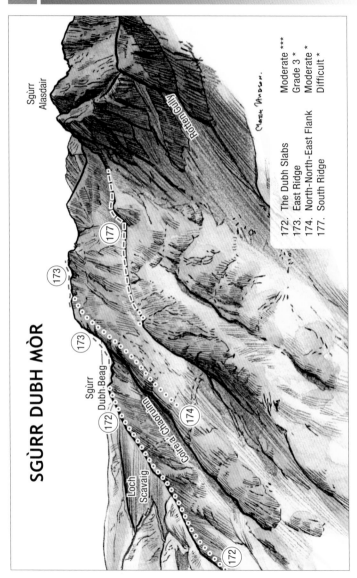

SGÙRR DUBH MÒR

Sgùrr Alasdair

Rotten Gully

Sgùrr Dubh Beag

Coire a' Chaol**uinn**

Loch Scavaig

172. The Dubh Slabs — Moderate ***
173. East Ridge — Grade 3 *
174. North-North-East Flank — Moderate *
177. South Ridge — Difficult *

SGÙRR DUBH MÒR 944m

(NG 457 205) Map p325

The mighty mountain of Sgùrr Dubh Mòr lies to the east of the main Cuillin ridge. It has a long summit ridge running east–west and an extensive north-north-east flank. The mountain is linked by a fine ridge to its small eastern top, Sgùrr Dubh Beag (733m).

173 East Ridge   Grade 3 *

(NG 465 203)   Alt 695m   Map p325   Diagrams pp322 & 326

The ridge which continues onto Sgùrr Dubh Mòr from Sgùrr Dubh Beag is very different in character from the Dubh Slabs. A short distance along it, just after a small bump, there is a rather awkward steep descent. Interesting scrambling on the crest then alternates with easier ledges on the left. Higher up, a scar on the right side of the crest marks a recent rockfall.

Eventually the more intimidating rocks guarding the summit ridge are reached. The natural tendency is to follow sloping stony ledges up leftwards, taking higher options wherever possible. If this is done, it leads to an exposed move past a boulder perched on a slab. Immediately after this, there is an alcove with a very steep and tricky (Severe) groove above it. The easiest way avoids this groove by ascending a much less obvious line starting from a muddy and gritty slope further right and slightly lower down (i.e. before the boulder). Step rightwards at first, then go up a short distance before cutting back left to reach a slabby rake slanting left. Emerge on the crest of the ridge at a slight dip not far from the steep eastern end. Clamber along the crest with steep drops to the left and a gentler slope to the right. Cut back left to descend a steep drop before reaching the final section of mossy rocks forming the summit.

Turn left at the western end and descend the south-west nose with care (Route 152). A recent rockfall has left a green scar. Weave a way down to a small dip before a pinnacle. It is possible to descend grassy rakes slanting down leftwards into An Garbh-choire from this first dip. Otherwise continue to the lowest point on the ridge. (Do not descend the gully on the left at this point. It is horribly loose.) Then scramble up the east ridge of Sgùrr Dubh na Dà Bheinn. To return to a base at Coruisk from here, descend the south ridge (Route 153) to Bealach a' Gharbh-choire and continue down the extremely rough ground in An Garbh-choire. Eventually descend beside the unnamed stream immediately south of The Mad Burn to the shores of Loch na Cuilce.

174 North-North-East Flank   Moderate *

(NG 461 211)   Alt 500m   Map p325   Diagrams pp326 & 331

The broad northern flank of Sgùrr Dubh Mòr forms the eastern border of Coire an Lochain. It does not bear comparison with the previous route, but it does offer a fairly direct way to the summit from the upper end of Loch

Coruisk. The great majority of the outing is easy scrambling but one steeper section warrants the grade.

Approach

Follow the path along the south side of Loch Coruisk and slant left across the lower half of Coire a' Chaoruinn, crossing streams as necessary. Head for a fairly obvious slanting grassy terrace which cuts across the shoulder of Sgùrr Dubh Mòr at about the 500m level. This is the approach route to Coire an Lochain.

The Route

When in full view of the northern flank, set off up grass and slabby rocks to the main section of slabs. Ascend these without undue difficulty by any number of lines. A steeper nose high up gives the crux. Thereafter the angle soon eases and a broad slope can be ascended almost anywhere to reach the summit crest. Finish as for the previous route.

It is possible to descend into Coire an Lochain from the dip between Sgùrr Dubh Mòr and Sgùrr Dubh na Dà Bheinn. This is the way Sheriff Nicolson began his epic descent in 1873.

SGÙRR THEÀRLAICH 978m

(NG 450 207) Map p325

The delightful lochan in Coire an Lochain is rarely visited. Sgùrr Theàrlaich is the highest peak overlooking the corrie. A steep Difficult chimney (Aladdin's Route) on the left-hand side of the face leads up to the notorious T–D Gap. The north and south ridges of the peak make a fine traverse (Routes 126 and 127), but they are not usually approached from the Coruisk side.

175 East Face Grade 3
(NG 452 208) Alt 800m Map p325 Diagram p329

The east face of this peak is rather broken, and has no distinguished lines. A steep band of rock which cuts across its upper half has a slanting terrace beneath it. The face was first ascended by Harold Raeburn and party in 1913. Raeburn suggested that by descending to it from Bealach Coire an Lochain it could be used to avoid the T–D Gap. Nowadays the easy way on the other side of the mountain (Route 149) is much preferred.

Approach

From Bealach Coire an Lochain scramble down slightly awkward rocky ground before slanting leftwards to the foot of the face.

It can also be reached by descending the gully from Bealach MhicCoinnich. When starting this descent it is best to stay hard over by the left-hand wall on the MhicCoinnich side. After an awkward step to begin with there is some scree before a second awkward slabby section. Again stay left and descend a groove to gain a much easier scree slope.

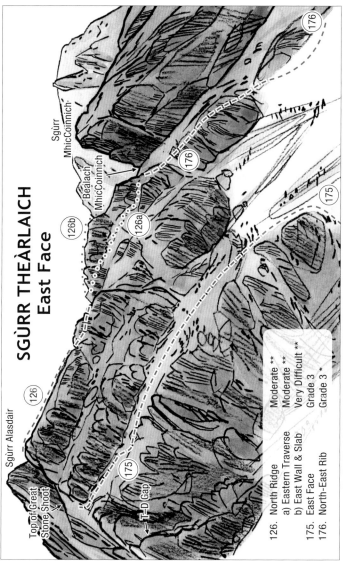

SGÙRR THEÀRLAICH
East Face

CORUISK

Sgùrr Alasdair

Top of Great
Stone Shoot

T–D Gap

Sgùrr
MhicCoinnich

Bealach
MhicCoinnich

126. North Ridge — Moderate **
   a) Eastern Traverse — Moderate **
   b) East Wall & Slab — Very Difficult **
175. East Face — Grade 3
176. North-East Rib — Grade 3 *

From Coruisk approach as for Route 174. From the start of that route continue further right along the grassy terrace and follow the stream uphill to the lochan in Coire an Lochain. Ascend the right-hand slope behind the lochan and so gain a dip on the south ridge of Sgùrr Coire an Lochain. Turn left and follow the broad crest easily, over a minor top (787m), and slant left across scree to the foot of the face.

The Route
It is possible to head up a diagonal rightwards break through the lower apron of rocks. Otherwise skirt beneath the lowest rocks before ascending scree for some distance. Follow the terrace leftwards. This gradually gets harder. Eventually scramble up a steeper step and traverse left in a very exposed position to gain the south ridge. This is at the point where it can easily be crossed to join the scree slope leading to the top of the Great Stone Chute.

 176 North-East Rib   Grade 3   *
(NG 451 210)   Alt 800m   Map p325   Diagrams pp329 &331

There is a prominent slabby rib on the left side of the gully leading to Bealach MhicCoinnich. It offers a more interesting way of reaching the bealach from the Coruisk side.

Approach
Gain the easy ground at the start as for the previous route.

The Route
Avoid the first boss of rock on the left-hand side, and return to the crest by a rightwards slanting grassy ramp. Climb knobbly slabs left of centre weaving to and fro. At an overlap with greasy slabs to the right make a steep move up left to a good high handhold and so break through to rougher slabs on the left. These give pleasant scrambling but soon ease off. After a slight flattening easier rocks soon lead to the steeper rocks marking the start of the north ridge (see variations 126a & 126b). Bealach MhicCoinnich lies a short distance down to the right.

SGÙRR COIRE AN LOCHAIN 759m

(NG 454 214) Map p325

There are several minor bumps on the low ridge forming the west side of Coire an Lochain. At the northern end of this ridge there is a high point (759m) followed by a steep descent to a small gap (712m), and then a tiny top (729m) with steep rock on three sides. This top is thought to have been the last mountain summit to be conquered in the British Isles, when Collie, Howell, Mackenzie and Naismith first climbed its north face in 1896. They made a day of it by also climbing the Inaccessible Pinnacle and continuing along the ridge to Sgùrr a' Mhadaidh, before descending by the Thuilm ridge.

SGÙRR COIRE AN LOCHAIN

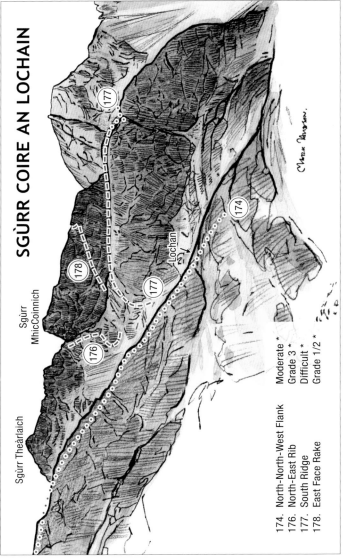

Sgùrr Theàrlaich

Sgùrr
MhicCoinnich

Lochan

174. North-North-West Flank — Moderate *
176. North-East Rib — Grade 3 *
177. South Ridge — Difficult *
178. East Face Rake — Grade 1/2 *

Coire an Lochain

Bidein Druim
nan Ràmh

Glac
Mhòr

D

177

Coire an Uaigneis

Sgùrr a' Mhadaidh

Sgùrr a' Ghreadaidh

Bealach
MhicCoinnich
and 176

SGÙRR COIRE AN LOCHAIN

177. South Ridge   Walk/Difficult *

D   Descent route

177 South Ridge Difficult *
(NG 453 211) Alt 720m Map p325 Diagrams pp331 & 332

The grade only applies if the top itself is reached. The ridge is only a walk as far as the high point (759m) before the gap.

Approach

Follow the same approach as for the previous route, but turn right on reaching the crest of the ridge behind the lochan.

The Route

The crest is followed without difficulty until the drop into the gap. Climb down carefully into the gap (712m), then scramble more easily onto the small summit – a superb viewpoint. Return the same way, or (much harder) pick a way carefully down the gully and bordering rocks on the east side of the gap.

SGÙRR MHICCOINNICH 948m

(NG 450 210) Map p325

There are two main ways of reaching the summit of Sgùrr MhicCoinnich from the Coruisk side. One option is to gain Bealach MhicCoinnich, either by the obvious gully with some short Grade 2/3 rock steps, or by Route 176. Then follow Hart's Ledge (Route 124) or King's Chimney (Route 125) on the west face. The other main option is to gain the north ridge by the next route.

178 East Face Rake Grade 1/2 *
(NG 451 211) Alt 800m Map p325 Diagram p331

This is a surprisingly easy way onto the summit ridge of Sgùrr MhicCoinnich. It joins the north ridge at a prominent notch.

Approach

Gain the south ridge of Sgùrr Coire an Lochain as for Route 175. Slant rightwards across a bouldery slope to the left-hand end of the east face of Sgùrr MhicCoinnich. Start below Forgotten Groove – a Very Difficult climb with a slabby face and a vertical right-hand wall.

The Route

A scree gully slants rightwards through small rock buttresses. The worst of the scree can be avoided by traversing right along a terrace for a short distance, and then ascending slabs trending slightly left. Follow an easy, rightward-slanting grass rake for some distance with only one slightly awkward rocky section.

Eventually a prominent pinnacle can be seen on the skyline with a scree gully to its left. Again the worst of the scree at the bottom can be avoided by traversing right a short distance. Scramble up the right-hand side of a rib, and then cut back left into the gully. Ascend scree and boulders to a notch on the north ridge (see Route 122).

CORUISK

'The best rock in the world for climbing...' Peridotite Buttress (Grade 3)
Scrambler: George Archibald

SRÒN BHUIDHE 878m

(NG 443 219) Map p325

The small top just north of Bealach Coire na Banachdaich has a ridge, called Sròn Bhuidhe, projecting into Coireachan Ruadha. This ridge is distinguished at half-height by a buttress of peridotite – the most northerly outcrop of the band that crosses the Cuillin.

 179 Peridotite Buttress   Grade 3 *
(NG 447 220)   Alt 620m   Map p325   Diagram p337

The superb rock which characterises this route justifies making the rather lengthy approach. The scrambling is reminiscent of Honeycomb Arête on Barkeval (Rum), and although very short-lived it is very enjoyable.

Approach
The best approach is from Glen Brittle via Bealach Coire na Banachdaich (see Route 111). From the bealach, drop down steep scree into Coireachan Ruadha for 250m, and slant left by some massive boulders to reach a broad terrace at the 600m level.

A prominent orange/brown buttress is situated a short distance above the terrace. It has a V-shaped central face and a leftward-leaning slabby section to the left. The scramble ascends the central face.

The Route
Clamber over boulders to reach the central depression. Start quite close to a rightward-slanting groove. Scramble up fairly directly, but make some steep moves left early on to get past some small overlaps. Then take a direct line up the steep face using reassuringly deep slots for the hands and feet. The rock is superb and the situation is exhilarating. The buttress peters out all too soon.

Continue up the ridge more easily until near the steep upper rocks. Then follow an obvious narrow ledge across the right flank to easier ground. It would be possible to scramble up from here to the dip between the 878m top and the south top of Sgùrr na Banachdaich (917m). However, the best option now is to traverse a long way right along a terrace to the start of the next route.

SGÙRR NA BANACHDAICH 965m

(NG 440 224) Map p325

The east face of Sgùrr na Banachdaich, which overlooks Coireachan Ruadha, is impressively steep. Unfortunately the rock here is generally not as good as elsewhere. However, the next route has character, and makes a fine continuation to the previous one.

CORUISK

180 Midget Ridge Difficult *
(NG 442 221) Alt 810m Map p325 Diagram p234

This fine little ridge was first climbed by Patey and Brooker in 1953. They did three other routes hereabouts on the same day. There are occasional loose holds and the climb could do with more traffic.

Approach
The ridge is best done after the previous route, but it can also be reached by dropping down from the dip on the ridge north of the 878m top. Traverse along the terrace to the foot of a rightward-leaning arête with a gully on its left-hand side.

The Route
Make some steep moves to get established on the front of the arête. Continue slightly more easily. A second pitch up the arête leads to a stance below an alcove. Bridge up carefully by suspect blocks and make some strenuous moves to exit from the alcove. Take a stance after half a rope-length to avoid rope drag. Continue up a slightly broader section of ridge with some fine climbing. An easier arête then leads to the main ridge a few metres north of the south top.

A good continuation is to traverse Sgùrr na Banachdaich (Route 111).

SGÙRR A' GHREADAIDH 973m

(NG 445 231) Map p325

The south-east face of this mountain dominates the head of Coir'-uisg. It has a long route up its south-east ridge which may appeal to climbers seeking a full day's mountaineering in secluded surroundings. On the lower left-hand side of the face are twin buttresses of excellent rock split by a long gully. A sizeable terrace, which gives the buttresses their names, is situated immediately above at half-height on the face.

181 Terrace Buttress West Difficult *
(NG 446 225) Alt 530m Map p325 Diagram p337

This is one of three climbs done on the twin buttresses by Steeple and Barlow in the early 1920s. It catches the sun and gives a pleasant outing. It is a long way to the start, but you are very likely to have the whole crag to yourself.

Approach
It is nearly 6km from the Coruisk Hut along the side of Loch Coruisk. Perhaps the best approach from the Glen Brittle side is via Bealach Coire na Banachdaich (851m). Although it does entail gaining and losing a lot of height, halfway down the Coruisk side there are excellent views of what you are letting yourself in for. Cut left at the level of Peridotite Buttress (Route 179) and drop down to the stream in the floor of the corrie. Look for a way through a short but steep rock band guarding the base of the face.

SGÙRR A' GHREADAIDH

Coire an Uaigneis

Terrace Gully

The Terrace

CORUISK

179. Peridotite Buttress   Grade 3 **
181. Terrace Buttress West   Difficult *
182. South Face   Grade 2/3 *
183. South-East Ridge   Very Difficult **

Looking down the curving chimney/gully on Terrace Buttress West (Difficult)
Climber: Willie Jeffrey

The Route
The normal start begins near Terrace Gully on the right-hand side of the buttress. There is a long, steep section before slabs are gained. An alternative start begins much further left and makes a rising rightwards traverse on less steep rock to the same point.

The main feature of the climb is a leftward curving gully/chimney system, roughly parallel to Terrace Gully. This is followed to a big ledge, from where a variety of lines can be followed to an ancient cairn on the summit.

 182 South Face Grade 3 **
(NG 446 227)   Alt 750m   Map p325   Diagram p337
This is a straightforward way of gaining the main ridge from The Terrace. It makes a natural continuation of the previous route. It also offers an easier finish to the next route.

Approach
Reach The Terrace by the previous route. Go up to the obvious leftward-slanting slabby rib in the centre of the south face. It would also be possible to reach this suntrap by making a long but interesting traverse from Bealach na Glaic Moire all the way across Coire an Uaigneis.

The Route
The initial rocks give sustained but pleasant scrambling. They gradually get easier as height is gained. Continue in the same general direction on a narrower grassy line for some distance. Eventually head up a gully slightly more steeply to reach the crest of the south ridge at around two-thirds height.

The natural continuation is to traverse over the south top and then descend from the main summit by the north-north-east ridge. However, the easiest way off is to traverse Sgùrr Thormaid to Sgùrr na Banachdaich.

 183 South-East Ridge Very Difficult **
(NG 451 227)   Alt 380m   Map p325   Diagrams pp337 & 340
This is reputed to be one of the longest rock climbs in Scotland, although in fact it is a rather disjointed outing. The lower third gives good climbing on ice-smoothed slabs, whilst the middle section is just a walk. The upper section is more nerve-racking. It weaves an intricate line up a narrow ridge on some rather suspect rock. The route was pioneered by Collie and Howell in 1896.

Approach
It is a long way to the start of this route. Perhaps the quickest approach is to cross Bealach na Glaic Moire from upper Glen Brittle. Another option is to use Bealach Coire na Banachdaich from lower Glen Brittle as for Route 181. One attraction of an approach by Loch Coruisk is that a quick return can be made to Coir'-uisg from Bealach Thormaid.

The climb starts at a height of some 380m, where a stream from a prominent gully meets two other tiny streams in a slabby depression. A short way up the slope to the left there is a recess with a rowan tree. When this part

CORUISK

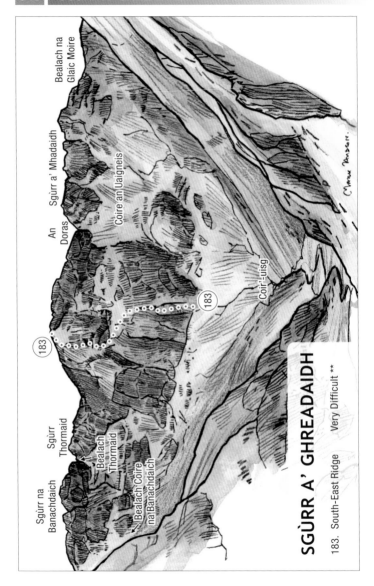

Bealach na
Glaic Moire

Sgùrr a' Mhadaidh

Coire an Uaigneis

An
Doras

Coir'-uisg

Sgùrr na
Banachdaich

Sgùrr
Thormaid

Bealach
Thormaid

Bealach Coire
na Banachdaich

SGÙRR A' GHREADAIDH

183. South-East Ridge   Very Difficult **

High up on the South-East Ridge of Sgùrr a' Ghreadaidh (Very Difficult)
Climber: George Archibald

CORUISK

of the face is viewed from Loch Coruisk, the prominent gully is seen to curve rightwards higher up and join with another gully to form an inverted U.

The lower part of the route is open to variation. The original start goes up the prominent left-hand gully or the rocks to the left of it. A later direct start begins further up the slope to the left. However, another alternative start is now described which climbs the rocks inside the inverted U.

The Route

Climb a pitch up a slabby rib immediately to the right of the prominent left-hand gully. Continue on slightly easier rock, then cross a cleft with water in it and belay below steeper rocks.

The next pitch gives the crux. Traverse right and then back left across a wall. Follow slanting slabby rocks with scant protection for some distance to a stance with a poor belay. Step right and follow a slanting groove. Then break right and soon reach easier ground. Slant diagonally right across slabs and continue to a ledge with an overlap above.

Traverse right over blocks towards a long gully (a continuation of the right-hand leg of the inverted U). Continue up a groove on the left side of the gully. Break left onto superb slabs and follow these, eventually passing to the left of a big boulder, and so reach easy ground. Walk a long way leftwards and pass to the left of the lowest rocks forming the bottom of the south-east ridge.

From the south side of the ridge – with good views of the extensive terrace further left – cut back right very slightly to gain the crest. Follow the crest then continue by climbing a series of short walls linked by leftward-slanting cone-sheets. Great care is needed with the rock at times, and the easiest way is not always obvious. Eventually make a slightly longer traverse left, and ascend a recess directly to reach somewhat easier ground. Continue up the crest for some distance on more mossy rock and join the main ridge a short distance before the south top (see Route 102).

COIRE AN UAIGNEIS

Map p325

This high-level corrie has something of a Shangri-La feel. It extends from the south-east ridge of Sgùrr a' Ghreadaidh across beneath the summit of Sgùrr a' Mhadaidh to a broad ridge on the south side of Bealach na Glaic Moire which leads to the first top of Sgùrr a' Mhadaidh. The corrie can be entered most easily from the east side by Glac Mhòr or from the west by following a watercourse up to The Terrace from just beyond the slabs below Bealach Thormaid.

The first route recorded here (Brown's Climb) was done in 1897 on the horribly wet SMC summer meet. The various gullies were subsequently explored by Steeple and Barlow, and sometimes Doughty, in 1910–13. They can only be ascended by climbing. The one leading to Eag Dubh has eight or nine pitches (Difficult) and the one to An Doras has several short tricky pitches and is far from easy. The gullies which lie between the tops of Sgùrr a' Mhadaidh also give climbs and are named according to the numbers of the neighbouring tops. The only scrambling route up to the ridge is by a prominent ramp (Grade 2/3) which starts near the bottom of the 2–3 Gully and slants leftwards to the 3–4 Nick. See the diagrams on pp210 & 332.

BIDEIN DRUIM NAN RÀMH 869m

(NG 456 239) Map p325

Druim nan Ràmh is the longest side ridge projecting from the main Cuillin chain. It overlooks the north-east side of Loch Coruisk and leads to the complex triple peaks of Bidein Druim nan Ràmh.

 **184 Druim nan Ràmh   Grade 2 ** or Difficult **
(NG 490 205)   Alt 100m   Map p325   Diagrams pp343 & 344
This 5km long ridge is the easiest continuous stretch of ridge in the Cuillin. It is mainly a walk, apart from short problems at the start and near the finish. It offers superb views of the whole Cuillin range.

Approach
From the eastern end of Loch Coruisk, cross the Allt a' Choire Riabhaich and head up the hillside to the start of the ridge. If approaching from the north

Sgùrr nan Gillean

BIDEIN DRUIM NAN RÀMH

Sgùrr a' Ghreadaidh

Loch Coruisk

184

184

184b

184a

Difficult Walk

184. Druim nan Ràmh **
a) Direct Start
b) Right-hand Start

CORUISK

BIDEIN DRUIM NAN RÀMH
South-West Flank

Druim Pinnacle

184c

184d

184

West Top

184

184. Druim nan Ràmh **
    c) Coruisk Flank
    d) Direct Route

Grade 2
Difficult

drop down from Duim Hain and eventually cross the stream in the floor of Coire Riabhach before slanting down across the hillside to the start.

The Route

a) **Direct Start   Difficult**

Start steeply from the lowest rocks and soon reach a platform. Follow a blunt rib (crux) weaving from side to side as necessary. Continue on more slabby rocks. When possible move left and break out onto easier ground. Follow pleasant slabs for some distance with fine views of the Coruisk basin.

b) **Right-hand Start   Walk**

Ascend a grassy gully on the right flank of the ridge without any difficulty.

Both starts then join. Continue along the crest for some distance. The ridge broadens out as the high point of 500m is reached at one-third distance. There are a number of tiny lochans scattered about the summit plateau, and fine views in all directions. The ridge gently undulates then narrows as it drops to a low point of 450m.

The final third of the ridge rises more steeply to a small top. At a tiny dip there is a prominent gully on the western flank. Then continue to another minor top, beyond which a deep cleft gives the main unavoidable difficulties of the day. There are two options from here:

c) **Coruisk Flank   Grade 2**. The easiest way is to turn left and descend the Coruisk flank for a short distance until a very narrow grassy break (crux) can be followed round into the gully below the gap. Cross the gully without any difficulty, and slant out the other side along a narrow ledge.

d) **Direct Route   Difficult**. Climbers may prefer to descend more directly into the gap. This option is quite intimidating. Look right and descend a very narrow and exposed slab overlooking the gully on the Harta Corrie side, then cut back left and descend a steep wall into the gap. Traverse out of the gap along a narrow ledge and soon join the slightly lower ledge taken by the easier option.

Continue on the Coruisk side of the crest and skirt the west flank of the Druim Pinnacle. (It is only a minor diversion for climbers to bag this top and return down the Coruisk flank – Difficult.)

A little way beyond the Druim Pinnacle it is possible to scramble down to the right and join the normal descent route from Bealach Harta. However, the Central Peak of Bidein Druim nan Ràmh lies straight ahead. This can be ascended by making a rising traverse across the west face to join the upper part of the normal route from the Bridge Rock (Route 83b) at the dyke chimney. Otherwise follow horizontal ledges leading left to the gully below the West Peak. Then slant out left up slabs to gain the ridge immediately west of the West Peak. It is possible to continue up the gully itself, but it has some Difficult climbing and finishes at a hole beneath the Bridge Rock. The north side has a short, but unpleasantly loose, scree gully.

To return to Coruisk descend a short way to Bealach na Glaic Moire. Slant down easy scree and then descend by a stream to Coir'-uisg.

CORUISK

CUILLIN MAIN RIDGE TRAVERSE

The traverse of the Cuillin main ridge is undoubtedly the finest outing of its type in the British Isles. No other ridge is as narrow, as rocky and of such sustained difficulty. To complete the full traverse demands a high level of physical fitness, agility and mountaineering skill, as well as good fortune with the weather. An ability to scramble comfortably in exposed situations is essential. The direct route along the crest involves climbing of Very Difficult standard, and even taking all the easier options will still involve making some moves graded Difficult. The sustained level of difficulty can take its toll mentally as well as physically in the later stages of the outing.

The ridge is usually done from south to north, but a good case can be made for doing it in the opposite direction. Both of these options involve problems with transport at the finish. It is slightly easier to complete the circuit on foot by starting from a base at Coruisk. Bivvying out on the ridge is a wonderful experience in settled weather, but this does mean carrying extra gear.

May and June are generally the best months for the ridge weather-wise, although this is far from being true every year. In warm weather dehydration can also become quite a problem. Two litres of water is a popular amount to carry, but this may not be enough in heatwave conditions.

Fuller details of the individual sections of the ridge can be found earlier in this guide, but a brief summary is given here of the main difficulties encountered when making a south to north traverse.

The normal approach from Glen Brittle follows the first part of the 'coastal' route to Coruisk. Start up the path to Coire Lagan, and after 750m turn right and cross a stream. Some 1.3km later, cross the rather bigger Allt Coire Lagan. Once below the flank of Sròn na Cìche, the path forks. Take the right-hand fork and after a further 1.4km reach the moor below the mouth of Coire a' Ghrunnda. The path from hereon is much fainter. Eventually cross the Allt Coire nan Laogh and ascend the unpleasant bing-like south-western flank of Gars-bheinn. The normal tendency is to arrive on the ridge some distance west of the summit. Cross two very minor tops to reach the summit of Gars-bheinn. There are several possible bivouac sites just below the summit.

Another option is to ascend into Coire nan Laogh and follow Route 161 to gain the ridge at the bealach (774m) west of Sgùrr a' Choire Bhig. More comfortable bivouac sites are available in upper Coire nan Laogh, or on the lowermost section of the north-west ridge of Sgùrr a' Choire Bhig.

Gars-bheinn to Sgùrr nan Eag – mainly pleasant ridge walking with only short sections of Grade 1 scrambling.

Sgùrr nan Eag to Bealach a' Gharbh-choire – Grade 2 scrambling if the crest is followed, otherwise mainly rough walking and scrambling below the crest on the Coire a' Ghrunnda side.

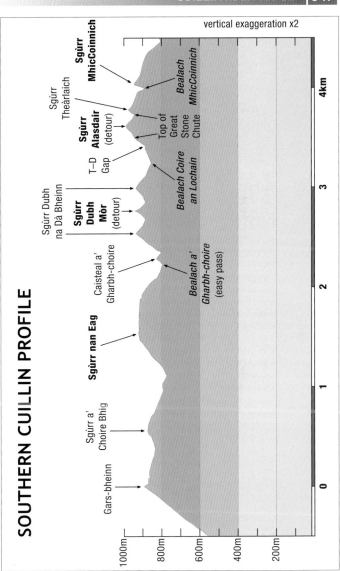

SOUTHERN CUILLIN PROFILE

vertical exaggeration x2

Gars-bheinn

Sgùrr a' Choire Bhig

Sgùrr nan Eag

Caisteal a' Gharbh-choire

Bealach a' Gharbh-choire (easy pass)

Sgùrr Dubh na Dà Bheinn

Sgùrr Dubh Mòr (detour)

Bealach Coire an Lochain

T–D Gap

Sgùrr Alasdair (detour)

Top of Great Stone Chute

Sgùrr Theàrlaich

Sgùrr MhicCoinnich

Bealach MhicCoinnich

1000m
800m
600m
400m
200m

0
1
2
3
4km

On the south ridge of Caisteal a' Gharbh-choire (Moderate)
Scramblers: George Archibald and Archie Marshall

Caisteal a' Gharbh-choire – this fine rock bastion is easily bypassed on its eastern side. Purists will need to be competent climbers to ascend the south ridge and descend by the north-east or north-west ends (Difficult).

Bealach a' Gharbh-choire to Sgùrr Dubh na Da Bheinn – a pleasant Grade 2 scramble. Not exposed, but on very rough rock. A cracked wall right of the crest is worth a short diversion early on.

Sgùrr Dubh na Dà Bheinn to Sgùrr Dubh Mòr (and return) – this is becoming an obligatory detour. Be prepared for up to Grade 3 scrambling on the steep south-western nose of Sgùrr Dubh Mòr.

Sgùrr Dubh na Dà Bheinn to Sgùrr Alasdair – although Sgùrr Alasdair is not on the main ridge, it is rarely missed out, since it is the highest peak on the island. The easiest option skirts below the south-west face of Sgùrr Theàrlaich and ascends the south-west ridge of Sgùrr Alasdair by a Grade 3 chimney.

The classic option is to climb a short rock step to reach the lip of the Theàrlaich–Dubh Gap. Then abseil a short wall directly into the gap and climb out the other side by one of the hardest pitches on the ridge (Very Difficult). The crux chimney may seem harder in windy or damp conditions. Continue up the ridge more easily. After a short distance, it is an easy matter to walk

Marieke Dekker abseils down the short side of the Theàrlaich–Dubh Gap
Photo: Dave Fisher

off the ridge on the left and then ascend on scree to the top of the Great Stone Shoot. A pleasant scramble (Grade 2) then leads up a short section of ridge to the summit of Sgùrr Alasdair – the highpoint of the day. There are superb views from the top. Then descend to the top of the Great Stone Shoot.

Sgùrr Theàrlaich to Bealach MhicCoinnich – not a section that should be underestimated. Starting from the top of the Great Stone Shoot, either descend the path in the scree mentioned earlier until it is possible to walk back onto the south ridge of Sgùrr Theàrlaich, or climb more directly up the wall at a much higher standard. The south ridge is a Grade 3 scramble.

The main part of the north ridge from the summit is very pleasant; however, the descent at the north end to Bealach MhicCoinnich is at least Moderate. The traverse on the Coruisk side perhaps gives the least troublesome route-finding, but the crucial step down is awkward and very exposed. Slant rightwards shortly after the second gap on the crest and descend rightwards, go round a corner on the left and follow a ledge to the awkward crucial wall (Moderate/Difficult in descent). Follow a ledge to another short descent. Continue round on a continuation of the ledge system to a small terrace at the upper bealach. Then scramble down on the right to arrive just below the main bealach.

There are two other ways of descending at the north end, but they are not

Andy Nisbet climbs the long side of the T–D Gap (Very Difficult)
Photo: Gillian Carruthers

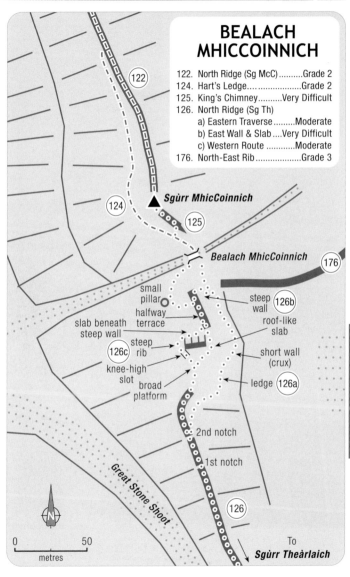

BEALACH MHICCOINNICH

122. North Ridge (Sg McC).........Grade 2
124. Hart's Ledge.....................Grade 2
125. King's Chimney.........Very Difficult
126. North Ridge (Sg Th)
    a) Eastern Traverse.........Moderate
    b) East Wall & Slab....Very Difficult
    c) Western Route...........Moderate
176. North-East Rib..................Grade 3

▲ *Sgùrr MhicCoinnich*

Bealach MhicCoinnich

small pillar

steep wall (126b)

halfway terrace

slab beneath steep wall

roof-like slab

(126c)

steep rib

short wall (crux)

knee-high slot

broad platform

ledge (126a)

2nd notch

1st notch

(126)

Great Stone Shoot

N

0   50

metres

To
Sgùrr Theàrlaich

CUILLIN MAIN RIDGE

King's Chimney (Very Difficult)
Climber: Peter Duggan

*L to R: Sgurr Dubh Mòr, Sgùrr MhicCoinnich, Sgùrr Theàrlaich, and Sgùrr
Alasdair – viewed from Bealach Coire na Banachdaich   Photo: Peter Duggan*

as easy to find. The more popular of the two goes past the second gap on
the crest to where the ridge widens out to a broad flattening. Do not go down
gullies to the left, but look for a small slot (with knee-high rocks either side)
which trends north-west. Face in and descend a short rib for some 5m to a
ledge. Then turn left (still facing in) and traverse across slabs beneath a steep
wall staying high where possible. Go behind a boulder to gain an easy, level
section of ridge. Descend diagonally leftwards on loose rock as far as a small
pillar. Descend a chimney/groove immediately to its right and slant rightwards
across strange, rubbly rock. Ascend slightly to gain the bealach.

Bealach MhicCoinnich to Sgùrr MhicCoinnich – either follow Hart's Ledge
across the Coire Lagan face at Grade 2 and backtrack along the north ridge
to the summit, or part-way along Hart's Ledge scramble up to a higher ledge
and climb the spectacular King's Chimney (Very Difficult) more directly to
the summit.

Sgùrr MhicCoinnich to An Stac – the descent of the north ridge of Sgùrr
MhicCoinnich is an enjoyable Grade 2 scramble. The top section is very
exposed and there are some awkward moves by huge blocks towards the

CENTRAL CUILLIN PROFILE

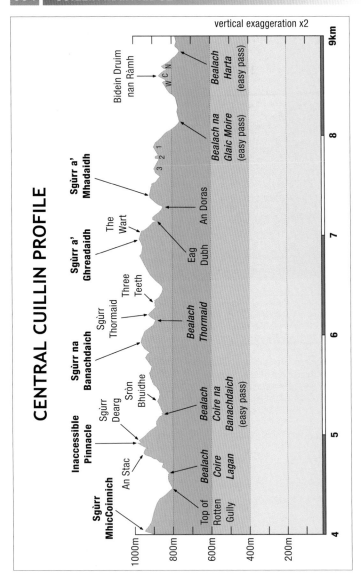

vertical exaggeration x2

*The West Ridge of the Inaccessible Pinnacle (Very Difficult)
– before the lightning strike   Climber: Rob Richardson*

bottom. Go past a dip in the ridge and ascend to a broad flattening which soon leads to Bealach Coire Lagan. The best continuation is to take the direct route up the east ridge of An Stac (upper Grade 3), but an easier slabby ramp can be followed around the base of the south face at Grade 1/2.

The Inaccessible Pinnacle – can easily be avoided on the left, but this is not a very satisfying option unless there are long queues. The East Ridge is surely the most sensational, but also one of the easiest, of Moderate rock climbs. Not to be missed. Most climbers will then abseil down the shorter, but more difficult, western end.

Sgùrr Dearg to Sgùrr na Banachdaich – an easy descent down a broad scree slope from the summit of Sgùrr Dearg is followed by scrambling down to Bealach Coire na Banachdaich – an important crossing point over the main ridge to Coruisk. The south ridge of Sgùrr na Banachdaich gives a superb Grade 2 scramble over two tops before the major summit is reached.

Sgùrr na Banachdaich to Sgùrr a' Ghreadaidh – this is one of the most committing sections of the ridge. Scramble down loose ground well left of the crest to Bealach Thormaid. From there follow the crest with interest, staying slightly right at one point. (Do not be tempted by ledges leading left.) Soon reach the summit of Sgùrr Thormaid. Descend pleasant slabs and then bypass the Three Teeth by a path on the east side of the crest (or climb the Teeth direct at Difficult/Very Difficult). Then follow the long south ridge of Sgùrr a' Ghreadaidh with increasing interest. An absorbing section of Grade 3 scrambling links the south top and the main summit.

Sgùrr a' Ghreadaidh to An Doras – rather easier scrambling leads down from the main summit of Sgùrr a' Ghreadaidh passing the Wart on the left-hand side. Eventually descend into a narrow gap called Eag Dubh which has an impressive cleft (and a possible escape route) on the Glen Brittle side. A little further down the ridge, a short but tricky Grade 3 scramble down a steep ramp just a short distance down the Glen Brittle side leads into the gap of An Doras, from where escape is also possible into Coire a' Ghreadaidh.

The four tops of Sgùrr a' Mhadaidh – another committing and difficult section, best done in this direction. From An Doras, scramble up to the main summit without any great difficulty. Follow the narrow ridge crest northwards to where it takes a sharp turn to the east. Scramble down into a notch and then climb up and over a small rock tower (Moderate). This is easier and probably quicker than cutting the corner via some smooth slabs and a gully.

Descend a pleasant ridge with fine views of Coruisk to the gap below the third top. The steep rocks above the gap can be climbed immediately right of the crest on good holds (Moderate). Move round a slight nose to the right and traverse more easily right to finish. A more popular and less intimidating

*On the south top of Sgùrr a' Ghreadaidh (Grade 3)
looking towards the main summit*

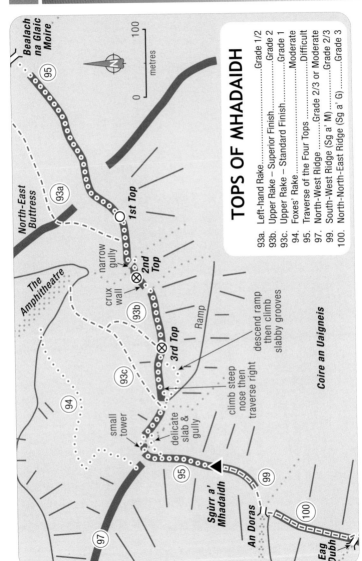

Bealach na Glaic Moire

95

North-East Buttress

93a

1st Top

narrow gully

2nd Top

crux wall

93b

The Amphitheatre

3rd Top

Ramp

93c

descend ramp then climb slabby grooves

94

climb steep nose then traverse right

small tower

delicate slab & gully

95

99

Sgùrr a' Mhadaidh

97

An Doras

100

Eag Dubh

Coire an Uaigneis

N

0   100
metres

TOPS OF MHADAIDH

93a. Left-hand Rake.....................Grade 1/2
93b. Upper Rake – Superior Finish.......Grade 2
93c. Upper Rake – Standard Finish.......Grade 1
94. Foxes' Rake........................Moderate
95. Traverse of the Four Tops.........Difficult
97. North-West Ridge ......Grade 2/3 or Moderate
97. South-West Ridge (Sg a' M) ....Grade 2/3
100. North-North-East Ridge (Sg a' G) .....Grade 3

The direct way up the west end of the Third Top (Moderate). Sgùrr a' Mhadaidh Scramber: Peter Duggan

*Finishing the crux wall on the south-west face of the Second Top (Difficult),
Sgùrr a' Mhadaidh   Photo: Peter Duggan*

way can be found by descending rightwards a short distance from the gap and then ascending slabby grooves.

It is relatively easy then as far as the steep rock wall that guards the second top. Start on the left and slant up left before cutting back right. The final moves climbing directly to the summit give the crux (Difficult).

Descend from the second top easily at first. Then scramble down into an awkward gap by moving right at first, and traversing back left into a narrow gully. Climb out of the gap by a short steep wall. The traverse of the first (and final!) top proves more straightforward until a tricky section of slabs is reached near the bottom. Slant leftwards down these and follow an easy scree path down to Bealach na Glaic Moire – a broad, easy pass between Glen Brittle and Coruisk. It is the lowest point on the ridge.

Bidein Druim nan Ràmh – this complex peak has three tops. The West Peak is bypassed with ease on the south side, but there is a troublesome slabby step (Moderate) to get down onto the Bridge Rock in the gap before the Central Peak. Then scramble up the other side. Traverse right for a short section and descend slightly before ascending again and cutting back left more easily. Climb a dyke chimney before continuing more easily again and soon reach the split block that forms the highest Central Peak.

The descent from the Central Peak to the gap below the North Peak is the crux. It calls for careful route-finding. It is at least Difficult unless the two awkward sections are abseiled. Head north on the left side of a wall to start with then cross over to the right and descend slabs which are sustained and exposed. Reach a ledge and go to the left of a rock boss, before crossing over to the right on slabs. Then cut back left and descend an overhanging wall at full stretch (crux, Difficult). A short descent leads to the bottom of the gap.

The North Peak can be avoided by scrambling round the right-hand (Harta Corrie) side. Otherwise spiral up leftwards by a cone-sheet before taking steeper rock directly to summit (Grade 3). The descent of the North Peak proves relatively straightforward and finishes at Bealach Harta – a fairly easy, but rarely used, pass over the main ridge.

An Turaid and An Caisteal – a short distance above the bealach the way is blocked by a steep boss of rock, here called An Turaid. If taken direct it gives a fine stiff scramble, otherwise follow ledges which slant up to the right rather more easily. The narrow ridge which follows leads to the summit of An Caisteal. It gradually gets harder with height. This section of ridge is famous for its three gaps, the last of which can be crossed by a bold leap.

The descent at the north end of the peak is quite tricky and may seem quite hard for Moderate. Head off on the left-hand (north-west) side to start with. From a short section of horizontal arête descend slabs on the right. Scramble down short drops slanting leftwards before eventually arriving at a steep drop. Descend a steep corner slightly to the left at first. Then traverse back right, before making some steep moves (crux) down the wall into the gap.

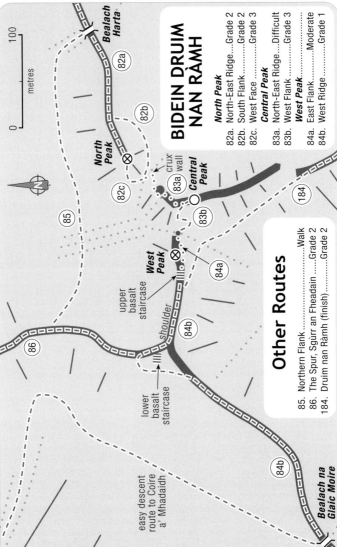

BIDEIN DRUIM NAN RÀMH

North Peak

82a. North-East Ridge....Grade 2
82b. South Flank............Grade 2
82c. West Face ....Grade 3

Central Peak

83a. North-East Ridge....Difficult
83b. West Flank..............Grade 3

West Peak

84a. East Flank..............Moderate
84b. West Ridge.............Grade 1

Other Routes

85. Northern Flank.........................Walk
86. The Spur, Sgùrr an Fheadain ......Grade 2
184. Druim nan Ràmh (finish)............Grade 2

Bealach Harta

North Peak

crux
83a wall

Central Peak

West Peak

upper basalt
staircase

shoulder

lower basalt
staircase

easy descent
route to Coire
a' Mhadaidh

*Bealach na
Glaic Moire*

0   metres   100

Peter Duggan abseiling the top section on the north-east ridge of the Central Peak (Difficult), Bidein Druim nan Ràmh

NORTHERN CUILLIN PROFILE

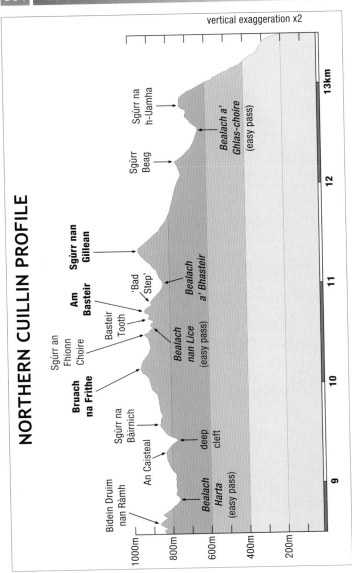

*On the northern section in gathering gloom. The summit of Bruach na Frìthe is
in the foreground with the top of Sgùrr nan Gillean in the cloud on the right.*

Sgùrr na Bàirnich and Bruach na Frìthe – the technical difficulties relent
for the next kilometre, and nothing more than very pleasant Grade 2
scrambling need be encountered. The summit of Bruach na Frìthe – with the
Cuillin's only trig pillar – is a welcome sight. A good place for a breather
before the final leg. Head east on easy ground towards the small peak of
Sgùrr an Fhionn Choire.

Sgùrr an Fhionn Choire – although it can be bypassed easily on the north
side, this fine peak is well worth traversing. The west ridge has an awkward
step on it (Grade 2/3). An easy scramble down a gully on the north flank
leads to Bealach nan Lice – another easy pass over the ridge.

Basteir Tooth – the ascent of this peak is for climbers only. Many a tired
climber has been fazed by the sensational face climbing on Naismith's Route
(Very Difficult). Lota Corrie Route (Moderate) is an easier but much longer
alternative which starts at the bottom of the south face of Am Basteir.
 The continuation onto Am Basteir is a real sting in the tail. It is significantly
harder than the Lota Corrie Route. From the Basteir Nick head to the right
and scramble up a short rift, then follow ledges round as far as a gully that

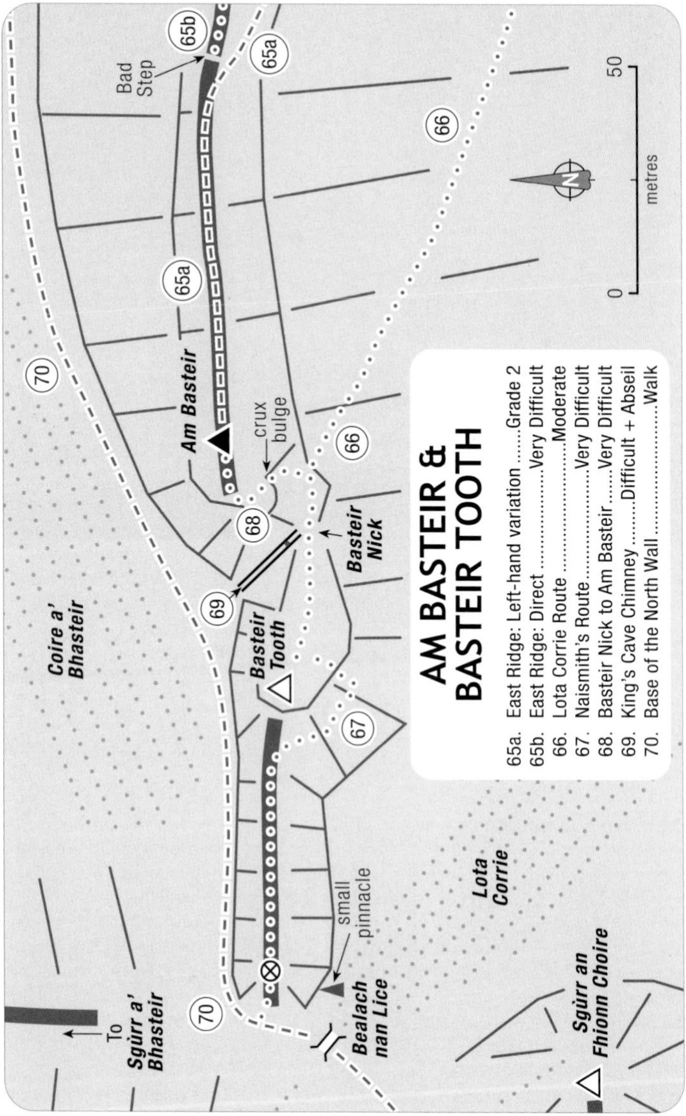

65b

65a

Bad
Step

66

50

65a

70

metres

Am Basteir

crux
bulge

66

N

68

Basteir
Nick

69

66

Bastier
Tooth

0

AM BASTEIR &
BASTEIR TOOTH

67

65a. East Ridge: Left-hand variation......Grade 2
65b. East Ridge: Direct.........................Very Difficult
66. Lota Corrie Route.........................Moderate
67. Naismith's Route.........................Very Difficult
68. Basteir Nick to Am Basteir......Very Difficult
69. King's Cave Chimney......Difficult + Abseil
70. Base of the North Wall.........................Walk

Coire a'
Bhasteir

small
pinnacle

Lota
Corrie

70

⊗

To
Sgùrr a'
Bhasteir

Bealach
nan Lice

Sgùrr an
Fhionn Choire

A climber at the crux on Naismith's Route (Very Difficult), Basteir Tooth
Photo: Mike Hutton

slants back left. The first part is fairly straightforward, but it leads to an undercut alcove just left of a corner. This is strenuous (at least Very Difficult), but soon leads to an easier section of gully above. Other options can be found on the rocks just to the right of the corner. The ledge on the left leads to even greater difficulties. The masses avoid the Basteir Tooth altogether by following a path in the scree below the north face of Am Basteir to Bealach a' Bhasteir.

Am Basteir – the simplest way up to this summit is by the east ridge from Bealach a' Bhasteir, but a rockfall late last century has turned a fairly easy step down on the crest into a formidable Bad Step. This can be down-climbed at Very Difficult standard by those with a long reach. It is also possible to climb down a Difficult wall just back from the step on the Lota Corrie side. However, with careful route-finding it is possible to avoid this problem by traversing round on the Lota Corrie side at a lower level (Grade 2).

Sgùrr nan Gillean – there are a number of options at the start of the west ridge. A very popular option is to climb Tooth Groove followed by the exposed and rather tricky Tooth Arête (Moderate) past the stump of the former Gendarme. Another popular option is to climb an obvious chimney

Looking east from the summit of Am Basteir, towards Sgùrr nan Gillean
Photo: Roger Robb

The END! Marieke Dekker on the summit of Sgùrr nan Gillean celebrates completing the Cuillin main ridge traverse. Photo: Dave Fisher.

(Tooth Chimney, Difficult) on the left side of the alcove. This is harder, but avoids doing the very narrow Tooth Arête. The remainder of the west ridge has little more than Grade 2 scrambling, and there is an optional window high up. The very shapely summit makes a superb finale.

The first part of the descent by the south-east ridge involves very exposed Grade 3 scrambling, but it eases fairly quickly lower down. Most parties then descend northwards and pick up a path back across Coire Riabhach to Sligachan. The chance of a drink before closing time is an added spur, but purists will visit two extra peaks first.

Sgùrr Beag and Sgùrr na h-Uamha – a narrow but straightforward ridge is followed to the first top, from where an easy descent leads to Bealach a' Ghlas-choire. After crossing a small northern top, some careful route-finding and a step of Moderate grade soon bring the final summit underfoot.

The time taken for the traverse will obviously depend, among other things, on exactly which tops are visited and which route is taken. The time of 12 hours 18 minutes from first peak to last taken by Shadbolt and McLaren on the first complete traverse of the ridge in 1911 is still a good time to aim for.

There have been some remarkable times achieved by subsequent parties. Eric Beard set an amazing time of 4 hours 9 minutes in 1967, though his exact route is unknown. When Andy Hyslop bettered this time by 5 minutes in 1984 he took pains to specify his route in some detail. He also included Sgùrr Dubh Mòr. Del Davies and Paul Stott smashed the 4-hour barrier by some 10 minutes just two years later. They finished their traverse by descending Pinnacle Ridge. By 1994 Martin Moran and Andy Hyslop had both lowered the record even further to just over 3 hours 32 minutes. Then, in May 2007, Es Tresidder managed to better this time by a quarter of an hour. The current record is held by Finlay Wild who set a staggering time of 2 hours 59 minutes in October 2013.

These times are all from first to last peak. They were achieved by soloing all the climbing sections and running wherever possible.

Greater Traverse

Those looking for a more extended challenge can go on to complete a traverse of the Cuillin Outliers as well. This was first done by Charleson and Forde in 1939, when they added Clach Glas and Blàbheinn in a total ridge time from first to last peak of 20 hours. It is more usual nowadays to include Garbh-bheinn as well. A fair amount of willpower is needed to set off again from the floor of Glen Sligachan to tackle the eastern peaks.

Cuillin Round

The ultimate Cuillin circuit, which combines a traverse of the Red Hills overlooking Glen Sligachan with the Cuillin Outliers and all the Cuillin main ridge, was first done in a day by Rob Woodall in June 1999. He took 23 hours 28 minutes to complete the round, which started and finished in Glen Sligachan. He had a team of nine people to resupply him at various points.

His route included Glamaig, the Deargs, Marsco, Belig, Garbh Bheinn, Sgùrr nan Each, Clach Glas, Blàbheinn, Sgùrr Hain, Sgùrr na Strì and all the Munros and Tops of the Cuillin main ridge, plus many others including Sgùrr Beag and Sgùrr na h-Uamha – 59 tops in all.

A year later, Yiannis Tridimas – one of Rob Woodall's supporters – extended the Cuillin Round to include Sgùrr a' Bhasteir as well. He started from Coruisk and visited a total of 60 summits in 21 hours 22 mins – a total distance of 55km and 7920m of ascent.

A remark made by Colin Kirkus to Alf Bridge on the summit of Sgùrr Alasdair puts the case for a more relaxed approach to enjoying the mountains:

> *You know, Alf, going to the right place, at the right time, with the right people is all that really matters. What one does is purely incidental.*

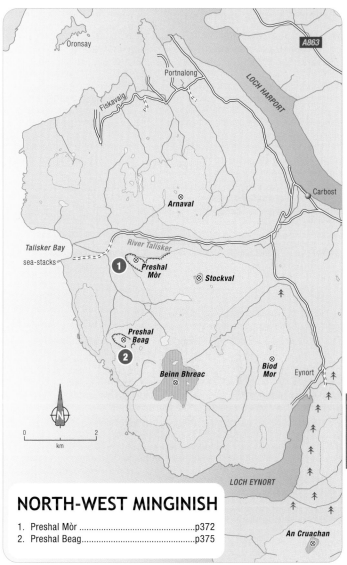

NORTH-WEST MINGINISH

1. Preshal Mòr p372
2. Preshal Beag p375

NORTH-WEST MINGINISH

There are other attractions in Minginish beyond the Cuillin – notably in the more desolate northern part of the region where there are some spectacular sea cliffs. About 7km west of Carbost lies beautiful Talisker Bay and its two sea-stacks. This is an idyllic place to visit on a fine summer's evening. Access is through the grounds of Talisker House. It is 1.5km from the parking place to the sandy beach. A circuit can be made by walking back beside a stream.

Boswell and Johnson were guests at Talisker during their tour of the Hebrides in 1773. Boswell noted that 'Talisker is a better place than one commonly finds in Sky[e]'. Towering above Talisker House is the steep western end of a basaltic hill called Preshal Mòr. Boswell ascended Preshal Mòr with Donald Maclean, the young Laird of Coll. He remarked on the fine views from the summit.

PRESHAL MÒR 317m

(NG 333 300) Map p371

This hill and its companion Preshal Beag are distinctive hills in the north-western part of Minginish. Most of the basalt lavas on Skye are only 10–15m thick, but these two hills are built from single flows over 120m thick. This came about because the lava erupted into deep canyons which had been eroded by rivers on the surface of the earlier flows.

 185 Boswell's Buttress Grade 2/3 *
(NG 329 300) Alt 160m Map p371 Diagram p373
This route finds a way up the western end at a surprisingly amenable grade.

Approach
Park on the right immediately before the tiny road bridge over the River Talisker. Go over a cattle grid and head up a faint track to the left soon after. Slant right and traverse around the western end of the hill. Start at the lowest rocks, near the bottom end of a prominent leftward-slanting earthy ramp.

The Route
Scramble up a small buttress with leftward-leaning columnar rocks. Stay on the crest when the rocks steepen slightly near a rock scar. Continue to a sloping ledge with junipers. Then move up diagonally leftwards, passing just to the right of a detached 2m high pillar. Care is needed with the rock for 4m. The going gradually eases above. Follow a long, leftward-slanting slope on broken rock, scree and heather to reach a heathery shoulder.

Head up the superb rock directly above. Start by trending right slightly and then back left. Instead of slanting easily left higher up, a more interesting option is to make a delicate traverse diagonally rightwards on excellent rock. Then trend back left slightly. Numerous lines are possible as the angle gradually eases.

PRESHAL MÒR

185. Boswell's Buttress   Grade 2/3 *
186. Summit Buttress   Grade 3 **
187. Finger Wagging Buttress   Grade 2/3 *

MINGINISH

Summit Buttress, Preshal Mòr (Grade 3)
Scramblers: John Temple and Andrew Wielochowski

Reach a large heathery ledge with views of the big craggy face further right. Higher up, at a slightly steeper final section, move right and ascend a short rock step by a pleasant V-groove. The western summit is close by. There are superb views of Talisker Bay below. To the north-west there are distant views of MacLeod's Tables, as well as the sea stacks near Idrigill Point.

Continue easily along undulating ground, cross a higher summit, then head south for about 150m. Look for a depression on the edge of the south face which points to the top of an easy scree gully. There is no mistaking the correct gully, because there is a prominent pinnacle well down the gully on the right-hand side.

 186 Summit Buttress   Grade 3   **
(NG 330 299)   Alt 190   Map p371   Diagram p 373

This striking buttress leads directly to the western summit. The route is quite sustained and the rock has to be treated with some care.

Approach
Go round to the right of the previous route and ascend diagonally rightwards for some distance to the second obvious long buttress left of a grassy gully.

The Route
Climb the broken basalt columns by the easiest line, going right and then back left in the middle. After some distance the angle starts to ease slightly. A short section of grassy ground leads to the same finish as the previous route.

 187 Finger Wagging Buttress   Grade 2/3   *
(NG 332 298)   Alt 250   Map p371

This route ascends a broad, but slightly easier-angled buttress a short distance to the west of the descent gully. There is much loose rock, but it should improve with traffic.

PRESHAL BEAG 345M

(NG 329 278) Map p371

This is a similar hill to Preshal Mòr. It lies 2km further south across Sleadale. Despite its name it is marginally higher than its companion. It has some spectacular columnar jointing on its hidden south-western side.

 188 Southern Flank   Grade 1
(NG 329 276)   Alt 270   Map p371

This hill is just a walk, but some minor sport can found by crossing a grassy saddle at its south-eastern end. The south-facing buttress just beyond the saddle gives some pleasant, but very short-lived scrambling. Continue easily to the summit. With careful route-finding it is possible to descend by heathery ledges at the north-western end (Grade 2). On the way home it is worth heading north for just over a kilometre to visit the ruined broch in Sleadale.

MINGINISH

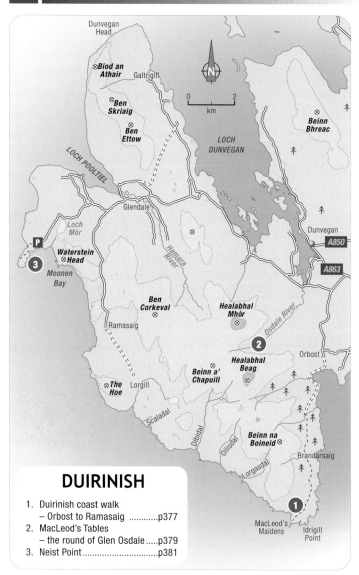

DUIRINISH

1. Duirinish coast walk
   – Orbost to Ramasaig p377
2. MacLeod's Tables
   – the round of Glen Osdale p379
3. Neist Point................................p381

DUIRINISH

The most westerly peninsula of the island, known as Duirinish, is accessed by a single-track road just south of Dunvegan. It leads over a high ridge to the small community of Glendale which looks out on Loch Pooltiel. A little further on, a side road extends to a small car park on the cliff top from where a popular walk leads out to the lighthouse on Neist Point.

The area is built mainly of flat-lying basalt lavas. These have been eroded to produce two very distinctive flat-topped hills, Healabhal Mhòr and Healabhal Bheag – better known as MacLeod's Tables. The area is also renowned for its spectacular coastal scenery.

189 Duirinish coast walk – Orbost to Ramasaig   21km ***
(NG 257 431)   High Point 200m   Map p376

This very long cliff-top walk is quite a serious undertaking. It follows the coast around the southern half of the peninsula. It is worth the effort, however, for it visits some of the most dramatic sections of coastline in the country. The distance from the finish back to the start by road is 20km, so a dropoff or pickup will need to be organised.

MacLeod's Maidens, near Idrigill Point
with The Cuillin and Red Hills in the distance

DUIRINISH

The arch and sea-stacks at Lorgasdal

Approach

Turn off the main A863 road at Heribost – 4km before Dunvegan – and drive through Roag. Park in a small square by some buildings at Orbost Farm.

The Route

Go to the far corner of the square and walk south down a rough track past Orbost House. Continue along beside Loch Bharcasaig. Cross the Abhainn Bharcasaig and follow the track into the forest. The track eventually peters out after a kilometre or so. Cross a stream and follow a good path through further forestry plantations. Pass over a small col and take the uphill side of a deer fence for a short distance. Descend slightly to cross Brandarsaig Burn near some crofting ruins, and continue for a further kilometre to the ruins of the larger community of Idrigill. It is worth diverting from here to see the natural arches and sea-caves directly below, although good views are also obtained looking back north if a diversion is made further south to ascend Ard Beag.

Some will be content to return to Orbost after viewing the three sea-stacks known as MacLeod's Maidens to the west of Idrigill Point. The continuation to the north-west takes on a different character. The ground underfoot is generally firm and grassy, but the route lies close to the edge of high sea-cliffs, and the path is not always obvious. Numerous short diversions have to be made inland to cross streams and rivers flowing from the various dals.

Round about the halfway mark a fine arch and several sea-stacks can be seen where the Lorgasdal River plunges over the cliffs in a waterfall. About 2km further on it is worth diverting inland to visit the Ollisdal bothy. This makes a welcome stopping place. (It is possible to take a route back to Orbost from here, via Healabhal Bheag, which avoids problems with transport.)

The last difficulty is crossing the ravine of the Scaladal Burn. Then crest a rise before dropping down a slope by Lorgill Bay. Slant up the floor of Lorgill past the ruins of the homes of ten families who were cleared from here in August 1830. Cross the Lorgill River and climb 70m (it seems more!) up the sloping hillside to pick up a rough track for the last 3km to Ramasaig.

The coast west of Ramasaig is also very spectacular, and if you have any energy left you can extend the walk by a further 4km to visit Waterstein Head. However, Waterstein Head and nearby Neist Point are more conveniently reached on a separate visit from the north. See Routes 191 & 192.

190 MacLeod's Tables – the round of Glen Osdale   11km   **
(NG 247 460)   High Point 489m   Map p376

An ascent of either Healabhal Mhòr or Healabhal Bheag alone is an enjoyable outing, but a circuit which includes them both is particularly rewarding.

Approach

Park near a small bridge over the Osdale River (GR 248 459).

The Route

Follow a fence on the west bank of the river at first, then cross heather moorland, which is boggy in places. Ascend gently rising ground on the north

DUIRINISH

MacLeod's Tables – Healabhal Beag and Healabhal Mhòr

side of Glen Osdale for some distance. Follow sheep tracks which zigzag up the first section of steeper slope. Continue up a series of long, gentle stretches succeeded by short steeper slopes. Go to the left of a rock band with a rockfall at its left-hand end. Eventually ascend steepish grass to gain the summit plateau of Healabhal Mhòr. It is a further 300 metres up a very gentle slope to the pile of rocks marking the summit (469m). The ground is slightly boggy in places and the views are rather disappointing, although Waterstein Head stands out to the north-west.

Leave the summit plateau and descend the grassy south-western flank to An Sgurran. Small rock bands are easily dealt with on the way. Negotiate a route through some peat hags, then either ascend a small rounded top or contour across its eastern face to reach the bealach below the steep north-west flank of Healabhal Bheag.

Ascend the long grassy slope to reach the summit plateau. There is a trig pillar inside a stone wall in the centre of the plateau, but the highest point (489m) lies at the southern end. It is marked by a cairn, which is almost completely overgrown by grass. There are excellent views of the glen below and all the islands in Loch Bracadale.

Return to the trig pillar and head north-east to leave the summit. The ridge gradually pinches down. Continuing over a slight rise leads to a fearsome drop, so backtrack slightly and drop down steep broken ground on the north-west flank. Zigzag down, then curve round to the right and gain easier grassy ground. A long descent over the moor, on the east side of a large stream, eventually leads back to the start.

191 Waterstein Head (296m)   4km   ***
(NG 137 479)   High Point 296m   Map p376
The short walk out to this dramatic headland makes a splendid outing.

Approach
The side road to Neist Point reaches a high point of just over 110m before it descends on the north side of Loch Mòr. Either start from this high point or from anywhere on the last stretch of road to the Neist Point car park.

The Route
The first start heads south up the hillside eventually following a grass wall and then a fence to the summit. The second option is the same distance but slightly more interesting. Slant down the hillside leftwards and cross the stream from Loch Mòr. Then ascend relatively straightforward grassy ground to an obvious easy way up onto the escarpment.

On the final section up to the summit the headland gradually gets narrower. The views from the top do not disappoint, but don't get too close to the edge.

192 Neist Point & Oisgill Bay   4km   ***
(NG 133 478)   High Point 123m   Map p376
The very scenic headland of Neist Point has a lighthouse on its tip. It is an extremely popular walk. An extension to the north makes a visit here especially worthwhile, though a short section of it is rather scary because it follows exposed and very narrow sheep tracks.

Approach
From the car park on the cliff top overlooking Neist Point.

The Route
Descend a long flight of steps to a flatter area below. Follow a good path over the back of An t-Aigeach and continue to the lighthouse.

Instead of going back up the steps on the return go slightly left through a stone wall and head north. The first section is bouldery and the route is close to the cliff top. The ground then becomes grassy and opens out for a bit. Eventually when boulders become more common again, do not stay by the cliff edge, but head uphill near a stone wall, and continue northwards along the foot of the upper crag.

Go round a corner on steeply-sloping grassy ground and cross a gully (Tower Gully). Continue on similar ground the other side, then head up to the base of the crag above. Follow this along to a 30m high stack known as The Green Lady. Just before reaching this feature turn right and ascend to the top of the cliff arriving not far from a lochan. On the way back seek out a tower feature close to the cliff top. Its top can be visited by making an exciting leap.

Waterstein Head and Moonen Bay

DUIRINISH

Neist Point – An t-Aigeach with the lighthouse behind

Pete Hunter leaps Tower Gap, north of Neist Point

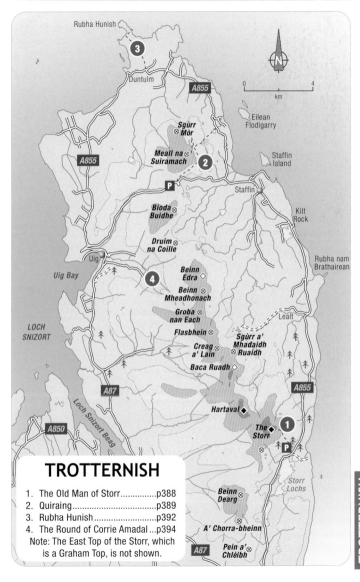

Rubha Hunish

3

Duntulm

A855

N

0   4
km

Eilean
Flodigarry

Sgùrr
⊗ Mòr

Meall na ⊗
Suiramach   2

Staffin
Island

A855

P

Staffin

Kilt
Rock

Bioda ⊗
Buidhe

Druim ⊗
na Coille

Uig

Uig Bay

4

Beinn ◇
Edra

Rubha nam
Brathairean

Beinn ⊗
Mheadhonach

Groba ⊗
nan Each

Lealt

LOCH
SNIZORT

Flasbhein ⊗

Sgùrr a'
Mhadaidh
Creag ⊗ ⊗ Ruaidh
a' Lain

Baca Ruadh ◇

A87

A850

Loch Snizort Beag

Hartaval ◆

The
Storr ◆   1

P

A855

TROTTERNISH

1. The Old Man of Storr...............p388
2. Quiraing....................................p389
3. Rubha Hunish...........................p392
4. The Round of Corrie Amadal...p394
Note: The East Top of the Storr, which
is a Graham Top, is not shown.

Beinn ⊗
Dearg

Storr
Lochs

A' Chorra-bheinn ⊗

A87

Pein a' ⊗
Chlèibh

TROTTERNISH

TROTTERNISH

The great northern finger of Skye has the longest continuous ridge on the island – the Trotternish Ridge. It forms the crest of a 30km long, east-facing escarpment, on the east flank of which are numerous massive landslides – the largest in Britain. The landslipped masses have been eroded to form some extraordinary scenery.

Trotternish lies to the north of Portree – the principal town on the island. A short distance further south, and just outwith Trotternish proper, there is a hill which offers a delightful excursion.

BEN TIANAVAIG   413m

(NG 511 410)   OS Explorer 409 or 410

This modest hill is clearly seen when travelling north to Portree. It gives a surprisingly enjoyable outing.

 193   South Ridge   7km   **
(NG 508 389)   High Point 413m

The crest of this splendid hill has firm grassy ground which gives easy walking. There are fine views from it of Raasay, Portree and The Storr.

Approach
A few kilometres south of Portree, take a minor road leading to the Braes. Turn off to Camastianavaig and park in a layby by Tianavaig Bay. The best route onto the hill is not obvious. Continue along the road and round the head of the bay for about 150m. The road turns sharply through 90° to the north-west by a red letterbox.

The Route
Follow a small sign straight ahead between the houses, cross a stile and pass through a narrow gap between a wall and fence to gain the rear of the house plots. At the foot of steep ground take the right fork and follow this to the termination of the south ridge. Other popular options follow the left fork.

Ascend the steepish slope using sheep tracks where possible. Cross more heathery ground and eventually reach the closely-cropped, grassy ground leading up the crest. There are splendid views to the south of Raasay Sound. A possible return route can also be seen on the shore below. Continue up the delightful ridge to the summit trig point. On a good day the views are superb.

One option now is to descend the same way and look for a route off on the right which eventually leads back to the left fork in the path. Alternatively, descend the north ridge and, at a height of about 350m, cut down to the right to reach an eastern shoulder. Head back southwards through landslipped terrain and make for a finger-like pinnacle. Continue south and eventually descend fairly steeply in a south-easterly direction. Pick up a path around the coast and follow this – slightly exposed in places – back to Tianavaig Bay.

The Old Man of Storr

The next five outings wander among some of the gigantic landslides on the eastern flank of the Trotternish Ridge. Countless other possibilities exist.

THE STORR 719m

(NG 495 540) Map p385

This peak is the highest summit on the whole Trotternish escarpment, so it is a conspicuous feature from several parts of the island.

194 The Old Man of Storr 3km ***
(NG 508 529) High Point 450m Map p385

This giant obelisk is situated among some amazing landslipped terrain below and to the east of the main Storr cliffs. A visit to the Old Man is one of the most popular walks on Skye. It is well worth the effort. Parking may be a problem at busy times.

Raeburn and Russell ascended 'a small pinnacle near the Old Man' in 1898, but it wasn't until 1955 that the Old Man itself was first climbed by Don Whillans. Although other routes have been added since, it is still very rarely ascended, because of the difficulty of the climbing and the appalling rock.

Approach

The walk starts at a car park by a large forest plantation 10km north of Portree. A circuit can be made by starting on the north-east side of the plantation and ascending open, but slightly boggy ground. This leaves the well-constructed path through the forest for the descent.

The Route

Follow the rather boggy path directly up the hillside. Once above the forest join the other approach route and continue up steeper ground. The 50m high pinnacle known as the Old Man lies straight ahead. Routes go up to the left and to the right of the pinnacle. It is better to take the left-hand route on the way up and visit an area known as 'The Sanctuary'. This gives excellent views of the Old Man and the other pinnacles.

Follow a track on the uphill side of the Old Man beneath towering cliffs of basalt. A little further north another distinctive pinnacle with window-like holes in it is known as both 'Needle Rock' and 'The Cathedral'.

Now find a steep route back on the east side of the Old Man and eventually follow the good path down through the forest plantation. However, in good weather, and with plenty of time available, it is well worth extending the outing to include The Storr as described for the next route.

195 The Storr – Northern Flank 7km ***
(NG 508 529) High Point 719m Map p385

This is a rather more demanding outing, but very enjoyable. It continues beyond the high point of the previous route.

Approach
Reach the Old Man as described in the previous route.

The Route
Continue northwards beyond the Needle Rock until the cliffs diminish in size and there are views of Loch Scamadal below. The shortest option now is to turn back hard left and ascend the upper scoop of Coire Scamadal near to the left-hand rim overlooking the Storr cliffs. Skirt round the tops of gullies, and trend right near the top to find a way up to the summit. The summit trig pillar is 100m back from the eastern plateau rim. A tiny peak (Graham Top, 710m) is situated 200m due east of the main summit with a gap to its west.

A more circuitous option after turning the corner above Loch Scamadal is to head in a north-westerly direction and join the north ridge at a slight flattening. If time allows it is worth making a detour to the north for a further kilometre to view the amazing boulder-field below the steep cliffs of Carn Liath. This is the debris from an unusually large rock avalanche. Otherwise turn back left and ascend the north ridge pleasantly to the summit.

After enjoying the views of the whole Trotternish ridge from the summit, the simplest option is to return the same way. A more appealing option is to descend the steep south-western flank of The Storr to Bealach Beag. Drop down from the escarpment by the left bank of a stream. Slant across the boggy hillside and follow the south-west edge of the forest to the road.

MEALL NA SUIREAMACH 543m

(NG 445 695) Map p385

This hill lies on the north side of the road between Staffin and Uig. The escarpment to the east of it harbours some of the most remarkable scenic features on the island, and more than justifies making the long journey north.

196 The Quiraing – The Needle & The Table   5km   ***
(NG 439 679)   High Point 500m   Map p385

This outing visits an extraordinary section of landslipped ground called the Quiraing (pillared enclosure) that is hidden from normal view. Although just a walk, the ground up to the Needle is rough and very steep.

Approach
The most popular approach starts from a sharp bend near the high point on the Staffin–Uig road. An alternative approach can be made from lower down the same road from a tiny parking space (GR 444 682).

The Route
Head in a north-westerly direction below the increasingly impressive cliffs. The first sizeable knoll below the main path is called Cnoc a' Mhèirlich, *hill of the robber*. Both approaches join before the next significant feature, called 'The Prison', is reached on the right-hand side of the path. It is worth

The Quiraing and The Table

ascending this impressive hillock to get a good view of the way up to the Quiraing proper. An ascent of the highest tower involves a tricky scramble.

A tall, slender pinnacle in the cliffs high above, called 'The Needle', points the way into the hidden sanctuary above. Ascend the steep slope directly below the Needle and then pass around it on the left-hand side. Ascend a narrow rocky gully to the right and weave a way up through the cliffs behind. Eventually slant left and ascend a short distance to the right onto the flat, grassy surface of a colossal landslipped block known as 'The Table'.

There is no easy way of reaching the plateau above from here, so either return by the same route or drop down from the middle of the eastern rim of The Table and descend a gully leading north. Continue down to join the path taken by the next route. Turning right leads back round to The Prison.

197 North–South Traverse 6km ***
(NG 439 679) High Point 543m Map p385

Although this outing can be done independently it makes a natural continuation to the previous route.

The Route
Follow the path from the car park on the Staffin to Uig road as for the

Looking north from Leac nan Fionn to Sròn Vourlinn

previous route. Instead of heading up the steep ground to the Needle continue round the corner and head north for just over a kilometre. Take the left fork in the path and cross a stone wall. Eventually the path rises gently to gain the crest of the ridge on the left. Then turn left and follow the rising rim of the escarpment back south. There are fine views overlooking the Quiraing just before the highest point on the rim. The summit of Meall na Suireamach lies about 350 metres back from the edge. Descend the long south-western flank, then drop down steeply southwards back to the road.

SRÒN VOURLINN 378m

(NG 451 708) Map p385

This fine summit has a fiercesome precipice on its eastern side. It overlooks a fascinating area of landslipped ground some 1.5km north of the Quiraing.

198 Leac nan Fionn & Sròn Vourlinn 5km **
(NG 463 710) High Point 378m Map p385

This very enjoyable outing is slightly less frequented than the ones around the Quiraing. It explores some impressive landslipped ground.

TROTTERNISH

Approach

Instead of taking the road over to Uig, continue north on the Duntulm road for just over 3km. Look on the west side of the road for a gated entrance with a faint track, which leads in a short distance to a hidden loch – the delightful Loch Langaig. Park a short distance further north.

The Route

Follow the track round the north side of Loch Langaig and continue by a path which ascends in a south-westerly direction to Loch Hasco. Above this second loch are the cliffs of Leac nan Fionn. These are too steep to take direct, so continue on the path and cross a fence by a stile. Shortly after the path cuts back to the right, leave the path and ascend steeply northwards. Find a way up onto the sloping table-top of Leac nan Fionn (Fingal's Tombstone) by the more amenable ground on its western side. Go to its northern end to view the sheer cliffs of Sròn Vourlinn, below which is a hollow peppered with pinnacles.

Return down the western side of the plateau and head west for a dip on the main escarpment edge gained by the previous route. Turn right and ascend the crest, which overlooks Coire MhicEachainn, in a north-easterly direction to the summit. There is a horrifying drop on the eastern side.

Return the same way to the dip, then find a way down on the north side of Leac nan Fionn to the hollow with the pinnacles seen earlier. There are scrambling possibilities here. Head east to rejoin the route of approach.

———

Trotternish has some very spectacular sea-cliffs, particularly along its eastern coast. There is a very popular viewing place for Kilt Rock, for example, by Loch Mealt just to the south of Staffin. This feature is so named because a thick dolerite sill has prominent columnar jointing which resembles the pleats of a kilt. The name Staffin means 'place of the pillars'.

MEALL TUATH 117m

(NG 412 762)

The next outing visits some remote sea-cliffs at the northern tip of the island. This lowly summit can easily be included as part of the outing.

199 Rubha Hunish 7km **

(NG 422 742) High Point 117m Map p385

This walk visits a beautiful, hidden headland forming the most northerly tip of the island. On a fine day, the views of the Shiants and the Western Isles are superb.

Approach

Take the road to Duntulm. There is a car park just to the east of a telephone

The cliffs of Rubha Hunish – Meall Tuath and Meall Deas

box by a bend in the road (NG 422 742). There are two possible starts. Either head north-west from the carpark on a fairly well-used path or walk west along the road for 600m and drop down to the right on a track past some former coastguard buildings on the west side of a lochan (NG 415 741). This route eventually descends to the coast and is not as well worn. A good combination is to go out by the coastal route and return by the inland path.

The Route
Follow the track by the lochan, go through a gate and turn right shortly after. Go along the right-hand (east) side of a wall and cross a fence by a small stile. Eventually slant down to the shore in Tulm Bay. After about a kilometre, cross a fence and ascend a steep slope. Continue over heathery ground to the summit of Meall Deas (101m). There are very steep cliffs immediately below with fine views across Loch Hunish. Turn right and follow the cliff top along to a trench-like hollow. There is a way down from here to the headland below starting on the near side of the depression by a large boulder.

Slant down rightwards through the cliffs on rocky ground with some minor scrambling to the headland beyond. There are old lazybeds here and several sea-stacks are hidden on the north-east side of the headland.

After returning to the cliff top make a short detour by turning left to visit

a former coastguard lookout on the summit of Meall Tuath. Then follow the path which runs along the depression between the summits. After one rather boggy section continue in the same general direction back to the start.

BEINN EDRA 611m

(NG 455 627) Map p385

This fine peak lies on the main escarpment, but it can be ascended independently by approaching from the west along the delightful Glen Uig.

200 Beinn Edra & the round of Corrie Amadal   12km **
(NG 417 630)   High Point 611m   Map p385
The approach to this peak follows a narrow single-track road on the south side of Glen Uig which leads to a section of landslipped ground which is sometimes referred to as The Fairy Glen. The rather dull terrain in Corrie Amadal contrasts with the spectacular views from the main escarpment.

Approach
Turn off the main road shortly before Uig and just south of the River Conon.

Glen Uig – The Fairy Glen

Looking south along the Trotternish Ridge from Grobha nan Each towards Sgùrr a' Mhadaidh Ruaidh

Follow the road for about 2km and park discreetly a little way before the buildings at the road end.

The Route

Follow the tarmacked road and just before it ends at farm buildings slant off to the right on a track. Go through a couple of gates and continue on an earthy track to the Lòn an t-Sratha. Cross this stream and continue on its north bank for over a kilometre. Then head east-north-east and cross the Abhainn Dhubh. Continue in the same general direction and soon cross the line of a low turf dyke (grass wall). This slants rightwards to Bealach a' Mhòramhain. However, continue straight ahead more directly to the picturesque summit.

Follow the escarpment pleasantly to the south. Then head west from Groba nan Each and follow the broad ridge over Beinn an Laogh. Continue west until it is convenient to drop down to the north and rejoin the outward route.

201 The Trotternish Ridge   33km ***
(NG 439 708)   *High Point 719m*   *Map p385*

The traverse of the whole Trotternish Ridge is a major undertaking, which is normally done north to south. Purists will start from Conista in the north and finish at Portree. The going underfoot is generally quite delightful, so, despite being almost three times the length of the Cuillin main ridge, the outing described can be completed in a similar time.

It is perhaps best done in lightweight style as an extended hill jog. It can also be completed at a more leisurely pace by backpacking along it over a couple of days. There is a welcome spring on the western slope of The Storr above Bealach a' Chuirn.

Approach

The northern route starts from Conista, fords the Kilmaluag River and then ascends the steep north-west shoulder of Sgùrr Mòr. A more popular option starts from Flodigarry by Loch Langaig and follows the path up past Loch Hasco. Eventually gain the escarpment as for Route 197. A 2km detour then has to be made to bag Sgùrr Mòr.

The Route

Starting from the summit of Sgùrr Mòr, follow the crest of the escarpment all the way south! After visiting the flat summit of Meall na Suiramach, go east to the cliff edge to view the Quiraing. Then descend the south-west flank before dropping south more steeply to the Staffin–Uig road. A good place for second thoughts, especially if the weather is dubious.

The crest which rises to the south is quite worn to start with as far as a tiny top (396m). The route from Bioda Buidhe onwards is relatively unspoilt. No special problems should be encountered. It is possible to escape into Coire Leacaich and pick up a track from the old diatomite workings to Lealt. It is also possible to descend from The Storr as described for Route 195.

The steep north-eastern flank of Beinn Dearg gives one of the hardest sections on the ridge. The heathery ground on the final leg is also hard going.

INDEX OF ROUTES – listed mainly by nearest peak/location name

Allt Darach Gorge	83
Am Basteir	167
Base of the North Wall	175
Basteir Nick to Am Basteir	171
East Ridge	167
King's Cave Chimney	175
Amphitheatre Arête	273
An Caisteal	184
East Face: Central-South Buttress	189
East Face: North Butress	190
North Ridge	184
South Ridge	184
West Buttress	186
An Diallaid: North Rib	226
An Stac	245
An Stac Chimney	247
East Buttress	245
see also Sgùrr Dearg: SE Flank	243
An Turaid	184
Arrow Route	271
Banachdaich Slab	237
Basteir Gorge: Cooper's Gully	156
Basteir Tooth	169
Lota Corrie Route	169
Naismith's Route,	171
Bealach na Glaic Moire Slabs	203
North Buttress	203
South Buttress	205
Tuppenny Buttress	205
Beinn Dearg Mhòr	86
North-East Ridge	86
Round of the Beinn Deargs	87
Beinn Edra	394
Beinn na Caillich	82
Round of Coire Reidh	82
Belig	97
North Ridge	97
South-East Ridge	97
South-West Ridge	99
Ben Tianavaig	386
Bidein Druim nan Ràmh	192
Central Peak	195
North Peak	192
Northern Flank	198
West Peak	195
Blàbheinn	117
Dog-Leg Gully	122
Dyke Route	129
East Flank	127
East Ridge	125
Forked Pinnacle Ridge	117
Great Gully Slabs	129
North Face	120
North-East Face	124
Scupper Gully	125
South Ridge	133
South-East Flank	131
South-West Buttress	135
Southern Buttresses (A-D)	131
Boreraig – *see* Suisnish & Boreraig	72
Bruach na Frìthe	178
East Ridge via Fionn Choire	180
North-West Ridge	180
South Ridge via Sgùrr na Bàirnich	182
Caisteal a' Gharbh-choire	291
North-East Ridge	291
South Ridge & West Face	291
Camasunary to Coruisk	143
see also Elgol to Camasunary	77
see also Kilmarie to Camasunary	76
see also Sligachan to Camasunary	141
Cioch – *see* Sròn na Cìche	268
Clach Glas	101
Athain Slab Route	116
North Ridge	104
Pilkington's Route	116
Ramp Route	112
Sid's Rake / Slapin the Face	109
South Ridge	106
Coire a' Ghreadaidh	223
Bealach Thormaid	226
Headwall (Greta/Thormaid Col)	225
Coire na Seilg Slabs	93
Coire nan Laogh	299
Eastern Route	302
Western Slabs	300
Collie's Ledge – *see* Hart's Ledge	250
Coruisk	309
see Camasunary to Coruisk	143
see Glen Brittle to Coruisk	144
see Sligachan to Coruisk	142
Cuillin Main Ridge, The Traverse of	346
Cuillin Outliers, The Traverse of	137
Druim Eadar Dà Choire	93
Druim nan Ràmh	342
Duirinish	377
Coast Walk (Orbost to Ramasaig)	377
MacLeod's Tables	379
Neist Point & Oisgill Bay	381
Waterstein Head	381

Dubh Slabs, The	320
Elgol to Camasunary	77
Fiaclan Dearg – see Marsco	88
Forked Pinnacle Ridge (Blàbheinn)	117
Foxes' Rake	208
Garbh-bheinn (Cuillin Outliers)	99
North Ridge	99
North-East Ridge	101
South-East Ridge	101
Gars-bheinn	305
North-East Ridge	317
North-West Ridge	305
Glàmaig	85
South-East Rib	85
Glen Brittle to Coruisk via the coast	144
see also Sligachan to Glen Brittle	145
Glen Uig	394
Hart's Ledge	250
Healabhal Bheag & Healabhal Mhòr	379
Idrigill Point – see Duirinish: Coast Walk	
Inaccessible Pinnacle, The	244
East Ridge	244
West Ridge	244
Kilmarie to Camasunary	76
King's Chimney	250
Knight's Peak via 4/5 Gully	162
Leac nan Fionn & Sròn Vourlinn	391
MacLeod's Maidens	
see Duirinish: Coast Walk	377
MacLeod's Tables	379
Marsco	88
Fiaclan Dearg: NW Shoulder	88
Fiaclan Dearg: Odell's Route	91
South-East Ridge	91
Meall a' Mhaoil	83
Meall Dearg	95
North Buttress	95
Meall na Suireamach	389
Meall Teath (Rubha Hunish)	392
Midget Ridge	336
Naismith's Route (Basteir Tooth)	171
Nead na h-Iolaire	156
Needle, The (Quiraing)	389
Neist Point	381
Nicolson's Chimney	164
Old Man of Storr, The	388
Orbost to Ramasaig	377
Pinnacle Rake	281
Pinnacle Ridge	158
Preshal Beag	375
Preshal Mòr	372
Boswell's Buttress	372
Summit Buttress	375
Finger Wagging Buttress	375
Prison, The	389
Quiraing, The	389
Ruadh Stac	94
South Face	94
Rubha an Dùnain	306
Rubha Hunish	392
Sgùrr Alasdair	258
South-East Ridge	258
South-West Ridge	261
Sgùrr an Fheadain	198
Edgeway	200
Spur, The	198
Pipeline	202
Waterpipe Slabs	202
Sgùrr a' Bhasteir	176
Traverse via the North-East Ridge	176
North Face	176
Sgùrr a' Choire Bhig	302
North-East Ridge	319
North-West Ridge	302
South Ridge	305
Sgùrr an Fhionn Choire	178
Traverse via W Ridge & N Face	178
Sgùrr a' Ghreadaidh	217
Diagonal Buttress	223
North-North-East Ridge	217
South Face	339
South Ridge via Sgùrr Thormaid	223
South-East Ridge	339
Terrace Buttress West	336
West Flank	219
Sgùrr a' Mhadaidh	206
Foxes' Rake	208
NW Buttress & Upper Rakes	206
North-West (Thuilm) Ridge	215
South-West Ridge via An Doras	217
Traverse of the Four Tops	209
West Face	215
Sgùrr Beag	151
North–South Traverse	151
South-East Flank	152
Sgùrr Coire an Lochain	330
South Ridge	333
Sgùrr Dearg	237
Banachdaich Slab	237
North-West Flank	238
South Flank: Central Buttress	241
South-East Flank	243
South-West Ridge	241
Window Buttress	238